25 YEARS
OF MOUNTAIN BIKING

words MARK**RIEDY**   design **VEHICLE**sf

Table of Contents

FIG. 07

20 hours, 20 days, 20 years ago—it's hard not to remember that first mountain bike ride. The crunching of leaves and bark. Front tire squirting and smashing through, over, past nearly everything in its way. Nearly. Moving through the wilds with the ease and grace of a big cat. Covering ground like an XR-250. That first good endo or pedal to the shin, a bit of a warning, but mostly an exhilarating pain. It was too good to be true—an impossibly sweet first kiss, a prelude to a beautiful addiction.

The mountain bike did this. It's got that kind of power. Sassy, but approachable, dangerous but, with wide, high-set handlebars, soft saddle and gangly chassis, lovable all at the same time. Not happy simply injecting new feelings and thoughts, the mountain bike drew people together—doctors from the suburbs with plumbers from the city and teachers from the country—and took them places they'd never have known existed. Even if it was just around their own block. The mountain bike has kept people, people like us, coming back by elevating endorphins and guaranteeing adventure.

The story on these pages could've been a tale of technology, but the mountain bike has never really been about technology. Sure we'll all squint our eyes to see what kind of derailleur or fork is on a bike, but that's more culture and obsession. Thanks to passion, inspiration and insight, the Stumpjumper was originally envisioned as a simple way to stretch smiles across more faces. Happily, people noticed and have kept the Stumpjumper and the rest of this sport and culture rolling strong for more than 25 years.

Thanks to everyone that ever slung a leg over a mountain bike. You've made this book, this culture and this life possible.

WHERE DOES THE SHREDDING START?

Wait, are these guys from the VCCP mountain biking? Although it's something like twenty years before the invention of the mountain bike, it sure looks like they might be. After all, they're riding on the dirt, they've got fat tires and they're definitely smiling from ear to ear.

What about John Finley Scott and the 1953 Schwinn Varsity that he used to cover thousands of off-road miles, including an ascent of 14,260-foot White Mountain in California's Sierra Mountains way back in the '60s?

Or we could go way back to the 20 Buffalo Soldiers who, in 1897, rode a 1,900-mile loop through the West that included an excursion into what is now Yellowstone National Park. They definitely weren't road biking across the old Wild West. Then again, they weren't exactly shreddin' it for credit, either.

So, when exactly did people stop simply riding off-road and start mountain biking? Was it on December 1, 1974, when San Francisco Bay Area rider Russ Mahon first slapped a derailleur on a Clunker and showed up at a local cross race? Was it when Joe Breeze first piloted a custom, multi-gear fat-tire bike of his own making down the legendary Repack downhill in October 1977? Maybe it was a few years later, when Tim Neenan, the designer of the first-ever Stumpjumper, hopped on an early prototype and grunted up into the hills behind the Specialized office near San Jose?

Tough to say. Finding the answer to the question of where the clunking stopped and the shredding actually started is best left to university professors or the crew of bike fiends you'll find on any given afternoon in San Francisco's Zeitgeist saloon.

Members of the Velo Club Cross Paris buck their homemade rigs between heats of a motocross race in 1955.

ANNUAL PEARL PASS KLUNKER TOUR

SAT. SEPT. 22ND

START

CRESTED BUTTE
TO
ASPEN

GRUBSTAKE SALOON

CRESTED BUTTE .... ASPEN

When the first outsiders, a gang of five Clunker junkies from Marin, rolled into Crested Butte in 1978 for the "third annual, second actual" Pearl Pass Tour, they found, in the words of Joe Breeze, "A run-down old coal-mining town, its last remaining black-lung coal miners slumped on benches, while on foot and by bike youth danced by." A mining town since the **Colorado** Gold Rush of 1859, the Crested Butte of the late 1970s looked more than a bit bedraggled, but, with its early embrace of telemark skiing and wheatgrass therapy, it was thought to be on the cutting edge of hippiedom. The frequently dreadlocked and often dirty nouveau locals preferred names like Cloud, Star, Plank and Suitcase (whose son was Briefcase—seriously).

Thanks to a long history in outdoor sports—the town has the distinction of being home to the first ski lift in Colorado—both the hippies and the old-timers showed a distinct bent for outdoor exhilaration, including a long love affair with the bike. Of course those who rode bikes pre-1978 weren't cyclists per se; they just rode bikes, usually bikes of the Denver dump variety: old Schwinn, Hawthorne and BFGoodrich Clunkers on their second or even third wind. Even without an eight-month blanket of snow and ice, nearly all the streets of Crested Butte were made of dirt, so balloon tires proved to be best for cruising the city.

In the summer of 1976, on a late night at C.B.'s Grubstake Saloon, it was decided that the Clunkers would be perfect for a push over 12,692-foot Pearl Pass and down to the bar at the Jerome Hotel in Aspen. In September of that year, 15 hearty and well-lubricated souls saddled up on their Clunkers and headed north toward Aspen. After partying on Pearl Pass for a night—according to a report in the Crested Butte Pilot, riders and support staff consumed one keg of beer, three bottles of schnapps, two gallons of wine and three big bottles of champagne—they clunked, crashed and crawled their way down to the Jerome Hotel where more drinks were drunk and legends were cemented.

ALL HAIL!

THE KING

OF THE CLUNKERS

THE KING OF THE CLUNKERS

Every man, woman and child who owns a mountain bike should raise a glass, sing a song, shout at the sea or say a prayer in the name of Charles R. Kelly (a.k.a. SeeKay). Holed up in the supremely crusty community of Fairfax, California, Sir Charles started the first mountain bike magazine—Fat Tire Flyer—even before there were mountain bikes. While many claim to having invented something to do with fat—first frame, first bike, first race—Charlie was the one who defined the Clunker crew's particular point of view. It was he who spelled out to the world exactly what Clunking was.

"While Clunkers somewhat resemble lightweight dirt motorcycles, the similarity is in appearance only and cornering at high speed is a unique form of body art. A motorcycle has large tires and shock absorbers, but a Clunker does not. It consequently tends to become airborne when it hits even slight projections in the road surface. On a tight corner a Clunker does not have the instant acceleration that a motorcycle uses to bring the rear end around, and without shock absorbers it skitters. Nevertheless, expert riders take curves much faster than you could imagine.

"Sliding into an off-camber, eroded turn, you miscalculate. Out of control, you must make a rapid decision: off the edge or lay it down. Lay it down...damn...torn shirt, bloody elbow. No time to mess with that now (the shirt was old, so was the elbow), how's the bike? OK...jump on it and feed the chain back on with your hand as you coast the first few yards. Back in gear, you really stand on it to make up time."

—Charles Kelly
Bicycling Magazine 1979

Specialized founder Mike Seynard [like it says on the box] hanging with early employees Demi Moore, Sean Penn & Axl Rose in the Campbell, California warehouse circa 1976.

FIG. 17

YEARS 1974 1979

SPECIALIZED STOKED THE FAT TIRE REVOLUTION WITH BITS & PIECES

"Looking back now, things moved slow, but it felt fast to me," says Mike Sinyard (a.k.a. Mr. S) of the first years after hanging out the Specialized shingle.

Long before people made websites devoted to their collections of chainring tattoos (it's true: blackbirdsf.org), being so obsessed with bikes that you would sell your only valuable possession (a Volkswagen Microbus in the case of Mr. S.) and use the profits to fund a bike trip on another continent was certifiably lock-up-able. Hell, it's still strange, but back in 1973, when Mr. S. packed his blue-and-white Bob Jackson touring bike and flitted off to Europe, it was straight crazy.

After pedaling through the U.K., Amsterdam (wink-wink) and Barcelona, Mr. S. arrived on the flat plains of Northern Italy's Po Valley having no idea what he was doing, but with a gut sense that something great could happen at any minute. And happen it did, in the form of a young lady that Mr. S. chanced to meet in a Milan youth hostel. She had a connection to the don of the Italian cycling universe, Signore Cino Cinelli, founder of an eponymous frame and component company that Mr. S. held in highest regard.

Within a month, Mr. S. was back in his San Jose single-wide trailer with a boatload of Cinelli components. He'd spent every dime he had on Cino's famed bars, stems and frames. Now, with no car and nothing like eBay to help him move his Milanese merchandise, he pedaled to bike dealers in the Bay Area, towing a trailer full of hardware and selling his equipment as he went.

By the Bicentennial, Specialized was a full-blown bike and component importer, one whose stock-in-trade was the niche and hard-to-find parts favored by fat-tire riders: European ephemera like Huret Duopar derailleurs, Mafac brakes and Columbus frame tubing. With a clientele that included mostly West-coast frame builders, Specialized was at the center of the booming bike business. Artisan framesmiths like Joe Breeze, Albert Eisentraut and Tom Ritchey (who would later do contract work for Specialized like custom-drilling tandem hubs), were counted as regular customers and, as their orders for oddball equipment like TA cranks and cantilever studs escalated, the small crew at Specialized wondered what they were up to. What they were up to was reinventing the bicycle.

FIRST YEAR SALES: $60K
1975 YEAR SALES: $128K
1976 YEAR SALES: ....$200K+

The first Stumpjumper ad, 1981.

THE BIKE FOR ALL REASONS.

More fun per mile than anything you can ride. The Stumpjumper combines balloon tires with modern road racing technology to create a bike for all reasons. Only 28 lbs., the 15 speed Stumpjumper's great handling, super brakes, and bomb-proof wheels will take you anywhere you have the nerve to go. Rediscover the fun of riding. Ride a Stumpjumper.

WILDERNESS

DIRT RIDING

STUMPJUMPER

by SPECIALIZED

FIELD GUIDE v01

1981 Stumpjumper - The Original
1TJ0001-400

FRAME 01 — DESIGNED BY TIM NEENAN OF LIGHTHOUSE BIKES IN SANTA CRUZ, CA, THE ORIGINAL STUMPJUMPER FRAME WAS TIG-WELDED. IF YOUR EARLY STUMPJUMPER FRAME HAS LUGS, IT'S AN '81 NOT AN '82. THE BLUE PAINT? IT WAS PICKED BECAUSE IT WAS SIMILAR TO THE BLUE ALREADY IN USE ON SPECIALIZED'S SEQUOIA TOURING BIKE.

STEM 02 — THE LEGENDARY GOLF CLUB STEM, THIS GEM WAS A MODIFIED VERSION OF A BMX STEM MADE AT THE TIME. THE ORIGINAL STEEL STUMPJUMPER HANDLEBAR WAS BASED ON MAGURA MOTORCYCLE BARS.

BRAKE LEVERS 03 — STANDARD ON ALL EARLY STUMPJUMPERS, TOMASELLI RACER BRAKE LEVERS WERE DESIGNED FOR USE ON LATE-'70S CAFÉ-RACER MOTORCYCLES. THEY WENT OUT THE DOOR WITH HEAVY-DUTY CABLES THAT IMPROVED THE FEEL AND PERFORMANCE OF THE STOCK MAFAC CANTILEVER BRAKES.

TIRES 04 — SPECIALIZED USED THE KNOWLEDGE GAINED IN CREATING ITS SUCCESSFUL LINE OF ROAD TIRES TO MINT THE FIRST LIGHTWEIGHT, MOUNTAIN BIKE-SPECIFIC TREAD, THE STUMPJUMPER. IF YOU'VE STILL GOT A PAIR, HANG ONTO 'EM; 25-YEAR-OLD MOUNTAIN BIKE TIRES ARE HARD TO FIND.

CRANK 05 — AN ITEM THAT SPECIALIZED HAD BEEN IMPORTING INTO AMERICA FOR USE ON TOURING BIKES, THE TA CYCLOTOURIST CRANK HAD A HIGHLY POLISHED FINISH AND ALLOWED FOR ULTRALOW GEARING. FAILURES WERE COMMON THOUGH, AS THEY WEREN'T MADE FOR OFF-ROAD USE.

FEATURES:

SPECIFICATIONS:

ORIGINAL RETAIL PRICE	$750 complete; $395 frame only
APPROXIMATE NUMBER SOLD	500
WEIGHT	29-lbs
FRAME	Custom chro-moly Touring tubing; TIG welded
FORK	Rigid steel with (clunky) cast crown
HEADSET	Specialized steel
STEM	Specialized aluminum 'Golf Club' model
HANDLEBAR	Specialized Model IV steel rise bar
GRIPS	Foam
BRAKES	Mafac Deluxe Tandem Cantilevers
BRAKE LEVERS	Tommaselli Racer
FRONT DERAILLEUR	Suntour ARX GT
REAR DERAILLEUR	Suntour ARX GT
SHIFT LEVERS	Suntour Thumbshift MS1 & MS2
FREEWHEEL	Suntour 5-speed (14, 17, 20, 24, 28)
CHAIN	Shimano
CRANKSET	TA Cyclotourist Triple (26/36/46)
BOTTOM BRACKET	Chro-moly spindle with precision-ground races
PEDALS	Alloy BMX
RIMS	Araya 7X aluminum
FRONT HUB	Suzue 36-hole sealed small flange
REAR HUB	Suzue 36-hole sealed small flange
SPOKES	DT 14-gauge stainless steel (laced by Wheelsmith)
FRONT TIRE	Specialized Stumpjumper 26 x 2.125
REAR TIRE	Specialized Stumpjumper 26 x 2.125
SEAT	Stumpjumper Anatomic
SEAT POST	SR La Prade 26.8 with blue painted flutes
SEAT BINDER	Cut-down Campagnolo-style wheel quick-release
ACCESSORIES	Specialized water bottle
DESIGNED BY	Tim Neenan

1st time
I Saw A Stumpjumper

JOE BREEZE *mountain bike pioneer, frame builder, author* "I saw it at Bike Odyssey in Sausalito, California near my home. "I thought, 'What's up with that golf-club stem,' and I also wondered why they used Tomeselli brake levers instead of Magura, but at $750, I thought they'd probably sell lots of them." **TOM RITCHEY** *mountain bike pioneer, frame builder, inventor, national caliber racer* "It (the Stumpjumper) was crude and it was basically something that represented the level of technology that was available through Japan at that time. Our bikes were twice as expensive (and lighter), but the Stumpjumper was reasonably priced and had interesting parts for the time." **RICHARD CUNNINGHAM** *founder of Mantis Cycles and Editor at Mountain Bike Action.* "The Stumpjumper was heavy, bouncy and didn't corner all that well, but seeing one for the first slapped me in the face and yelled: "This mountain bike thing is the real stuff...get on it!" I built my first mountain bike shortly afterwards." **DON COOK** *mountain bike pioneer, co-director of the Mountain Bike Hall of Fame.* "At the time a handmade Ritchey was $1,200 to $1,500. We saw the Stumpjumper and thought 'Now we're talking.' Suddenly you didn't have to spend an arm or a leg or wait three or four months to get a bike from Tom (Ritchey) and Gary (Fisher)."

GARY FISHER *mountain bike pioneer, racer; founder of Gary Fisher bikes* "One day I drove down to buy some parts from Mike and he says 'Hey, I want to show you something.' So he takes me in the back of his shop and I was like 'HOLY SHIT.' He had the first Stumpjumper and it was almost identical to what we were doing for $1,320, but it was only $750. That was like November 1981. I went to Japan right after that because I saw that you could get containers of nice bikes for a good price." **JACQUIE PHALEN** *mountain bike pioneer, WOMBATS founder, author* "I saw Stumpjumpers, but didn't know what they were. At the time I was going with Gary Fisher and he described them as "copies". I CAN'T SEE ANYONE LETTING THAT GET IN THE BOOK THOUGH." **VICTOR VINCENTE** OF AMERICA *mountain bike pioneer, Olympic road racer, race promoter, artist.* "My memory is a little faded here, but I belive my reaction to it was to recognize it as a standard, functional design that would appeal to the masses, not so much like the custom bikes that had been available before." **RICHARD HEMINGTON**, UK *The first person to sell a Stumpjumper outside of the USA.* "The Stumpjumper came in a box and had to be built almost from scratch. I can still see all of the pieces spread out on the floor and it taking an age to put together. I remember thinking what trouble we'd be in if it actually started to sell! Of course it did and we were." **JOE MURRAY** *early racer, bike designer, test rider* "The 1981 Stump I had was quite a sled, but I remember liking it even though I needed a certain style to get it down the curvy fire roads in the Marin hills. Once I started racing for Gary Fisher, he gave me a bike, so I sold the Stumpjumper. I wish I still had it though." **MERT LAWWILL** *motorcycle legend, early mountain bike designer* "When I saw what it (the Stumpjumper) was selling for and how much better a bike it was than mine, I figured the game was up and I should just go back to motorcycles."

StumpJumper

IT'S NOT JUST A NEW BICYCLE, IT'S A WHOLE NEW SPORT.

Used to be, there were two kinds of bikes. To go fast, you had your skinny 10-speed. For everything else you got a Paperboy Special, with maybe a horn built into the tank.

But, hey, that's ancient history.

Mafac cantilever brakes feature extra-long pivots, huge 5-stud pads and tandem calipers.

TA alloy triple crankset offers a flawless 15-speed pattern over a range of 25-89 gear inches.

Tommaselli forged brake levers with recurved design were developed in Europe for motorcycle racing.

Anatomic saddle has quick-release seat post binder. SR Laprade fluted alloy seat post.

Take a look at the beast on the opposite page. What we have here is high technology taken to the max, born in the backyards of America and tweaked til it breathes fire.

THE THRILL IS BACK.

The StumpJumper. 15 speeds. Superlight. Monster brakes. Fat knobbys. The essence of adventure engineering, with an appetite for the Great Outdoors.

The possibilities are awesome.

You can really get *out there* on one of these things. Down trails you never dreamed you could ride. Quickly. Safely. Silently.

And that same surefooted agility and same lightning braking response that puts the thrill in fat tire flying, gives you a tremendous defensive advantage in city commuting.

CONQUER THE ASPHALT JUNGLE.

When traffic forces you into the rough stuff, the StumpJumper's wide footprint and motorcycle bars really give you something to work with. And when you're out there every day, that much technology between you and the road can be pretty reassuring.

Examine, for a moment, the comfortable, upright riding position. This vehicle puts *fun* back into riding. Even down to the store, you'll find you're riding more and driving less.

Across town. Or out of town. On or off the pavement, the StumpJumper lets you point it more places than any bike you've ever owned.

But look closer. We didn't arrive at this level of performance by just guessing. We took prototype after prototype to the woods. And discovered the hard way what one wimpy part can do to you when you're goin' full tilt.

ONLY THE STRONG SURVIVE.

So we didn't compromise. We started from scratch: a custom chrome-moly frame with radical geometry and raked forks, Mafac cantilever brakes, Tommaselli motorcycle levers, ratchet thumb shifters, TA triple crankset, Suntour ARX componentry, Wheelsmith "dishless" alloy wheels with DT stainless spokes, precision sealed bearings and oversized axles.

Very exotic stuff. From France, Italy, Japan, and Switzerland.

And when the best wasn't good enough, we built it. Our own investment-cast fork crown. Our own massive four-point stem. Our own contact-seal headset. Our own chrome-moly handlebars. Our own aggressive 26" knobbys.

The result? 29 pounds of bulletproof performance, a race-bred machine that'll take you anywhere you've got the nerve to go. The best of everything. The StumpJumper. See for yourself at your local SPECIALIZED dealer.

Specialized Bicycles 844 Jury Court, San Jose, CA 95112 (408) 297-6026

StumpJumper

© 1982 Specialized Bicycle Components.

ARCHETYPE ADVERT

A NEW TYPE OF BIKE CALLED FOR A NEW TYPE OF ADVERTISING: ONE THAT'S LASTED FOR 25 YEARS.

Not all that many years before, Mr. S. was living in a trailer (a single-wide at that), writing his catalog on yellow legal paper and coaxing employees to sleep overnight cozyed up to piles of tires that couldn't be squeezed into what little storage there was at Specialized world headquarters. Suddenly, he was struggling to hang on to the tiger's tail otherwise known as the Stumpjumper.

A production bike unlike anything Specialized or anyone else had ever made, the old standards for selling it just weren't going to work. Before the Whole New Sport campaign Specialized adverts were mostly black and white, and were all a halfpage or even less. That changed with this dark, glossy beauty that became the archetype for Specialized print ads for the next 25 years. Shot by Jack Christensen in the same garage where he snapped the first Apple Computer brochure, and designed by longtime Specialized collaborator Patrick Mountain, Whole New Sport was impossible to miss in the largely black-and-white magazines of the day.

As groundbreaking as it was, most people take one look at Whole New Sport and think 'Why is the guy in the ad heading out on a ride wearing tube socks and overalls? The guy in question is the designer of the original Stumpjumper, Tim Neenan, and he remembers it this way: "Back then, there was no specific mountain bike uniform, nothing that you were supposed to wear. I had some overalls that I wore when I worked, so I threw 'em on and we just kinda went with it."

NATIONAL CHAMPIONSHIPS
START   NORBA   FINISH
★★★ 1985 ★★★

1984

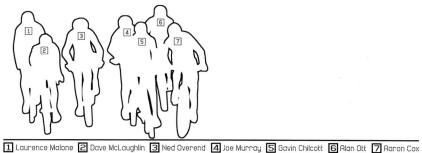

| 1 Laurence Malone | 2 Dave McLaughlin | 3 Ned Overend | 4 Joe Murray | 5 Gavin Chilcott | 6 Alan Ott | 7 Aaron Cox |

Start Your Engines

Racing in the first half of the 1980's was a lot like NASCAR back the second half of the 1940's: Stake out a course in a random field, line 'em up and let the flag drop. Racers were known to sleep in their cars, bounce their entry fee checks and smoke their energy bars. It was raw, it was real, it was two-wheeled racing with a purity that hadn't been seen in a hundred years. It was also too good to keep a secret. Between its initial meeting in a house in Danville, California in 1983 and the first UCI World Championships in 1990, the National Off-Road Bicycle Association (NORBA) grew from zero to over 20,000 members.

TEAM S.J.
THE O.G.

Back in 1984 there was no such thing as a normal mountain bike team, but even if there had been, Team Stumpjumper, the first professional squad ever, wouldn't have been considered normal. They rode pink bikes with dropped bars and used proper cycling shoes at a time when many of the best mountain biker racers rode laid-back rigs and made due with sneakers like the Nike Lava Dome. Organized by Specialized's road racing guru Bill Woodul, Team Stump was an off-road experiment. "Woody (Woodul) brought a bunch of us Elite road and cross racers together and applied the same ideas and methods he had developed on the road," says former Team Stumpjumper rider Dave McLaughlin.

In the team's first year, Woodul's hand picked talent consisted of cyclo-cross upstart McLaughlin, Gavin Chilcot (who'd later race for the famed 7-11 road team), Northern California locals Mark Michel and Alan Ott and the godfather of American 'cross, Laurence Malone. "Bill Woodul understood that we needed to be well-supported and compensated for our efforts," says Team Stump's Gavin Chilcot, "He saw our value and made it possible for us to pursue excellence." Packed into a Specialized van, they traveled the US, hitting the handful of big races that existed in those days: the Suntour Pacific States Challenge Series, the Gant Challenge Series, the Ross Stage Race and one-day classics like the Rockhopper, Rumpstomper and the NORBA National Championships. "The races were a little uneven in those days. Mostly it wasn't as competitive as it is today, but when Joe Murray or a few pro road racers like Andy Hampsten and Steve Tilford would show up, things would get pretty serious," says McLaughlin of racing's crawling-before-it- could-walk period.

Just a few seasons of rough-and-tumble racing later and Team Stumpjumper had evolved into Team Specialized, the world's best, most well equipped mountain bike squad. Early editions of Team Specialized featured World Champions Ned Overend, Lisa Muhich and Sara Ballantyne as well as cross-country phenom Daryl Price and downhill demons Elladee Brown and Paul Thomasberg. Later versions of Specialized's fat tire team got rid of the pink bikes, but kept the swagger.

Swagger...Team Stumpjumper Had Plenty
You'd have it too if you showed up to the starting line on a pink bike.

FIG. 29

Talk about swagger? Five-time US National Cyclo-Cross Champion Laurence Malone (far left, bottom & far right) had it in spades. Dave McLaughlin and Gavin Chilcott (top & middle) rockin' the drop bars in 1985.

1984

1984 Specialized Stumpjumper Team

If you're on a pink bike, you better be fast!

FRAME 01 — DESIGNED BY JIM MERZ FROM JAPANESE-MADE TANGE PRESTIGE TUBING, THE 1984 TEAM STUMPJUMPER FRAME WAS THE LIGHTEST SPECIALIZED HAD MADE TO THAT POINT.

FORK 02 — THE PINK STUMPJUMPER TEAM ALSO FEATURED SPECIALIZED'S FIRST UNICROWN FORK, WHICH WAS MUCH LIGHTER AND EASIER TO MAKE THAN THE LUGGED FORKS USED UNTIL THAT TIME.

REAR BRAKE 03 — FORTUNATELY, UNDER-THE-BOTTOM-BRACKET-MOUNTED U-BRAKES, LIKE THE SUNTOUR ROLLERCAM FEATURED ON THE TEAM, WERE A SHORT-LIVED FAD. A MAGNET FOR MUCK, THE U-BRAKE IS REMEMBERED AS ONE OF THE BIGGEST COLLECTIVE MISTAKES MADE BY THE BIKE WORLD.

TIRES 04 — IN 1984 THE TRICROSS TIRE REPLACED THE STUMPJUMPER AS THE TREAD OF CHOICE FOR HIGH-END MOUNTAIN BIKES. ITS LOW-PROFILE KNOBS PROVIDED GREAT GRIP IN DRY, DUSTY CONDITIONS.

FREEWHEEL 05 — A WORKS-LEVEL MACHINE IN EVERY SENSE OF THE WORD, THE STUMPJUMPER TEAM FEATURED SHIMANO'S 600 ROAD FREEWHEEL WITH A TALL COG OF JUST 26 TEETH—NOTHING LIKE THE 30-TOOTH COGS FAVORED BY MOST OFF-ROADERS OF THE DAY.

FEATURES:

SPECIFICATIONS:

ORIGINAL RETAIL PRICE	$949
APPROXIMATE NUMBER SOLD	500
WEIGHT	27-lbs
FRAME	Tange Prestige MTB chro-moly double-butted tubing
FORK	Unicrown style with chro-moly blades
HEADSET	Specialized sealed
STEM	Specialized MTB-3
HANDLEBAR	Specialized Model IV alloy
GRIPS	Specialized
BRAKES	Shimano Deore XT front; Suntour Rollercam rear
BRAKE LEVERS	Tommaselli Racer
FRONT DERAILLEUR	Shimano Deore XT
REAR DERAILLEUR	Shimano Deore XT Superplate
SHIFT LEVERS	Shimano Deore XT
FREEWHEEL	Shimano 600 [14/26]

FREEWHEEL	Shimano 600 [14/26]
CHAIN	Shimano 8-speed
CRANKSET	Specialized touring [28/38/48]
BOTTOM BRACKET	Specialized cup-and-cone
PEDALS	Suntour mp 1000 bmx
RIMS	Saturae HX-22
FRONT HUB	Specialized sealed quick-release
REAR HUB	Specialized sealed quick-release
SPOKES	Wheelsmith stainless straight gauge
FRONT TIRE	Specialized Tri-Cross
REAR TIRE	Specialized Tri-Cross
SEAT	Specialized Mountain
SEAT POST	Suntour XC
SEAT BINDER	Specialized Campagnolo style
DESIGNED BY	Jim Merz

1990 Inductees

IF STREAKERS AND UKULELE PLAYERS CAN HAVE ONE, WHY CAN'T WE?

MBHoF

Google the phrase 'Hall of Fame' and you'll get 47,400,000 responses. 47 million. Yep, there's a Mining hall of fame, a cowgirl hall of fame, a home computer hall of fame, a streaker hall of fame, a Ukulele hall of fame. A Ukulele hall of fame! Mother of this good earth, what could possibly be in the Ukulele hall of fame? Probably more than is in the Streaker hall of fame, that's for sure.

There's something undeniably universal about wanting to honor those who've contributed to a culture and, in that way, fat tire fanatics are no different than cowgirls, streakers or lovers of the ukulele. Housed rather fittingly in an old gas station on Crested Butte's Elk Avenue, the Mountain Bike hall of fame was the brainchild of Carole Bauer. In the mid-1980's long-time Butte local Bauer was worried that the architects of the mountain bike culture were destined to be forgotten without an institution to honor their accomplishments and the sport they helped to create.

By 1988 the MBHoF was ready to accept its first batch of inductees. Not surprisingly, fat tire pioneers with names like Breeze, Fisher, Kelly, Cunningham, Ritchey and Murray were among that first class. So was Mr. S., who was flattered, flabbergasted and fully honored to be held in the same esteem as such a select group of peers. After Mr. S. at least three other Specialized-centric mountain bikers were honored by the MBHoF, including The Captain (a.k.a. Ned Overend), frame designer Jim Merz and race support guru Tom Hillard.

These days the MBHoF keeps the lights on and the culture thriving with support from the bike industry and mountain bike fans from around the world. mtnbikehalloffame.com

Bill's rides nearly every day on one of his two Stumpjumpers (two Stumpjumpers! How sweet is Bill?), for a total of about 150 miles per week. Not bad for a 65-year-old guy, right?

A few years ago when Bill's teenage grandson started hitting the singletrack, he knew he'd have to upgrade his old Stump if he wanted keep pace with Jr. It didn't take many rides for Bill to realize that his FSRxc suspension bike helped him to keep up with the little whippersnapper. Bill says that, thanks to his FSR, he can now carry more speed than ever through the rough stuff.

Bill's daily driver is a 1982 lugged steel Stumpjumper (the one with the sweet bi-plane crown) that he bought used a few years ago. "It's one of my favorite bikes to cruise around on," says Bill "It's great for making my way to the local fishing holes."

As much as we'd like to say otherwise, Bill's not getting any younger. But he says he can still do all the things he likes—like playing short stop—thanks to the fitness he finds on two-wheels. "Simply put," says Bill, "My bikes are my life.

150 Miles | Bill Hennion

2 Stumpjumpers, 65 Years-Young & 150-Miles Per-Week

FIG. 95

SPECIALIZED FREE WRENCHING

AT THE RACES SINCE 1985

FREE TECH SUPPORT?
IS SPECIALIZED CRAZY?

Backindaze before they even said back in the day—somewhere around 1985 in fact—the mountain bike thing was just beginning to go bonkers. There weren't a whole lot of events, but every year there were more excited promoters and pumped-up racers and a whole lot of room for error. So Specialized, who'd already sold a whole, whole lot of Stumpjumpers and been to a whole lot of races, decided to lend a hand, to help the promoters promote and racers race. Like they'd done on the road racing side of things since at least 1982, they decided to hand out tech support to any racer on any kind of bike—free of charge. They also decided to help promoters by lending a hand wherever possible, setting a course, sweeping a course, popping a tent, driving a lead moto, running registration. Whatever it took, the mob from Morgan Hill was ready to do it.

To guarantee success, they hired one of the most seasoned race technicians alive, Sonoma County, California's Tom Hillard, co-author of the NORBA rule book, promoter of the Punk Bike Enduro and a man who claims to have made his first mountain bike way, way backindaze (1961). So, someone at Specialized flipped him the keys to a van and Tom headed off to races with legendary names like Rockhopper, Rumpstomper, Reseda-To-The-Sea, Kamikaze and Whiskeytown.

Whether it was a NORBA National, Cactus Cup or Tuesday night club race in Texas, riders always seemed stoked when one of Specialized's mechanics, friendly and hard working guys like Tom Hillard or Dave Meyers, Steve Mosher or Joe Buckley wheeled off their busted bike for a quick (and most often free) repair. You better believe the overwhelmed and understaffed promoters loved it too, "Things just went smoother when the Specialized truck showed up," said one old-time race director. So smooth that Specialized self-published a book on race promotion and organization.

Of course having trucks and mechanics on the road wasn't cheap, but the people at Specialized never thought of it as a one-way street. Of course running good races helped grow the sport, but being out in the field, wrenching on bikes that people were riding hard and fast and often was better than having 1,000 engineers stuck in a lab trying guess what kinds of off-road abuse a bike might see.

Free race and tech support? Cheap R&D? Who wouldn't agree that the Specialized tech support situation was a good thing.

Tom Hillard (on the motorcycle) gassed up the Specialized tech support team in the early days.

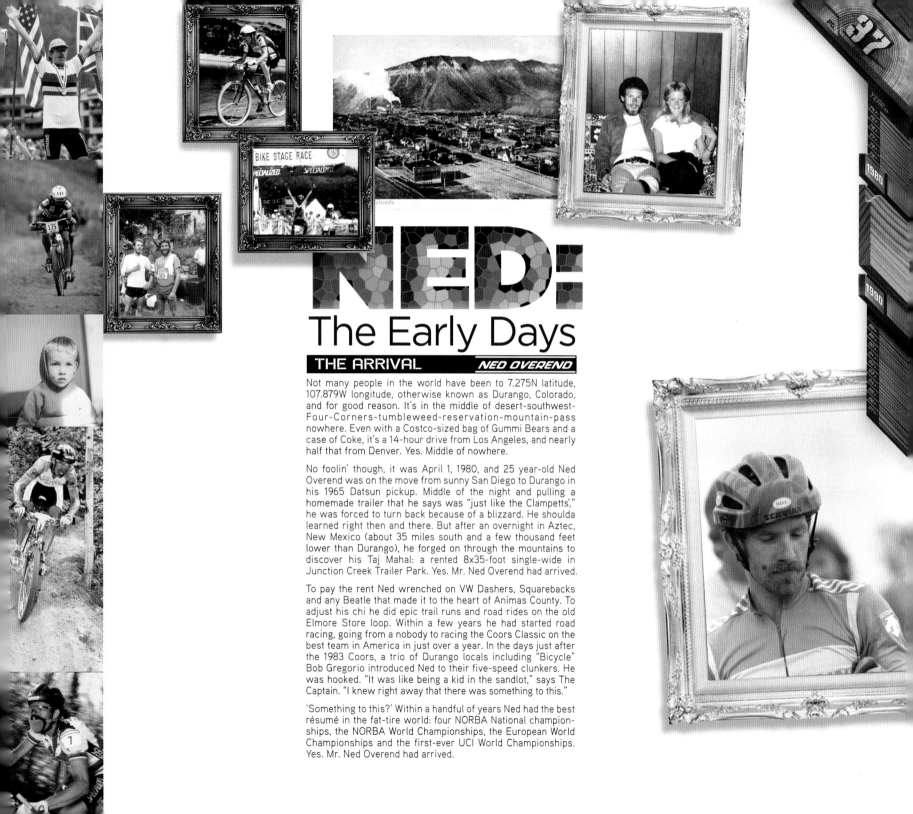

NED:
The Early Days

THE ARRIVAL — NED OVEREND

Not many people in the world have been to 7.275N latitude, 107.879W longitude, otherwise known as Durango, Colorado, and for good reason. It's in the middle of desert-southwest-Four-Corners-tumbleweed-reservation-mountain-pass nowhere. Even with a Costco-sized bag of Gummi Bears and a case of Coke, it's a 14-hour drive from Los Angeles, and nearly half that from Denver. Yes. Middle of nowhere.

No foolin' though, it was April 1, 1980, and 25 year-old Ned Overend was on the move from sunny San Diego to Durango in his 1965 Datsun pickup. Middle of the night and pulling a homemade trailer that he says was "just like the Clampetts'," he was forced to turn back because of a blizzard. He shoulda learned right then and there. But after an overnight in Aztec, New Mexico (about 35 miles south and a few thousand feet lower than Durango), he forged on through the mountains to discover his Taj Mahal: a rented 8x35-foot single-wide in Junction Creek Trailer Park. Yes. Mr. Ned Overend had arrived.

To pay the rent Ned wrenched on VW Dashers, Squarebacks and any Beatle that made it to the heart of Animas County. To adjust his chi he did epic trail runs and road rides on the old Elmore Store loop. Within a few years he had started road racing, going from a nobody to racing the Coors Classic on the best team in America in just over a year. In the days just after the 1983 Coors, a trio of Durango locals including "Bicycle" Bob Gregorio introduced Ned to their five-speed clunkers. He was hooked. "It was like being a kid in the sandlot," says The Captain. "I knew right away that there was something to this."

'Something to this?' Within a handful of years Ned had the best résumé in the fat-tire world: four NORBA National championships, the NORBA World Championships, the European World Championships and the first-ever UCI World Championships. Yes. Mr. Ned Overend had arrived.

81 ↑ 06

MOUNTAIN BIKE FAMILY

GROWTH & DIVERSITY

Since the introduction of the Stumpjumper in the fall of 1981, the team at Specialized has designed hundreds of mountain bike models, two wheelers for every type of riding imaginable. Here's a few of Morgan Hill's greatest hits.

96 · M2 GROUND CONTROL FSR
FIRST SPECIALIZED SUSPENSION BIKE TO FEATURE A METAL MATRIX FRONT TRIANGLE.
▶ TRAIL ◀

93 · S-WORKS FSR
THE FIRST SPECIALIZED SUSPENSION BIKE. IT DEBUTED THE ENDURING FSR SUSPENSION SYSTEM.
▶ TRAIL ◀

84 · TEAM STUMPJUMPER
THIS BIKE WAS THE FIRST EVER MADE WITH TANGE PRESTIGE TUBING.
▶ XC/RACE ◀

88 · EPIC
FIRST PRODUCTION CARBON MOUNTAIN BIKE EVER MADE.
▶ XC/RACE ◀

97 · GROUND CONTROL AIM
3-BAR SUSPENSION. LIGHT WITH MINIMAL TRAVEL. IT WAS PRECURSOR TO THE FSRXC.
▶ XC/RACE ◀

90 · EPIC ULTIMATE
FIRST PRODUCTION BIKE TO EVER USE TITANIUM AND CARBON TOGETHER.
▶ XC/RACE ◀

91 · STUMPJUMPER M2
FIRST CONSUMER PRODUCT TO BE MADE FROM METAL MATRIX COMPOSITE.
▶ XC/RACE ◀

81 STUMPJUMPER
THE ORIGINAL STUMPJUMPER WAS ALMOST CALLED THE BIG MAX. OUCH.

▶ TRAIL ◀

MTB CHRONO:81.08

04 F DEMO 9
THE LONGEST TRAVEL, MOST CAPABLE FREERIDE BIKE EVER MADE BY SPECIALIZED.
▶ DH/FREERIDE ◀

01 ◇ P3

MUTANT BIKE THAT SOLIDIFIED THE 26-INCH DIRT JUMPING CATEGORY.
▶ DIRT JUMP ◀

05 F DEMO 8
AS BURLY AS THE DEMO 9, BUT WITH A LITTLE LESS TRAVEL AND A LOT LESS GIRTH.
▶ DH/FREERIDE ◀

02 ◆ ENDURO PRO
THE ENDURO PRO CAME WITH A PROPRIETARY "ITCH" SWITCH FOR ON-THE-FLY ADJUSTABLE TRAVEL BETWEEN 4" AND 5.2".
▶ TRAIL ◀

06 ◆ S-WORKS CARBON EPIC
A BRAIN SHOCK AND PROPRIETARY FACT CARBON MADE THIS THE MOST TECHNOLOGICALLY ADVANCED AND FASTEST RACE BIKE EVER.
▶ XC/RACE ◀

99 ◆ ENDURO PRO
AN INCH MORE TRAVEL THAN THE FSRXC, BUT PLENTY LIGHT AND EFFICIENT. THE ENDURO MARKED THE BEGINNING OF EXPERIENCE ORIENTED SEGMENTATION.
▶ TRAIL ◀

03 ◆ S-WORKS EPIC
THE FIRST APPEARANCE OF SPECIALIZED'S PATENTED BRAIN SHOCK TECHNOLOGY.
▶ XC/RACE ◀

99 ◆ S-WORKS FSR XC
THE FIRST XC RACE ORIENTED SUSPENSION BIKE. ONE PROTOTYPE WEIGHED 20.6 LBS (PRODUCTION BIKES WERE JUST OVER 24 LBS).
▶ XC/RACE ◀

06 ◆ S-WORKS CARBON HARDTAIL
PROPRIETARY FACT CARBON MADE THIS THE LIGHTEST HARDTAIL EVER MADE BY SPECIALIZED.
▶ XC/RACE ◀

HOW DO YOU TAME AN 800 POUND GORILLA?
YOU GET ORGANIZED

FRONT-AND-CENTER, FRIENDS

On the first page of the first edition of the first mountain bike magazine ever published, Charlie Kelly's Fat Tire Flyer, in August 1980, there was a clear call to action. "Without an organization to protect our interests we will have no interests to protect," pleaded SeeKay. Even before you could find a mountain bike at your local shop, trail access was an 800 pound gorilla.

Jump to the summer of 1987 and, while most of the country was just discovering the joys of mountain biking, trail-access issues were blowing up in the heart of Clunker country. "Two-Wheeled Terrors," howled the September 28, 1987, issue of Newsweek. From the American River Parkway near Sacramento to the Santa Monica mountains in Los Angeles, bikes were being banned from singletrack or kicked off public lands altogether. The National Park Service had closed all of its trails and the Bureau of Land Management was booting bikes from forests. If mountain biking was to have a future, mountain bikers needed to band together and organize. Quick.

That fall, representatives from five California-based advocacy groups (Bicycle Trails Council of Marin, Bicycle Trails Council of the East Bay, Sacramento Rough Riders, Concerned Off Road Bikers Association of Los Angeles and Responsible OffRoad Mountain Pedalers of San Jose) put their heads together at Interbike, the annual bicycle trade show in Long Beach. Within six months, these groups had chartered under the moniker, International Mountain Bike Association (IMBA), and were battling for access on all fronts.

Thanks to the vision of Linda DuPriest and Eric Eidsmo, then on Specialized's marketing staff, a grant of $1,000 was given to IMBA in the company's name. It was the first major move that Specialized (or any big bicycle company) would make for advocacy and access. Soon after, Linda convinced the company to sponsor an industry-wide meeting at the 1989 Interbike show, one that would encourage other companies to jump on the advocacy bandwagon. A turning point in the development of IMBA, the Interbike meeting helped raise awareness and funds for the struggle for singletrack and served to jump-start a wide range of efforts, including early mountain bike advocacy conferences in Washington, D.C., and Durango. DuPriest would end up on the board of IMBA for a decade, helping the early advocates polish their presentations and business plans and serving as IMBA's liaison to the bike industry.

RIGHT NOW, THERE'S A GUY WITH A ROUTER CARVING A WOODEN SIGN THAT WILL UNCEREMONIOUSLY BE POSTED AT A TRAILHEAD SOMEWHERE. It's a simple sign. And very easy to comprehend: No bikes.

Perhaps even more disturbing is the fact that this sign is not limited to just a handful of trails in just a handful of areas around the country.

From Marin to Moab to New Hampshire, trail access to mountain bikes is being threatened at an alarming rate. One estimate has one trail closing for every single day of the year. And up on Mount Tamalpais, the birthplace of mountain biking, it's no big secret that park rangers, armed with radar guns, lie in ambush hoping to "discourage" cyclists with $200 speeding tickets.

CHECKPOINT : REALITY

So how did this happen? How did a sport that started innocently enough on a couple of fat tire bikes end up the target for the biggest quarantine since smallpox? And more importantly, who's responsible?

Oops, there go all the fingers. Hikers pointing at bikers. Bikers pointing at equestrians. And isn't it funny, no one is pointing at themselves. Maybe that's the problem. Maybe we as mountain bikers need to take a long hard look at ourselves.

Hikers will tell you they've been around forever and that they've paid their dues by helping secure land, by building and maintaining trails and by educating the public to help insure a more respectful wilderness experience. And who can argue? After all, most of us ride on trails the hikers and equestrians helped establish. But what, if anything, are we contributing in return? Oh sure there are mountain bike clubs and groups working for land access but how many of us are actively involved? How many of us know there's a problem out there? How many of us even care?

We're not suggesting that everyone jump on the bandwagon nor are we suggesting that everyone who rides a mountain bike become a martyr for the sport. We're merely suggesting that, as cyclists, we need to start becoming more aware of what's going on; that we're not the only ones on the trail and that, when it comes to land access, there are a lot of legitimate gripes concerning everyone involved—not just hikers.

There is no simple solution to any of this but maybe, just maybe, by first trying to understand the various points of view out there we can all start to get a handle on this thing.

Meanwhile the guy with the router is filling orders as fast as he can.

FIND OUT WHERE EVERYONE'S AT ON THE TRAIL.

International Mountain
Bicycling Association
(IMBA)
PO Box 412043
Los Angeles, CA 90041
(818) 792-8830

American Hiking Society
(AHS)
PO Box 20160
Washington, D.C. 20041-2160
(703) 385-3252

American Horse Council
(AHC)
1700 K Street NW #300
Washington, D.C. 20006
(202) 296-4031
Contact: Amy Mann

Brought to you as a public service by Specialized and this publication.

Fueled by funding and support from every major player in the bike industry as well as its more than 35,000 members, IMBA has since educated trail users and fought for trail access in all areas of the world. Without IMBA, we'd have no trails to protect. *You've heard the gospel, now please pass the collection plate: imba.com*

Bolinas Ridge on the western edge of Mt. Tamalpais, a view worth protecting.

AIL CLOSED

SHARE THE TRAIL

SPECIALIZED

Denise, a 36 year-old registered veterinary technician, started riding on the suggestion of her doctor. A bad knee ruled out running or even walking on a treadmill, so her doc suggested she take up riding to lower the stress on her knee and help her regain fitness. Once she hopped on a two-wheeler her life changed forever.

In search of a little extra motivation, Denise started racing about 6 months after that first fateful ride. It took just a few moments in the heat of battle, before Denise realized that she needed something lighter and more reliable if she was going to be competitive. So she bought a Specialized Rockhopper and, after rollin' it for a few seasons, she upgraded to a used Stumpjumper. "It fits me perfectly and now I'm absolutely hooked," she says. "Suddenly I have speed and confidence like never before." Denise, who does some road riding for basic fitness, admits that there's nothing like being on her Stumpjumper, sailing through the woods in the early morning.

These days her knee has strengthened to the point that she no longer needs a brace, even when cross-training. Not that she runs very often though, "I'd rather be on my Stumpjumper, after all I'm a mountain-bike racer now."

REWRITING THE RULE BOOK, ONE PAGE AT A TIME

In the space of five years, Specialized completely rewrote the mountain bike book. Between '88 and '93, Specialized became the first company to put together production frames in steel and carbon, titanium and carbon, and metal matrix (not to mention the first suspension fork ever with carbon-fiber legs and the first production frame designed entirely in the digital ether). A lot of rules were rewritten back in the days when the Cold War was closing down, and the guy holding the pen for most of it was Mountain Bike Hall of Famer and Specialized engineer Jim Merz.

When Reagan asked Gorby to pull down that wall, it opened up a flood of materials and technologies that had been tucked in the military's closet. Thanks to his love of a good scientific journal and experience working with then-novel 3-D modeling software (which Specialized kicked down a cool $250,000 to purchase in 1985), Merz was perfectly positioned to pick up on the latest materials and methods.

After a group of engineers who had been working with composites at a subsidiary of Prince tennis racquets in El Cajon, California, introduced him to carbon, Merz set about optimizing the composite tubing and designing a set of lugs to join them into a frame. "I went through hell working the whole thing out," says Merz. After much testing and toil at his Applicon-powered workstation, he came up with a chro-moly lugset that was precision-welded by Specialized's long-time frame-building partner in Japan. As much labor as building an entire bike, the lugs made the Epic a wallet-wasting $2,400 for a frame and Direct Drive rigid fork. The steel lugs were then shipped to Specialized world headquarters in Morgan Hill where they were bonded to a brace of carbon tubes and stuffed into a jig to cure. With only two jigs for each size, building the approximately 2,000 Epics that were made proved to be just that, Epic.

Never satisfied, Merz quickly moved past chro-moly lugs and right on to titanium. Not just any titanium though, titanium machined by the experts at Merlin Metalworks in Cambridge, Massachusettes. That, though, is a whole other Epic.

★ ★ ▶ WITH THE PRESSURE ON

★ ➡ THE CAPTAIN DID THE DEED ➡ IN DURANGO

HELLO
my name is
MR. AMERICA

/RACE: **XC** /SPECTATORS: **10,000** /START: **8,800'** /CLIMBING: **4,800'** /RACERS: **130** /DISTANCE: **32 MI**

If you flipped on a radio or TV in Colorado's Four Corners region during the early days of September of 1990 you'd probably hear Ned Overend's name or see his mustached mug on the screen. He was the subject of daily articles in the Durango Herald and could be seen on the cover of the official program for the race. Someone had even gone to the trouble of silk-screening T-shirts showing The Captain winning the (upcoming) worlds. Durango wasn't happy to just host the first-ever UCI worlds, they wanted their boy to win too.

The Captain could've made a whole lot of dough racing as a professional on the road or suffering through triathlons, but he decided on dirt for the simple reason that it was more fun than cycling's other options. Still, a week before those first-ever UCI "unified" world championships, America's cross-country king didn't feel like he'd chosen the easy way out. The pressure to become the first-ever UCI world champion was sitting squarely on the Durango local's shoulders.

Then it was happening. Thirty-five-year-old Ned, racing on a prototype Epic Ultimate with titanium lugs and a BBQ-black RockShox suspension fork, had dropped his only challengers in the 130-rider field, Tim Gould of Great Britain and Thomas Frischknecht of Switzerland, and was speeding toward a win at the base of Purgatory ski hill. Save for the nearly 10,000 screaming spectators, The Captain was alone. "It was really more of a relief," he'll say if you ask him today, but like Greg Herbold, another Durango local and winner of the downhill at those first-ever world championships, said, *"Standing up there, getting that medal that I worked so hard for, I felt like Miss America."* Ned's probably more of a Mr. America, though.

The Captain wasn't Specialized's only rainbow winner in Durango — Lisa Muhich grabbed the win in the women's vet class and Sara Ballantyne narrowly missed victory in the elite women's race.

FIG. 49

YEAR
1990

STUMPJUMPER **M2**

THE DEPARTMENT OF DEFENSE LIGHTENS UP

"Who ever heard of metal matrix composite?" asked the April 1 edition of the San Francisco Chronicle back in 1991. Because its very existence was kept in the dark thanks to the Munitions Control Act (which limited the exchange of information about the aluminum-aluminum oxide hybrid) not too many people without a security clearance were tuned in to the aluminum material. There wasn't a single consumer product in the world at the time made with metal matrix and it was nearly impossible to form or weld, but Jim Merz, Mark Winter, Mark DiNucci and the rest of the crew at Specialized cracked the code of the space-race material. The result was the first anything not pointed at Moscow made from metal matrix composite, the Stumpjumper M2.

Dreamed up for nose cones of satellites and driveshafts of tanks, M2 was said to be 10 percent stronger and 20 percent stiffer than typical aluminum. According to the big brains in the Pentagon, its strength came from chunks of aluminum oxide, a ceramic that was laced into the microscopic lattice of the material's 6000-series aluminum base. As light and strong as it was, though, making it into a bike frame would prove to be no easy task.

So, just as the year before, when the Specialized team had partnered with DuPont to create the three-spoke carbon wheel (yeah, the exact same design that a certain American used at some point during every one of his seven Tour de France victories), they turned to an industrial giant for help. The dance partner for the M2's MMC material was Duralcan, a subsidiary of the world's second-largest aluminum company, whose San Diego-based MMC scientists dialed in the right recipe for the tubing, while the guys in Morgan Hill designed the new frame (including the task of butting the super hard stuff) and figured out how to weld it. At the end of the day, Specialized teamed with partner Anodizing Inc. to create a new production facility in Portland, Oregon, made just to extrude M2 tubes and weld them into frames. Ultimately the duo would completely reinvent the butting process, making M2 frames increasingly lighter as time went on.

Certainly not the fast-and-cheap route to a lighter and stiffer frame, but since when did anyone at Specialized ever take the easy way out?

BECAUSE IT'S **BITCHIN'**

There's one thing that just about anyone at Specialized will tell you: If you want to win, play a game that you've got a feel for, a game that you're passionate about.

So, back in '89 when Specialized needed a storyteller, they went looking for someone who was every bit as passionate about telling stories as they were about making bikes. One bit of luck led to another and, boom! (click fingers as you slap your right fist into your left palm for a magical effect), they hooked-up with one of the best tellers to ever take on a story: Goodby, Silverstein and Partners. You've never heard of GSP? Two words: Got milk? It turns out that the 'S' in GSP, Rich Silverstein, was and still is, a dedicated cyclist, a wiry guy who could often be seen riding from his home in Marin County, over the Golden Gate Bridge and into GSP's San Francisco world headquarters.

The rest, is a fine bit of storytelling history. While busy with their many clients like Morgan Stanley, Haagen-Dazs, Saturn, Anheuser-Busch and Hewlett-Packard, GSP has also made most of Specialized's advertising that you can remember.

The lesson here: whether it's bikes, Bud Light ads or baking bread, you'll have a very tough time doing it right if you don't do it with passion.

BALLANTYNE RACES GRUNDIG WITH AIRLOCK TUBE, DOESN'T BLOW IT.

we didn't make it lighter so you could carry the damn thing.

With all due respect to President Bush,

TEAM STUMPJUMPER GOES TO PURGATORY, RIDES LIKE HELL.

SPECIALIZED, 1974. A DREAM. A VISION. A GREAT EXCUSE NOT TO GET A REAL JOB.

IF WINNING ISN'T EVERYTHING THEN WE SURE SCREWED UP WHEN WE DESIGNED THIS TIRE

OVEREND WINS OVERALL.

IT CAME FROM OUTER SPACE

DON'T TRY THIS
AT HOME.

GOD IS IN
THE
DETAILS

Ned's had a
better four years.

BECAUSE
IT'S BITCHIN'
THAT'S WHY.

WHEN WE STARTED SPECIALIZED,
NOTHING COULD STOP US.
EXCEPT MAYBE OUR BELL BOTTOMS.

TRUTH
AND
BEAUTY

YEAH, IT WORKS.

FutureShock

HAPPILY RISKING LIFE AND LIMB
FOR YOUR RIDING ENJOYMENT

LIKE FATHER.   LIKE SON.

DIRECT DRIVE

Carbon

Titanium

COMPUTER

FIELD GUIDE *v03*

1992 S-Works Epic Ultimate*
*Bike shown here is a test mule that was never sold in this trim.

FRAME 01 — FROM 1990 TO 1995 SPECIALIZED HAND-BUILT APPROXIMATELY 1,500 SUB-THREE-POUND EPIC ULTIMATE TITANIUM AND CARBON FRAMES IN THEIR MORGAN HILL HEADQUARTERS. THE EPIC ULTIMATE'S TI-AND-CARBON CONSTRUCTION, WOULD BE IMITATED BY HIGH-END CUSTOM BUILDERS FOR WELL OVER A DECADE.

LUGS 02 — AN UPGRADE TO THE STANDARD EPIC, THE EPIC ULTIMATE USED TITANIUM LUGS THAT WERE MACHINED BY MERLIN METALWORKS OF CAMBRIDGE, MASSACHUSETTS. THE EXPENSE OF RAW MATERIALS AND THE COST OF SUBCONTRACTING THE WORK MADE THE FRAMES A COMPLETE MONEY LOSER FOR THE COMPANY.

TUBING 03 — EARLY EPIC ULTIMATE FRAMES USED A SUPER-HIGH-MODULUS COMPOSITE MATERIAL THAT PROVED TO BE TOO BRITTLE TO BE PRACTICAL; A LOWER-MODULUS MATERIAL FROM MACLEAN QUALITY COMPOSITES OF SALT LAKE CITY, UTAH, WAS USED FOR MOST OF THE EPIC ULTIMATE FRAMES PRODUCED.

FORK 04 — ALTHOUGH SHOWN WITH A SPECIALIZED-DESIGNED CARBON-AND-TITANIUM FUTURE SHOCK FSX, THE EPIC ULTIMATE, WHICH WAS PRODUCED UNTIL 1995, WAS NEVER SOLD WITH A SUSPENSION FORK. INSTEAD IT CAME WITH A FEATHERY DIRECT DRIVE CHRO-MOLY MODEL.

LIMITED 05 — IN 1995, THE FINAL EPIC ULTIMATE FRAMES, ALL BUILT BY BRIAN LUCAS IN MORGAN HILL, WERE PRODUCED. EACH OF THE 60 FRAMES HAS A UNIQUE SERIAL NUMBER DISPLAYED ON A PLAQUE ON ITS TOP TUBE. NED OVEREND WAS GIVEN #1 TO COMMEMORATE HIS 1990 WORLDS WIN ABOARD A PROTOTYPE ULTIMATE.

FEATURES:

SPECIFICATIONS:

ORIGINAL RETAIL PRICE	$3,800 (frame and fork only); approximately $6,000 as shown
APPROXIMATE NUMBER SOLD	1,500 between 1990 and 1995
WEIGHT	2.6 pounds (frame only); 24 lbs as shown
FRAME	High-modulus carbon tubing; machined & welded titanium lugs
FORK	Specialized Direct Drive heat-treated chro-moly
HEADSET	Specialized alloy Aheadset, 1-inch diameter
STEM	Specialized Team
HANDLEBAR	Specialized Team aluminum
BRAKES	Shimano XTR
BRAKE LEVERS	Shimano XTR
FRONT DERAILLEUR	Shimano XTR
REAR DERAILLEUR	Shimano XTR
SHIFT LEVERS	Shimano XTR
CASSETTE	Shimano XTR 8-Speed 12/32
CHAIN	Shimano XTR
CRANKSET	Shimano XTR 24/36/46
BOTTOM BRACKET	Shimano XTR
PEDALS	Shimano XT clipless
RIMS	Specialized X23
FRONT HUB	Hugi
REAR HUB	Hugi
SPOKES	DT 14/15 gauge
FRONT TIRE	Specialzied Cannibal S 1.95
REAR TIRE	Specialzied Cannibal S 1.95
SEAT	Specialized ProLong w/titanium rails
SEAT BINDER	Specialized quick-release
DESIGNED BY	Jim Merz & Mike Lopez

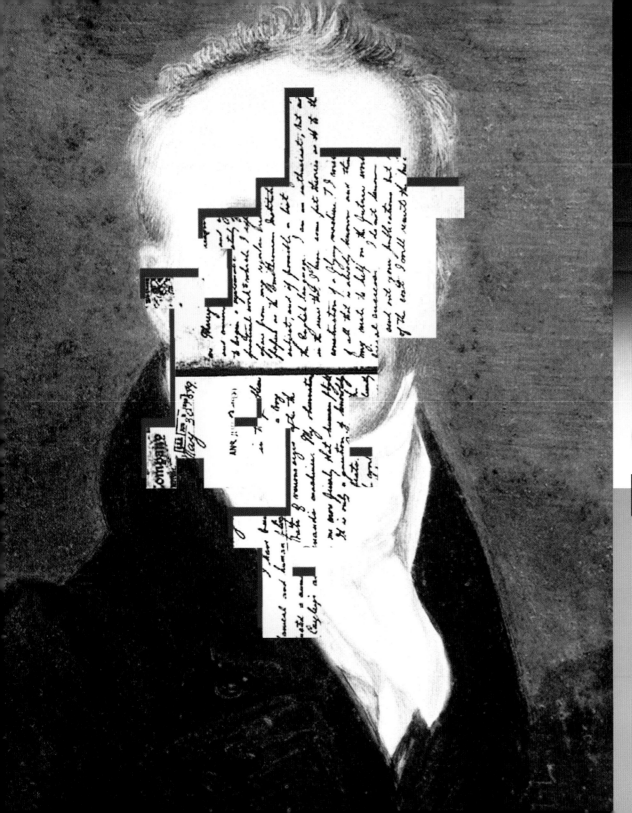

STUM
SMI

PJUMPER IN THE HSONIAN

MUSEUMS AND MOUNTAIN BIKES?

What, you're probably asking, does a renowned cultural institution created in Washington, D.C., more than 100 years ago thanks to an endowment from an ambitious British aristocrat have to do with shredding singletrack? As it turns out, just enough.

James Smithson, a scientist and explorer who left just over a half-million bucks to the people of the United States to build an institution that would promote "the increase and diffusion of knowledge," was a diligent young student, dedicated scientific researcher and, above all, a guy who loved a bit of adventure. He was known to have risked life and limb, including a near-drowning while gathering geological observations on a tour of the Hebrides islands off the Northwest coast of Scotland, and would've appreciated the energy and inventiveness of mountain biking's early pioneers.

These days, the institution that Smithson funded has evolved into the world's largest museum complex, the Smithsonian, and it houses America's most important national collections and research centers such as the National Air and Space Museum, the National Museum of Arts and Industries and, in one little corner of National Museum of American History, the Specialized Stumpjumper.

Sometime around 1990, the Smithsonian discovered the mountain bike and, with its mandate to catalog the best examples of transportation, picked up the phone and dialed Specialized's office in Morgan Hill. "'Can we send a bike?' sure," said Tom Hillard, who picked up the phone that afternoon. Now, along with everything from steamships to spaceships, there's a Stumpjumper collecting dust in the Smithsonian. Let's hope they're keeping the tires properly inflated.

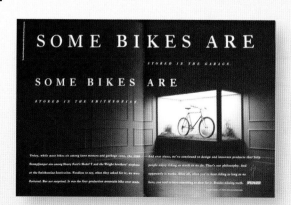

SOME BIKES ARE *STORED IN THE GARAGE.*

SOME BIKES ARE *STORED IN THE SMITHSONIAN.*

Q: HOW DO YOU PURSUE **PERFECTION?**

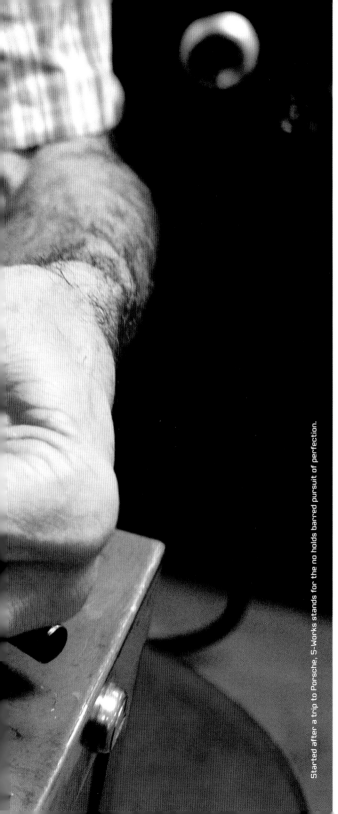

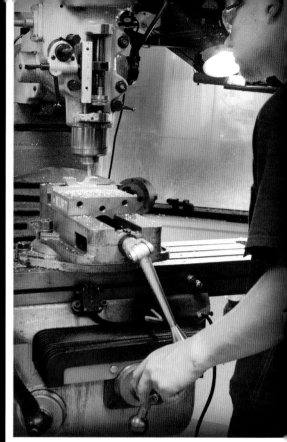

A: TAKE NOTES FROM PORSCHE

The call came from Harm Lagaay himself. Being a Dutchman with a German accent, it was tough to believe whether the head of Porsche's design department was for real. Can Specialized send some engineers to the super secretive workshop in Weissach to talk about a Porsche Spider version of the 2.6-pound carbon-and-titanium Epic Ultimate? Hard to say no to an offer like that.

So, a few S team members packed their bags, pulled out their passports and went to the workshop the good Dr. had built. What they saw at Weissach was an atelier packed with more than a thousand of the world's best engineers, all obsessed with one glorious goal: to design and build the best. Cars built purely for racing, cars built to investigate alternative fuels or new materials, cars done purely as design studies. The budget seemed as endless as did the outpouring of outstanding ideas and, although legendary cars and other consumer products regularly came out of Weissach, there was no mandate that anything directly marketable flow from the factory. It was R&D in its purest form. Ultimately the Porsche Spider bike never came to fruition, but the boondoggle in the Black Forrest did spawn something: Specialized's own version of Weissach right in Morgan Hill.

From the first, the plan was to allow Specialized's most talented designers and engineers indulge themselves completely. To lift all restraints and put to rest all preconceptions. To ignore economies, traditions and timelines in pursuit of one simple goal: to make the best bikes available anywhere. Has it been a success? S-Works bikes have rocketed riders to victories in World Championships on the road and mountain, riders who've won stages and worn the coveted Yellow Jersey in the Tour de France, riders who've taken Olympic and X Games medals and riders who've captured the Ironman. There's also a big pile of bikes and parts that have never made it out of the shop; some good ideas in there and many will likely end up in other bikes at other times, but that's not the point of S-Works. The point is to pursue perfection, regardless.

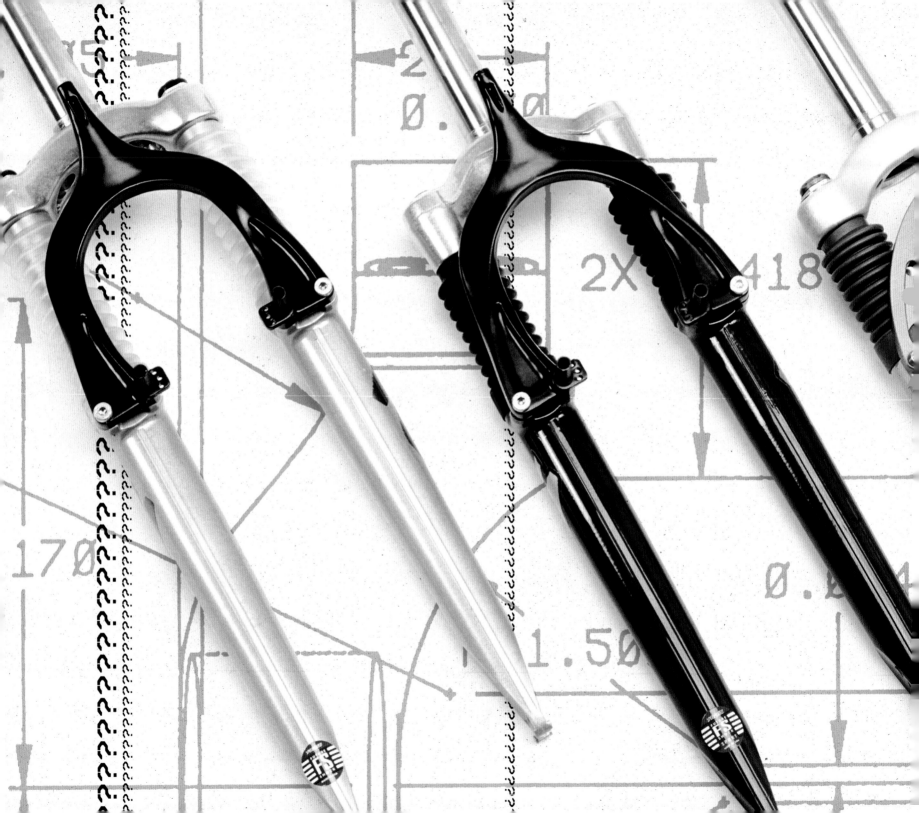

Preload Adjuster

Fork Crown

Stanchion Tube

Fork Brace

Elastomers (6)

Fork Bushing

ner Lug

Carbon Lower Fork

Damper Cartridge

Lower Fork Bushing

Valving Assy

FUTURE SHOCK

When the Captain won the 1990 Worlds in Durango he had a prototype RockShox RS-1 suspension fork hanging off the front of his Specialized Epic Ultimate. The fact that Ned and other top riders (like DH Champ Greg Herbold) relied on the new fangled part for such a monumental race sent a clear message: suspension forks were the future.

Sensing the opportunity, Specialized set to work on their own sus fork. After test riding and tearing into a few early RS-1's, the engineering team in Morgan Hill realized that it was going to be tough to beat the air-and-oil internal components that RockShox founder Paul Turner had created. So, they drove up to the RockShox factory in Mountain View, California and struck a deal: Specialized engineers, led by Mark Winter, would create many of the external parts and RockShox would supply the intricate internals and manufacturing muscle.

By 1992 the fruits of the Specialized-RockShox partnership appeared: Future Shock forks were featured on Specialized's own bikes. The first few years was nothing spectacular, but then came the Future Shock FSX. Designed by Winter, the FSX was a cost-is-no-object analog to Specialized's carbon-and-titanium Epic Ultimate frame (although the two were never sold together). Riding on air-and-oil RockShox Mag21 internals, the FSX was the first suspension fork to ever use carbon lower legs, which were developed, designed and manufactured just for that purpose. Sounds expensive and it was; word has it that each carbon leg cost Specialized over $100. The composite tubes and CNC machined aluminum brace made the FSX both lighter and more expensive than any production fork on the market. "We knew at the time that Specialized's fork was actually better than ours," says Special-ized's suspension guru Mike McAndrews who was then working at RockShox with boyhood friend Turner. "But it was also something we just couldn't afford to produce."

Eventually though, the race between suspension manufacturers made it clear that keeping up in the fork business was not in the cards for Specialized. So, as with derailleurs, rims and pedals, they went back to choosing the best parts they could find from a range of companies. Does that mean they're out of the game forever? Hard to say, but with McAndrews and his team of designers and engineers working in Morgan Hill, nothing is out of the question.

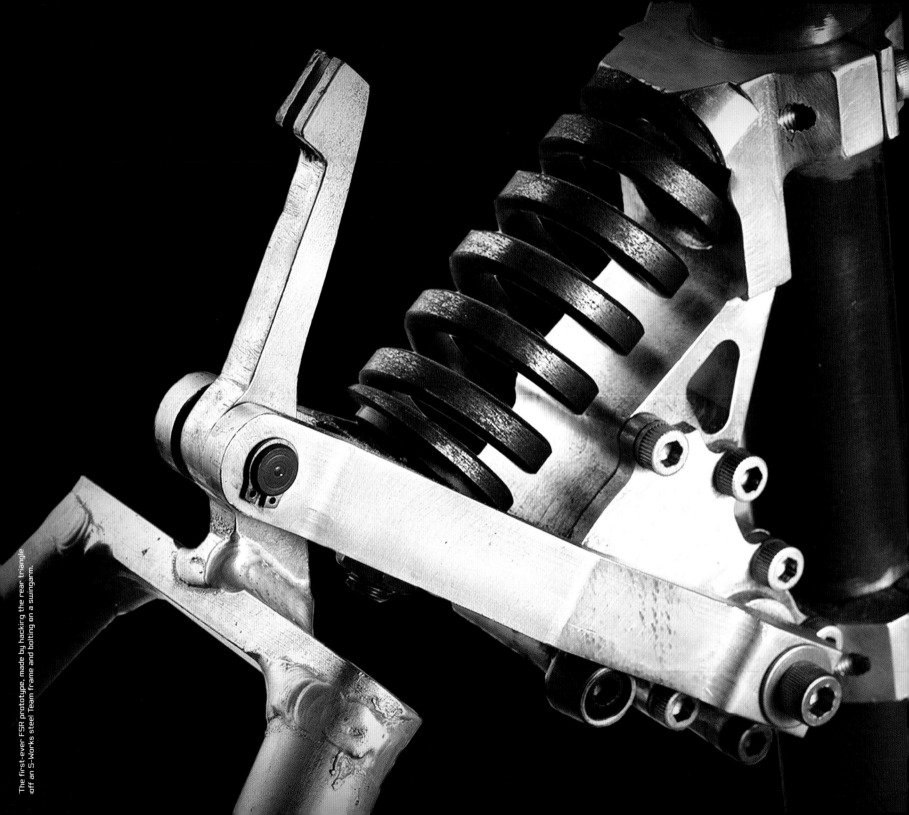

The first-ever FSR prototype, made by hacking the rear triangle off an S-Works steel Team frame and bolting on a swingarm.

FSR

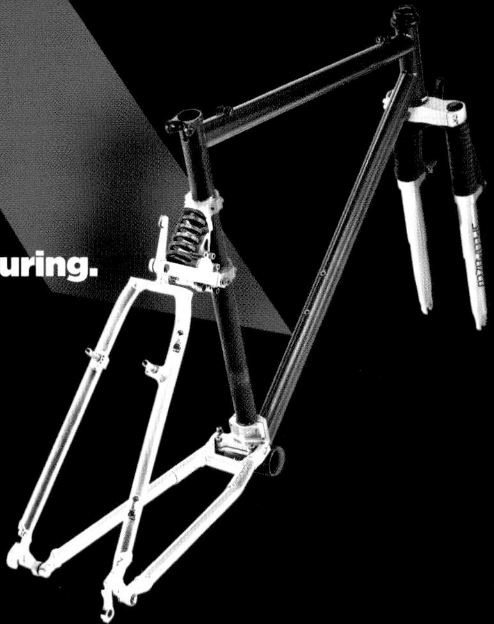

Unique. Masterful. Enduring.

FIG. 67

1993

Thank God There Are People Who Stayed In The Science Club.

While you were learning how to French kiss, they were learning how to manipulate gravity. Introducing the S-Works FSR? The most thought-out, dialed-in, thoroughly tested, fully suspended mountain bike there is. See your nearest physicist (*or your local S-Works™ dealer*) for a thorough explanation.

FUTURE SHOCK /\/\/\/REAR

WHAT HAPPENS WHEN SPECIALIZED'S ENGINEERS GET THEIR HANDS ON AN AUSTRIAN'S REAR END?

We'll call it 1991-ish. In the decade since the launch of the original Stumpjumper, the off-road world and the technology that made it possible had blown up in ways nobody could have imagined. Rear suspension designs were popping onto the radar like UFOs over the Nevada desert. Trouble was, most were heavy and inefficient alien monstrosities. At the time, bike suspension was so complicated and undependable that many inside Specialized headquarters weren't even convinced it was a good thing.

Still, thinking not of what was, but what could be, Specialized sent their top team on a quest for a true no-compromises suspension bike, one that pedaled properly when you poured on the gas, remained under control and comfortable at all times, was light (less than 27 pounds was the number thrown around), dependable and easy to service. Even today it'd be a BHAG (Big, Hairy, Audacious Goal), but back in '91 much of the technology that would make such suspension possible didn't even exist.

Spending over a year on the project, engineers John O'Neil, Mark Winter and Mark DiNucci mocked up and mowed through every design they could get their hands on. Some were good, but none were perfect. So they kept fabricating Frankenbikes and listening to any other Frankenbikers who came through their door (hey, it's how Nike found Air). Eventually Austrian engineer Horst Leitner, who'd worked for European auto and motorcycle giants in the 1970s, filled the team's head with a magical multi-link design that would become the FSR. To DiNucci and the designers, Horst was a motorcycle-design guru with a pile of patents to his name; to Horst, Specialized had the resources to fine-tune his design and repeat what they'd done with the Stumpjumper.

DiNucci and Co. made early FSRs by hacking the rear ends off existing Stumpjumper frames and replacing them with Horst's swingarms. With a stadium-sized heap full of busted bikes (and a new team of test riders that had been recruited exclusively for the project), development quickly moved into production. Perhaps a bit too quickly: In the summer of 1993 the first few hundred production frames had to be scrapped when it was discovered that the original seat-tube shock mount wasn't substantial enough. Like DiNucci says, *"It was pretty much everyone's experience getting thrown into the pot and making some decisions based on gut feeling. We didn't have the kind of sophisticated testing and development that we needed for a bike as complex as the FSR."* Which is one reason the FSR is so important in the world of Specialized—it's the bike that broke the machine and forced the folks in Morgan Hill to rethink their research and development process. *"All of a sudden the cocktail napkin just wasn't enough; you needed real engineering and testing,"* says Specialized's longtime R&D and marketing man Chris Murphy.

Racers, both pro and amateur, made the Cactus Cup the kick-off to their season.

CACTUS CUP

A SPECIALIZED SPONSORED SPRING BREAK

MTB STAGE RACE

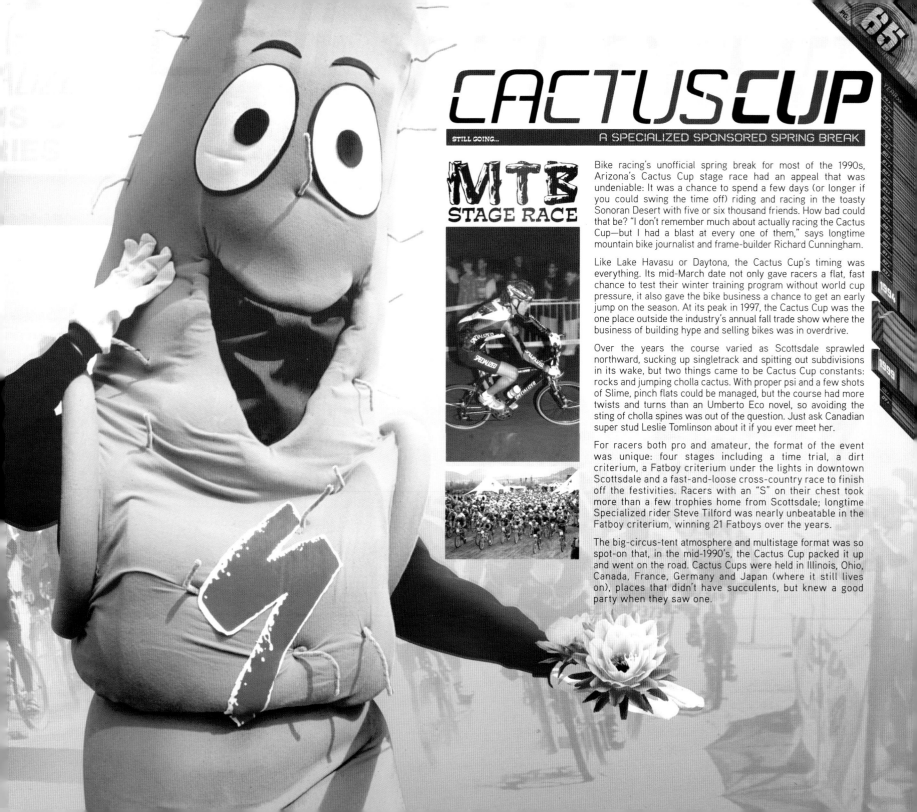

Bike racing's unofficial spring break for most of the 1990s, Arizona's Cactus Cup stage race had an appeal that was undeniable: It was a chance to spend a few days (or longer if you could swing the time off) riding and racing in the toasty Sonoran Desert with five or six thousand friends. How bad could that be? "I don't remember much about actually racing the Cactus Cup—but I had a blast at every one of them," says longtime mountain bike journalist and frame-builder Richard Cunningham.

Like Lake Havasu or Daytona, the Cactus Cup's timing was everything. Its mid-March date not only gave racers a flat, fast chance to test their winter training program without world cup pressure, it also gave the bike business a chance to get an early jump on the season. At its peak in 1997, the Cactus Cup was the one place outside the industry's annual fall trade show where the business of building hype and selling bikes was in overdrive.

Over the years the course varied as Scottsdale sprawled northward, sucking up singletrack and spitting out subdivisions in its wake, but two things came to be Cactus Cup constants: rocks and jumping cholla cactus. With proper psi and a few shots of Slime, pinch flats could be managed, but the course had more twists and turns than an Umberto Eco novel, so avoiding the sting of cholla spines was out of the question. Just ask Canadian super stud Leslie Tomlinson about it if you ever meet her.

For racers both pro and amateur, the format of the event was unique: four stages including a time trial, a dirt criterium, a Fatboy criterium under the lights in downtown Scottsdale and a fast-and-loose cross-country race to finish off the festivities. Racers with an "S" on their chest took more than a few trophies home from Scottsdale; longtime Specialized rider Steve Tilford was nearly unbeatable in the Fatboy criterium, winning 21 Fatboys over the years.

The big-circus-tent atmosphere and multistage format was so spot-on that, in the mid-1990's, the Cactus Cup packed it up and went on the road. Cactus Cups were held in Illinois, Ohio, Canada, France, Germany and Japan (where it still lives on), places that didn't have succulents, but knew a good party when they saw one.

1994

1999

FIELD
GUIDE v04

1994 Specialized S-Works FSR*
*1994 bike with 1993 shock shown

FRAME 01 — ENGINEERED BY MARK DINUCCI AND MARK WINTER, THE LIGHT, BUT RIGID DIRECT DRIVE FRONT TRIANGLE USED ON THE 1994 FSR WAS THE PINNACLE OF SPECIALIZED'S WORK IN FERROUS FRAMES.

SUSPENSION 02 — CO-DEVELOPED WITH AMP RESEARCH FOUNDER HORST LEITNER, THE FSR SUSPENSION WAS DESIGNED TO BE FULLY ACTIVE AND FULLY INDEPENDENT IN ORDER TO MAXIMIZE COMFORT, CONTROL AND EFFICIENCY.

FORK 03 — CO-DEVELOPED WITH AND MANUFACTURED BY ROCKSHOX, THE FSX USED MODIFIED ROCKSHOX MAG21 INTERNALS WITH A SPECIALIZED-DESIGNED CARBON LOWER LEGS AND M2 ALLOY BRAKE BRACE.

SHIFTER 04 — FIRST PRODUCED IN 1993, THE SRAM SRT 500 8-SPEED TWIST SHIFTERS WERE THE FIRST HIGH-END, RACE-SPECIFIC SHIFTERS MADE BY THE CHICAGO-BASED COMPANY AND SPECIALIZED WAS THE FIRST BIG BIKE COMPANY TO SPEC THEM.

TIRES 05 — NAMED AFTER A PINK FLOYD ALBUM, UMMA GUMMA WAS THE FIRST SOFT-COMPOUND RUBBER EVER INTRODUCED. PERHAPS AHEAD OF ITS TIME, IT NEVER FOUND MUCH OF A FOLLOWING AND WAS EVENTUALLY DISCONTINUED.

FEATURES:

SPECIFICATIONS:

ORIGINAL RETAIL PRICE	$2,800
APPROXIMATE NUMBER SOLD	1,000 in 1994 (calendar year)
WEIGHT	26 lbs
FRAME	Prestige chromoly steel main triangle/machined aluminum linkage
SHOCK	FOX Alps 4 (shown with non-stock shock)
FORK	Specialized Future Shock FSX
HEADSET	Aheadset 1-inch diameter
STEM	Specialized investment cast titanium
HANDLEBAR	SBC Team double butted alloy
GRIPS	Grip Shift with Umma Gumma rubber
BRAKES	Avid Hollow-Core cantilevers
BRAKE LEVERS	Dia-Compe PC-8 Power Control
FRONT DERAILLEUR	Shimano XTR
REAR DERAILLEUR	Shimano XTR
SHIFT LEVERS	Grip Shift SRT500
CASSETTE	Shimano XTR 8-speed (12/32)
CHAIN	Shimano XTR 8-speed
CRANKSET	Shimano XTR (26/36/48)
BOTTOM BRACKET	Specialized Direct Drive w/ titanium spindle
PEDALS	Shimano 737 SPD clipless
RIMS	Specialized Z 21 Pro
FRONT HUB	Shimano XTR
REAR HUB	Shimano XTR cassette
SPOKES	DT Comp 15/16 gauge with alloy nipples
FRONT TIRE	Pro Control/S 1.95 w/ Umma Gumma rubber
REAR TIRE	Pro Control/S 1.95 w/ Umma Gumma rubber
SEAT	Specialized Prolong/S with titanium rails
SEAT POST	Specialized alloy single-bolt
SEAT BINDER	alloy quick-release
ACCESSORIES	pump for shock and fork
DESIGNED BY	Mark DiNucci, Horst Leitner, Jim Merz, Mark Norris and Mark Winter

Winning Is Easy With SPECIALIZED On Your Chest.

Not Just Racing. WINNING.

Plane tickets? You wanna talk about buying some plane tickets? Ever since some fool in the Specialized marketing department threw Laurence Malone, Specialized's first sponsored off-roader, the keys to their van, Morgan Hill has spent millions of dollars to send hundreds of riders and support staff all over the world in search of one thing: the top step of the podium.

Crack the cover on the record book, and you'll see that the men and women with an "S" on their chest have hit their mark with the ferocity of a Detroit pit bull and the efficiency of a Toyota Prius. The score? Specialized mountain riders have won five UCI elite world championships, dozens of UCI world cup races and world cup titles, and so many NORBA nationals and national championships we lost count back when Ned was sportin' Factory Pilots and winning everything in sight.

While winning is everything for the riders in red, for Specialized, supplying the pickiest riders on the planet with gear that's designed exclusively to help them go fast is a worthy obsession. No question that without the team, there'd be no S-Works, and without S-Works there'd be no feathery Stumpjumper Carbon hardtail frame or Brain-it-knows-the-difference-between-a-bump-and-a-bicep suspension.

SPECIALIZED OFF-ROAD RACERS

Alban Lakata	Gavin Chilcot	Marga Fullana
Allan Ott	Golden Brainard	Mark Jordan
Anneke Beerten	Wayne Crossdale	Mark Michelle
Barbara Blatter	Jasen McRoy	Mike Kluge
Bart Brentjens	Jay Henry	Mikki Douglass
Bas Van Dooren	Jeff Osguthorpe	Ned Overend
Caroline Alexander	Jeremy Horgan-Kobelski	Nick Waite
Chris Powell	Jimmy Mortonsen	Oscar Saiz
Cindy Whitehead	John Devine	Paola Pezzo (1)
Conrad Stolz	Kelli Emmit	Sabine Spitz (3)
Dara Marks-Merino	Kirt Vories	Sam Jurekovic
Daryl Price	Kyle Straight	Sam Schultz
Dave McLaughlin	Laurence Malone	Shaun Palmer
David Vazquez	Liam Killen (5)	Sid Tabarlay
Derek Wilkerson	Lisa Muhich	Silvia Furst
Elladee Brown	Lori Bowden	Susy Pride
Elsbeth Vink	Luca Bramati	Tara Llanes (4)
Filip Meirhaeghe (2)	Magen Long	Todd Tanner
Frank Mapel	Marcel Garretson	Todd Wells

Refugee | Vedran Novak

One-Time Refugee Bounces Back To Normalcy On A Stumpjumper

30 year-old Verdan Novak used to live in Zagreb, Croatia. When civil war hit the country in the 1990s, he became one of the thousands of refugees who found safe haven in Serbia. You don't see a lot of racing bikes in refugee camps for the simple reason that people leaving home with everything they have on their backs don't have room for two-wheelers. Once in Serbia, Verdan and the rest of the Croatians were under the oppressive rule of Slobodan Milosevic, and with even the basic necessities hard to come by, life was anything but easy and a bike was a luxury that nobody could afford. "Things were so bad that I couldn't even imagine a time when I would ride again," says Vedran of the time in Serbia.

Fortunately for Vedran (and the rest of the world), Milosevic was deposed and life in the Balkans slowly returned to normal. Vedran scrimped and saved and was able to buy a used Stumpjumper Pro that he says was in excellent condition. He's been riding it every day since and says he just doesn't want to stop. "Before my new Stumpjumper came along, I really didn't know that so much fun could be packed into two wheels! My bike is a constant reminder of how good life can be."

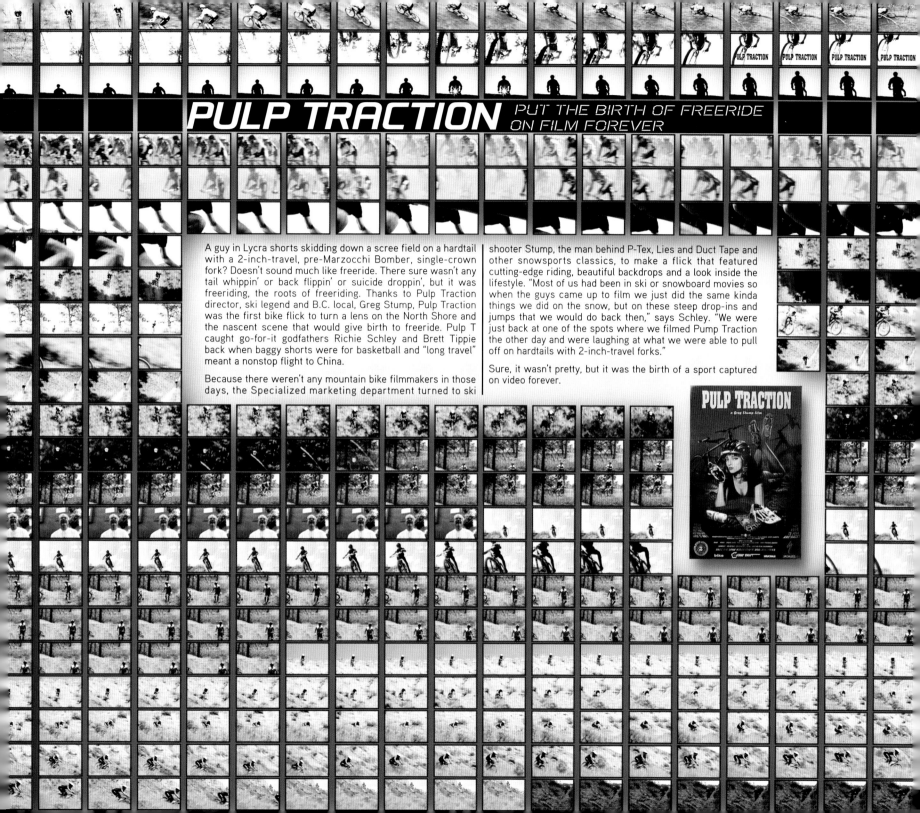

PULP TRACTION
PUT THE BIRTH OF FREERIDE ON FILM FOREVER

A guy in Lycra shorts skidding down a scree field on a hardtail with a 2-inch-travel, pre-Marzocchi Bomber, single-crown fork? Doesn't sound much like freeride. There sure wasn't any tail whippin' or back flippin' or suicide droppin', but it was freeriding, the roots of freeriding. Thanks to Pulp Traction director, ski legend and B.C. local, Greg Stump, Pulp Traction was the first bike flick to turn a lens on the North Shore and the nascent scene that would give birth to freeride. Pulp T caught go-for-it godfathers Richie Schley and Brett Tippie back when baggy shorts were for basketball and "long travel" meant a nonstop flight to China.

Because there weren't any mountain bike filmmakers in those days, the Specialized marketing department turned to ski shooter Stump, the man behind P-Tex, Lies and Duct Tape and other snowsports classics, to make a flick that featured cutting-edge riding, beautiful backdrops and a look inside the lifestyle. "Most of us had been in ski or snowboard movies so when the guys came up to film we just did the same kinda things we did on the snow, but on these steep drop-ins and jumps that we would do back then," says Schley. "We were just back at one of the spots where we filmed Pump Traction the other day and were laughing at what we were able to pull off on hardtails with 2-inch-travel forks."

Sure, it wasn't pretty, but it was the birth of a sport captured on video forever.

PULP TRACTION
a Greg Stump film

FSRXC

NOTHING EXTRA. NOTHING.

THE FINAL NAIL
IN THE HARDTAIL COFFIN.

Train and train and train to be fast on a cross-country bike, and you'll find that other than a set of king-sized quads, you're as sparse as a supermodel. That was the idea behind the FSRxc: Strip a suspension bike down to nothing but that which was necessary, just like an XC-racer's body.

The timing, though, was the real genius: Back in the late 90s suspension bikes were gaining additional travel, but were also packing on a whole lot of extra weight. In the process, they lost a lot of appeal for people who were more concerned about speed and efficiency than bombing off house-high boulders.

So Specialized team members Ben Capron, Mark Norris, Mike Ducharme and Jeff Pint decided to zig when everyone else was zagging. They shaved and optimized and cut and trimmed and came up with the 3-inch-travel FSRxc: a chassis that had nearly as much travel as a standard FSR, but weighed less and still had razor-sharp handling. Ducharme, Capron and crew obsessed over every square millimeter of the frame, trimming tube diameters, shortening butting profiles and shaving the seatpod design.

The result was one of the most innovative bikes Specialized has ever produced and lightest pivoted suspension bikes that had ever been built. When saddled up with a boxful of good parts, the FSRxc tipped the scales at well under 25 pounds and a raceable sample that weighed just 20.6 pounds floated around the 1998 Interbike tradeshow.

Why take this narrator's word for it though? Check out one rider's review from MTBR.com that was posted way back in 1999: "I will never go back to a hardtail. One ride on this bike, and you won't, either."

Shaun Palmer, game face fully intact.

!@#!?#!@!

NAPALM!

WHEN THE WORLD'S GREATEST ATHLETE ENTERED THE MOUNTAIN BIKE SCENE HE LEFT ONLY

SCORCHED EARTH &
CRUMPLED BAIL BONDS IN HIS WAKE

He wasn't a mountain biker

He wasn't a mountain biker. That was the thing. He never really considered himself a biker, he just came in and hauled ass on a mountain bike just as he would've on a snowboard or a moto or one of his dozen Cadillacs.

He wasn't a mountain biker; he was a rock star the likes of which had never been imagined in pedal-powered circles. Since his first day on a board at Donner Ski Ranch, the man they called Mini-Shred owned the snow-sports world outright. Then he truly blew up; in his words: "In 1992 my grandmother died and it led to me being a compete idiot, fighting in bars, drinking, going nowhere. So I turned it around, started to vent all my anger about her death by putting the energy into sports. It was like 'Shit, I am going to win everything.'" So Mini-Shred morphed into Napalm and set out to beat anyone he could find at their own game. "It made me feel good," he says.

By '96 he had moved into mountain biking and, with the river of Olympic and tech money flowing into the sport, his timing absolutely could not have been better. Palmer soaked up the accolades and the limelight, and ultimately was the beginning and the end of everything that millennial mountain biking will be remembered for. A gold lamé suit, a Troy Lee-painted Prevost bus and a six-figure contract (although the size of said contract was more than vastly overstated.) "The guy never took it seriously enough to win the big races, but he sure stirred up a lot of shit," says former mechanic and Shaun Palmer's bail bondsman Joe "Buck" Buckley.

ENDURO

Because it's called "all mountain," not "easy mountain"

As the end of the millennium came into view, people predicted chaos. Y2K was on everyone's lips. "End times are nigh," claimed certain religious sects. Well, apparently they weren't, but that's a whole other story.

For off-road riders the chaos was reflected in the way they were thinking of bikes and trails and how the two came together. Thanks to the popularity of the mountain bike, the spots that were easy to get to (those with trailside parking) were under an incredible amount of stress, if not completely closed due to overuse. Core mountain bikers wanted to get away from the masses and were calling for bikes that would rail on the tougher trails that most folks couldn't handle, but because those trails were farther away, additional weight or a loss in efficiency was out of the question.

A lot of trail time—luckily, riding is research at Specialized—and a rethink of the time-tested four-bar rear suspension design that the engineers in Morgan Hill had codeveloped with suspension guru Horst Leitner beginning in 1991 resulted in the first Enduro. Launched, literally, off rocks and loading docks in the summer of 1999, the original Enduro Pro frame featured a burly MAX (Manipulated Aluminum eXtrusion) Backbone chassis with 4.6 inches of adjustable travel that was just 250 grams heavier than a shorter-travel FSR from the previous year. The Enduro also had a low-slung, V-shaped top tube that lent riders an incredible standover height for a bike with loads of travel. For 2000 the chassis was lightened and refined even more; fenders were added for an unmistakable moto appeal. The upshot was a line of all-trail bikes that would come to be known as a stalwart in the Specialized line.

Product manager Ben Capron drops in on a 2000 Enduro.

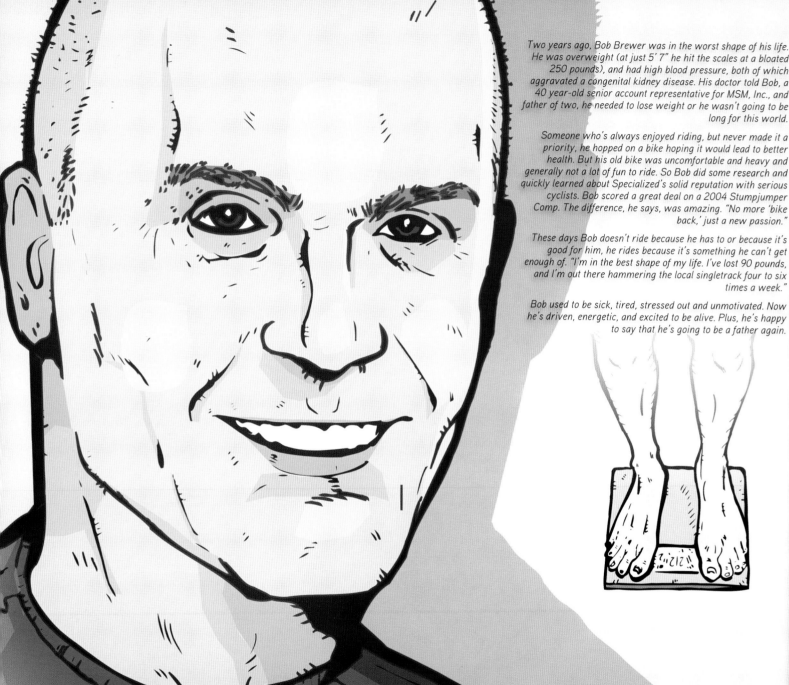

Two years ago, Bob Brewer was in the worst shape of his life. He was overweight (at just 5' 7" he hit the scales at a bloated 250 pounds), and had high blood pressure, both of which aggravated a congenital kidney disease. His doctor told Bob, a 40 year-old senior account representative for MSM, Inc., and father of two, he needed to lose weight or he wasn't going to be long for this world.

Someone who's always enjoyed riding, but never made it a priority, he hopped on a bike hoping it would lead to better health. But his old bike was uncomfortable and heavy and generally not a lot of fun to ride. So Bob did some research and quickly learned about Specialized's solid reputation with serious cyclists. Bob scored a great deal on a 2004 Stumpjumper Comp. The difference, he says, was amazing. "No more 'bike back,' just a new passion."

These days Bob doesn't ride because he has to or because it's good for him, he rides because it's something he can't get enough of. "I'm in the best shape of my life. I've lost 90 pounds, and I'm out there hammering the local singletrack four to six times a week."

Bob used to be sick, tired, stressed out and unmotivated. Now he's driven, energetic, and excited to be alive. Plus, he's happy to say that he's going to be a father again.

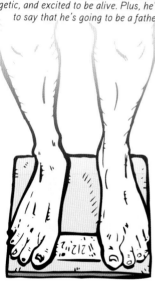

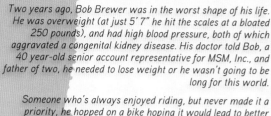

MY STUMPJUMPER

From Fullback To Flyweight, Bob Lost 90lbs On His Stump

Fullback | Bob Brewer

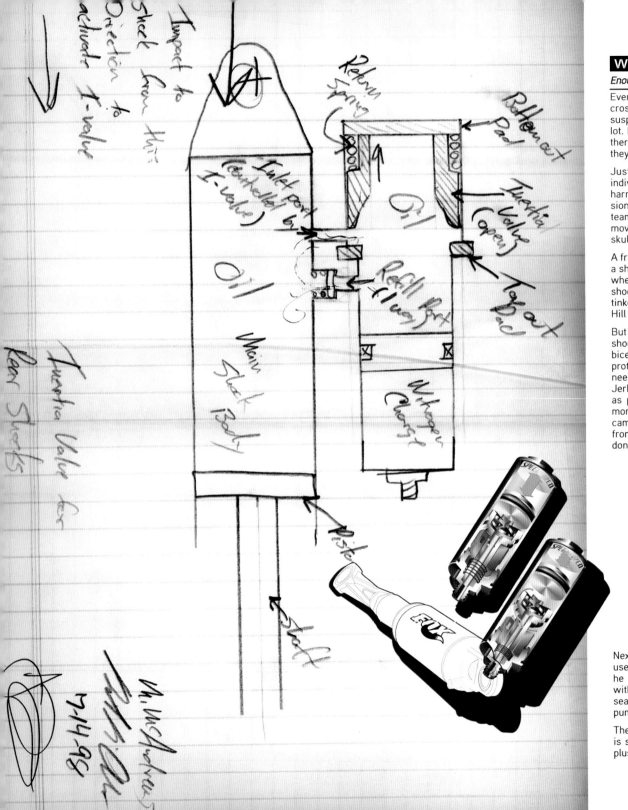

Impact to Shock from this Direction to activate I-valve

Return Spring

Bottom out Pad

Inertia Valve (open)

Oil

Inlet port (controlled by I-valve)

Oil

Impact Pad

Refill Port

Inertia Valve box

Rear Shocks

Main Shock Body

Nitrogen Charge

Piston

Shaft

M. McAndrews

7-14-98

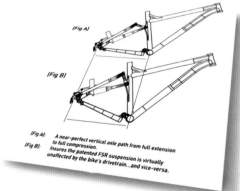

WHAT CAN YOU LEARN FROM A JERK?

Enough to make your suspension work only when you want it to

Ever pushed up and down on the handlebar or saddle of a pro cross-country racer's bike? Tell you this much: The so-called suspension fork on the front of that bike doesn't move a whole lot. In fact, many racers have their forks pumped up so much there's just about zero travel. Hey, if that's how they like it, and they can win, what's the harm? Right?

Just ask Mike McAndrews, a lifelong suspension-obsessed individual and engineer at Specialized. He'll tell you about the harm. He's spent years and years and years making suspension that works—really good. So when a group of Specialized team riders said they wished they had suspension that would move only when they hit a good-sized bump, Mick, with his skull full of suspension solutions, had just the right idea.

A friend who was an engineer at FoMoCo once told Mick about a shock he'd designed that would only compress when a car's wheel hit a big bump. Back in Detroit they called it the Jerk shock because it took a jolt to activate it. So, Mick started tinkering with his own version of a Jerk shock, but in Morgan Hill they jokingly called it The Jerk's Shock.

But Mick thought it was a pretty smart idea, and because the shock knew the difference between input from a bump and a bicep, he dubbed the project "the Brain." He developed a prototype that immediately worked, but not as dependably as it needed to. Then, he had a Eureka moment: If the heart of the Jerk shock—the Inertia valve—was moved as close to the axle as possible, the whole thing would work better, faster and more dependably. He did, and it did, and that auxiliary chamber came to be known as the Brain. With no small amount of help from the FOX crew on the finer points and production, it was a done deal.

[Fig A]

[Fig B]

[Fig A]: A near-perfect vertical axle path from full extension to full compression.
[Fig B]: Insures the patented FSR suspension is virtually unaffected by the bike's drivetrain...and vice-versa.

Next thing you know Filip Meirhaeghe—one of the guys who used to race hardtails and keep his fork pumped up as hard as he could—won a World Championship on an Epic equipped with a Brain shock. (OK, Meirhaeghe was popped the following season for a certain chemical imbalance, but the Brain wasn't pumped up on anything illegal.)

These days Mick's Brain shock with trailside tuning technology is smart enough to be found on many race bikes and even a plush Stumpjumper trail bike.

EPIC
with
BRAIN

2003

Kamloops kid Matt Hunter smokes a berm for Sterling Lorence's lens.

BIKE BUILT FOR BUSTING THE WORLD'S SICKEST TRICKS
ALL STARTED WITH A PILE OF LEGOS

The guy on this spread, Darren Barrecloth, lord of new-school freeriding, he needed a weapon in his battle against limits, laws and preconceptions. So, Specialized came up with the Demo, a series of bikes that BearClaw said needed to have a load of plush, active travel; geometry balanced enough for the steepest steeps and the skinniest skinnies; a super-low center of gravity; a dropped top tube for enhanced maneuverability; and, oh yeah, superb shifting including accommodations for a front derailleur. No problem, says the team at Specialized, we can do that.

So a team of Specialized engineers, designers and product managers, including Jason Chamberlin, Brandon Sloan and Robert Egger dove into the project by playing with a pile of Lego building blocks. Snapping together Lego blocks allowed the team to build a quick and easy model of the Demo's basic suspension concept, one that the whole team could tune and tweak and revise before superstar engineer Chamberlin hunkered down at his computer to grind out the tough engineering work.

It doesn't take a rocket scientist to know that playing with Legos was the easy part. Creating a working design with Pro/E 3-D modeling software, building prototypes in the machine shop at Specialized headquarters in Morgan Hill and huck-testing the Demo design took years literally, two of 'em and hundreds of thousands of dollars.

The initial result of Chamberlin's computer genius, and multiple sorties to the North Shore for product manager Brandon Sloan, was a 9-inch travel, four-bar suspension frame with a regular swingarm augmented by a sub-swingarm and six pivot points. To make the Demo stiff and sturdy Chamberlin and Co. designed the most expensive set of cold forgings ever used on a bike, including the single most complex forging ever the central rib cage that houses the shock and takes a five-million-pound press to manufacture.

Who'd have guessed that a bike made for the deepest drops, gnarliest gaps and hardest hits all started with a pile of Legos?

DEMO

30 YEARS OF RIDING FAST AND TAKING CHANCES

Who you callin' long in the tooth?

The Big Three-O. Used to be a wake more than a celebration; adios to the kid and on to the adultlike things. These days, it's just time to freshen up your flip-flops and cut back on the beers before the crack of noon (on weekdays, anyway). Still, nobody wanted to mention it. The little guy that started as a scrappy company selling stems and such from a single-wide in San Jose was turning 30. The Big Three-O.

It's OK though. These days you're just catching your stride at 30. Right? Thirty is the new 25.

To commemorate their 30th year in *STUMPJUMPER* business, the guys at Specialized put together a very special Stumpjumper and there's no denying it looked better than ever. Its timeless, ride-me-anywhere-a-sane-person-would-ride smile fully intact. And the body? Just look at the Dream Silver brickshithouse of a chassis. Like Specialized's legendary lead designer Robert Egger is fond of saying, "If it looks right, it is right." And with the Italian Dolomites as a backdrop, is it ever. "The bike needed lots of strong shapes that, when combined, looked stronger than the sum of the parts," says Egger, the designer behind such Specialized gems such as the Enduro, Hemi and Tarmac.

Kevin Franks treads lightly in Italy's Dolomites aboard a 2004 Stumpjumper.

LIFE AT THE HEAD OF THE PACK

◆ RIDE ON, CAPTAIN NED

Yet another Saturday night for The Captain. Holed up in the latest of a world class string of $99-per-night hotels. Ice on his injured right foot and an episode of Speedvision flickering at the foot of the bed. He'll watch the late local news and drink his last bit of secret energy elixir even though he's got a 7AM start. That's The Captain's way.

Ned OFFICIALLY RETIRED back in 1996, but he doesn't seem to remember that. Since Specialized threw him a retirement party in the fall of '96 he's continued to race World Cups and NORBA Nationals, road races, hill climbs, downhills (yeah, and he beat his teenage son), duathlons, triathlons, X-terras, marathons, trail runs, adventure races and just about anything else you can imagine. If it involves elevated levels of lactic acid and an excess of endorphins, The Captain has been there. Hell, on the very day of his 50th Birthday he finished 4th in the brutal Mt Washington Hillclimb.

A lot of the kids he routinely leaves in his rear-view weren't even born when Ned finished the 1980 Ironman, or in 1983 when he won his first-ever mountain bike race and rode the Coors Classic with the legendary Ti-Raleigh team (the one with Andy Hampsten, Roy Knickman and Steve Tilford) or even when he won both the European and NORBA World Championships in 1987.

But Ned doesn't want any special treatment or extra praise, The Captain sees less than ideal lodgings, sore appendages and 7AM starts as his lot in his life. *"I'm not out there trying to prove that I'm faster than the young guys,"* he says *"I'm just out there because I love to mix it up at the front—I love the competition."*

1976
California All State Cross Country Selection

1980
28th Hawaii Ironman Triathlon; 1st College All State Cross Country Selection

1981
3rd Estes Park Marathon; 1st Kendall Mountain Run; 1st Kendall Mountain Triathlon; 1st Kendall Mountain Run;

1982
2nd Estes Park Marathon; 4th Fountain Mountain Triathlon

1983
1st Grand Junction Stage Race
1st Morgul Bismarck Road Race
1st Fountain Mountain Triathlon (2nd Overall Stage Race)
1st Iron Horse Road Race
3rd Colorado State Road Race
35th Coors Classic
2nd Mt. Evans Hill Climb
1st Road Apple Rally
Colorado State Best All-Around Rider

1984
4th Iron Horse Road Race (2nd Overall Stage Race)
2nd Colorado State Road Race
1st Pacific States Suntour MTB series
1st Crested Butte MTB Stage Race
2nd NORBA National Championships

1985
2nd Iron Horse Road Race
1st Iron Horse MTB Race
2nd Colorado State Road Race
1st Mt. Evans/Bob Cook Memorial Road Race
5th Munsingwear Bicycle Classic
1st Pacific States Suntour MTB series
1st Crested Butte MTB Stage Race
1st Road Apple Rally
5th NORBA National Championships
1st NORBA National Points Series (Road)
Colorado Best All-Around Rider

1986
1st Iron Horse Road Race
1st Iron Horse MTB Race
1st Colorado State Championships
1st Mt. Evans/Bob Cook Memorial Road Race
16th National Road Race Championships
2nd Munsingwear International Stage Race
World Cycling Road Championships
1st NORBA National Championships

1987
1st Iron Horse Road Race
2nd Nevada City Road Race
4th Mt. Evans/Bob Cook Memorial Road Race
1st Rage in the Sage Bicycle Classic
1st Revenge of the Siskiyous
1st Colorado State Championships (MTB)
1st NORBA National Champion
1st NORBA National Points Championships
1st European World Championships
1st NORBA World Championships (XC and Hill Climb)

1988
1st Iron Horse Classic MTB Race
1st Colorado State Championships
2nd NORBA National Championships
2nd European World Championships
1st NORBA World Championships (XC and Hill Climb)
1st Road Apple Rally

1989
1st NORBA National Championships
4th NORBA World Championships

1990
1st Mammoth NORBA National
1st King of the Rockies MTB Stage Race
UCI World MTB Champion
1st NORBA National Championships
Inducted: Mountain Bike Hall of Fame

1991
1st NORBA National Championships
1st Park City MTB World Cup

1992
1st NORBA National Championships
1st Road Apple Rally

1994
1st Place Swiss MTB World Cup
1st Place Italian MTB World Cup

1996
3rd XTerra Triathlon World Championships

1997
2nd XTerra Triathlon World Championships

1998
1st XTerra Triathlon World Championships

1999
1st XTerra Triathlon World Championships

2000
1st U.S. National Winter Triathlon Championships

2001
U.S. National XTERRA Series Champion

2002
U.S. National XTERRA Series Champion

2004
1st Colorado State Road Championships
4th Road Apple Rally

2005
1st Red Bull Divide & Conquer
4th Bob Cook Memorial Mt. Evans Hill Climb
4th Mt. Washington Auto Road Hill Climb
5th NORBA National Championships
11th USA Cycling Elite Road Championships

2006+

05
04
01
02
03

FIELD GUIDE v05

2006 S-Works FSR Carbon
For finding the flow on the smoothest carbon bike ever made

FRAME 01 — MADE FROM PROPRIETARY FACT Y570 COMPOSITE, AT THAT POINT THE STRONGEST CARBON USED TO MAKE A BIKE FRAME. THE S-WORKS CARBON STUMPJUMPER WAS PRIZED FOR ITS BLEND OF EFFICIENCY AND RAZOR-SHARP HANDLING.

SHOCK 02 — BRAIN WITH BRAIN FADE, THE FIRST SHOCK TO KNOW WHEN TO BE ACTIVE FOR MAXIMUM COMPLIANCE AND WHEN TO BE FIRM FOR ENHANCED EFFICIENCY. THE 2006 FEATURED BRAIN FADE TECHNOLOGY, WHICH ALLOWED RIDERS TO CUSTOM-TUNE THE FEEL OF THE BRAIN SHOCK.

TIRES 03 — DEVELOPED JUST FOR A FAST, FULL-TRAVEL BIKE LIKE THE CARBON STUMPJUMPER, THE ADRENALINE PRO 26X2.0 TIRES USED A 120 THREADS-PER-INCH CASING TO KEEP WEIGHT TO A MINIMUM AND HAD DUAL-COMPOUND RUBBER FOR THE BEST COMBINATION OF EXCELLENT ROLLING RESISTANCE AND TRACTION.

HANDLEBAR 04 — THE PERFECT COMPLEMENT TO THE CARBON STUMPJUMPER'S COMPOSITE FRAME, THE SPECIALZIED OS CARBON RISE BAR WAS LIGHT AT JUST 175 GRAMS AND FEATURED THE PERFECT COMBINATION OF UPSWEEP (6 DEGREES) AND BACKSWEEP (8 DEGREES).

SADDLE 05 — NEW FOR THE 2006 MODEL YEAR, THE RIVAL FEATURED SPECIALIZED'S EXCLUSIVE BODY GEOMETRY TECHNOLOGY, WHICH IN LAB TESTING WAS SHOWN TO ENHANCE BLOOD FLOW TO SENSITIVE AREAS.

FEATURES:

SPECIFICATIONS:

ORIGINAL RETAIL PRICE	$7100
APPROX. NUMBER SOLD	750
WEIGHT	26-lbs
FRAME	FACT 10M carbon/M5 Premium aluminum
SHOCK	FOX remote Brain Fade with Trail Tune setting
FORK	FOX Talas RLC with 90-130mm adjustable travel
HEADSET	threadless integrated alloy
STEM	Thomson CNC alloy 31.8mm clamp, 5-degree rise
HANDLEBAR	Specialized OS Carbon Rise, 6" rise, 8" backsweep
GRIPS	Specialized MTB grip
BRAKES	Shimano XTR hydraulic disc with 6-inch rotor
BRAKE LEVERS	Shimano XTR hydraulic disc
FRONT DERAILLEUR	Shimano XTR 34.mm clamp diameter
REAR DERAILLEUR	SRAM X.0 9-speed
SHIFT LEVERS	SRAM X.0 trigger with carbon housing
CASSETTE	Shimano XTR M960 (11/34) with titanium cogs
CHAIN	Shimano XTR 9-Speed
CRANKSET	Shimano XTR M960 (22/32/44)
BOTTOM BRACKET	Shimano XTR M960
RIMS	Mavic Crossmax SL Disc
FRONT HUB	Mavic Crossmax SL Disc
REAR HUB	Mavic Crossmax SL Disc
SPOKES	Mavic Crossmax SL Disc
FRONT TIRE	Specialized Adrenaline Pro 26 x 2.0 dual compound tread
REAR TIRE	Specialized Adrenaline Pro 26 x 2.0 dual compound tread
SEAT	Specialized Body geometry Rival with titanium rails
SEAT POST	Thomson aluminum 30.9mm diameter
SEAT BINDER	7075 hard anodized alloy w/ quick release
ACCESSORIES	chainstay protector, derailleur protector
DESIGNED BY	Jason Chamberlin

2⊔

SJ 81

THE FUTURE?

Tough to say where this or anything else is all headed. Greater people have tried and, well, you remember Y2K.

No question that the cycle that's gotten all of us this far will continue: Specialized will crank out great bikes, we'll find new and different ways to ride and break them, Specialized will crank out even better bikes, we'll find new and different ways to ride and break them. ad infinitum.

Since we all agree that both the trails and the architects of this culture need to be protected, Specialized has agreed to donate 100% of the profits from this book to IMBA and The MTB Hall of Fame. That's something to look forward to.

DB recycles a 500 year-old Fir tree.

FRENCH/Translation

6 & 7

DEDICACE

20 heures, 20 jours, 20 ans en arrière—c'est difficile de ne pas se souvenir de cette première sortie
en Mountain Bike. Le pneu avant qui fend la terre, et domine n'importe quel obstacle, franchissant tout sur son passage avec la douceur et la grace d'un enorme chat, Avalant les chemins comme un XR 250. Cette première gamelle ou retour de pédale dans le tibia, un avertissement, mais surtout une douleur transcendante.c'était trop bon pour être vrai, un premier baiser impossible ou le prélude d'une magnifique addiction.

Le mountain bike a cette de force; Insolent, mais accessible; dangereux mais, avec un large guidon relevé, une selle douce et un cadre articulé, prenant et attachant. Plus satisfait de juste vous apportez de nouvelles sensations et pensées, le Mountain Bike rapproche les docteurs de banlieue d'avec les plombiers de la ville et les instituteurs de provinces, et leur fait découvrir des endroits dont ils ignoraient l'existence. Même si c'est à deux pas de chez eux. Le Mountain Bike fidélise les gens apportant aventure et endorphine.

L'histoire de ce livre aurait pu être un simple comte technologique, mais le Mountain bike c'est bien plus que ça. Evidemment qu'on louchera toujours pour voir quelle sorte de dérailleur ou de fourche est sur ce vélo qui passe, ça tient plus de la culture et de la passion. C'est grace à la passion, la perspicacité et l'inspiration, que le Stumpjumper fut envisagé à l'origine comme un simple moyen d'étirer des sourires sur plus de visages. Heureusement, tous s'en sont aperçut et ont permis au Stumpjumper et au reste de ce sport et de cette culture de perdurer et d'évoluer sur plus de 25 ans. Pour ça, nous remercions tous ceux qui ont jamais enjambé un Mountain Bike. Vous avez rendu ce livre, cette culture et cette vie possible.

8 & 9

PRE-MONTAIN BIKE OFF-ROAD

Attendez, est ce que ces types sont en train de faire du mountain bike? Bien que ce soit une vingtaine d'années avant l'invention du Velo Tout Terrain, c'est bien l'impression qu'ils donnent. Après tout, ils roulent sur la terre, ils ont de gros pneus et affichent clairement de francs sourires d'une oreille à l'autre.

OK, mais alors qu'en est il de John Finley Scott. Lui qui a parcouru des milliers de kilomètres de pistes tout terrain, poussant jusqu'à l'ascension de White Mountain, à 4 456 m dans les Sierra Mountains de Californie dans les années 60 et le tout sur un Schwinn Varsity de 1953. Pouvons nous dire qu'il faisait du VTT ?

Et si nous faisions un petit voyage dans le passé jusqu'aux 20 Buffalo soldiers qui, en 1897 ont parcouru une boucle de presque 3000 km à travers l'ouest. La boucle en question les faisait traverser ce qui est devenu le Yellowstone National Park. Il est clair que ce n'était pas du vélo de route qu'ils faisaient à travers le vieil ouest sauvage.

Donc, quand exactement, les gens ont ils arreté de rouler sur les chemins et commencé à faire du mounatin bike ? était-ce le 1er decembre 1974 lorsque Russ Mahon, un pilote de la baie de San Francisco fut le premier à flanquer un dérailleur sur son Clunker ? ou alors lorsque Joe Breeze fut le premier à participer à la legendaire Repack Downhill en Octobre 1977 au guidon d'un vélo de sa fabrication avec des gros pneus et un derailleur? Ou bien quelques années plus tard lorsque Tim Neenan, le designer du tout premier Stumpjumper, a enfourché un de ses prototypes se propulsant sur les collines dérriere les bureaux de Specialized à San Jose?

Trouver la réponse à la question : quand la révolution a-t-elle réellement commencé? C'est une tache qu'il est préférable de laisser aux profs d'universités, ou bien aux groupes d'acharnés du vélos que vous trouverez n'importe quel après-midi de l'année squattant le Zeitgeist saloon à San Francisco.

10 & 11

CRESTED BUTTE

Quand les premiers outsiders, une bande de cinq marlous en Clunker venant de Marin, débarquèrent à Crested Butte en 1978, c'était pour le troisième annuel "second actual Pearl Pass Tour". Ils trouvèrent en les moto de Joe Breeze, "une course à travers une vieille mine de charbons avec ses derniers mineurs les poumons noirs de charbons qui squattent les bancs, tandis que la jeunesse danse et pédale." une ville minière depuis la ruée vers l'or de 1859. Le Crested Butte de la fin des années 70 ressemblait plus à un trou à rat, mais avec un interêt appuyé pour le telemark et la thérapie par les plantes, la station prenait des allures de royaume pour hippies. Les nouveaux locaux qui peuplaient la ville, fréquemment craints et bien souvent sales portaient des noms bizarres tels que nuage, étoile, planche ou valise.

Bénéficiant d'un passé historique dans les sports de plein air –la ville à la fierté d'être la première a avoir installé un télésiège dans le Colorado—autant les hippies que les anciens ont montré un certain penchant pour les réjouissances en plein air, dont une longue histoire d'amour avec le vélo. Évidemment, ceux qui faisaient du vélo avant 1978 n'étaient pas des bikers, ils faisaient juste du vélo. Des vélos qu'on trouvait dans la décharge de Denver, des vieux Schwinn, Hawthorne ou BF Goodrich Klunkers dans une deuxieme voire troisième renaissance. Les rues de Crested Butte n'étaient presque pas goudronnées, les pneus ballons ont donc toujours été ce qu'il y avait de mieux pour se ballader dans la ville.

Été 1976. Lors d'une longue soirée au Grubstake Saloon de Crested Butte, il fut décidé que les Klunkers seraient parfaits pour une ascension du pearl pass à 3 966 mètres puis une descente jusqu'au bar du Jerome Hotel à Aspen. En septembre de la même année, 15 âmes vaillantes et courageuses enfourchèrent leur Clunkers et prirent la direction du nord vers Aspen. Après avoir festoyer à Pearl Pass toute la nuit (d'après un compte-rendu dans le "Crested Butte Pilot", les bikers et leur équipe technique ont descendu un tonneau de bière, trois bouteilles de Schnapps, 7 litres de vin, et trois bouteilles de champagne) ils ont rejoint comme ils ont pu entre coups de pédales et gamelles, limite à la nage le Jerome Hotel où encore plus de verres furent descendus alors que la légende s'écrivait.

14 & 15

LE ROI DES CLUNKERS

Chaque Homme, Femme ou enfant qui possède un VTT devrait lever un verre, chanter une chanson, ou dire une prière au nom de Charles R Kelly (a.k.a SeeKay). Planqué dans la super hippie commune de Fairfax, Monsieur Charles créa le tout premier magazine de mountain bike –Fat Tire Flyer--bien avant même qu'il y ait des mountain bikes. Alors que chacun prétendait avoir inventé quelquechose (le premier cadre, le premier vélo, la premiere course), Charlie fut celui qui répandit un point de vue particulier propre aux gonzes qui roulaient sur ces Clunkers. C'est lui qui dicta au monde exactement ce qu'était la pratique du Clunker.

"Tandis que les Clunkers ressemblaient à de légères moto de cross, la similitude n'était que visuelle, et prendre une courbe à haute vitesse devenait une sorte de gymnastique périlleuse. Une moto a de gros pneus et des suspensions, mais un Clunker, non". Forcément, la moindre imperfection du sol rendait son pilotage délicat, voir aérien. Dans un virage serré, le Clunker n'a pas l'accélération qu'utilise une moto pour partir en glisse et se remettre dans l'axe, et sans amortisseur c'est tendu. Et pourtant, des pilotes acharnés arrivaient déja à négocier les courbes et en ressortir plus vite qu'on aurait pu l'imaginer.

"Glissez en déhanché, dans un virage en ornière, et c'est la panique. Perte totale de controle, vous devez prendre une décision dans l'urgence : sauter dans le vide ou se coucher. Se coucher…foutu…t.shirt déchiré, le coude sanguinolant. Fini la rigolade (le t.shirt était vieux…et le coude aussi), comment va le vélo ? OK …remonte dessus, remets la chaine avec ta main tout en continuant en roue libre. La chaine réenclenchée, accroche toi, t'as intéret a rester sur le vélo pour assurer un temps."
--Charles Kelly
Bicycling Magazine 1979

16 & 17

SPECIALIZED ALIMENTA LA RÉVOLUTION DU TOUT TERRAIN AVEC DES PIÈCES DÉTACHÉES

Total des ventes la première année: 60 000$
L'année suivante: 128 000$
L'année suivante: plus de 200 000$

"En regardant en arrière aujourd'hui, les choses sont allées doucement, mais ça m'a paru sacrement rapide," dit Mike Sinyard, le fondateur et président de Specialized, à propos des premières années après avoir batti les fondations de la marque et de l'entreprise.

Bien avant que des gens consacrent des sites internet à leurs collections de tatouages en chaines de vélos (en plus c'est vrai, blackbirdsf.org), être autant obsédé par le vélo au point de vendre votre seul objet de valeur (un combi VW dans le cas de Mike) et se servir de l'argent récolté pour se payer un trip en vélo sur un autre continent était un truc de bargeot. C'est toujours incroyable, mais en 1973 lorsque Mike a empaquetté son Bob Jackson bleu et blanc de cyclo-tourisme et a décollé pour l'Europe, c'était complètement fou.

Après avoir pédalé à travers la Grande Bretagne, Amsterdam (hum hum)et Barcelone, Mike se retrouva sur les plaine de la vallée de PO dans le nord de l'Italie. Se laissant porter, n'ayant aucune idée de ce qu'il était en train de faire, mais avec la certitude que quelquechose de formidable pouvait arriver à n'importe quel instant. C'est alors qu'il fit la rencontre d'une jeune femme dans une auberge de jeunesse de Milan. Il se trouve que la demoiselle en question connaissait le parrain de l'univers du cyclisme Italien, Signore Cino Cinelli, fondateur d'une marque de cadres et d'accessoires à son nom que Mike appreciait et convoitait particulièrement.

Moins d'un mois plus tard, Mike était de retour à San Jose, seul avec une cargaison de pièces Cinelli. Il avait dépensé jusqu'à son dernier cent pour se payer un stock de guidons, potences et cadres Cinelli. Désormais, sans voiture, ni l'existence d'Ebay pour écouler sa marchandise Milanaise, il se mit en route pour la tournée des revendeurs de vélos de la baie de SF. Le tout à vélo, bien sûr, tractant une remorque pleine à ras bord de composants, qu'il vendait aux boutiques sur sa route.

En 1976, Specialized était devenu l'importateur de pièces qui cartonne. Son stock était le lieux de prédilections des Fat Tire Riders qui pouvaient y trouver les composants tant recherchés qui leur permettaient de faire leurs spads, surtout des pièces européennes tels les dérailleurs Huret, les freins Mafac et les tubes Columbus. Avec une clientèle faite principalement de constructeurs de cadres de la côte ouest, Mike se retrouvait au cœur de l'émergence d'une révolution industrielle naissante dans le cyclisme. Des concepteurs de cadres artisans comme Joe Breeze, Albert Eisentraut et Tom Ritchey (qui travailla pour Specialized comme perceur de moyeux de tandems), comptaient parmis les clients réguliers. À la vue de leurs commandes particulières de vieux matos comme des manivelles TA et des cantilevers, Mike commençait à se poser des questions et se demander ce qu'ils manigançaient. Ce qu'ils manigançaient, ils étaient simplement en train de réinventer le vélo, et Mike se retrouvait fatalement impliqué dans le jeu.

20 & 21

STUMPJUMPER FIELD GUIDE/1981 STUMPJUMPER

Toutes les illustrations de la fiiche technique auront cinq détails spécifiques. Ils changeront selon le vélo mais il seront toujours au nombre de cinq Pour le SJ 1981, ce sont les suivants :

Cadre : conçu par Tim Neenan de chez Lighthouse Bikes à Santa Cruz, le premier cadre Stumpjumper avait des soudures TIG. Si votre cadre de 1981 a des raccords, c'est un cadre de la fin de l'année. La peinture bleue ? elle fut choisie car c'était similaire au bleu déja utilisé sur le vélo de tourisme Sequoia.

Potence : la légendaire potence Golf Club, ce bijoux était une version modifiée d'une potence de BMX de l'époque. Le guidon originel du Stumpjumper, en acier était inspiré d'un guidon de moto Magura.

Leviers de Freins : modèle standard sur tous les premiers Stumpjumpers, les leviers de freins Tomaselli Racer était conçus pour être montés sur des motos type café-racer de la fin des années 70. Pour ne pas lésiner, ils y ont associé de gros cables de freins renforcés qui amélioraient les sensations et performances du freinage.

Pneus : Specialized à mis à profit ses connaissances acquises dans la création de leur gamme de pneus de route, qui rencontrèrent un franc succès, pour accoucher du premier pneu léger pour le tout terrain: le Stumpjumper. Si vous en possedez encore une paire, gardez les précieusement, c'est une denrée rare et recherchée.

Pédalier : un produit que Specialized importait aux Etats-Unis pour être monté sur les vélos de cyclotourisme, les manivelles TA avait une finition polie. Les casses ou félures étaient courantes du fait qu'elles n'étaient pas originallement conçues pour une utilisation tout-terrain.

22 & 23

LA PREMIÈRE FOIS QUE J'AI VU UN STUMPJUMPER

JOE BREEZE; pionnier du Moutain Bike, fabricant de cadres, auteur
Je l'ai vu à Bike Odyssey à Sausalito, pas très loin de chez moi. "j'ai pensé, 'c'est quoi cette potence en club de golf', et j'ai aussi été emerveillé par la monte de freins Tomaselli à la place de Magura. Mais à 750$, je me suis dit qu'ils allaient sûrement en vendre un paquet.

TOM RITCHEY; pionnier du Mountain Bike, fabricant de cadres, inventeur, coureur de niveau national
Il (le Stumpjumper) était grossier représentait tout simplement le niveau de technologie dont disposait le Japon à cette époque. Nos vélos à nous étaient deux fois plus cher (et plus légers), mais le Stumpjumper avait un prix raisonnable et était tout de même équipé de pièces intérressantes pour l'époque.

RICHARD CUNNINGHAM; fondateur de Mantis Cycles et rédacteur à Mountain Bike Action
Le Stumpjumper était lourd, tenait pas la route et était dur à placer dans les virages, mais quand j'en ai vu un pour la première fois, ça m'a sauté aux yeux, je me suis écrié "ce Mountain Bike, c'est le vrai truc…sautez dessus" j'ai construit mon premier Mountain Bike peu de temps après.

DON COOK; pionnier du Mountain Bike, co-directeur du Mountain Bike Hall of Fame.
À l'époque, un Ritchey fait main coutait entre 1200$ et 1500$ juste pour le cadre. On a vu le Stumpjumper et on a pensé 'voila du lourd'.' itement, tu n'avais plus à attendre trois ou quatre mois pour avoir un vélo fait par Tom (Ritchey) ou Gary (Fisher).

JACQUIE PHELAN; pionnière du Mountain Bike; fondatrice de WOMBATS, auteur.
J'ai vu des Stumpjumpers, sans trop savoir ce que c'était. À cette époque, je roulais avec Gary Fisher, et il les décrivait comme des "copies". Je ne vois personne capable de laisser publier ce que je viens de dire dans ce livre.

VICTOR VICENTE OF AMERICA; pionnier du Mountain Bike, coureur cycliste Olympique, organisateur de courses, artiste.
Ma mémoire est un peu floue là, mais je crois que ma réaction face au Stumpjumper était de le reconnaitre comme un standard, son design fonctionnel attirerait les masses, pas vraiment comme les vélos artisanaux qui étaient disponibles avant.

RICHARD HEMINGTON, GRANDE BRETAGNE; la première personne à vendre un Stumpjumper en dehors des USA.
Le Stumpjumper arrivait dans une boite et il fallait le monter de toutes pièces. Je revois encore toutes les pièces étalées sur le sol, je passais une éternité à le monter. Je me souviens me demander dans quel pétrain on serait si les ventes décollaient! Évidemment ça s'est produit et on s'est retrouvé dedans.

JOE MURRAY; un des premiers coureurs, designer de vélos, pilote d'essais
Le Stump de 1981 que j'avais était une sacrée luge, mais je me souviens que je l'aimais même si je devais opter pour un certain style pour arriver en bas des pistes par feu dans les collines de Marin. Quand j'ai commencé à rouler pour Gary Fisher, il m'a donné un vélo, alors j'ai vendu mon Stumpjumper. J'aimerais tellement l'avoir encore.

MERT LAWWILL; légende de la moto, un des premiers designer de mountain bikes "lorsque j'ai vu ce pour quoi il était vendu et à quel point il était mieux que le mien, j'ai pensé que le dés étaient lancés et que j'allais devoir me remettre dans la moto."

24 & 25

COMMUNICATION CIBLÉE

Une nouvelle génération de vélos pour un nouveau style de publicités. Et ça dure depuis 25 ans.

Pas tant d'année que ça avant, Mike vivait dans une caravane, écrivant son catalogue sur des formulaires types de papier jaune, et n'avait même pas la place de faire rentrer dans son petit entrepot les piles de pneus à stocker. Il surfait désormais sur la vague Stumpjumper, et ça commençait à devenir sacrément confortable.

Un vélo de production. Contrairement à tout ce que Specialized ou n'importe qui d'autre n'avait jamais fait. Les vieilles méthodes pour le vendre n'allaient tout simplement pas fonctionner. Avant la campagne "Whole New Sport", telle qu'elle était connu au QG de la marque, les publicités Specialized étaient principalement en noir et blanc et toujours des demi-pages, voir moins. Tout changea avec cette beauté noire et glacée qui devint l' archetype des publicités presse de la marque pour les 25 années à venir. Shootées par le photographe Jack Christensen dans le même garage où il pris les photos de la première brochure des ordinateurs Apple, et mis en page par un collaborateur de longue date en la personne de Patrick Mountain, la campagne "Whole New Sport" ne laissait personne indifférent dans les pages des magazines en noir et blanc de l'époque.

Évidemment c'est grandiose et tout et tout, mais pourquoi donc, le type en action sur la photo portait il de grandes chaussettes et une salopette . le mec en question était le designer du premier Stumpjumper. Tim Neenan. Voici ce dont il se rappelle: "à l'époque, il n'y avait pas de vêtements spécifiques au mountain bike, rien que tu étais censé porter pour rouler. J'avais une salopette avec laquelle je travaillais, on a fait avec sans se poser trop de questions."

26 & 27

FAITES CHAUFFER LES MOTEURS

Courir dans la première moitié des années 80, c'était vraiment comme les courses de NASCAR de la deuxième moitié des années 40. Tracer un circuit dans un champs au hasard, aligner les coureurs et abaisser le drapeau. Les compétiteurs étaient connus pour dormir dans leur voiture, frauder les entrées et fumer leurs 'barres énergetiques'. C'était brut, c'était vrai, c'était de la compétition sur deux roues avec une pureté qu'on avait pas vu en cent ans. C'était aussi trop bon pour le garder secret. Entre le premier meeting dans une maison de Danville,Californie en 1983 et les NORBA de 1989, le nombre de participants est passé de zero à 20 000. "les choses sont passés d'un secret entre potes à un phénomène d'envergure mondiale en quelques années" confia Scot Nicol, fondateur de la marque Ibis Bicycles. "je pense que personne n'aurait pu s'y attendre."

28 & 29

LE TEAM STUMPJUMPER ÉTAIT PLEIN DE MACHOS

T'avais plutôt interêt à en imposer quand tu te pointais sur la ligne de départ avec un vélo rose.

En 1984, il n'y avait pas de team établi et vraiment installé. Et même si ça avait été le cas, on aurait pas pu considérer le team Spe comme un team normal. Ils étaient la toute première équipe pro, roulaient sur des vélos roses avec des guidons de routes et des chaussures de cyclistes, à une époque ou bon nombre des meilleurs pilotes de VTT avaient plutôt tendance à rouler leurs vitamines dans du OCB, et prenaient le départ des courses avec des pompes comme les Nike Lava Dome. Géré par Bill Woodul, un guru de la course sur route, le team Stump était une sorte d'experimentation tout terrain. "Woody (Woodul) nous a pris en mains et a appliquer les même idées et methodes qu'il avait développées pour la route," confia Dave McLaughlin, ancien pilote du team Stumpjumper. "désormais, nous étions entrainés, organisés, et mettions en place des stratégies pendant les courses."

Durant la première année d'existence du team, Woodul séléctionna des coureurs prometteurs de cyclo-cross tels que McLaughlin, Gavin Chilcot (qui plus tard roula pour la célèbre équipe 7-11), Mark Michelle et Alan Ott des locaux de Californie du nord et Laurence Malone. Bien tassés dans un van Specialized, ils ont parcourus les Etats Unis, participants à un bon paquet de grosses courses qui existaient à l'époque: le Suntour Pacific States Challenge Series, le Gant Challenge Series (courses urbaines à Seattle, Chicago, Golden, Tampa et Miami), le Ross Stage Race et des courses classiques comme la Rockhopper, Rumpstomper et les championnats Nationaux NORBA. " les courses étaient un peu inégales en ces jours. En gros, ce n'était pas aussi sérieux et compétitif que ça l'est aujourd'hui, mais quand Joe Murray ou quelques pros de la route comme Andy Hampsten et Steve Tilford vont se pointer, les choses sérieuses vont commencer," confia Maclaughlin à propos des compétitions qui rampaient à cette époque, juste avant de se mettre à marcher.

Juste quelques saisons de courses un peu à l'arrache plus tard et le team Stumpjumper s'était transformé en Team Specialized, le meilleur du Monde, l'escadron des mountain bikes les mieux équipés. À ses débuts, le Team comprenait des athlètes tels que le Champion du Monde Ned Overend, Lisa Muhich et Sara Ballantyne, tout comme le phénomenal Daryl Price, et les démoniaques Elladee Brown et Paul Thomasberg en descente. À cette saison, et pour les suivantes, le team Specialized a abandonné les vélos roses, mais pas l'attitude de guerriers.

30 & 31

STUMPJUMPER FIELD GUIDE/1984 STUMPJUMPER TEAM

Si tu roules sur un vélo rose, t'as interet à être rapide!

Toutes les illustrations de la fiiche technique auront cinq détails spécifiques. Ils changeront selon le vélo mais il seront toujours au nombre de cinq.

Le cadre fut conçu par Jim Mertz à partir de tubes Tange Prestige provenant du Japon, faisant du Team Stumpjumper de 1984, le cadre le plus léger que Specialized ait fabriqué jusqu'ici.

Fourche : le Stumpjumper Team, rose, était ainsi équipé de la première fourche uni-crown qui était bien plus légère et plus facile à fabriquer que la fourche à raccords en té utilisée jusqu'alors.

Freins Arrières :Sur le Team, des U-brakes montés sous le boitier de pédalier comme les Suntour Rollercam. Ces aimants à boue ne furent qu'une passade, heureusement. On se souvient des U-Brakes comme une des plus grosses erreurs collectives qu'ait pu faire le monde du vélo.

Pneus : en 1984, le pneu TriCross remplaçat le Stumpjumper plus performant pour des vélos haut de gamme. Il était réputé pour son adhérence sur le sec et les conditions très poussiéreuses grace à ses petits crampons.

Roue Libre : le Stumpjumper Team était équipé d'une roue libre Shimano 600 avec un grand pignon de 26 dents-rien de comparable avec les pignons de 30 dents appréciés par la plupart des vététistes de l'époque.

32

MBHOF

Si les fanas de Ukulele en ont un, pourquoi pas nous?

Si vous tapez sur Google 'Hall of Fame', vous aurez 47,400,000 réponses. 47 millions. Yep, il y a un Hall of Fame des mineurs, un Hall of Fame des cowgirls, un Streaker Hall of Fame un Hall of Fame du ukulele. Un Hall of Fame du Ukulele! Incroyable, mais que peut il bien y avoir dans le Ukulele Hall of Fame? Probablement plus de choses que dans le streaker Hall of Fame, c'est certain.

Il est indéniable, qu'il y a quelquechose d'universel dans le besoin d'honorer ceux qui ont contribué à une culture, et les fanatiques du gros pneus à crampons ne sont pas différents des cowgirls, streakers, ou des amoureux du Ukulele. Bien installé dans une vieille station service sur Elk avenue à Crested Butte, le Mountain Bike Hall of Fame est l'invention de Carole Bauer. Résidente de longue date de Crested Butte, Bauer était soucieuse que les architectes de la culture mountain bike ne soient déstinés à être oubliés sans même qu'il y ait une institution pour honorer et saluer leurs accomplissements et le sport qu'ils ont aidé à créer.

En 1988, le MBHoF était pret à acceuillir sa première fournée d'intronisés. Personne ne fut surpris de voir parmis cette première promotion les pionniers du gros pneus, des noms comme Breeze, Fisher, Kelly, Cunningham, Ritchey et Murray. Tout comme Mr. S, qui fut époustoufflé, surpris et carrément honoré d'être tenu dans la même estime qu'un groupe aussi select de ses pairs. Après Mr. S, au moins trois mountain bikers qui portaient le S sur leur poitrine furent honorés par le MBHoF, dont The Captain (Overend), Jim Merz, et Tom Hillard.

De nos jours, le MBHoF continue de vivre et de prospérer avec le soutien de l'industrie du vélo et des fans de mountain bike du monde entier. Mtnbikehalloffame.com

33

MON STUMPJUMPER N.1

Bill Hennion

2 Stumpjumpers, 65 ans et 240 km par semaine.

Bill roule quasi quotidiennement sur l'un de ses deux Stumpjumpers (deux Stumpjumpers! Cool le Bill) pour un total de 240 kms par semaine. Pas mal pour un type de 65 ans, non?

Il y a quelques années, lorsque le petit fils de Bill s'est mis à enchainer les singletracks, il savait qu'il allait devoir améliorer son vieux Stump s'il voulait garder le rythme avec Junior. Ça n'a pas pris longtemps à Bill pour réaliser que son moderne FSRxc suspendu l'aidait sacrément à tenir l'allure du petit enragé. Bill depuis, remercie la gémoétrie de son FSR, il peut désormais passer plus vite que jamais dans les endroits cabossés.

Son vélo de tous les jours, est un Stumpjumper 1982 acier qu'il a acheté d'occase il y a quelques années. "c'est l'un de mes vélos favoris pour me ballader dans le coin," confia Bill "c'est parfait pour faire la route jusqu'à mes spots de peche."

Contrairement à ce que l'on préfererait, Bill ne rajeunit pas. Mais il assure qu'il peut toujours faire tous les trucs qu'il aime (comme freiner le plus tard possible) grace à son habileté sur deux roues. selon Bill, "mes vélos, c'est ma vie.

34-35

ASSISTANCE TECHNIQUE GRATOS?

Specialized serait il devenu fou?

À l'époque, bien avant qu'ils disent à l'époque—quelque part vers 1985—La folie pour le Mountain Bike voyait tout juste le jour. Il n'y avait pas des masses d'évenements, mais chaque année il y avait plus de promoteurs motivés et de coureurs affutés. Alors Specialized, qui avait déja vendu un paquet, un énorme paquet de Stumpjumpers et qui était allé à beaucoup de courses, décida de tendre la main pour aider les promoteurs à promouvoir et les coureurs à courir. Ils décidèrent de mettre en action un support technique pour n'importe quel vélo— gratuitement. Ils aidèrent aussi les organisateurs en donnat un coup de main où c'était utile. Tracer le circuit, nettoyer la piste, monter une tente, conduire la moto de tête, gérer les engagements. Quoique ça demandait, le gang de Morgan Hill était pret à le faire.

Pour s'assurer le succès, ils engagèrent Tom Hillard, de Sonoma County en Californie, un des techniciens de courses les plus chevronné encore en vie; l'auteur du livre des règles de la NORBA, le promoteur du Punk Bike Enduro, mais surtout un homme qui revendique avoir fabriqué son premier mountain bike il y a des années lumières (1961). Alors, Mr. S lui fila les clefs d'un van et Tom se mit en route pour les courses qui portent des noms désormais légendaires comme Rockhopper, Rumpstomper, Reseda To The Sea, Kamikaze et Whiskeytown.

Bien sûr avoir des camions et des mécanos sur la route, ça coûte du blé, mais Mr. S à toujours su ce que cela rapporterait. Il est sûr que faire de bonnes courses aide à faire évoluer le sport, qu'être à l'air libre dans les champs à s'arracher sur les vélos que des gens pilotent dur, vite et souvent est meilleur que d'avoir 1000 ingénieurs coincés dans un labo à se demander à quelles sortes de contraintes le vélo peut être exposé.

Courses gratuites et support technique? R&D peu couteux? Qui ne serait pas daccord que le support technique Specialized était une bonne chose.

36-37

LA CONSÉCRATION

Peu de gens dans le monde se sont déja rendu au point 7.275 lattitude nord—107.879 longitude ouest autrement dit Durango dans le Colorado pour une bonne raison. La ville se trouve perdue au milieu de nulle part à quelques enjambées des légendaires et terrifiants "Four Corners", le point de croisement de quatre états : Colorado, Nouveau Mexique, Arizona et Utah. Même avec une malle pleine de cookies et de bonbons, et une cargaison de Coca, c'est un trip de 14h de route depuis Los Angeles et environ la moitié depuis Denver…bel et bien au milieu de nulle part.

Nous sommes le 1er avril 1980, Ned est sur la route. Il a quitté San Diego direction Durango au volant de son pick-up Datsun de 1965. En pleine nuit, il est contraint de faire demi tour à cause du blizzard. C'est là qu'il aurait dû renoncer, mais après une nocturne à Aztec, Nouveau Mexique (a 20 km au sud et quelques milliers de mètres au-dessus de Durango) il traverse les montagnes pour découvrir son Taj Mahal : une caravane d'environ 10 mètres de long dans le trailer-park de Junction Creek. Eh oui, Mr ned Overend était dans la place.

Pour payer son loyer, Ned a réparé les moteurs de coccinelles VW de tous les modèles qui aient traversé Animas County. Pour ajuster son chi, il se lançait dans des virées épiques sur le spot d'Elmore Store.

En quelques années, il s'est mis à la compétition sur route, passant du statut d'inconnu à celui de coureur de la Coors Classic au sein du meilleur team des Etats-Unis en juste une année.peu de temps après la Coors de 1983, un trio de locaux de Durango (dont Bob 'bicycle' Gregorio) fit découvrir à Ned leurs clunkers à 5 vitesses. il fut immédiatement emballé. "je me sentais comme un gamin dans un bac à sable," dit le Captain. "j'ai su immédiatement qu'il y avait un truc à faire."

Un truc à faire? En quelques années, Ned avait le meilleur palmarès de l'histoire du Mountain bike: quatre titres de champion National NORBA, les NORBA World Championships, les European World Championships et les tout premiers Championnats du Monde UCI à son actif. Oui, Mr. Ned Overend était dans la place.

40 & 41

COMMENT DOMPTER UN GORILLE DE 400 KG?

Tu t'organises.

Sur la première page du premier numéro du tout premier magazine de mountain-bike jamais publié, le Fat Tire Flyer de Charlie Kelly d'août 1981, il y avait un appel à la mobilisation très clair. "si nous ne nous organisons pas pour protéger nos interêts, nous n'aurons plus d'interêts à protéger"' plaidait See Kay. Bien avant même que vous puissiez trouver un VTT chez votre revendeur local, les accés aux chemins devenaient un véritable parcours du combattant.

Un bon en avant vers l'été 1987. Alors que la plupart des pays du monde découvraient à peine les joies du mountain-bike, le problème des accés aux pistes et chemins prenait une ampleur démeusurée et nuisait considérablement les adeptes du VTT. "Two Wheeled Terrors" titrait la une de Newsweek le 28 sept 1987. Des collines de Sacramento aux montagnes de Santa Monica à Los Angeles, les vélos se voyaient bannis des singletracks et virés des parcs nationaux et régionaux. Le National Park Service s'empréssait de fermer l'accès à tous ses chemins tandis que le BLM expulsait les vélos de toutes les forêts. Si le mountain-bike avait un futur, les vététistes avait besoin de se regrouper et de s'organiser…et rapidement.

Cet automne là, des représentants de cinq groupes de plaidoirie basés en Californie –le Bicycle Trails Council of Marin, le Bicycle Trails Council of the East Bay, les Sacramento Rough Riders, les Concerned Off-Road Bikers Association de Los Angeles et les Responsible Off-Road Mountain Pedalers de San Jose –ont unis leurs forces à l'occasion du salon du cycle de Long Beach. En moins de six mois, l'IMBA (international Mountain Biking Association) avait établi une charte et se battait activement sur tous les fronts pour réhabiliter l'acces des VTT aux forêts et autres parcs et chemins.

Grâce à la vision de Linda DuPriest et d'Eric Aidsmo, qui faisaient alors partie de l'équipe Marketing de Specialized, un don de 1000$ fut versé à l'IMBA au nom de la société. C'est le premier mouvement marquant que Specialized (ou n'importe quelle grosse marque) fit pour défendre les droits des vététistes. Peu de temps après, Linda convint la société de sponsoriser une réunion regroupant tous les acteurs de l'industrie au salon Interbike de 1989. L'implication de Specialized dans ce combat encouragea fortement les autres marques à se jetter dans le groupe de plaidoyer. C'est un tournant marquant dans le développement de l'IMBA. La réunion aux sommets permit de rassembler des fonds, d'éveiller les consciences pour mener à bien la lutte pour la libération du singletrack. Ce fut également le point de départ d'une large brassée d'efforts qui donna naissance, entre autres, à des conférences défendant la pratique du mountain bike à Washington D.C et Durango. Dupriest se retrouvait naturellement à la tête de l'IMBA et ce pour une décennie, apportant son aide aux jeunes défenseurs afin qu'ils soignent leurs interventions et leurs business plans tout en servant de relais avec l'industrie du vélo.

Alimenté autant par des dons et le support de chacun des acteurs importants de l'industrie, que par les 35 000 membres de l'association, l'IMBA s'est depuis battue pour éduquer les administrations et pour rendre accessibles les chemins sur l'étendue du territoire américain, et du reste du Monde. Sans l'IMBA nous n'aurions aujourd'hui pas de chemins à protéger.

Vous avez entendu la sainte parole, désormais, faite tourner la quête : imba.com

42

MON STUMPJUMPER N.2

Denise Weber

Jamais trop tard pour la compétition

Denise, une vétérinaire de 36 ans se mit à faire du vélo sur une suggestion de son médecin. Un mauvais genou la pénalisait dans ses déplacements.

Alors son doc' lui suggera qu'elle devrait se mettre à rouler pour regagner de l'agilité et soulager un peu son genou. Une fois ses fesses posées sur un deux roues, sa vie changea à jamais.

À la recherche d'une petite motivation supplémentaire, Denise se mit à la compétition environ six mois après cette première sortie révélatrice. Il ne fallut pas longtemps à son tempérament de battante pour comprendre qu'elle avait besoin de quelquechose de plus léger et fiable si elle voulait devenir compétitive. Alors elle alla s'acheter un Rockhopper, et après l'avoir utilisé quelques temps, elle passa la vitesse supérieur avec un Stumpjumper. "il me va comme un gant, et maintenant je suis complètement mordue," dit elle. "soudain, j'ai la vitesse que je ne pensais pas avoir et une confiance nouvelle." Denise, qui fait aussi de la route pour la forme, avoue qu'il n'y a rien de tel qu'être sur son Stumpjumper à voguer au travers des bois tôt le matin.

Aujourd'hui, son genou s'est renforcé au point qu'elle n'a plus besoin d'atelle, même pour courir. C'est pas qu'elle court beaucoup "je préfere être sur mon Stumpjumper, après tout, je suis une pilote de mountain bike désormais.

43

RÉECRIRE LES RÈGLES DE JEU PAGE APRÈS PAGE

En l'espace de cinq ans, Specialized a complètement réécris les codes et règles du VTT. Entre 88 et 93, Specialized devint la première marque à mettre sur le marché des cadres en acier et carbone, titanium et carbone et métal matrix (sans oublier la première fourche suspendue avec des fourreaux en fibre de carbone, et le premier cadre de production entièrement conçu sur ordinateur). Un bon nombre de règles établies ont volées en morceaux lorsque la guerre froide prit fin et que l'homme qui tenait en main le stylo pour la plupart d'etre elles n'était autre que l'ingénieur Specialized Jim Merz du Mountain Bike Hall of Fame.

Lorsque Reagan a demandé à Gorby d'abattre ce mur, ça ouvrit l'accès à une large palette de matériaux et de technologies qui avaient été mises de coté dans les quartiers de l'armée. Grace à l'amour qu'il portait pour une revue scientifique et son implication dans l'expérimentation d'un nouveau logiciel de modellisation 3D (Specialized à du se delester de 250 000 $ pour l'obtenir en 1985), Merz était le mieux placé pour découvrir avant les autres les dernières méthodes et matériaux.

Puis, un groupe d'ingénieurs, qui avaient travaillé avec des composites dans une filliale de la marque de raquette de tennis Prince à El Cajon en Californie, l'initièrent au carbone. Merz travailla à optimiser les tubes en composite et dessiner un jeu de raccords pour rassembler le tout et former un cadre. "j'ai vécu l'enfer pour y arriver" dit Merz. Après plus de testing à son atelier, il mit au point un jeu de raccords soudés avec précision par les partenaires japonais de la marque. Autant de travail que pour construire un vélo complet. Les raccords et les tubes conçus et réalisés sur mesure faisaient du Epic un ensemble cadre et fourche digne de la place vendôme, à 2400 $. Les raccords étaient envoyés au QG mondial de Specialized où ils étaient collés avec des tubes optimisés de carbone compressés dans un gabarit afin qu'ils sèchent. Avec seulement deux gabarits par taille, la construction des 2000 Epic fut, justement, épique.

Jamais satisfait, Merz laissa tomber les raccords de tubes en cro-mo pour se diriger sur le titane. Pas du simple titane, bien sûr, mais du titane usiné par les experts de chez Merlin Metalworks à Cambridge. Le résultat donnait un tout nouvel Epic radicalement different.

46 & 47

MR. AMERICA

Comment le Captain a rempli son contrat à Durango.*

Si vous tourniez le bouton ON d'une radio ou d'une télé dans la région des Four Corners au Colorado en septembre de cette année là, vous auriez à coup sûr entendu le nom de Ned. Ou aperçu sa geule moustachue sur les écrans. Il était le sujet quotidien d'articles du Durango Herald et sa photo était sur la couv' du programme officiel de la course. Certains étaient même allés jusqu'à faire sérigraphier des t.shirts à l'éffigie du "Captain" gagnant les championnats du monde (avant même la course). La ville de Durango ne se contentait pas de la fierté d'accueillir les tous premiers championnats du monde de Mountain Bike, elle voulait en plus que l'enfant du pays les remportent.

Le Captain aurait pu se faire un paquet de fric en tant que pro sur route ou en souffrant sur les triathlons, mais il opta pour le tout terrain pour la simple et bonne raison qu'il trouvait ça plus cool et bien plus amusant que les autres disciplines cyclistes. Pourtant, une semaine avant les premiers championnat du Monde UCI en 1990, le roi americain du cross-country se demandait s'il avait choisi la meilleure option. La pression à l'idée de (peut être) devenir le premier champion du Monde historique UCI pesait plus lourd qu'un peterbuilt sur les épaules du local de Durango.

Puis ça arriva. Ned, 35 ans, courant sur un prototype Epic Ultimate avec raccords titane et une fourche suspendue RockShox noire, avait semé ses seuls concurrents sérieux et inquiétants parmis les 130 participants, Tim Gould, l'anglais et Thomas Frischknecht, le suisse. Il fonçait ainsi loin devant vers la victoire au pied de Purgatory Ski Hill. Hormis les 10 000 spectateurs déchainés, le Captain était seul. "me retrouver en tête était bien plus qu'un soulagement", c'est ce qu'il dirait si vous lui posiez la question aujourd'hui, mais comme Greg Herbold, un autre local de Durango et vainqueur en descente aux premiers championnats du Monde à dit "se tenir là, obtenir cette médaille pour laquelle j'ai travaillé si dur, je me sentais comme miss America." Ned serait probablement plus un Mr America.

*le Captain n'était pas le seul vainqueur de l'arc en ciel à Durango –Lisa Muhich décrocha la victoire dans la catégorie véteran femme, et Sara Ballantyne a loupé de très peu la victoire de la course élite femme.

48 & 49

STUMPJUMPER M2

Le secret défense dévoilé.

"Qui a deja entendu parler du composite Metal Matrix?" titrait la une du San Francisco Chronicle du 1er Avril 1991. Sa simple existence était maintenue secrète en raison du Munitions Control Act (qui limitait l'échange d'informations à propos de l'hybride d'oxyde d'aluminium), peu de non-initiés étaient mis au courant. Aucun objet de consommation au monde n'était à l'époque construit à partir du Metal Matrix et il était quasiment impossible à souder ou faire fondre. Mais Jim Merz, Mark Winter, Mark DiNucci et le reste du crew Specialized ont décortiqués le code du matériau destiné à l'exoploration spatiale. Le résultat : le premier objet non pointé sur Moscou fabriqué à partir du composite Metal matrix : le Stumpjumper M2

Élaboré pour être utilisé sur les satellites et les commandes de tanks, le M2 était considéré comme 10% plus résistant et 20% plus rigide qu'un alu traditionnel. Selon les gros cerveaux du Pentagone, sa force viendrait de morceaux d'aluminum oxydé, une céramique dans un treillage microscopique sur une base d'alu 6000. Aussi léger que résistant comme présenti, en faire un cadre de vélo ne devrait pas être si evident.

Donc, comme pour les roues en carbone à trois batons (oui, le même design qu'un certain américain à utilisé à des moments précis de chacun de ses sept Tour de France remportés), que le S team avait crée en partenariat avec DuPont l'année précédente, ils se sont tourné vers un géant industriel pour obtenir de l'aide. Le partenaire pour le projet était Duralcan. Une filliale de la deuxième plus grande société d'Aluminum. Les scientifiques MMC basés à San diego ont trouvé la bonne recette pour le tubing tandis que les gars de Morgan Hill ont créé le design, trouvé un moyen de travailler cette matiere ultra-résistante et réussi à la souder

À la fin de la journée, Specialized fit équipe avec Anodizing Inc comme partenaire, afin de créér une nouvelle usine à Portland uniquement destinée à extruder les tubes M2 et les souder en cadres. Le duo allait plus tard réinventer l'extrusion et le boutage, fabricant des cadres de plus en plus légers.

Ceratinement pas la route la plus rapide et la moins chère vers le cadre de rêve le plus solide et léger, mais quand est ce que Mike a dit qu'il fallait opter pour la facilité ?

50 & 51

PASSION

Une histoire de slogans.

Il y a une chose que Mike vous dira avoir appris de toutes ces années : si tu veux gagner, joue à un jeu qui te plais, un jeu qui te passionne.

Donc, retour en arrière en 89 quand Specialized avait besoin d'un publicitaire. Ils sont partis à la recherche de quelqu'un qui était en tous points aussi passionné pour trouver des slogans qu'ils pouvaient l'être pour construire des vélos. Un morceau de chance vous mène à un autre et, boom! (claque tes doigts en frappant ton poing droit dans ta paume gauche pour un effet magique), Ils ont fait appel à des spécialistes : Goodby, Sylverstein et Partners. Des inconnus ? Non. Ces publicitaires sont devenus mondialement célèbres pour avoir conçu la campagne pour le lait "Got Milk ?". Le S de GSP, Rich Silverstein, était un cycliste assidu, un gars assez ouvert qu'on pouvait voir sur son vélo venir de chez lui à Marin County, par le Golden Gate Bridge jusqu'au QG de GSP à San Francisco. Le reste, c'est de la légende.

Tandis qu'ils étaient plutôt très pris avec des clients comme Anheuser-Busch, Morgan Stanley, Haagen-Dazs, Saturn et Hewlett—Packard, GSP s'est aussi chargé de presque toutes les campagnes de pub Specialized dont vous pouvez vous souvenir encore aujourd'hui.

La leçon à en retenir? Peu importe que ce soit pour des vélos, des Budweisers ou du pain de mie, vous en baverez pour le faire correctement si vous ne le faites pas avec passion.

52 & 53

STUMPJUMPER FIELD GUIDE/1992 SPECIALZIED S-WORKS EPIC ULTIMATE*

*Le vélo montré ici est un vélo de tests, qui n'a jamais été vendu dans cette configuration.

Cadre : de 1990 à 1995, Specialized à construit à la main environ 1500 cadres en-dessous de 1,5 kg Epic Ultimate en carbone et titane au QG de la marque à Morgan Hill dans le nord de la Californie. La méthode de fabrication de ce cadre, une innovation à l'époque, fut immitée par les meilleurs fabricants de cadres pendant une décennie.

Raccords : une évolution de l'Epic standard, l'Epic Ultimate utilisait des raccords en titane usinés par Merlin Metalworks of Cambridge dans le Massachusetts. Les frais en matériaux bruts, et de sous-traitance faisaient perdre de l'argent à la société qui produisait à perte.

Tubes : les premiers cadres Epic Ultimate étaient en carbone tres rigide, qui se sont avérés être trop fragiles; un carbone plus souple provenant de Mclean Quality Composites à Salt Lake City dans l'Utah fut utilisé pour la plupart des cadres Epic Ultimate produits.

Fourche : bien que présenté avec une fourche Specialized carbone-titane Future Shock FSX, le Epic Ultimate, qui fut produit jusqu'en 1995, n'a jamais été vendu avec une fourche suspendue. À la place, il était proposé avec une fourche Chromoly Direct Drive.

Limited : en 1995, les derniers cadres Epic Ultimate, tous assemblés par Brian Lucas à Morgan Hill, étaient produits. Chacun des 60 cadres à un numéro de série unique affiché sur une plaque se situant sur le tube supérieur du cadre. Le cadre portant le numero de série 01 fut donné à Ned Overend en mémoire de sa victoire aux Championnats du Monde de 1990 au guidon d'un Ultimate.

54 & 55

SMITHSONIAN

Musées et VTT? Vous voulez sûrement me demander ce qu'une institution culturelle qui vit naissance il y a plus de 100 ans à Washington D.C, grace à la dotation d'un aristocrate Anglais, à à voir avec l'invasion des singletracks? Vu la tournure que prennent les évènements, juste ce qu'il faut.

James Smithson était un scientifique et un explorateur. Ce jeune élève assidu, chercheur scientifique invésti, qui cultivait un certain gout pour l'aventure, avait laissé plus d'un demi million de dollars aux Etats-Unis pour établir une institution. Laquelle aurait pour but de promouvoir "l'amélioration et la diffusion des connaissances". Il était connu pour avoir risqué sa vie, échappant de peu à la noyade lors d'observations géologiques dans les iles Hebrides de la côte nord de l'Ecosse. Il aurait certainement apprécié l'énergie et la créativité sans limite des pionniers du mountain-bike.

De nos jours, l'institution que Smithson a fondé a évolué pour devenir le plus grand complexe de musées au Monde. Il est composé d'un groupe de musées Nationaux et de centres de recherches tels que le National History Museum, le American History Museum, le National Zoo, the National Air and Space Museum, le National Museum of Arts and Industries, et dans un coin du musée National de l'histoire americaine, le Specialized Stumpjumper.

Aux alentours de 1989, le Smithsonian decouvrit le mountain Bike et, avec leur mandat pour répertorier les meilleurs exemples de transports qui ont changé l'Amérique, ils ont décroché leur téléphone et composé le numéro du bureau de Specialized à Morgan Hill. 'est ce qu'on peut envoyer un vélo?' bien sûr répondit Mike. Désormais, il y a donc un Stumpjumper qui goute un autre type de poussière au milieu de bateaux à vapeurs ou autre navette spaciale. Esperons qu'ils garderont au moins les pneus gonflés.

56 & 57
S-WORKS STORY
Comment vendre une Obesssion?
En prenant exemple sur Porsche.
L'appel provint de Harm Lagaay lui-même. Être hollandais avec un accent Allemand, c'était dur à croire et pourtant, c'était bien le boss du département design de Porsche. Est ce que Specialized peut envoyer des ingénieurs à Weissach dans l'atelier super secret afin de discuter d'une version Porsche Spider du Epic Ultimate carbone et titane? Difficile de dire non à une offre pareil.

C'est ainsi que quelques membres du S team plièrent baggages, passeports en poche en direction du fameux atelier tant convoité. Ce qu'ils ont vu à Weissach était un atelier rempli de plus de mille des meilleurs ingénieurs. Tous obsédés par un objectif glorieux : concevoir et construire ce qu'il y a de mieux. Des voitures fabriquées juste pour la course, d'autres construites pour enquêter sur des carburants alternatifs ou de nouveaux matériaux ou réalisées purement comme une étude de style et de design. Le budget semblait aussi infini que leur déferlante d'excellentes idées et, bien que les voitures légendaires et autres accessoires sortaient régulièrement de Weissach, il n'y avait pas de mandat permettant de mettre sur le marché un produit directement depuis l'usine. C'était de la recherche et developpement dans sa plus pure forme. Le vélo Porsche Spider n'aboutira jamais, mais l'éscapade sauvage dans la foret noire engendra autrechose puisque Specialized mit en place sa version perso de Weissach à Morgan Hill.

Dès le départ, le plan était d'autoriser les ingénieurs et designers les plus talentueux de chez Specialized à se faire plaisir, à se lacher complètement. Lever toutes réstrictions et préjugés, ignorer les facteurs économiques, traditionnels et les impératifs de délais dans la quête d'un seul objectif simple : faire le meilleur vélo sur le marché. Est ce que ce fut un succès ? les vélos S-Works ont propulsé les athlètes vers les victoires aux championnats du monde sur route et tout terrain. ces athlètes ont remporté des étapes et porté le fameux maillot jaune du tour de France tant convoité, obtenus des médailles Olympiques, des médailles aux X Games, et se sont emparés de Ironman. Il y a aussi un bon paquet de vélos et de pièces qui n'ont jamais franchi la porte de l'atelier; quelques bonnes idées qui finiront peut être plus tard par être exploitées sur d'autres vélos, mais là n'était pas le but pour les S-Works. Le but était de faire ce qu'il y a de mieux, coûte que coûte.

58 & 59
SUSPENSION SPECIALIZED?
Amortisseur du futur?
Quand le Captain a gagné les Championnats du Monde à Durango en 1990, il avait à l'avant de son Specialized Epic Ultimate une fourche RockShox RS-I. Le fait que Ned et d'autres top-pilotes (comme Greg Herbold et Juliana Furtado) se fièrent à ce nouvel accéssoire sur une course si monumentale, envoyait comme un message liminale au monde du VTT: les fourches suspendues sont le futur.

Flairant l'opportunité, Specialized se mit à travailler sur sa propre fourche suspendue. Après des séances d'essais et de maltraitance sur quelques RS-1, il ne fallut pas longtemps à l'équipe d'ingénieurs de Morgan Hill, pour comprendre qu'il allait être difficile de battre le systeme interne (air et huile) que Paul Turner, le fondateur de RockShox avait créé. Alors, ils sont allés à l'atelier de Turner à Mountain View, California et ont conclu un accord: les ingénieurs Specialized, avec à la tête Mark Winter, devraient créer la plupart des pièces externes, et RockShox fournirait le contenu interne complexe et la puissance de fabrication.

Dès 1992, une ligne de fourches Future Shock étaient montées sur les vélos Specialized, mais pour dire la véritée, les premières fourches ressemblaient étrangement à ce que RockShox produisait sous son propre label. Puis vint la Future Shock FSX. Dessinée par Winter, la FSX était comme le cadre Epic Ultimate Carbone et Titane, un produit dont le soucis de prix n'était pas une prioritée (d'ailleurs les deux n'ont jamais été vendus ensemble). Fonctionnant avec l'intérieur air et huile d'une RockShox Mag21, la FSX fut la première fourche suspendue à utiliser des fourreaux en carbone, qui ont du être déssinés, développés et fabriqués dans ce seul objectif. Ça a l'air de coûter cher, et pas que l'air: pour preuve, chaque fourreau coutait plus de 100$. Les tubes en composite, l'arceau et les pattes de fourche en alu CNC rendaient la FSX plus légère et plus chère que n'importe quelle fourche sur le marché. "nous avions connaissance à ce moment que la fourche Specialized était meilleure que la notre," confia récemment Mike McAndrews, guru de la suspension chez Specialized qui travaillait à l'époque chez RockShox avec son pote Turner. "mais c'était également un produit que nous n'avions pas les moyens financiers de produire."

Finalement, la bataille que se livraient les fabricants de fourches suspendues rendait évident que rester dans la course n'était pas dans les cartes de Morgan Hill. Donc, comme pour les dérailleurs, jantes et pédales, ils sont repartis à la quête du meilleur modèle qu'ils pourraient trouver parmis diverses marques. Est ce que ça signifie qu'ils seraient hors de ce business à jamais? Dur à dire, mais Mr. S à toujours été homme à saisir opportunité.

62 & 63
FUTURE SHOCK REAR
Quand Specialized rencontre un génie autrichien, ça fait des étincelles.
Depuis le lancement du premier Stumpjumper, le monde du velo tout terrain à totalement explosé prenant une dimension que personne n'aurait pu imaginer. Dans les années 90, les plans de suspensions arrière clignotaient sur les radars comme les OVNIs au dessus du desert du Nevada. Le problème était que la plupart des vélos étaient d'inefficaces monstruositées dignes d'un alien. À ce moment, les suspensions de vélos étaient un truc tellement compliqué que pas mal de gens au sein même de Specialized n'étaient même pas convaincus que c'était une bonne idée.

Comme à son habitude, ne s'arretant pas à ce que c'était, mais se focalisant sur ce que ça pouvait être, Mike, envoya son équipe vers une quête du vélo suspendu sans compromis aucun. Un qui avancerait normalement lorsque l'on appuie sur les pédales, qui améliorerait le pilotage, ait un rendement satisfaisant à tout instant, serait léger (12 kg était le chiffre référence), fiable et facile à entretenir. Encore aujourd'hui, ce serait un POTA (Putain d'Objectif de Taré Audacieux), mais en 91 la plupart des technologies qui rendraient possible une telle suspension n'existaient même pas.

Passant plus d'un an sur le projet, les ingénieurs John O'Neil, Mark Winter et Mark DiNucci ont éprouvé tous les plans qu'ils avaient dessiné. Certains étaient bons, mais aucun n'était parfait. Alors ils ont continué de fabriquer des Frankenbikes et d'écouter tous les frankenbikers qui passaient les voir (hey, c'est comme ça que Nike à trouvé leur systeme Air). Finalement, Horst Leitner, un ingénieur Autrichien, qui avait officié pour des grands noms de la moto et de l'auto dans les années 70, rejoint la tête de l'équipe avec un design magique de suspension à articulations multiples qui deviendra le FSR. Pour DiNucci et les autres designers, Horst représentait un guru du design de moto avec une tonne de brevets à son actif.; pour Horst, Specialized avait les ressources nécéssaires pour mettre au point ses plans et refaire ce qu'ils avaient brillament fait avec le Stumpjumper.

Avec le prototype de la partie arrière du multi-link en main, DiNucci and Co ont fait les premiers FSR en coupant la partie arrière d'un cadre de Stumpjumper existant pour la remplacer avec un des bras oscillant dessiné par Horst. Avec une poubelle grande comme un stade de foot pleine à craquer de vélos démantibulés (et un nouveau team de pilotes d'essais mis en place exclusivement pour ce projet), le développement se transforma finalement en production. Peut-être un poil trop vite: l'été 1993, la première centaine de vélos en production à du être foutue à la benne lorsqu'il fut découvert que le tube de selle n'était pas assez solide. Comme dit DiNucci "c'était un peu l'expérience de chacun mélangée dans la casserolle, en prenant des décisions avec ses tripes. Nous n'avions pas la structure nécessaire pour le développement et le testing que demandait un vélo aussi complexe que le FSR." Une raison de plus pour laquelle le FSR est si important dans le monde de Specialized, c'est un vélo qui fit s'emballer la machine et força l'équipe de Morgan Hill à repenser totalement son processus de recherches et développements. "itement, les croquis sur des coins de tables ne suffisaient plus, nous avions plus que tout besoin d'une rèélle ingénierie et de tests à la hauteur" dit Chris Murphy Mr.marketing et R&D depuis des années chez Specialized.

64 & 65
CACTUS CUP
Spring break à la sauce Specialized.
Le charme de la Cactus Cup en Arizona est indéniable. La course était, dans les années 90, un rendez-vous hors calendrier officiel immanquable : passer quelques jours (voire plus si il y avait moyen d'arrêter l'horloge), rouler, courrir dans le desert bouillant avec cinq ou six mille amis ? ne serait ce pas mortel ? "je ne me souviens pas de grand chose à propos de la véritable course de la Cactus Cup en elle-même—mais je me suis éclaté à chacune d'elles" se souvient Richard Cunningham, un des premiers soudeurs de cadres, et journaliste de mountain bike de longue date.

C'était comme se pointer au Lake Havasu ou à la Bike Week de Daytona, les dates de la Cactus Cup étaient critiques. Son positionnement sur le calendrier à la mi-mars offrait non seulement au coureurs la possibilité de mettre en pratique leur programme d'entrainement hivernal sans la pression d'une Coupe du Monde, mais permettait aussi à l'industrie du vélo de sentir un avant gout de la saison à venir. A son apogée, la Cactus Cup était l'endroit mis a part les salons de l'automne, ou les tendances s'affichaient et les ventes de vélos se démultipliaient.

Au fil des années, le parcours varia mais il restait toujours de la rocaille et des Cholla cactus à perte de vue. Avec une bonne pression des pneus, et du slime, il était possible de gérer les crevaisons, mais avec plus de virages et d'épingles, il était impossible d'éviter une épine de Cholla Cactus.

Pour les coureurs, autant pros que amateurs, le format de l'épreuve était unique : 4 étapes incluant un contre la montre, un criterium tout terrain, le Fatboy criterium sous les lumieres du centre ville de Scottsdale et une course de x-country, qui quelques années plus tard se vit embellie de virages relevés et de tables. Les coureurs portant le fameux S rouge sur le torse ont ramené plus d'un trophée de Scottsdale; Steve Tilford, pilote Specialized de longue date est invaincu au Fatboy criterium avec 21 victoires depuis le début.

L'atmosphère bon esprit avec le campement de tentes de cirque, et le format de l'évènement en plusieurs courses était tellement attirant, que mi-90, la Cactus Cup s'offrit un petit tour du Monde. Des Cactus Cup furent organisées dans l'Illinois, l'Ohio, au Canada, en France, en Allemagne et au Japon (où la course à toujours lieu), des endroits qui ont toujours su acceuillir cette grande célébration du vélo.

66 & 67
STUMPJUMPER FIELD GUIDE/1994 S-WORKS FSR
Cadre : mis au point par Mark DiNucci et Mark Winter, le triangle avant Direct Drive léger mais pas moins rigide utilisé sur le FSR de 1994 était l'apogée du travail de Specialized dans les cadres ferreux.

Suspension : co-développée avec le fondateur d'Amp Research Horst Leitner, la suspension FSR fut dessinée pour être pleinement active et indépendante dans le but d'optimiser le confort, la maniabilité et les performances. Au fil des années, le design FSR s'est prouvé être incroyablement versatile.

Fourche : co-développée et fabriquée par RockShox, la FSX était composée d'un intérieur modifié de Mag21 avec des fourreaux en carbone dessinés par Specialized et un arceau de frein en alliage M2.

Commandes : produits pour la première fois en 93, les SRAM SRT 500 à poignées tournantes de 8 vitesses étaient les premiers changements de vitesses haut de gamme conçus spécialement pour la compétition par la société de Chicago.

Pneus : leur nom provient d'un album des Pink Floyd, l'Umma Gumma fut le premier à utiliser une combinaison de gommes tendres. Peut-être en avance sur son temps, il n'a jamais suscité un interet suffisant et fut arrété.

70 & 71
IL NE SUFFIT PAS DE PARTICIPER, IL FAUT GAGNER
Facile de voler quand tu portes le S sur la poitrine.

Billets d'avion? Vous voulez parler de billets d'avion? Depuis le jour où Mike balança les clefs du van à Laurence Malone, le premier pilote VTT sponso par la marque, Specialized a dépensé des millions de dollars pour envoyer des centaines de pilotes et d'équipes techniques à travers le monde à la quête d'une seule chose: la plus haute marche du podium.

Ouvrez donc un livre des records, et vous verrez que les hommes et les femmes portant le S sur leur poitrine ont atteint leurs buts avec la ferocité d'un pitbull de Détroit et l'éfficacité d'une Toyota Prius.le score? Les pilotes sponsorisés par Specialized ont remporté 5 titres Mondiaux UCI elite, des douzaines de manches de Coupe du Monde, des titres de Coupe du Monde, et tellement de NORBA nationaux et de championnats nationaux que nous avons arreté de compter depuis l'époque où Ned portait encore des Oakley Eyeshades gagnant tout sur son chemin.

Alors que gagner était tout pour les coureurs en rouge, pour Specialized, engager les pilotes les plus aiguisés de la planète avec l'équipement le plus perfectionné dans le but de les aider à aller plus vite était une noble obsession. Bien sûr, sans l'existence du team, il n'y aurait pas eu de S-Works, et sans S-Works, il n'y aurait pas eu de Stumpjumper Carbone rigide super léger, ou même de Brain.

72
MON STUMPJUMPER N.3
Vedran Novak
Un réfugié Croate libéré grace à son Stumpjumper.
Vedran, 30 ans habitait à Zagreb en Croatie. Lorsque la guerre civile frappa le pays dans les années 90, il devint l'un des milliers de réfugiés qui trouvèrent asile en Serbie. Vous ne voyez pas trop de vélos de compétition dans les camps de réfugiés pour la simple raison que les gens qui quittent leur maison avec uniquement ce qu'ils ont sur leur dos n'ont généralement pas de place pour un vélo. En Serbie, Vedran et les autres Croates étaient sous les règles oppressantes de Slobodan Milosevic. Les premières nécéssités étant déja dures à obtenir, un vélo était un luxe auquel personne ne pouvait accéder. " les choses allaient si mal, que je ne pouvais même pas imaginer quand je pourrais à nouveau rouler," dit Vedran à propos de cette époque en Serbie.

Heureusement pour Vedran (et le reste du Monde), Milosevic fut renversé et la vie dans les Balkans revint lentement à la normale. Vedran, se serra fortement la ceinture et économisa suffisamment pour s'offrir un Stumpjumper Pro d'occasion qui, selon lui était en excellent état. Depuis ce jour, il roule dessus tous les jours et dit ne jamais vouloir arrêter. "avant d'avoir mon Stumpjumper, je ne savais pas que tant de plaisir pouvait sortir d'un deux roues! Mon vélo est le moyen de me rapeller en permanence combien la vie est bonne."

73
DÉCOLLAGE
Pulp Traction immortalisa la naissance du freeride à jamais.
Un type en lycra qui dérape une pente abrupte et cahotique sur un vélo rigide avec une fourche à simple té Marzocchi et ses 5 cm de débattements? Ça ressemble pas trop à du freeride. Certes il n'y avait aucun tail whip, back flip ou autre drops en suicide, mais c'était bel et bien du freeriding. Les racines du freeride même. Un grand merci au réalisateur de Pulp Traction, Greg Stump, une légende du ski et local de BC, car Pulp Traction fut la premiere video à orienter sa caméra sur le North Shore, et la scene naissante qui qui accouchera du freeride. Pulp T captura les parrains du 'je me jette' Richie Schley et Brett Tippie à l'époque ou les baggy shorts étaient réservés aux basketteurs et Long Travel signifiait un vol direct pour la Chine.

Etant donné qu'il n'y avait pas vraiment de cinéastes spécialisés dans le mountain bike à l'époque, le département Marketing de chez Specialized se tourna vers le filmeur de ski Stump, l'homme dérrière P-Tex, Lies And DuctTape et d'autres videos classiques de sports de glisses, pour réaliser une vidéo avec du pilotage extreme, de gros sauts de corniches et un regard sur le lifestyle des riders. "la plupart d'entre nous avions déja tourné dans des films de ski ou de snowboard, alors quand les gonzes sont arrivés pour filmer, on a juste fait le même genre de trucs qu'on faisait sur la neige…mais sur des vélos", dit Schley. "on était justement de passage récemment sur un spot où nous avions filmé Pulp Traction et on s'est marré en pensant à ce que l'on avait pu faire avec des spads rigides et quasi aucun débattement à l'avant."
Certes, c'était pas très beau, mais c'était la naissance d'un sport capturé sur pellicule pour toujours.

74 & 75

RIEN DE PLUS. RIEN

L'heure est venu de refermer le cercueil sur les rigides.

Entraine toi encore et encore pour être le plus rapide sur un vélo de cross-country, et tu te rendras compte qu'à part un trèfle à quatre feuilles géant, tu es aussi rare qu'un super topmodel. Telle était l'idée dérrière le FSRxc. Dénude un vélo suspendu au maximum en ne laissant que ce qui est indispensable, comme le corps d'un pilote de XC.

De plus, le timing était le bon : en 1996, les vélos suspendus gagnaient du débattement et prenaient donc du poids. Ils perdaient du coup pas mal d'ineterets aux yeux des gens plus portés sur la vitesse et les performances que par les sauts énormes depuis des rochers hauts comme des immeubles.

Donc les membres du S team Ben Capron, Mark Norris, Mike ducharme et Jeff Pint prirent la décision de zigger alors que tout le monde zaggait. Ils ont rasé, optimisé, coupé et taillé pour nous sortir le FSRxc avec 3pouces de débattement, un ensemble plus léger qui avait 1 pouce de débattement en moins que le FSR standard, et qui se maniait avec la précision d'une lame de rasoir. Ducharme, Capron et l'équipe obsédés par chaque millimètre carré du cadre, racourcissaient le diamètre des tubes. La partie sur laquelle ils gagnèrent le plus de poids fut la suspension sur le FSRxc, puisque l'articulation principale et les haubans pivotaient sur un seul axe, utilisant moitié moins de matériaux.

Le résultat fut un des vélos suspendus à pivot les plus léger jamais construit; assemblé avec tout ce qu'il faut de bonnes pièces, le FSRxc passait sous la barre des 11, 25 kg. Une version ultra-light fit du bruit au salon Interbike de 1998 avec 9, 27 kg au compteur.

Pourquoi me croiriez vous? Jettez donc un coup d'œil au message posté sur MTBR. com en 1999, " je ne roulerais plus jamais sur un rigide, une sortie sur ce spad et vous en ferez de même."

76 & 77

NAPALM!

Le plus grand athlète au monde est arrivé sur la scène du mountain bike. Là où il est passé, l'herbe a cessé de pousser.

Il n'était pas vététiste. C'était là le truc. Il ne s'est jamais considéré comme un biker, il se pointait juste et déchirait tout sur un VTT, comme il l'aurait fait sur un snowboard, une moto ou l'une de ses Cadillacs.

Il n'était pas vététiste, c'était une rock star du genre qu'on ne pouvait pas imaginer dans le milieu de la pédale. Depuis son premier jour sur une board à Donner Ski Ranch, l'homme qu'on appelait Mini-Shred maitrisait clairement ce sport. Puis il a littéralement explosé. " en 1992 j'ai perdu ma grand mère et ça m'a mené à devenir un parfait idiot, me battant dans les bars, buvant, zonant. Alors je me suis mis à cogiter, et j'ai commencer à me débarrasser de la colère que j'éprouvais depuis la mort de ma grand-mère en mettant toute mon energie dans le sport. C'était genre 'fais chier, je vais tout gagner'." Alors Mini Shred mua en Napalm et mis en place le défi de battre n'importe qui à son propre jeu. "ça me fait me sentir bien," dit il.

En 96, il a délaissé un peu le snowboard pour se lancer dans le mountain bike, son timing n'aurait pas pu être meilleur, car avec l'entrée du sport aux J.O, l'argent s'est mis à circuler plus massivement. Palmer allait vite, très vite, il était tellement charismatique et télégénique qu'il révolutionna à jamais le monde du mountain bike en ce changement de millénaire.
Un costard doré, un bus Prevost décoré par Troy Lee et un contrat juteux, même si Mike et tous ceux présent affirment que le contrat était plus modeste que ce qu'on croit : "Il n'a jamais pris tout ça suffisamment au sérieux pour gagner la grande course, mais par contre, foutre la merde, ça, il l'a fait", raconte Joe 'Buck' Buckley, son ancien mécano et garde fou.

80

ENDURO

Qui a dit que ça devait être facile?
Alors que la fin du millénaire arrivait, les gens prédisaient le chaos. L'an 2000 était sur les lèvres de tout le monde. 'la fin est proche,' clammaient certaines.

Pour les mountain bikers, le chaos se ressentait dans le manière de penser les vélos et les chemins. Grace à la popularité du VTT, les spots facilement accéssibles (ceux avec des parkings aux bords des sentiers) étaient saturés de monde lorsqu'ils n'étaient pas fermés pour avoir étés trop exploités. Les puristes qui voulaient se démarquer de la masse se mirent à exprimer le besoin d'avoir un vélo qui pourrait passer dans les chemins les plus dur et les plus cabossés.

Beaucoup de pratique (heureusement, rouler c'est faire de la recherche chez Specialized) et une remise en question du design de suspension que les ingénieurs de Spe avaient co-développé avec le gourou de la suspension Horst Leithner en 91, se concrétisa par le premier Enduro.

Lancé à l'été 1999, le cadre Enduro Pro était bardé d'une encombrante structure appelée en MAX (Manipulated Aluminum eXtrusion), avec un débattement réglable de 4,6 pouces le vélo ne pesait que 250 grammes de plus que FSR de l'année précédente. L'Enduro avait également un tube supérieur en forme de V qui permettait d'avoir une hauteur de selle respectable pour un vélo avec tant de débattement.

Pour 2000, le cadre fut encore plus allégé et affiné, tandis que des garde-boue étaient ajoutés donnant une touche motocross.

81

MON STUMPJUMPER N.4

Bob Brewer

De poids lourd à poids plume, Bob a perdu 45 kg sur son Stump
Il y a deux ans, Bob Brewer était au plus mal physiquement. pour tout juste 1m70, il atteignait les 130 Kgs, et sa forte tension artérielle participait activement à aggraver une maladie congénitale du rein. Son médecin dit que Bob, un comptable de 40 ans pour MSM inc, et père de deux gamins, devait absolument perdre du poids et se remettre en forme ou bien il ne tarderait pas à clamser.

Bob avait toujours apprécié faire du vélo, mais n'en fit jamais une priorité. Pour le coup, il sauta sur son spad en espérant que ce serait le ticket pour la santé. Mais sa vieille enclume de vélo n'était pas confortable et pas vraiment fun à rouler. Bob se ballada alors sur le web, effectua des recherches et découvrit rapidement la solide réputation de Specialized. Un peu chanceux, il trouva un bon deal et acheta un Stumpjumper comp 2004. La différence, dit il, était hallucinante. "c'est pas un retour au vélo, mais juste une nouvelle passion"

De nos jours, Bob ne roule pas parcequ'il le doit ou parceque c'est bon pour lui, il fait du vélo car c'est quelquechose dont il ne peut plus se passer. " je n'ai jamais été aussi en forme de toute ma vie. J'ai perdu 45 kilos, et je suis dehors à marteler les singletracks locaux quatres à six fois par semaine."
Bob était malade, fatigué, stréssé et démotivé. Désormais il est énergique, inspiré et heureux de vivre. De plus, il est heureux de dire qu'il va à nouveau être père. On dirait que le Stumpjumper a encore frappé.

82 & 83

QU'EST CE QU'ON PEUX APPRENDRE D'UN BOURRICOT?

Juste ce qu'il faut pour faire fonctionner la suspension quand vous le voulez.

Avez vous déja essayé de pomper, en appuyant sur le guidon, la fourche du vélo d'un pilote de cross country avant le départ d'une Coupe du Monde? La vérité, c'est que la soi-disant fourche suspendue à l'avant de leur vélo ne bouge pas d'un poil. En fait, beaucoup d'entre eux ont leur fourche tellement gonflée qu'il n'y a quasi plus de débattement. Hey, si c'est comme ça qu'ils kiffent, et qu'ils peuvent gagner, où est le bleme?

Demandez donc à Mike Andrews, ingénieur chez Specialized et véritable acharné de suspensions, il vous en dira plus sur le bleme. Il a passé un nombre incalculable d'années à fabriquer des suspensions qui fonctionnent vraiment bien. Alors quand un des pilotes du S team souhaitent avoir des fourches qui bougent seulement lorsqu'ils percuttent une grosse bosse, Mick avec son crane rempli de schemas de suspensions, trouve l'idée adecquate.

Un ami de Mick qui était ingénieur chez FoMoCo lui a dit une fois, à propos d'un amortisseur qu'il avait dessiné, qu'il ne se compréssait que lorsque la roue de la voiture frappait un dos d'ane. De retour à Detroit, ils appelèrent ce nouvel amorto le Jerk shock car il lui fallait une secousse pour l'activer. Mick se mit à bricoler sa propre version.

Mick trouvait que c'était une brillante idée, et comme l'amorto était capable de faire la différence entre un choc provenant du sol de ceux provenant de la force du pilote, il le baptisa le 'Brain.' Il mit au point un prototype qui fonctionna immédiatement, mais qui n'était pas aussi fiable qu'il l'aurait souhaité. Il eut alors une illumination: si le cœur du jerk shock (une valve inertielle) était ramené au plus près de l'axe, tout fonctionnerait beaucoup mieux, plus vite et de façon plus fiable. Il y parvint, et cette chambre auxiliaire devint le Brain. Avec l'aide de Fox sur les points les plus précis de la production, l'affaire était dans le sac.

La suite à connaitre, Filip Meirhaeghe (un des types qui roulait en rigide avec sa fourche réglée au plus dur possible) remporta un titre de Champion du Monde au guidon d'un Epic équipé d'un Brain shock (OK, Meirhaeghe fut choppé la saison suivante pour un certain déséquilibre chimique, mais l'Epic, lui, n'était gonflé à rien d'illicite.)

De nos jours, l'amortisseur Brain n'est pas seulement réservé à la compétition, puisqu'il est de série sur les Stumpjumpers.

86 & 87

UN VÉLO FABRIQUÉ POUR RENTRER LES CASCADES LES PLUS DANGEREUSES ÉLABORÉ À PARTIR D'UNE PILE DE LEGOS

Ce type sur la double précédente. Darren Berrecloth. Seigneur du freeriding new school. Il avait besoin d'une arme dans son combat contre les limites, les lois et les préjugés. Alors, Mike commanda le Demo, un bike qui selon BearClaw avait besoin d'un maximum d'options. Gros débattement, une géométrie suffisament équilibrée pour les drops les plus raides, un centre de gravité ultra bas, un tube supérieur rabaissé pour enrichir la maniabilité , et, ben oui, de quoi accueillir un dérailleur avant.

C'est ainsi qu'une équipe d'ingénieurs, de designers et de chefs de produits Specialized comprenant Jason Chamberlin, Brandon Sloan et Robert Egger se sont plongés dans le projet en jouant avec une pile de Legos. Le team pu construire en un rien de temps un modèle du concept basique de suspension Demo juste en assemblant des Legos. Cette maquette était une sorte d'ébauche qui permit à l'équipe d'ajuster et de corriger certains détails avant l'arrivée de la superstar des ingénieurs Jason Chamberlin. Lequel se plongea dans son ordinateur pour concrétiser le projet grace à ses talents.

Pas besoin d'etre un scientifique de la Nasa pour conclure que jouer avec des Legos était la partie facile des recherches. créer un design qui marche, avec le logiciel de modélisation Pro/E 3-D, construire des protos dans l'atelier au QG de Specialized et tester le Demo design dans des spots réels démesurés pris des années (littéralement, deux) et des centaines de milliers de dollars.

Le résultat du génie informatique de Chamberlin et des multiples sorties test pour Brandon Sloan, le Product manager, se résuma en un cadre de 9 pouces de débattement, avec une suspension à quatre points d'encrages, et un bras oscillant classique renforcé par un sous-bras oscillant et six points de pivot. Pour rendre le Demo rigide et solide, Chamberlin and co. ont déssiné la pièce forgée à froid la plus chère jamais faite pour un vélo, dont la partie centrale qui enferme l'amortisseur fut la plus complexe à forger nécessittant une presse de plus de deux millions de kilos.

Qui aurait pu deviner qu'un vélo fait pour les énormes gaps, les pires drops et les plus violents crashs fut au début conçu à partir d'une pile de Legos.

88 & 89

30 ANS À ROULER À FOND, ET À PRENDRE DES RISQUES

Qui a les dents longues?

Trois decennies. C'était plutôt une veillée funéraire qu'une fête : kaput le gosse et on passe à des choses d'adulte. Il est temps de ranger les tongs et de se calmer sur les bières avant midi (du moins en semaine). De toute façon, personne ne voulait en parler. Le petit gars qui a commencé dans un petite entreprise vendant des potences et d'autres trucs depuis sa caravane à San Jose venait d'avoir 30 ans.
C'est pas grave, cela dit. Aujourd'hui, on commence à peine sa vie, pas vrai ?

Ce qui est indéniable, c'est que le stumpjumper du 30ème anniversaire de la fondation de Specialized est plus beau que jamais. Il est éternel, son sourire prêt à dévaler toutes les pistes toujours intact. Et le corps ? Il suffit de regarder le chassis Dream Silver bâti comme un tank. Comme le designer en chef de Specialized Robert Egger dit toujours : "si ça a de la gueule, c'est bon." Avec les Dolomites d'Italie en guise de décor, ça a de la gueule. "Il faut beaucoup de formes nettes à un vélo, qui, assemblées, ont l'air plus robuste que séparées les unes des autres" selon Egger, le designer responsable de bijoux Specialized tels que l'Enduro, le Hemi et le Tarmac.

90 & 91

RIDE ON CAPTAIN

Difficile de freiner une vie passée en tête de peloton.
Un samedi soir de plus pour le Captain. Terré dans un hotel à 99$ la nuit, seul, avec de la glace sur son pied droit blessé. Ce soir, il regardera la dernière édition des infos locales, et boira son ultime gorgée d'elixir énergétique secret, même s'il a un départ de course à 7 heure du mat'. C'est la méthode du Captain.

Ned s'est officiellement retiré en 1996, mais il n'a pas l'air de s'en souvenir. Depuis que Specialized lui a organisé une fête de départ à la retraite cet automne là, il a continué à courir des Coupe du Monde et des NORBA, des courses sur route, des ascension de cols, s'est inscrit à des courses de descente (yeah, et il a battu son ado de fils), des duathlons, triathlons, marathons, et en gros tout ce que vous pouvez imaginer exister. Pourvu que ça implique un niveau élevé d'acide lactique et un exces d'endorphine, le Captain sera présent. Le jours de ses 50 ans, il a carrément fini 4ème à la sévère ascension du Mt Washington!

Bon nombre des minots qu'il sème dans le sillon de sa roue arrière, n'étaient même pas nés lorsque Ned finit l'Ironman de 1980 à la 24ème place, ou lorsqu'en 1983, il remporta sa toute première course de VTT et couru la Coors Classic au sein de l'équipe légendaire Ti-Raleigh (celle composée de Andy Hampsten, Roy Knickman et Steve Tilford) ou même lorsqu'il remporta en 1987 les championnats Europpéen et NORBA.

Seulement Ned n'accepte aucun traitement de faveur ou louange supplémentaire, le Captain considère que les blessures, les hotels miteux et les départs de courses à 7 h du mat' font partie du jeu dans sa vie de compétiteur. C'est sa destiné et il l'accepte entièrement "je ne suis pas la dehors à tenter de prouver que je suis plus rapide que les jeunes,"dit il "je suis juste là dehors parceque j'adore être à la tête du peloton"

92 & 93

STUMPJUMPER FIELD GUIDE/2006 S-WORKS STUMPJUMPER

A la recherche de la fluidité sur le vélo en carbone le plus onctueux.

Cadre : fait en composite de propriété FACT Y570, jusqu'ici le carbone le plus résistant utilisé pour un cadre de vélo. Le Stumpjumper S-Works carbone était prisé pour son mélange de performances et de maniabilité ultra précise.

Amortisseur : brain avec brain fade, le premier amortisseur à savoir quand s'activer pour une meilleure absorption des chocs, et quand être ferme pour accroitre le rendement. Comprend la technologie Brain Fade 2006 qui offre la possibilité aux riders de régler à leur gout le comportement de l'amortisseur Brain.

Pneus : développé juste pour un vélo suspendu rapide tel que le Stumpjumper Carbone, le pneu Adrenaline Pro 26 x 2.0 a 120 "TPI" pour un poids minime, et deux densitées de caoutchouc pour combiner rendement et adhérence.

Cintre : le Specialized OS Carbon Rise s'assorti à merveille avec le cadre du Stumpjumper Carbone. À peine 175 grammes offrant la meilleure combinaison avec un cintrage de 6 degrés vers le haut et 8 degrés vers l'arrière.

Selle : la Rival, nouveauté pour le modèle 2006, est dotée du système exclusif Specialized Body Geometry qui, suite aux tests en labo a prouvé qu'il améliorait la ciculation sanguine dans les zones sensibles.

94 & 95

LE FUTUR?

Dur de dire ou cela, ou n'importe quoi d'autre va nous mener.
Des personnes plus importantes ont déjà éssayé, et, vous vous souvenez du passage à l'an 2000.
Nous sommes certains d'une chose, c'est qu'autant les épreuves, et les architectes de cette culture ont besoin d'être protégés. Nous faisons ainsi don de 100% des bénéfices de ce livre à l'IMBA et le Mountain Bike Hall of Fame.

DEUTCH/GERMAN/Translation

6 & 7

DEDICATION

20 Stunden, 20 Tage, 20 Jahre vorher – es ist schwer, die erste Mountainbike-Tour zu vergessen. Die knirschenden Laubblätter und Zweige. Der Vorderreifen rollt und drückt sich durch fast alles, was im Weg liegt. Fast. Wie eine Raubkatze tigert man leicht und elegant durch die Wildnis. Fast so schnell wie auf einem Motorrad. Der erste Überschlag, die erste Wunde am Schienbein von der Bärentatze, wie eine Warnung kam der Schmerz hoch. Und doch ein gutes Gefühl. Fast zu schön, um wahr zu sein. Wie der erste Kuss, das Vorspiel zu einer wunderbaren Sinfonie der Sucht.

Genau das löste ein Mountainbike in einem aus. Es war wie eine Macht, gefährlich, aber beherrschbar. Man musste es sofort lieben, mit seinem breiten Lenker, dem weichen Sattel, dem stabilen Fahrwerk. Ein Mountainbike löst nicht nur ganz neue Gefühle aus, es ist auch ein sozialer Faktor – Ärzte aus der Vorstadt treffen auf Klempner aus der Stadt und auf Lehrer vom Lande – und alle zusammen entdecken sie Gebiete, von deren Existenz bis dahin nichts ahnten. Selbst wenn diese gleich in der Nachbarschaft liegen. Mit dem Mountainbike entdeckt man die Natur immer wieder neu, weil die Endorphine ausgeschüttet werden und neue Abenteuer locken.

Die Geschichte dieses Buches könnte auch eine trockene Technikabhandlung sein, aber die Technik ist nicht das Entscheidende an einem Bike. Natürlich bückt man sich und schaut nach, welcher Umwerfer oder welche Gabel an diesem Rad montiert sind, aber dies hat seine Ursachen in der Leidenschaft. Dank Leidenschaft, Inspiration und Fachwissen entwarf man ursprünglich den Stumpjumper, um ein fettes Grinsen auf noch mehr Gesichter zu zaubern. Glücklicherweise funktionierte dies auch und so wurde der Stumpjumper und der ganze Sport über 25 Jahre am Leben erhalten und gestärkt. Ein Dank an alle, die sich jemals in den Sattel eines Bikes geschwungen haben. Erst sie haben dieses Buch, diese Einstellung und diesen Lebensstil ermöglicht.

8 & 9

FAT TIRE VORWORT

Wie begann das Shredden wirklich?
Moment mal, ist das Mountainbiken, was die Jungs da machen? Eigentlich dauert es noch rund zwanzig Jahre, bis das Mountainbike erfunden wird, aber es schaut schwer danach aus. Sie fahren auf Schotter, die Bikes haben dicke Reifen und jeder grinst von einem Ohr zum anderen.

So gesehen hat John Finley Scott auf seinem 1953er Schwinn Varsity bereits in den Sechziger Jahren Tausende von Meilen offroad zurückgelegt und dabei den White Mountain mit seinen 4350 Metern Höhe in den kalifornischen Sierra Mountains bezwungen. War er der erste Mountainbiker?

Oder was ist mit den 20 Buffalo-Soldaten, die 1897 in Gebieten, die heute als Yellowstone National Park bekannt sind, an die 1900 Meilen auf Rädern runterstrampelten? Die Jungs waren garantiert nicht auf Straßenrädern im Wilden Westen unterwegs. Andererseits war es auch nicht ihre Absicht, als Mountainbiker berühmt zu werden.
Wann also genau war es nicht mehr einfach nur Radfahren im Gelände, sondern echtes Mountainbiken? Vielleicht am 1. Dezember 1974, als Russ Mahon in der Bucht von San Franzisko ein Schaltwerk an einen Clunker schraubte? Oder vielleicht als Joe Breeze im Oktober 1977 zum ersten Mal mit einem selbst gebauten Bike mit Gangschaltung und dicken Reifen den legendären Repack-Downhill hinunter raste? Oder begann das Ganze vielleicht ein paar Jahre später, als Tim Neenan, der Designer des allerersten Stumpjumpers, auf einen der Prototypen stieg, um die Hügel hinter dem Specialized-Büro in San Jose hinauf zu keuchen?

Die Antwort auf die Frage, wann das Shredden wirklich erfunden wurde, sollte man am besten Universitätsprofessoren überlassen, oder dem Haufen von Bike-Süchtigen, die sich jeden Sonntag in San Franziskos „Zeitgeist-Saloon" treffen.

10 & 11

CRESTED BUTTE

„Ein runtergekommenes altes Kohlengruben-Dorf, die letzten Kumpel mit ihren schwarzen Lungen lungerten auf Bänken herum, während junge Menschen zu Fuß und auf Bikes vorbei schwebten..." so beschreibt Joe Kelly das Kaff Crested Butte, wie es die ersten Aussteiger, eine Bande von fünf Bike-Fans aus Marin, bei ihrer jährlichen dritten (eigentlich zweiten) Pearl-Pass-Tour erlebten. Crested Butte war seit dem Colorado-Goldrausch von 1859 ein Gruben-Ort gewesen. Die Szenerie in den späten Siebzigern präsentierte sich kunterbunt, und mit den Anfängen des Telemark-Skiings und der Zubereitung von grünem Gras-Tee schrammte es knapp am Hippie-Dorf vorbei. Die Neuankömmlinge, meist mit Dreadlocks und auch ansonsten eher ungewaschen, gaben sich Namen wie Wolke, Stern und Koffer (dessen Sohn Geldbeutel hieß).

Dank seiner langen Tradition im Outdoorsport – dem Ort wird nachgesagt, den ersten Skilift Colorados besessen zu haben – liebten die Einheimischen und die Hippies gleichermaßen Aktivitäten in der freien Natur, wovon ein fester Bestandteil eine herzliche Beziehung zum Fahrrad war. Natürlich nannten sich diejenigen, die vor 1978 bikten, nicht Mountainbiker. Sie benützten einfach ein Fahrrad. Meistens Räder, die man in Denver bereits entsorgt hatte, alte Schwinns, Hawthorne und BF Goodrich Klunker, die ihren zweiten, eher schon dritten Frühling erlebten. Die Straßen von Crested Butte waren üblicherweise acht Monate im Jahr weiß von Schnee und Eis, die restliche Zeit braun von Sand und Schlamm, so dass man auf dicken Ballonreifen am besten durch die Stadt cruisen konnte.

In einer langen Nacht im Grubstake Saloon in CB im Sommer 1976 wurde beschlossen, dass man unbedingt einen Klunker über den 3870 Meter hohen Pearl Pass befördern müsse, um dann hinunter zur Bar des Jerome Hotels in Aspen düsen zu können. Im September des gleichen Jahres brachen 15 mutige Freiwillige, Ketten und Kehlen gut geölt, mit ihren Clunkern nach Norden Richtung Aspen auf. Nach einer heftigen Party auf dem Pearl Pass – Berichten des „Crested Butte Pilot" zufolge konsumierten Radfahrer und Supportcrew einen Kasten Bier, drei Flaschen Schnaps, fünf Liter Wein und drei Flaschen Champagner – schepperten, holperten und kullerten alle die Abfahrt hinunter ins Jerome Hotel, wo man in der gleichen Nacht weiter trank und zahlreiche Legenden geboren wurden.

14 & 15

DER KÖNIG DER CLUNKER

Jeder Mann, jede Frau und jedes Kind, das ein Mountainbike besitzt, sollte das Glas erheben, ein Lied singen, laut übers Meer brüllen oder einfach nur ein leises Gebet für Charles R. Kelly (auch genannt SeeKay) sprechen. Sir Charles, der sich damals in der eigenbrötlerischen Gemeinde von Fairfax, Kalifornien, verkrochen hatte, gründete das garantiert erste Mountainbike-Magazin – den Fat Tire Flyer – bevor es Mountainbikes überhaupt gab. Während jede Menge Leute behaupten, etwas mit der Erfindung von „Fat" zu tun zu habe (den ersten Rahmen, das erste Bike, das erste Rennen) war Charlie eindeutig der Erste, der den speziellen Standpunkt und die Ansichten der Clunker Crew definierte. Er war derjenige, der zum ersten Mal der Welt wirklich erklärte, was „Clunking" ist.

„Obwohl Clunker irgendwie leichten Cross-Motorräder ähneln, beschränkt sich diese Ähnlichkeit nur aufs Äußere. Damit Kurven zu kratzen ist eine einzigartige Kunstform. Ein Motorrad verfügt über dicke Reifen und Stoßdämpfer – ein Clunker nicht. Daher wird jede kleine Unebenheit auf der Strecke zum Katapult und der Clunker zum unfreiwilligen Flugobjekt. In engen Kurven fehlt einem Clunker die schnelle Beschleunigung eines Motorrads, um das Heck herum zu schleudern, und ohne Stoßdämpfer bockt es wie ein wilder Esel. Trotzdem rauschen gute Fahrer schneller um die Kurve, als man es sich vorstellen kann...
oh oh, zu schnell diesmal, das Bike rutscht in der Schotterkurve weg. Was tun? Ins Gelände rauschen oder hinschmeißen? Hinschmeißen... verdammt... T-Shirt kaputt, Ellbogen blutig. Keine Zeit darüber nachzudenken (das T-Shirt ist alt, der Ellbogen auch), ist das Bike in Ordnung? OK ... wieder drauf, die Kette mit den Händen aufgelegt, während man die ersten Meter rollt. Kaum läuft es wieder, trittst du voll rein, um die Zeit wieder reinzuholen."
--Charles Kelly
Bicycling Magazine 1979

16 & 17

SPECIALIZED SCHÜRT DIE FAT TIRE REVOLUTION MIT TEILE-NACHSCHUB

Die Verkäufe im ersten Jahr betrugen 60.000$
Im nächsten Jahr 128.000$
Im nächsten Jahr über 200.000$
„Wenn ich jetzt zurückblicke, bewegte sich alles langsam, aber mir kam es damals unglaublich schnell vor", sagt Mike Sinyard, der Gründer und Chef von Specialized über das erste Jahr, nachdem er offiziell die Firma Specialized eröffnet hatte.

Lange bevor es Leute gab, die Kettenblatt-Tattoos ganze Webseiten widmen (das stimmt wirklich, www.blackbirdsf.org) betrachtete man es als Wahnsinn, aus Liebe zum Fahrrad fahren das einzige Wertobjekt zu verkaufen (im Falle von Mike Sinyard ein VW-Bus), um mit dem Erlös eine Radreise in einen anderen Kontinent zu finanzieren. Genau genommen ist es auch heute noch eher ungewöhnlich. 1973, als Mike sein blau-weißes Bob Jackson Tourenrad einpackte, um damit nach Europa zu fliegen, erschien es anderen als komplett durchgedreht.

Nachdem er durch Großbritannien, Amsterdam (grins) und Barcelona getourt war, erreichte Mike die Po-Ebene in Norditalien mit einem Gefühl, das hoffentlich jeder von uns kennt. Er hatte keine Ahnung, was er eigentlich wollte, aber sein Bauch sagte ihm, dass jeden Augenblick etwas Großartiges passieren könnte. Und so kam es. Das Schicksal begegnete ihm in Form eines jungen Mädchens, das Mike zufällig in einer Jugendherberge in Mailand traf. Sie hatte Verbindungen zum „Paten" eines italienischen Rad-Universums, Signore Cino Cinelli, Gründer der legendären Rahmen- und Zubehörfirma, die Mike schon immer verehrte.

Binnen vier Wochen war Mike mit einer Ladung von Cinelli-Komponenten zurück in seinem kleinen Wohnwagen in San Jose. Er hatte jeden Cent, den er besaß, in Cinos berühmte Vorbauten, Lenker und Rahmen investiert. Ohne Auto und einem Phänomen wie eBay war er lediglich auf sein Fahrrad angewiesen, und so strampelte er mit einem Anhänger von Händler zu Händler, um seine italienischen Schmuckstücke anzupreisen und auf seiner Tour zu verkaufen.

Ein paar Jahre später war Specialized ein ausgewachsener Rad- und Komponentenimporteur, dessen Stärke im Angebot von seltenen und schwer zu findenden Teilen für die Fat-Tire-Fans lag. Es handelte sich um europäische Teile wie Huret DuoPar-Schaltwerke, Mafac-Bremsen und Rahmen aus Columbus-Rohren.
Als Lieferant für die meisten Rahmenbauer der Westküste befand sich Specialized genau im Epizentrum des neuen Bike-Booms. Rahmenkünstler wie Joe Breeze, Albert Eisentraut und Tom Ritchey (der Vertragsjobs für Specialized ausführte, wie die Bearbeitung von speziellen Tandemnaben) gehörten zu den festen Abnehmern. Als diese Schweißer immer mehr ungewöhnliche Teile wie TA-Kurbeln und Cantilever-Felgenbremsen bestellten, wunderte sich Mike Sinyard, was die Jungs damit wohl vorhatten. Was sie vorhatten? Die Jungs erfanden schlichtweg das Fahrrad neu und Mike hatte seine Bestimmung darin gefunden, dabei mitzuwirken.

20 & 21

STUMPJUMPER FIELD GUIDE/1981 STUMPJUMPER

Rahmen: Design von Tim Neenan, Lighthouse Bikes in Santa Cruz. Der ursprüngliche Stumpjumper-Rahmen war TIG-geschweißt. Besitzt ein 81er Rahmen Muffen, ist er von Ende 1981. Die blaue Lackierung? Die nahm man, weil man das Blau schon beim Sequoia Tourenrad verwendet hatte.

Vorbau: Der legendäre Golfschläger-Vorbau war die modifizierte Version eines damaligen BMX-Vorbaus. Die ursprünglichen Stahllenker des Stumpjumpers waren abgewandelte Magura-Motorradlenker.

Bremshebel: Die Standardhebel des Stumpjumpers waren Tomaselli-Rennbremsen, wie sie in den Siebzigern an Straßenmotorrädern verbaut wurden. Sie wurden mit Heavy-Duty-Zügen verkauft, die das Feeling und die Bremsleistung verbesserten.

Reifen: Specialized nutzte seine Erfahrung aus der Herstellung seiner erfolgreichen Straßenreifen, um die ersten leichten Mountainbikereifen mit Profil zu backen, den Stumpjumper. Falls du noch einen Satz davon besitzt, gib ihn nie her. 25 Jahre alte Bikereifen findet man nicht so leicht.

Kurbeln: Diese Teile hatte Specialized ursprünglich für Tourenräder nach Amerika importiert. Die TA-Kurbeln kamen glänzend poliert und konnten extrem kleine Kettenblätter aufnehmen. Leider traten viele Defekte auf, da sie nicht für den harten Geländeeinsatz konstruiert waren.

22 & 23

FIRST TIME I SAW A STUMPJUMPER

JOE BREEZE; Mountainbike-Pionier, Rahmenbauer, Autor
Ich sah ihn bei Bike Odyssey in Sausalito, da wo ich wohnte. Zuerst dachte, was soll denn dieser komische Vorbau, wie ein Golfschläger und wunderte mich, dass Tomaselli- statt Magura-Hebel dran sind. Aber für 750 Dollar werden sie jede Menge davon verkaufen, dachte ich mir.

TOM RITCHEY; Mountainbike-Pionier, Rahmenbauer, Erfinder, Rennfahrer
Er (der Stumpjumper) war eher grob und er verkörperte das technische Niveau, das damals in Japan möglich war. Unsere Bikes waren doppelt so teuer (und leichter), aber der Stumpjumper war günstig und hatte für damals interessante Komponenten.

RICHARD CUNNINGHAM; Gründer von Mantis Cycle und Redakteur bei Mountain Bike Action.
Der Stumpjumper war schwer, lief unruhig und sein Lenkverhalten war etwas störrisch, aber als ich das erste Mal einen sah, riss es mir die Augen auf und mir war klar: „Dieses Mountainbiken ist eine riesige Sache … das muss ich auch probieren!" Kurz danach baute ich mein erstes Mountainbike.

DON COOK; Mountainbike-Pionier, Co-Direktor der Mountainbike Hall of Fame.
Damals kostete ein handgefertigter Ritchey-Rahmen allein 1200 bis 1500 Dollar. Wir sahen den Stumpjumper und stellten fest: Das ist es. Auf einmal musste man nicht mehr drei bis vier Monate warten, um ein Bike von Tom (Ritchey) oder Gary (Fisher) zu bekommen.

JACQUIE PHELAN; Mountainbike-Pionier, Gründerin von WOMBATS, Autorin.
Ich sah einen Stumpjumper, wusste aber nicht, was es war. Damals war ich mit Gary Fisher zusammen und er nannte sie so eine Art „Raubkopie". Ich glaube ja nicht, dass sie das wirklich ins Buch bringen.

VICTOR VINCENTE VON AMERIKA; Mountainbike-Pionier, Olympischer Straßenfahrer, Rennveranstalter, Künstler.
Meine Erinnerungen sind etwas verblasst, aber so weit ich mich erinnere, fand ich es ein funktionelles gutes Design, das in der breiten Masse sicher gut ankommen würde, eher als die Custombikes zuvor.

RICHARD HEMINGTON, GB; Der erste Mensch, der einen Stumpjumper außerhalb der USA verkaufte.
Der Stumpjumper kam im Karton und musste fast vollständig aufgebaut werden. Ich erinnere mich noch, wie alle Teile ausgebreitet herum lagen und wir ewig brauchten, um ihn zu montieren. Wir bekommen ganz schön Ärger, wenn sich das Ding auch noch gut verkauft, dachte ich für mich. Und dann passierte es wirklich und wir saßen tatsächlich in der Patsche.

JOE MURRAY; Rennfahrer, Bike-Designer, Testfahrer.
Der 81er Stumpi, den ich besaß, war etwas störrisch, aber ich mochte ihn, obwohl ich ganz schön viel Technik brauchte, um ihn die Serpentinen in Marin County runter zu bringen. Als ich anfing, für Gary Fisher Rennen zu fahren, bekam ich von ihm ein Bike und verkaufte den Stumpjumper. Ich wünschte, ich hätte ihn behalten.

MERT LAWWIL; Motorradlegende, einer der ersten Mountainbike-Designer.
„Als ich merkte, wie günstig er (der Stumpjumper) verkauft wurde und um wie viel er besser als meine Bikes war, war ich kurz davor, aufzugeben und zu meinen Motorrädern zurück zu kehren."

24 & 25

DER UR-VATER ALLER ANZEIGEN

Ein komplett neues Rad braucht eine komplett neue Art von Anzeigenkampagne. Sie funktioniert seit 25 Jahren.

Nur wenige Jahre zuvor war Mike in seinem winzigen Wohnwagen gesessen und hatte seinen „Katalog" auf einen Schreibblock gekritzelt. Seine Angestellten nötigte er, auf Reifenstapeln zu schlafen, weil der Lagerraum mit Teilen überquoll. Jetzt versuchte er, ein ausgewachsenes Monster zu bändigen, das Stumpjumper hieß.

Ein völlig neues Rad aus einer Serienfertigung wie der Stumpjumper brach sämtliche bisherigen Gesetze, wie man so etwas verkaufen könnte. Vor der Zeit der „Whole New Sport"- Kampagne, wie sie im S-Hauptquartier heißt, bestand die Specialized–Werbung aus maximal halbseitigen Schwarz-Weiß-Anzeigen. Dies änderte sich mit einer schwarzen Hochglanz-Beauty, die der Ur-Vater aller folgenden Specialized-Anzeigen für die nächsten 25 Jahre werden sollte. Die Aufnahmen stammten von Jack Christensen, der sie in der gleichen Garage fotografierte wie seine Bilder für die ersten Apple-Computerbroschüren. Entworfen wurden die Anzeigen von Patrick Mountain, einem langjährigen Specialized-Mitarbeiter. Die „Whole New Sport"-Anzeige stach aus den damaligen grauen Magazinseiten hervor wie ein Ferrari auf einem Parkplatz voller VW-Käfer.

Klar schaut die Anzeige toll aus, aber warum, um Himmels Willen, trägt der Typ, der gerade auf seinem Bike losfährt, einen Overall und darüber gestülpte lange Strümpfe? Der „Typ" ist der Designer des Stumpjumpers, Tim Neenan, und er erklärt es folgendermaßen: „Damals gab es einfach keine Klamotten für Mountainbiker, nichts, was man irgendwie beim Shredden tragen konnte. Also fuhr ich einfach in meinem Arbeitsoverall, das ist alles."

26 & 27

START YOUR ENGINES

Die Rennen in den ersten Jahren der 80er waren wie die NASCAR-Rennen in den 40ern: Man suchte sich irgendwo eine Rennstrecke, ließ die Fahrer antreten und schwang die Startflagge. Damals schliefen die Fahrer im Auto, zahlten die Startgebühr mit ungedeckten Schecks und rauchten den Inhalt der Energieriegel lieber statt sie zu essen. Es war hart, es war ehrlich, es war alles so ehrlich, wie man es seit Jahren im Zweiradsport nicht mehr erlebt hatte. Es war einfach zu gut, um ein Geheimtipp zu bleiben. Von ihrer Gründung in einem Privathaus in Danville, Kalifornien 1983 wuchs die NORBA (National Offroad Bicycling Association) von Null auf 20.000 Mitglieder bis 1990.

28 & 29

SELBSTBEWUSSTSEIN – DAS STUMPJUMPER-TEAM HATTE JEDE MENGE DAVON

Das braucht man auch, wenn man auf pinkfarbenen Bikes antritt.
1984 gab es zwar so etwas wie ein normales Mountainbike-Team sowieso nicht, aber hätte es welche gegeben, hätte das Team Stumpjumper nicht dazu gehört. Es war das erste professionelle Team der Szene. Sie fuhren auf pinkfarbenen Bikes mit tiefem Lenker und mit richtigen Radschuhen, als die meisten ihre Energieriegel lieber inhalierten als aßen, und noch mit Turnschuhen antraten. Das Team Stump, organisiert von Straßen-Guru Bill Woodul, war ein echtes Experiment im Gelände. „Woody steckte einfach einige der Kategorie-I-Straßenfahrer wie uns und ein paar Cross-Fahrer zusammen und trainierte uns nach denselben Methoden und Ansätzen, wie er es mit dem Straßenteam gemacht hatte", sagt der ehemalige Team Stumpjumper-Fahrer Dave McLaughlin. „Wir haben richtig trainiert, wir waren durchorganisiert und wir hatten sogar eine Taktik für jedes Rennen."

Im ersten Jahr des Teams bestanden die handverlesenen Talente aus den Jungprofis im Cross McLaughlin, Gavin Chilcot (der später im berühmten 7-11-Straßenteam fuhr), den Nordkaliforniern Mark Michelle und Alan Ott und dem „Meister" der Amerikanischen Cross-Szene, Laurence Malone. In einen Specialized-Van gepfercht zogen sie durch die USA, überall hin wo damals die wenigen „großen" Mountainbike-Rennserien ihre Zelte aufschlugen: die Suntour Pacific States Challenge, die Gant Challenge-Serie (mit Städte-Rennen in Seattle, Chicago, Golden in Colorado und Tampa und Miami), das Ross-Stage-Rennen und Ein-Tages-Klassiker wie das „Rockhopper", „Rumpstomper" und die NORBA-Meisterschaften. „Es ging etwas rau zu damals. Die Konkurrenz war nicht so hart wie heute, aber wenn Joe Murray oder ein paar Straßenfahrer wie Andy Hampsten oder Steve Tilford auftauchten, ging es ganz schön zur Sache", meint McLaughlin über diese Zeit, als Bike-Rennen noch in den Kinderschuhen steckten.

Ein paar Jahre und holprige Rennsaisons später war aus dem Team Stumpjumper das Team Specialized geworden, das am besten ausgestattete und beste Bike-Team der Welt. In den frühen Konstellationen standen Weltmeister Ned Overend, Lisa Muhich und Sara Ballantyne auf den Gehaltslisten genauso wie das Cross-Country-Wunder Daryl Price und die Downhill-Helden Elladee Brown und Paul Thomasberg. Ab da fuhr man auch nicht mehr auf den pinkfarbenen Bikes, aber das Selbstbewusstsein wurde weiter hoch gehalten.

30 & 31

STUMPJUMPER FIELD GUIDE/1984 STUMPJUMPER TEAM

Ist dein Bike rosa, solltest du wirklich schnell damit sein.

Rahmen Design Jim Merz aus japanischem Tange Prestige-Rohr. Der 1984er Team Stumpjumper war der leichteste Rahmen, den Specialized bis dahin gebaut hatte.

Gabel Der rosafarbene Stumpjumper besaß die erste Unicrown-Gabel, die leichter und einfacher herzustellen war, als die bisherigen gemufften Gabeln.

Hinterbremse Glücklicherweise erwiesen sich die am Stumpjumper Team montierten U-Brakes, die unter den Kettenstreben saßen, als kurzlebige Modeerscheinung. Die Dinger zogen Dreck geradezu magnetisch an und gingen als einer der größten Irrtümer in die Geschichte des Mountainbikes ein.

Reifen 1984 ersetzten die TriCross-Reifen das Stumpjumper-Profil für High-End-Bikes. Das flache Stollenprofil wurde gerühmt für Supergrip in trockenen, staubigen Bedingungen.

Freilauf Als sprichwörtliches Arbeitstier besaß das Stumpjumper Team eine Shimano 600-Straßenkassette mit lediglich 26 Zähnen als größtem Ritzel – die meisten Biker bevorzugten damals allerdings schon ein 30er Ritzel.

32

MBHOF

Wenn es welche für Ukulele-Spieler und Flitzer gibt, warum nicht für Biker?
Gibt man bei Google den Begriff „Hall of Fame" ein, erhält man 47.400.000 Treffer. 47 Millionen. Wow. Es gibt eine Ruhmeshalle für Minen, für Cowgirls, für Computer, für Flitzer, und für Ukulele-Spieler. Unglaublich – Ukulele-Spieler. Was, um Himmels Willen, steht in einer Ukulele-Hall of Fame? Schwer zu sagen, aber definitiv mehr als in der Flitzer-Ruhmeshalle.
Es gibt wohl einen unstillbaren Wunsch der Menschheit, Menschen zu ehren, die etwas zu einer bestimmten Kultur beigetragen haben, und Fat-Tire-Fans unterscheiden sich darin nicht von Cowgirls, Flitzern oder Ukulele-Liebhabern. In den nicht gerade großzügigen Räumen einer ehemaligen Tankstelle findet man auf der Elk Avenue in Crested Butte die Mountainbike Hall of Fame, gegründet von Carole Bauer. Mitte der Achtziger Jahre befürchtete die seit langem in Crested Butte lebende Carole, dass die Gründer der Mountainbike-Bewegung in Vergessenheit geraten könnten, wenn man nicht mit einer Einrichtung ihre Verdienste würdigen und für die Nachwelt archivieren würde.

1988 war die MBHoF so weit, ihre ersten Mitglieder zu nominieren. In die erste Wahl kamen natürlich alle Pioniere wie Breeze, Fisher, Kelly, Cunningham, Ritchey und Murray. Kein Wunder, dass ein gewisser Mr. S. sich mehr als geschmeichelt, verblüfft und hoch geehrt fühlte, dass seine Person in diese erste Riege der Urväter mit aufgenommen wurde. Nach Mike Sinyard wurden mindestens drei weitere Personen mit dem großen „S" auf der Brust von der MBHoF geehrt, darunter der „Captain", Rahmendesigner Jim Merz und der Rennsupport-Guru Tom Hillard.

Bis heute wächst und gedeiht die MBHoF dank der Unterstützung der Bike-Industrie und der Mountainbike-Fans aus der ganzen Welt. www.mtnbikehalloffame.com

33

MY STUMPJUMPER N.1

Bill Hennion
2 Stumpjumper, 65 Jahre jung und 250 Kilometer pro Woche
Bill fährt nahezu täglich auf einem seiner zwei Stumpjumper (Zwei Stumpjumper! Ist er nicht toll?) ungefähr 250 Kilometer pro Woche. Nicht schlecht für einen 65-Jährigen, oder?
Als sein Enkel im Teenageralter vor ein paar Jahren das Biken anfing, dämmerte es Bill, dass er seinen alten „Stumpi" aufrüsten müsste, um mithalten zu können. Nach nur wenigen Touren war Bill klar, dass sein modernes FSRxc-Fully der Grund war, dass er dem jungen Raser überhaupt folgen konnte. Wie Bill meint, kann er mit seinem FSR einfach viel schneller übers Grobe heizen als je zuvor.

Das Alltagsrad von Bill ist ein 1982er Stumpjumper mit gemufftem Stahlrahmen (der mit der coolen Gabel), den er gebraucht vor ein Jahren kaufte. „Das perfekte Rad zum Rumfahren", meint Bill, „damit komme ich zu meinen besten Angelplätzen".

Wenn wir auch gerne etwas anderes behaupten würden, aber Bill wird nicht jünger. Wie er selbst meint, kann er immer noch alles machen, was er früher auch gemacht hat, wie Baseball spielen, weil er auf seinem Fahrrad einfach fit bleibt. „Einfacher gesagt", so Bill, „sind meine zwei Bikes mein Leben."

34 & 35

RENNSERVICE KOMPLETT UMSONST?

Spinnt Specialized jetzt komplett?
In den guten alten Zeiten (als es noch nicht mal schlechte neue Zeiten für Biker gab), also so ungefähr um 1985, drehte das ganze Bike-Dings ziemlich ab. Es gab zwar nicht viele Rennen, aber jedes Jahr tauchten immer mehr nervöse Veranstalter und aufgeputschte Rennfahrer auf, und es wurden immer mehr Fehler gemacht. Specialized beschloss, nachdem man ja schon jede Menge Stumpjumper verkauft und jede Menge Rennen besucht hatte, einzugreifen, also dem Veranstalter behilflich zu sein und die Rennfahrer zu unterstützen. Wie sie es bei den Straßenrennen schon seit 1982 praktizierten, boten sie jedem Rennfahrer, egal welches Bike er fuhr, technische Unterstützung an – komplett umsonst. Sie boten auch dem Veranstalter ihre Hilfe an, sei es bei der Gestaltung der Strecke, Absperrungen, dem Aufbau, dem Führungsmotorrad, der Organisation der Einschreibung und so weiter… Egal was anstand, einer aus dem Haufen aus Morgan Hill kümmerte sich darum.

Damit auch alles klappte, stellte man einen der erfahrensten Techniker an, den es damals gab: Tom Hillard aus Sonoma County, Kalifornien, war Verfasser des Regelwerks für die NORBA, Veranstalter des Punk Bike Enduro und einer der Menschen, der von sich behauptet, schon vor den guten alten Zeiten, so um 1961, sein erstes Mountainbike gebaut zu haben. Also schnappte sich Hillard die Schlüssel des Vans und fuhr los zu Rennen, die inzwischen zu Legenden wurden, wie das „Rockhopper", das „Rumpstomper", das „Reseda-To-The-Sea", der „Kamikaze" und das „Whiskeytown"-Rennen.

Egal, ob bei den NORBA-Rennen, dem Cactus Cup oder einem Dienstagabend-Rennen irgendwo in Texas, die Fahrer freuten sich immer tierisch, wenn einer der Specialized-Mechaniker, freundliche und fleißige Typen wie Tom Hillard, Dave Meyers, Steve Mosher oder Joe Buckley ihr verdrecktes demoliertes Bike in kurzer Zeit wieder voll funktionstüchtig machten, und das meistens umsonst. Kein Wunder, dass auch die gestressten Rennveranstalter, die immer zu wenige Leute hatten, genau so begeistert waren. „Es lief einfach alles ein wenig leichter, wenn der Specialized-Truck da war", erinnert sich einer der altgedienten Veranstalter.

Natürlich ist es nicht gerade billig, Trucks und mehrere Mechaniker ständig durch die Weltgeschichte zu schicken, aber für Mr. S. war das ganze nie eine einseitige Geschichte. Natürlich fördert man auch den Sport mit technischer Unterstützung, aber draußen bei den Rennen an Bikes von Leuten zu schrauben, die brutal und schnell unterwegs waren, brachte meist bessere Erkenntnisse, was an einem Bike kaputtgeht, als tausend Ingenieure in ein Labor zu stecken und darüber rätseln zu lassen, was wohl so ein Bike im Gelände aushalten muss.

Kostenlosen Renn-Service für alle? Billige Forschungsergebnisse? Egal, wie man es nennt, der technische Support Specializeds war einfach eine gute Sache für beide Seiten.

36 & 37

DIE ANKUNFT

Wenige Menschen auf diesem Planeten hatten einen guten Grund, die Position 7.275 Nördlicher Breite, 107.879 Westlicher Länge, auch bekannt als Durango in Colorado, aufzusuchen. Es befindet sich nämlich in der abgelegenen Ecke eines Niemandslands, wo Wüste, fliegende Dornbüsche, und eine Straße die auf einen Pass ins Nichts führt, zusammen treffen. Selbst mit einer Mega-Tüte Gummibärchen und einem 5-Liter-Becher Coke fährt man von Los Angeles 14 Stunden im Auto bis dorthin, von Denver aus ist es immer noch halb so weit. Wie gesagt, das Ganze liegt eher in einer der abgelegenen Ecken von Nirgendwo.

Achtung, kein Aprilscherz: Genau am 1. April 1980 startete Ned seinen Umzug vom sonnigen San Diego nach Durango, die Aktion ging bis spät in die Nacht. An seinem 65er Datsun Pick-up hing ein selbstgebauter Anhänger, der aussah wie frisch vom Schrottplatz. Als plötzlich ein Schneesturm aufzog (Ned hätte da schon merken müssen, das diese Gegend mehr als unwirtlich sein konnte), musste er umkehren und in Aztec, New Mexico, übernachten, das 35 Meilen weiter südlich und 300 Meter tiefer als Durango liegt. Am nächsten Tag dann entdeckte er sein „persönliches Taj Mahal": Ein Wohnwagen, drei mal zehn Meter, der im Junction Creek Trailer Park frei war. Es war soweit. Mr. Overend hatte sein Ziel erreicht.

Ned schraubte an VW Käfern, Variants und allen möglichen Modellen herum, die es bis Animas County geschafft hatten, um die Miete bezahlen zu können. Um sein „Chi" zu zentrieren, unternahm er endlose Läufe und Radtouren auf der Runde des alten Elmore-Ladens. Nach ein paar Jahren begann er mit Straßenrennen und schaffte es innerhalb von zwölf Monaten vom Nobody bis ins beste amerikanische Team, das an den Coors Classic teilnahm. Irgendwann nach dem Coors-Rennen 1983 setzten drei Durango-Locals, darunter „Bicycle" Bob Gregorio, Ned auf einen ihrer 5-Gang-Clunker. Ned wurde süchtig. „Ich fühlte mich wie ein Kind in einem riesigen Sandkasten", erzählt der „Captain". „Ich spürte sofort, dass an dieser Geschichte für mich mehr dran war."

Mehr? Nach ein paar Jahren war Ned einsamer Rekordhalter in der Fat-Tire-Welt: Vier NORBA-Meisterschaften, NORBA-Weltmeister, Worldcup-Sieger und der erste UCI-Weltmeister der Mountainbike-Geschichte. Es war soweit. Mr. Overend hatte sein Ziel erreicht.

40 & 41

WIE ZÄHMT MAN EINEN 300 KILO SCHWEREN GORILLA?

Man geht systematisch vor.

Das Problem mit den Trails gab es von Anfang an. Auf der ersten Seite des ersten je veröffentlichten Mountainbike-Magazins stand ein klarer Aufruf zu Aktionen. In Charly Kellys Fat Tire Flyer vom August 1980 stand: „Ohne eine Organisation, die unsere Interessen vertritt, brauchen wir gar keine Interessen anzumelden", argumentierte SeeKay. Es gab noch gar keine Mountainbikes zu kaufen, da bewachte schon ein 300-Kilo-Gorilla in Form von Restriktionen den Trail.

Wir springen ins Jahr 1987. Im Sommer, als in den meisten Teilen der USA die Freuden des Bikens gerade entdeckt wurden, entsprang im Herzen von Clunker-Country bereits der erste Streit über die Benutzung von Trails. „Terror auf zwei Räder" jaulte die Ausgabe des Newseek vom 28. September 1987 auf. Im Gebiet zwischen dem American River Parkway bei Sacramento bis zu den Santa Monica-Bergen von Los Angeles durften Bikes nicht mehr auf Singletracks oder gar nicht auf Wege der Nationalparks. Die Nationalpark-Behörde hatte die Wege geschlossen und das „Bureau of Land Management" die Wälder für Biker gesperrt. Sollte Mountainbiken eine Zukunft haben, mussten sich die Aktiven zusammenschließen und organisieren. Und das möglichst schnell.

Im Herbst steckten auf der Radmesse in Long Beach Vertreter von fünf Gruppen in Kalifornien ihre Köpfe zusammen. Sie kamen vom Bicycle Trails Council of Marin, dem Bicycle Trails Council of the East Bay, den Sacramento Rough Riders, der Concerned Off-Road Bikers Association of Los Angeles und den Responsible Off-Road Mountain Pedalers of San Jose. Innerhalb von sechs Monaten besaß die IMBA (International Mountain Biking Association) eine Satzung und kämpfte an allen Fronten für freie Trailbenutzung.

Dank der Weitsicht und dem Engagement von Linda DuPriest und Eric Eidsmo, die damals in der Marketing-Abteilung von Specialized arbeiteten, erhielt die IMBA eine Spende von 1.000 Dollar. Dies war der erste bekennende Schritt von Specialized (oder irgendeiner großen Radfirma) zu dieser Bike-Vereinigung, die für die Trailbenutzung kämpfte. Bald danach überzeugte Linda ihre Firma, ein Treffen der ganzen Radindustrie bei der Interbike-Messe 1989 zu sponsern, damit andere Firmen ebenfalls die Interessen wahrnähmen und sich für die Biker einsetzten. Dies wurde zu einem Wendepunkt in der Geschichte der IMBA. Das Treffen erregte große Aufmerksamkeit und brachte zahlreiche Gelder, mit denen mehrere Aktionen finanziert und gestartet wurde, darunter Konferenzen und Treffen von Verbandsmitgliedern in Washington D.C. und Durango. DuPriest arbeitete schließlich zehn Jahre lang im Vorstand der IMBA, wobei sie zu Beginn mithalf, das Image, die Präsentationen und die Geschäftspläne der Vereinigung professionell zu gestalten und als Bindeglied zur Fahrradindustrie fungierte.

Durch die finanzielle und ideelle Unterstützung aller wichtigen Radhersteller und ihrer 35.000 Mitglieder hat die IMBA seit ihrer Gründung für freie Trails für Biker in allen Gebieten der USA und des restlichen Planeten gekämpft. Ohne die IMBA gäbe es überhaupt keine Trails, für die man kämpfen müsste.

Du hast das Gebet gehört, reiche nun bitte den Klingelbeutel weiter: www.imba.com

42

MY STUMPJUMPER N.2

Denise Weber

„Ü30er" verdoppelt Lebensfreude und startet Rennkarriere

Denise, eine 36-jährige Tierarztassistentin, fing ebenfalls auf ärztlichen Rat das Biken an. Ein lädiertes Knie machte Joggen oder Step-Training im Studio unmöglich, also sollte mit Rad fahren die Belastung fürs Knie verringert und die körperliche Fitness gesteigert werden. Kaum war sie auf ein Rad gestiegen, änderte sich ihr Leben total.

Um sich ein wenig stärker zu motivieren, begann Denise sechs Monate nach ihren ersten Touren Rennen zu fahren. Im Wettkampf merkte Denise sehr schnell, dass sie ein leichteres und besseres Mountainbike brauchte. Sie kaufte einen Rockhopper und sattelte nach ein paar Jahren auf einen gebrauchten Stumpjumper um. „Das Rad passt mir perfekt und jetzt bin ich erst recht süchtig", sagt sie. „Ich bin auf einmal schneller als ich es mir je vorstellen konnte und dazu mutiger als je zuvor." Denise fährt auch ein wenig Rennrad für die allgemeine Ausdauer, aber es gibt nichts Schöneres für sie, als frühmorgens mit dem Stumpjumper durch den Wald zu rauschen.

Inzwischen ist ihr Knie so stabil, dass sie keinerlei Bandagen mehr braucht, selbst beim Cross-Training. Aber eigentlich läuft sie gar nicht so viel. „Ich bin lieber mit meinem Stumpjumper unterwegs, schließlich bin ich jetzt Rennfahrerin."

43

EPIC

Die Regeln werden neu geschrieben.

Innerhalb von fünf Jahren schrieb Specialized das Mountainbike-Buch komplett neu. Von 1988 bis 1993 war Specialized die erste Firma, die Serienrahmen in Stahl/Carbon, Titan/Carbon und Metal Matrix herstellte (ganz zu schweigen von der ersten Federgabel mit Carbon-Tauchrohren und dem ersten Rahmen, der komplett am Computer konstruiert worden war). Nach dem Ende des Kalten Krieges wurden jede Menge der alten Regeln über den Haufen geworfen, und einer der die meisten Regeln brach war Jim Merz, Mitglied der Mountainbike Hall of Fame und Specialized-Ingenieur.

Als Ronald Reagan „Gorby" dazu brachte, diesen ganzen Aufrüstungswahnsinn ein für alle Mal zu beenden, kamen plötzlich jede Menge Materialien und Verarbeitungstechniken auf den Markt, die zuvor in den Safes der Militärexperten versteckt lagen. Zum Glück liebte Merz wissenschaftliche Magazine und dank seiner Erfahrung mit der seinerzeit neuen 3-D-Konstruktionssoftware (für die Specialized damals lockere 250.000 Dollar hingeblättert hatte), war er perfekt gerüstet, sich die neuesten Materialien und Verarbeitungsmethoden anzueignen.

Dann brachte ihn auch noch eine Gruppe von Ingenieuren, die im kalifornischen El Cajon für Prince Tennisschläger bauten, auf den Werkstoff Carbon, und Merz machte sich daran, Verbundwerkstoffe für die Verarbeitung in Rohren zu optimieren und die entsprechenden Muffen für einen Rahmen zu konstruieren. „Ich musste durch die Hölle und zurück, als ich das Ganze konstruierte", meint Merz. Nach unzähligen Testphasen und endlosen Stunden an seinem Computer verwirklichte er einen Muffensatz aus Cromoly, der vom langjährigen japanischen Rahmenhersteller Specializeds geschweißt wurde. Da allein die Herstellung der Muffen und Rohre so viel verschlang wie ansonsten die Produktion eines Rahmens, kostete das Epic (Episch, bedeutet etwa ewig, unendlich) lockere 2.400 Dollar (Rahmen und Gabel). Damals transportierte man die Muffen ins S-Hauptquartier, wo sie mit optimierten Carbonrohren zu einem Rahmen verklebt und in einer Lehre gefestigt wurden. Da es für jede Rahmengröße nur zwei Lehren gab, wurde die Herstellung dem Namen mehr als gerecht: Es dauerte ewig.

Merz war immer weiter auf der Suche und kam bald von den Cromoly-Muffen ab und wollte Titanmuffen. Nicht irgendwelche Titanmuffen, nein, sie wurden von den Experten von Merlin Metalworks in Cambridge, Massachusetts, hergestellt. Das wiederum ist eine ganz andere unendliche Geschichte.

46 & 47:

MR. AMERICA

Was der Captain in Durango vollbrachte.*

Schaltete man damals, anfangs September, ein Radio oder einen Fernseher in Durango und Umgebung ein, hörte man garantiert Neds Namen oder sah seinen typischen Schnauzer auf dem Bildschirm. Täglich war über ihn in den Artikeln des „Durango Herald" zu lesen und er prangte auf dem Titel des offiziellen Programmhefts. Es hatte sogar jemand gewagt, T-Shirts zu bedrucken, die den „Captain" als Sieger der Weltmeisterschaften zeigten – und das vor der WM! Durango war nicht nur einfach stolz darauf, die allerersten offiziellen Mountainbike-Weltmeisterschaften zu organisieren, nein, ihr Local Ned Overend musste sie auf jeden Fall gewinnen. Der „Captain" hätte als Straßen-Profi oder beim Triathlon dickes Geld verdienen können, aber er entschied sich aus einem ganz einfachen Grund für die dreckige Variante des Radfahrens: Mountainbiken machte einfach mehr Spaß als alles andere. Eine Woche vor den ersten „echten" UCI-Weltmeisterschaften 1990 kam es dem Cross-Country-King Amerikas gar nicht mehr so spaßig vor, dass er sich fürs Biken entschieden hatte. Die Bürde, unbedingt der erste UCI-Weltmeister zu werden, lastete schwer auf den Schultern des Locals.

Und es kam, wie es kommen musste. Auf seinem Epic Ultimate-Prototyp mit Titanmuffen und einer rabenschwarzen RockShox-Federgabel, hatte der 35-jährige Overend seine stärksten Konkurrenten aus dem Feld der 130 Starter, den Briten Tim Gould und Thomas Frischknecht aus der Schweiz, abgeschüttelt und rollte als erster durchs Ziel am Fuße des Purgatory-Skihangs. Der „Captain" war total allein – natürlich mit Ausnahme der zehntausend jubelnden Zuschauer. „Es war mehr Erleichterung als Freude", antwortet er heute auf die Frage, wie er sich damals fühlte. Während Greg Herbold, der andere Local von Durango und Sieger des Downhills meinte: „Da oben zu stehen und die Medaille zu bekommen, für die ich so hart gearbeitet hatte – ich fühlte mich wie Miss America." Naja, Ned wäre dann wohl eher Mr. America.

*Der „Captain" war nicht der einzige, der für Specialized das Regenbogentrikot überziehen durfte – Lisa Muhich gewann die Frauen-Seniorenwertung und Sara Ballantyne verpasste bei den Frauen knapp die Goldmedaille.

48 & 49

STUMPJUMPER M2

Das Verteidigungsministerium macht sich locker

„Wer weiß, was Metal Matrix Composite ist?" fragte der San Francisco Chronicle in seiner Ausgabe vom 1. April 1991. Da die Existenz dieses Materials aufgrund des „Munitions Control Act" strengster Geheimhaltung unterlag und kaum Informationen über diesen Aluminium-Aluminiumoxid-Hybrid durchsickerten, hatten bis dahin nur Leute der höchsten Geheimhaltungsstufen davon gehört. Es gab bis dahin nicht ein einziges ziviles Produkt aus diesem Material und kein Mensch im normalen Leben wusste, wie man es schweißen oder verarbeiten konnte – aber Jim Merz, Mark Winter, Mark DiNucci und die anderen aus dem Specialized-Team knackten den Code dieses Raumfahrtmaterials. Das Ergebnis war das erste Gerät aus Metal Matrix, das nicht in Waffenform Richtung Moskau gerichtet war: der Stumpjumper M2.

Ursprünglich für Bauteile von Satelliten und Antriebswellen von Panzern entwickelt, galt M2 als 10 Prozent stärker und 20 Prozent steifer als normales Aluminium. Wie die Superhirne aus dem Pentagon erklärten, kam dies durch die Technik, Brocken von Aluminiumoxid, ein keramisches Material, in mikroskopisch dünne Schichten von 6000er Aluminium einzulagern. So leicht und steif dieses Wundermaterial war, genau so schwierig war die Aufgabe, einen Bikerahmen daraus zu bauen.

Also erinnerte man sich an eine andere fruchtbare Partnerschaft, als man zusammen mit DuPont das dreispeichige Carbon-Laufrad entwickelt hatte (ja, genau, das Ding, das ein berühmter amerikanischer Radfahrer mindestens einmal bei jedem seiner sieben Tour-France-Siege einsetzte), und nahm Kontakt mit einem Giganten der Branche auf. Der Wunschpartner für das M2 MMC-Material war Duralcan, eine Unterfirma des weltweit zweitgrößten Aluminiumherstellers. Die Spezialisten von Duralcan aus San Diego feilten am richtigen Rezept für die Rohre, während die Jungs vom S-Team in Morgan Hill daran forschten und ausarbeiteten, wie sich das Zeug schweißen ließ, inklusive wie man das superharte Material konifizieren könnte. Schließlich schloss sich Specialized auch noch mit Anodizing Inc. zusammen, um eine Produktionshalle in Portland, Oregon hinzustellen, die ausschließlich für die Herstellung von M2-Rohrsätzen und dem Rahmenschweißen vorgesehen war. Gemeinsam erfand man mehr oder weniger die Rohrproduktion und das Konifizieren neu und schuf damit noch leichtere M2-Rahmen als zuvor.

Das klingt garantiert nicht nach dem einfachsten und schnellsten Weg, einen leichteren und steiferen Rahmen zu bauen. Aber Mike hat auch nie jemandem vorgeschrieben, dass es einfach und unkompliziert sein müsse.

50 & 51

LEIDENSCHAFT

Das Märchen hinter den Märchenerzählern von Specialized.

Mike wird dir immer erzählen, dass er eine Sache gelernt hat in all diesen Jahren: Wenn du gewinnen willst, dann spiele ein Spiel, für das du ein Gefühl hast, ein Spiel das du mit Leidenschaft angehst.

Darum suchte Specialized 1989 einen Märchenerzähler, der mindestens so viel Leidenschaft in seine Geschichten steckte, wie Specialized in seine Bikes. Eines führte zum anderen, und „klack" (jetzt bitte laut mit den Fingern schnalzen, um den Effekt zu verstärken) landeten sie bei den besten Märchenerzählern, die sich je eine Geschichte ausdachten: Goodby, Silverstein und Partner. GSP ist dir kein Begriff? Die bekannteste Werbekampagne Amerikas: Got milk? Es stellte sich heraus, dass das „S" in GSP ein leidenschaftlicher Radfahrer war. Rich Silverstein, ein drahtiger Typ, radelte ständig von seinem Haus in Marin County über die Golden Gate Brücke ins Büro nach San Franzisko.

Der Rest ist eines der üblichen Märchen. Während GSP Großkunden wie Anheuser-Busch, Morgan Stanley, Haagen-Dasz und Hewlett-Packard betreute, entstanden auch sämtliche Anzeigen und Kampagnen für Specialized der letzten Jahre.

Was lernen wir daraus? Egal, ob es sich um Bikes, Bier oder Brot handelt – wenn der Job nicht mit Leidenschaft gemacht wird, wird auch nichts daraus.

52 & 53

STUMPJUMPER FIELD GUIDE/1992 STUMPJUMPER EPIC ULTIMATE

*Das hier abgebildete Bike war eine seltene Testversion, die in dieser Form nie verkauft wurde.

Rahmen Von 1990 bis 1995 baute Specialized von Hand rund 1500 Epic Ultimate Titan-Carbon-Rahmen (Gewicht unter 1400 Gramm) im Headquarter Morgan Hill, Kalifornien. Die Konstruktion der Carbonrohre mit Titanmuffen, damals absolut innovativ, wurde von erstklassigen Rahmenbauern noch jahrelang imitiert.

Muffen Als Upgrade zum Standard-Epic waren im Epic Ultimate Titanmuffen verbaut, die von Merlin Metalworks aus Cambridge, Massachusetts hergestellt wurden. Die Material- und Herstellungskosten waren so hoch, dass Specialized mit den Rahmen nie Geld verdiente.

Rohrsatz Die ersten Epic Ultimates wurden mit Super High Modulus-Verbundmaterial gebaut, das viel zu steif war und sich in der Praxis nicht bewährte. Dann benutzte man Material mit niedrigerer Dichte von Maclean Quality Composites aus Salt Lake City für die nachfolgenden Rahmen.

Gabel Obwohl es hier mit einer von Specialized entworfenen Future Shock-Gabel FSX aus Carbon/Titan gezeigt ist, verkaufte man das Epic Ultimate, das bis 1995 gebaut wurde, nie mit einer Federgabel. Es kam mit der normalen Direct Drive Cromoly-Gabel.
Limited 1995 wurden die letzten Epic Ultimate-Rahmen, alle von Brian Lucas in Morgan Hill gebaut, hergestellt. Jeder der 60 Rahmen trägt eine nur einmal vergebene Seriennummer auf einer Plakette am Oberrohr. Ned Overend erhielt die Nummer 1, um an seinen Weltmeistertitel 1990 zu erinnern, den er auf einem Ultimate gewann.

54 & 55

SMITHSONIAN

Ein Mountainbike im Museum? Wie kommt ausgerechnet ein Produkt, das man zum Shredden auf staubigen Straßen erfand, in ein ehrwürdiges kulturelles Institut, das durch eine Spende eines britischen Aristokraten vor hundert Jahren in Washington BC gegründet wurde? Das ist ganz einfach zu erklären.

James Smithson war ein Wissenschaftler und Forscher, der den Vereinigten Staaten eine halbe Million Dollar für eine Einrichtung überließ, die „Wissen fördern und verbreiten" sollte. Zudem war er in seinen Jugendjahren ein eifriger Student und engagierter Forscher und zudem ein echter Abenteurer. Er hatte seine Gesundheit und sein Leben riskiert – er wäre fast ertrunken – als er geologische Studien auf den Hebriden an der Nordwestküste Schottlands durchführte und er hätte mit Sicherheit die Energie und den Erfindungsreichtum der ersten Mountainbike-Pioniere zu schätzen gewusst.

Heute besteht das mit Smithsons Spende gegründete Institut aus dem größten Museumskomplex der Welt, der das bedeutendste Nationalmuseum Amerikas beherbergt und dazu Forschungszentren wie das Nationale Historische Museum, den Nationalen Zoo, das Nationale Luft- und Raumfahrtmuseum, das Nationale Kunst- und Industrie-Museum, das Smithsonian Magazin und, in einer kleinen Ecke des Nationalmuseums für Amerikanische Geschichte, den Specialized Stumpjumper.

Irgendwann im Jahre 1989 entdeckte das Smithsonian das Mountainbike, und weil seine Aufgabe darin bestand, die wichtigsten Transportmittel auszustellen, die Amerika veränderten, riefen sie das Specialized-Büro in Morgan Hill an. „Klar können wir euch ein Bike schicken", antwortete Mike Sinyard... Jetzt sammelt neben Dampfbooten und Raumkapseln auch ein Stumpjumper Staub in den Räumen des Smithsonian Museums an. Na, hoffentlich pumpen sie wenigstens regelmäßig die Reifen auf.

56 & 57

WIE VERKAUFT MAN LEIDENSCHAFT?

Porsche weiß, wie man es macht.
Der Anruf kam von Harm Lagaay persönlich. Als Hollander mit deutschem Akzent klang er etwas seltsam und es war nicht ganz sicher, ob der Chef des Porsche-Designcenters in Weissach es wirklich ernst meinte. Ob Specialized ein paar Ingenieure ins Geheimlabor nach Weissach schicken könnte, um eine Porsche Spider-Version des 1200-Gramm-Epic Ultimate aus Carbon und Titan zu besprechen? Dazu konnte man einfach nicht nein sagen.

Also packten ein paar aus dem S-Team die Koffer, schnappten sich ihre Pässe und flogen in die Werkstatt, die Dr. Porsche gebaut hatte. In Weissach erwartete die Jungs ein Studio mit über tausend der besten Ingenieure der Welt, die alle leidenschaftlich nur ein Ziel verfolgten: Das Beste vom Besten zu entwerfen und zu bauen. Superschnelle Rennwagen, oder Prototypen zur Erforschung von alternativen Antriebskonzepten, oder futuristische Designstudien. Das zur Verfügung stehende Budget erschien so unendlich wie der Output von neuen Ideen. Obwohl ständig legendäre Autos und andere Produkte ihren Ursprung in Weissach hatten, kam nichts aus dem Studio, das direkt verwertbar schien. Es war für Forscher und Entwickler das reine Paradies. Leider wurde das Porsche Spider-Bike nie verwirklicht, aber das Entwicklungszentrum im Schwarzwald war der Auslöser für etwas anderes: Specializeds eigene Version von Weissach in Morgan Hill.

Dahinter stand die Idee, den talentiertesten Designern und Ingenieuren von Specialized totalen Freiraum zu gönnen. Keine Limits, keine Erwartungen. Wirtschaftliche, historische oder zeitliche Auflagen wurden einfach ignoriert, um ein einziges Ziel zu erreichen: das beste Bike der Welt zu bauen. Hat es geklappt? S-Works-Bikes beförderten ihre Fahrer zu Erfolgen bei Weltmeisterschaften auf der Straße und im Gelände, es gaben Etappensieger und Träger des Gelben Trikots den Tour de France darauf, es gab Olympiasiege und X-Games-Medaillen, und Triathleten, die den Ironman gewannen. Es liegen auch kiloweise Material und Räder herum, die nie in den Laden kamen, aber das ist nicht das Ziel von S-Works. Ziel ist, das Beste herzustellen, was es gibt. Nichts anderes.

58 & 59

FEDERUNG VON SPECIALIZED?

Der Dämpfer der Zukunft?
Als der „Captain" 1990 die Weltmeisterschaften in Durango gewann, steckte der Prototyp einer RockShox RS-1 Federgabel im Rahmen seines Specialized Epic Ultimate. Die Tatsache, dass Ned und andere Topfahrer (wie Greg Herbold und Juliana Furtado) sich bei einem so wichtigen Rennen auf ein neues Teil wie eine Federgabel verließ, sprach eine deutliche Sprache: Federgabeln waren die Zukunft.

Specialized witterte die Gelegenheit und begann, an einer eigenen Federgabel zu arbeiten. Nach Testfahrten und der Demontage der ersten RS-1 war den Ingenieuren in Morgan Hill klar, dass man das delikate Innenleben aus Öl und Luft, das Paul Turner da geschaffen hatte, schwer besser machen konnte. Also schaute man rüber zu Turners Firma in der in Mountain View und vereinbarte einen Deal: Die Specialized-Ingenieure, allen voran Mark Winter, würden viele der äußeren Teile bauen, und RockShox lieferte dazu das komplizierte Innenleben und seine Produktionskapazitäten.

Zum ersten Mal kamen 1992 einige der Specialized-Modelle mit eigenen Future Shock-Gabeln. Aber um ehrlich zu sein waren die ersten Gabeln sehr, sehr ähnlich zu dem, was RockShox selbst produzierte. Dann kam die Future Shock FSX. Konstruiert von Winter, war die FSX das „Egal-was-es-kostet"-Gegenstück zum Carbon-Titan-Rahmen des Epic (auch wenn diese beiden Teile nie zusammen ausgeliefert wurden). Die FSX besaß die Öl-Luft-Konstruktion der Mag 21 und war die erste Federgabel mit Carbon-Holmen, die nur für diesen Zweck entwickelt, konstruiert und gebaut worden waren. Klingt teuer. War es auch. Angeblich kostete jeder Carbon-Holm über 100 Dollar. Die Verbundwerkstoffe und die CNC-gefertigte Aluminiumbrücke machten die FSX teurer als jede andere Gabel auf dem Markt. „Eigentlich war die Specialized-Gabel damals besser als unsere eigene", gibt Federungsguru Mike McAndrews zu, der damals mit seinem Kumpel aus Kindheitstagen, Paul Turner, zusammen arbeitete. „Aber wir selbst konnten uns nicht leisten, so etwas zu produzieren."

Schließlich stellte sich bei dem immer härteren Wettbewerb der Federgabelhersteller heraus, dass für Specialized in dieser Arena kein Platz mehr war. Deshalb tat man das Gleiche wie bei Felgen, Schaltwerken und Pedalen: Man wählte das beste Produkt einer Firma aus, das man finden konnte. War Specialized damit für immer aus dem Rennen? Schwer zu sagen, aber Mr. S. erkannte immer eine gute Gelegenheit, wenn sie ihm begegnete.

62 & 63

DIE ZUKUNFT DES FULLYS

Was passiert, wenn Specialized-Ingenieure Hand an das Hinterteil eines Österreichers legen?

Sagen wir mal, es war irgendwann nach 1991. In den zehn Jahren nach der Präsentation des Stumpjumpers hatte sich die Bike-Welt in Richtungen entwickelt, die keiner vorher gesehen hatte. Auf einmal tauchten Fullys so zahlreich auf wie UFOs auf den Radarschirmen in der Wüste Nevadas. Das Problem: Sie waren so schwer und praktisch wie Blei-Enten. Damals galten Heckdämpfungen als so kompliziert und unzuverlässig, dass viele Mitarbeiter des S-Hauptquartiers davon überzeugt waren, dass dies nicht der richtige Weg war.

Weil Mike aber eher darüber nachdachte, was möglich war, als darüber, was nicht funktionierte, sollte sein Team das kompromisslose Fullsuspensionbike erfinden. Ein Bike, das auch beim Pedalieren nicht wippte, gut zu kontrollieren war und mehr Komfort brachte, „leicht" (man erhoffte sich damals 12,3 Kilo) und leicht zu warten war. Selbst heute entspräche das noch der „Eier legenden Wollmilchsau", doch 1991 war die Technik noch gar nicht so weit, um so etwas auch nur ansatzweise zu bauen.

Über ein Jahr beschäftigten sich die Ingenieure John O'Neil, Mark Winter und Mark DiNucci mit dem Projekt. Sie spürten jedes existierende Design auf und testeten es. Einige waren gut, keines davon war perfekt. Also brauten sie weiter an einem „Frankenbike-Cocktail" und unterhielten sich mit jedem anderen „Frankenbiker", der zu ihnen kam (immerhin fand Nike auf diese Art zu seiner Air-Technik). Schließlich steuerte der österreichische Ingenieur Horst Leitner, der in den Siebzigern für große Auto- und Motorradfirmen gearbeitet hatte, sein magisches Multi-Link-Design bei, das zum FSR werden sollte. DiNucci und die Konstrukteure lernten Horst als Motorradfederungs-Guru kennen, der einen ganzen Stapel von Patenten auf seinen Namen besaß. Für Horst hatte Specialized die Ressourcen und die Fähigkeiten, sein Design zu verbessern und zu wiederholen, was sie mit dem Stumpjumper geschafft hatten.

Mit Prototypen des Multi-Link-Hinterbaus schufen DiNucci und Co die ersten FSRs, indem sie einfach das Heck von Stumpjumper-Rahmen amputierten und die Schwinge von Horst implantierten. Nachdem die geschrotteten Prototypenbikes ein ganzes Footballstadion füllten (es war eine eigene Test-Truppe dafür rekrutiert worden), lief endlich die Serienproduktion an. Vielleicht doch zu früh: Im Sommer 1993 mussten die ersten paar hundert der Produktionsbikes wieder zurückgeholt werden, da sich heraus gestellt hatte, dass die Anlenkung des Dämpfers am Sitzrohr nicht stabil genug war. Wie DiNucci dazu meinte „wurden wir alle ins kalte Wasser geworfen und mussten aus dem Bauch heraus schwimmen lernen. Für ein komplexes Rad wie das FSR waren unsere Test- und Forschungseinrichtungen nicht fein genug". Dies ist ein Grund, warum das FSR ein so wichtiger Bestandteil in der Specialized-Welt wurde – es war ein Rad, das alle Regeln ungültig machte und Morgan Hill dazu zwang, die Forschungs- und Entwicklungsmethoden neu zu definieren. „Auf einmal genügten die Skizzen auf den Servietten beim Mittagessen nicht mehr, man brauchte echte Test- und Ingenieurskriterien", sagt dazu der langjährige Marketing- und R&D-Mann Chris Murphy.

64 & 65

CACTUS CUP

Eine Spring Break, gesponsert von Specialized.
Die inoffizielle Spring Break (traditionelle Semesterpause der Studenten, bei denen wild gefeiert wird) der Bikebranche in den Neunzigern war eindeutig der Cactus Cup in Arizona: Hab' ein paar Tage Spaß auf dem Bike in der Wüste von Sonoma und das Ganze im Kreis von fünf- bis sechstausend Freunden, ach ja, und Rennen sind auch dabei. Klingt heftig? „Also, ehrlich gesagt kann ich mich nicht an die Rennen beim Cactus Cup erinnern", sagt der langjährige Bikejournalist und Rahmenbauer Richard Cunningham, „aber ich weiß, dass ich jede Menge Spaß hatte".

Wie in Havasu oder Daytona (dem Höhepunkt der Studentenfeten) war der Zeitpunkt des Cactus Cup perfekt gewählt. Die Racer konnten Mitte März bei den flachen Rennen checken, ob sie im Winter genügend Kondition für die neue Saison aufgebaut hatten, und das ganz ohne den Erwartungsdruck des Worldcups. Die Bike-Industrie konnte mit Vollgas in die neue Verkaufssaison starten. Neben den Herbstmessen war der Cactus Cup der perfekte Ort, um die neuesten Entwicklungen vorzustellen und den Hype und den Verkauf anzuschüren.

Im Lauf der Jahre veränderte sich die Rennstrecke immer mehr, da Scottsdale sich nach Norden ausbreitete und Wohnsiedlungen entstanden, wo sich zuvor Singletracks hindurch geschlängelt hatten. Doch zwei Dinge gab es beim Cactus Cup immer: Steine und Cholla-Kakteen, die immer in den Weg sprangen. Mit dem richtigen Luftdruck und der Antiplatt-Soße Slime konnte man vielleicht normale Platten bändigen, aber auf einer Strecke, die mehr Windungen und Ecken hatte als ein französischer Irrgarten, waren Dornenstiche unvermeidlich.

Die Art der Rennen war einmalig, sowohl für Amateure wie für die Profis: In vier Etappen absolvierte man ein Zeitrennen, ein Dirt-Kriterium, das Fat-Kriterium bei Flutlicht mitten im Zentrum von Scottsdale und ein Vollgas-Cross-Country-Rennen, das später noch mit Steilkurven und Sprungrampen aufgepeppt wurde, und den Höhepunkt zum Abschluss darstellte. Fahrer mit dem großen „S" auf der Brust sahnten nicht nur einmal in Scottsdale ab, der Specialized-Fahrer Steve Tilford war im Fatboy-Kriterium kaum zu schlagen und gewann diese Disziplin insgesamt 21 Mal.

Die Festival-Atmosphäre und die Art der Rennen schlug so ein, dass der Cactus Cup Mitte der Neunziger Jahre seine Zelte sogar an mehreren Orten aufschlug. Es gab Veranstaltungen in Illinois, Ohio, Kanada, Frankreich, Deutschland und Japan, wo er jetzt noch veranstaltet wird. Nicht dass es an diesen Orten immer Kakteen gegeben hätte, aber es gab auf jeden Fall genügend zu trinken – die Parties waren einfach unschlagbar.

66 & 67

STUMPJUMPER FIELD GUIDE/1994 SPECIALIZED S-WORKS FSR

Rahmen Konstruiert von Mark DiNucci und Mark Winter. Das leichte und steife vordere Direct Drive-Dreieck aus Stahl des 1994er FSR war Ausgangspunkt des Rahmendesigns.

Dämpfung Entwickelt zusammen mit dem Gründer von AMP, Horst Leitner. Die FSR-Dämpfung sollte voll aktiv und unabhängig von Antriebseinflüssen arbeiten, um maximalen Komfort, Kontrolle und Effektivität zu erzielen. Im Lauf der folgenden Jahre erwies sich das FSR-Design als erstaunlich vielseitig.

Gabel Zusammen mit RockShox entwickelt und dort produziert, arbeitete die FSX mit dem Innenleben der RockShox Mag21, in Carbon-Tauchrohren von Specialized und M2-Aluminium-Brücke.

Schalthebel Erstmals 1993 hergestellt, waren die SRAM SRT 500 8-Gang-Drehgriffschalter die ersten High-End-Schalthebel für Rennen, die man in Chicago produzierte.

Reifen Benannt nach einem Pink Floyd-Album. Der Umma Gumma war der erste Reifen mit weicher Gummimischung. Anscheinend war er seiner Zeit voraus, denn es gab nie einen Nachfolger und die Produktion wurde schließlich eingestellt.

70 & 71

RENNEN? SIEGE!

Ein „S" auf der Brust steht für Speed.

„Was? Flugtickets? Du willst Flugtickets kaufen? Hier..." mit diesen Worten warf Mike Sinyard dem ersten gesponserten Biker, Laurence Malone, die Schlüssel für den Specialized-Van zu. Seitdem hat Specialized Millionenbeträge ausgegeben für Fahrer, Techniker und Supportleute auf Veranstaltungen rund um den Globus, alles für ein Ziel: Auf dem Siegerpodest ganz oben zu stehen.

Schlägst du das Verzeichnis der Rennerfolge aller Fahrer mit dem S auf der Brust auf, wirst du feststellen, dass sie alle ihr Ziel mit der Entschlossenheit eines Pitbulls und der Effizienz eines Polo Diesels verfolgten. Die Ausbeute? Fahrer von Specialized holten 5 UCI Weltmeistertitel, Dutzende von UCI-Worldcup-Siegen und Worldcup-Gesamttiteln und so viele NORBA- und nationale Meisterschaften, dass wir aufgehört haben zu zählen, als Ned das Abonnement darauf eröffnet hatte.

Während für die Männer und Frauen im S-Trikot der Sieg alles bedeutet, haben wir den Ehrgeiz, den besten und wählerischsten Fahrern das Material zur Verfügung zu stellen, das sie wirklich schnell macht. Keine Frage, ohne das Team gäbe es S-Works nicht, und ohne S-Works gäbe es kein federleichtes Stumpjumper Carbon Hardtail oder den Brain-Dämpfer, der so schlau ist, den Unterschied zwischen einem Stein und dem Bizeps des Fahrers zu erkennen.

72

MY STUMPJUMPER N.3

Vedran Novak

Flüchtling findet auf Stumpjumper wieder ins Normalleben zurück

Der 30-jährige Vedran lebte in Zagreb in Kroatien. Als dort 1990 der Bürgerkrieg ausbrach, gehörte Vedran zu den Tausenden von Flüchtlingen, die sich in die Sicherheit eines serbischen Lagers retteten. In diesen Flüchtlingscamps sieht man nicht gerade viele Fahrräder, denn wenn man auf der Flucht nur das Allernötigste mitnehmen kann, gehört ein Fahrrad nicht gerade zu den handlichen Gegenständen. In Serbien litten Vedran und die anderen Kroaten unter dem Terror-Regime von Slobodan Milosevic. Selbst die täglichen Bedürfnisse waren schwer zu beschaffen, das Leben war hart und ein Fahrrad war absoluter Luxus, den sich niemand leisten konnte. „Die Zeiten waren so schwer, dass ich mir nicht mal vorstellen konnte, je wieder Rad zu fahren", erzählt Vedran über seine Zeit in Serbien.

Zum Glück (für Vedran und die restliche Welt) wurde Milosevic deportiert und das Leben auf dem Balkan normalisierte sich langsam wieder. Vedran kratzte jeden Cent zusammen, den er erübrigen konnte und kaufte sich einen gebrauchten Stumpjumper Pro, der in einem super Zustand war. Seitdem fährt er jeden Tag und möchte gar nicht mehr aufhören. „Bevor ich meinen neuen Stumpjumper hatte, wusste ich gar nicht, dass man auf zwei Rädern so viel Spaß haben kann! Mein Bike erinnert mich immer wieder daran, wie schön das Leben sein kann."

73

UND... ACTION

Pulp Traction: Der Beginn des Freeridens auf Zelluloid gebannt.

Ein Typ in engen Radlerhosen, der auf einem Hardtail mit einer Uralt-Federgabel mit 40mm Federweg einen Hang hinunterrutscht – das soll Freeriden sein? Zugegebenermaßen gab es noch keine Stunts wie den „Tail whip", den „Backflip" oder lebensgefährliche Drops, aber es war definitiv Freeriden. Zumindest der Beginn der Freeride-Bewegung. Durch den Verdienst des Regisseurs von Pulp Traction, Skilegende und British-Columbia-Local Greg Stump, wurden im ersten Bike-Film die Kamera auf die Spots der North Shore und die dortige Szene gerichtet, aus der Freeride entstehen würde. Pulp T filmte die unerschrockenen Paten der North Shore, Richie Schley und Brett Tippie, als Baggy-Shorts nur beim Basketball getragen wurde und „Long Travel" einen Non Stop-Flug nach China bedeutete.

Weil es damals keine Mountainbike-Filmemacher gab, wandte sich die Marketingabteilung des S-Teams an den Skispezialisten Stump, der bereits „P-Tex, Lies And Duct Tape" und andere Ski- und Snowboad-Klassiker gedreht hatte. So entstand ein Film, der extreme Fahraufnahmen, herrliche, entlegene Landschaften, und einen Einblick in den Lifestyle von Mountainbikern zeigte. „Die meisten von uns hatten schon in den Ski- und Snowboardfilmen mitgemacht. Als die Jungs mit ihren Kameras kamen, machten wir das Gleiche, was wir auf Schnee anstellten einfach mit den Rädern, an den gleichen steilen Stufen und Drops", erzählt Schley. „Wir waren gerade eben an einem der Spots, wo wir „Pulp Traction" filmten und haben uns kaputt gelacht, was wir mit den Hardtails mit 40mm Federweg damals zustande brachten."

Schön war was anderes, aber immerhin wurde die Geburtsstunde eines neuen Sports für immer auf Film festgehalten.

74 & 75

NICHTS ÜBERFLÜSSIGES. ABSOLUT NICHTS

Der letzte Nagel im Sarg des Hardtails.

Du kannst trainieren, trainieren, trainieren und noch mehr trainieren, um auf einem Bike schnell zu sein, aber mit Ausnahme von dicken Oberschenkeln wirst du so schlank bleiben wie Heidi Klum auf Null-Diät. Genau das war die Idee für das FSRxc: Nimm alles weg von einem Fullsuspension-Bike, was nicht nötig ist, um den Körper eines Cross-Country-Racers zu bekommen.

Noch besser als die Idee war allerdings das Timing: 1996 baute man die Federungsbikes mit immer mehr Federweg, leider wurden sie auch immer schwerer. Dadurch lehnten sie immer mehr Biker ab, die eher Wert auf Geschwindigkeit und Kraftumsetzung legten, als von haushohen Felsen zu droppen.

So beschlossen die S-Team-Leute Ben Capron, Mark Norris, Mike Ducharme und Jeff Pint gegen den Strom zu schwimmen. Sie schliffen und bohrten und kratzten und optimierten an allem herum, bis sie ein 75mm-FSRxc hatten: ein Fahrwerk mit nur 25mm weniger Federweg als das klassische FSR, aber weniger Gewicht und ein messerscharfes Handling. Dazu hatten Ducharme, Capron und alle anderen jeden Quadratmillimeter des Rahmens unter die Lupe genommen, die Rohrdurchmesser und die Konifizierungen überarbeitet und das Design der Sattelstützenaufnahme neu gestaltet. Doch das meiste holten sie an der Hinterradaufhängung heraus: Dämpfer, Hauptgelenk und die Sitzstreben drehten sich alle auf einer Achse – das sparte die Hälfte des Materials im Vergleich zum bisherigen Design.

Das Ergebnis war einer der leichtesten Fullsuspension-Viergelenker, den es gab. Ausgestattet mit den besten Komponenten blieb die Waage für das FSRxc bei knapp 11 Kilo und ein rennfertiges Modell mit nur 9,35 Kilogramm zeigte man stolz auf der Interbike-Show 1998.

Kaum zu glauben? Einer der Forumsbeiträge in www.mtbr.com von 1999 sagt alles: „Ich werde nie wieder ein Hardtail fahren. Nach einer Tour auf diesem Bike geht es dir genau so."

78 & 79

NAPALM!

Als der größte Sportler des Planeten in der Mountainbike-Szene aufschlug, hinterließ er verbrannte Erde und geplatzte Gerichtsbürgschaften.

Er war kein Mountainbiker. Das war das Besondere. Er betrachtet sich selbst nie als Biker, er zog einfach los und versägte jeden anderen auf einem Berg, genau so wie er es auf einem Snowboard, einer Motocross-Maschine oder in einem seiner Dutzende Cadillacs getan hätte.

Er war kein Mountainbiker, er war ein Rockstar, wie man ihn bis dahin in der Mountainbike-Szene noch nicht erlebt hatte. Seit seinem ersten Tag auf einem Board auf der Donner Ski Ranch dominierte der Typ, den sie Mini-Shred nannten, jeglichen Sport im Schnee. Dann jagte er sich selbst im wahrsten Sinne des Wortes ins Nirwana. „Als 1992 meine Großmutter starb, wurde ich zum kompletten Idioten. Ich prügelte mich in Bars, soff, und zog sinnlos herum. Dann schaffte ich die Kehrtwende und projizierte die ganze Wut über ihren Tod in positive Energie und in den Sport. Ich sagte zu mir selbst: Verdammt, ich werde einfach alles gewinnen, was ich anfange." So verwandelte sich Mini-Shred in Napalm und beschloss, jeden in dessen Disziplin zu schlagen, den er finden konnte. „Erst dann fühlte ich mich gut", sagt Palmer.

1996 fing er mit dem Mountainbiken an und da zu dieser Zeit durch die Olympischen Spiele richtig großes Geld in den Sport floss, war sein Timing perfekt. Palmer saugte den Ruhm und die Popularität auf wie ein Schwamm und wurde zur grandiosen Verkörperung des Mountainbike-Sports am Ende des Millenniums. Jeder erinnert sich an seine goldene Robe, den fetten Bus von Troy Lee lackiert, und den Vertrag in sechsstelliger Höhe (von dem Mike und alle anderen, die ihn kannten, sagten, dass er gnadenlos überschätzt wurde). „Dieser Typ war nie ernsthaft entschlossen, ein wirklich wichtiges Rennen zu gewinnen, aber er sorgte auf jeden Fall für jede Menge Aufregung", meint dazu der ehemalige Mechaniker Joe „Buck" Buckley.

80

ENDURO

Darum heißt es „All Mountain" und nicht „Easy Mountain".

Als das Millennium nahte, sagten alle ein Chaos voraus. Y2K war in aller Munde. „Das Ende ist nahe" prophezeiten manche religiösen Sektierer. Wie inzwischen klar ist, war dies keinesfalls der Fall, aber das ist eine andere Geschichte.

Für Mountainbiker bestand das Chaos eher in den Ansichten über Bikes und Trails, und wie diese beiden Dinge zusammen hingen. Durch die große Popularität des Sports wurden die Gebiete, die leicht zu erreichen waren (diejenigen, an denen man direkt parken konnte) erheblich belastet oder waren wegen Überlastung bereits geschlossen. Die echten Mountainbiker wollten sich von der Masse absetzen und verlangten nach Bikes, die auch Trails vertrugen, die für die meisten zu schwierig waren. Diese wiederum waren entlegen und schwer zu erreichen, deshalb durften die Bikes auf keinen Fall schwerer oder unhandlicher werden.

Jede Menge Zeit auf dem Trail – glücklicherweise zählt bei Specialized fahren als forschen – und ein Überdenken des Hinterbau-Federungsdesigns, das Specialized zusammen mit Guru Horst Leitner 1991 entwickelt hatte, ergaben das erste Enduro. Als das Enduro im Sommer 1999 auf den Markt geworfen wurde, sprichwörtlich geworfen, sowohl über Felsen wie auch über die Laderampen, war es mit seinem steifen MAX-Fahrwerk (Manipulated Aluminum eXtrusion) nur 250 Gramm schwerer als das FSR vom Vorjahr und hatte dabei mit 115mm einiges mehr an Federweg. Außerdem besaß das Enduro ein tiefgezogenes Oberrohr, das dem Fahrer jede Menge Schrittfreiheit schenkte. Im Jahr 2000 wurde das Enduro überarbeitet und noch leichter, und kam mit Schutzblechen, um den Motorrad-Look noch zu unterstreichen.

81

MY STUMPJUMPER N.4

Bob Brewer

Vom Schwergewicht zum Sprinter: Bob nahm mit seinem Stumpi 40 Kilo ab

Noch vor zwei Jahren war Bob Brewer in der schlechtesten Verfassung seines Lebens. Mit 120 Kilogramm bei 1,90 hatte er hohen Blutdruck und dadurch verursacht ein Nierenleiden. Sein Arzt meinte zum Gesundheitszustand von Bob, ein Angestellter und Vater von zwei Kindern, dass er schleunigst abnehmen und fit werden müsse, ansonsten bräuchte er keinen Urlaub fürs nächste Jahr mehr zu planen.

Eigentlich hatte Bob Fahrrad fahren immer gemocht, es war nur nicht seine beliebteste Sportart. Auf einem Rad würde er am schnellsten abnehmen, dachte sich Bob, leider war sein altes Bike unbequem, schwer und er hatte überhaupt keinen Spaß auf seinen Touren. Also stürzte sich Bob ins Internet, informierte sich und fand schnell heraus, dass ernsthafte Radfahrer Specialized-Räder ständig lobten. Mit Glück erwischte Bob auch noch ein richtiges Schnäppchen mit einem günstigen 2004er Stumpjumper Comp. Der Unterschied war unglaublich, sagt er. „Jetzt ging es nicht mehr darum, ein wenig zu radeln, auf einmal machte es richtig Spaß".

Jetzt sitzt Bob nicht mehr auf dem Bike, weil er muss oder weil es gut für seine Gesundheit ist. Er bikt, weil er einfach nicht genug davon bekommen kann. „Ich bin in der besten Form meines Lebens. Ich habe 40 Kilo abgenommen und habe vier bis sechs mal in der Woche Spaß auf den Singletracks bei uns zuhause."

Bob fühlte sich krank, erschöpft, gestresst und antriebslos. Jetzt ist er ehrgeizig, energiegeladen und hat Spaß am Leben. Außerdem freut er sich auf sein nächstes Kind, das gerade unterwegs ist. Eigentlich müsste es den Stumpjumper auf Rezept geben.

82 & 83

WAS KANN MAN VON EINEM IDIOTEN LERNEN?

Genügend, damit eine Federung nur arbeitet, wenn sie soll.

Hast du jemals das Bike eines Cross-Country-Profis kurz vor dem Start am Lenker oder Sattel nach unten gedrückt? Eins ist klar: die so genannte Federgabel vorne an so einem Bike bewegt sich kaum. Die meisten Fahrer haben ihre Gabel dermaßen hart eingestellt, dass der Federweg gegen Null geht. Na und? Wenn sie es so wollen und wenn sie auf diese Art einen Worldcup gewinnen, wen stört's? Genau.

Fragst du jedoch Mike McAndrews, der sich sein Leben lang mit Federung beschäftigt und bei Specialized arbeitet, wird er dir erzählen, dass es ihn störte. Er verbrachte Jahre und Jahre und noch ein paar Jahre damit, Federungen zu bauen, die funktionieren. Richtig gut funktionieren. Und dann erzählten ihm ein paar Fahrer des S-Teams, dass sie gerne eine Federung hätten, die nur anspricht, wenn sie gegen einen dicken Brocken fahren. Und Mike, der den ganzen Kopf nur voll mit Federungskonstruktionen hat, hatte eine Idee.

Ein befreundeter Ingenieur von FoMoCo erzählte Mike von einem Dämpfer, den er gebaut hatte, der nur reagierte, wenn der Autoreifen auf ein Hindernis stieß. In Detroit nannten sie das Ding nur den Idioten-Dämpfer, weil er einen richtig heftigen Stoß brauchte, um „aufzuwachen". Also begann Mike mit seiner eigenen Version des Idioten-Dämpfers, aber in Morgan Hill nannten sie das Projekt als Witz nur den Dämpfer des Idioten.

Mick fand das ganze aber eine ziemlich schlaue Idee und weil der Dämpfer unterscheiden konnte, ob der Schlag vom Untergrund oder vom Bizeps des Fahrers ausgelöst wurde, nannte er es „Brain" – das Gehirn. Er entwickelte einen Prototypen, der sofort funktionierte, aber nicht so zuverlässig wie er sollte. Dann hatte er einen Geistesblitz – Heureka! Würde das Herz des Idioten-Dämpfers, das Trägheitsventil, so nahe wie möglich an der Achse sitzen, würde das ganze besser, schneller und zuverlässiger funktionieren. Er versuchte es, schaffte es und die außenliegende Kammer wurde zum Gehirn – the Brain. Mit der Hilfe von Fox für ein paar Details und mit der Produktion klappte es schließlich.

Dann gewann Filip Meirhaeghe – einer der Typen, die am liebsten Hardtails fuhren und die Gabel so hart wie möglich einstellte – den Weltmeistertitel auf einem Epic mit einem Brain-Dämpfer (ok, Meirhaeghe wurde in der folgenden Saison wegen chemischer Unregelmäßigkeiten in seinem Körper gesperrt, aber am Epic wurden keinerlei illegalen Substanzen festgestellt).

Heutzutage ist der auf den Trail einstellbare Brain-Dämpfer von Mike so schlau, dass er in Rennen und auf einem serienmäßigen Stumpjumper eingesetzt wird.

86 & 87

DEMO

Das Bike für die verrücktesten Stunts, das aus einem Haufen Lego-Steine entstand. Da gibt es diesen Typen aus Kanada. Darren Berrecloth. Der Obermeister des New School Freeriding. Er brauchte eine Waffe im Kampf gegen Grenzen, Gesetze und Vorurteile. Also gab Mike das Demo in Auftrag, ein Bike das gemäß „Bearclaw" extrem weich, mit aktivem Fahrwerk und einer sehr ausgeglichenen Geometrie ausgestattet sein sollte, um die steilsten Stufen und die schmalsten Rinnen damit befahren zu können. Ach ja, und einen extrem tiefen Schwerpunkt, ein tiefes Oberrohr für bestes Handling und die Schaltung soll optimal funktionieren, dazu bitte noch einen Umwerfer vorne. „Kein Problem", sagte Mike, „machen wir."

Also machten sich Ingenieure, Designer und Produktmanager von Specialized, darunter Jason Chamberlin, Brandon Sloan und Robert Egger, an die Aufgabe und begannen – mit Lego-Steinen zu spielen. Mit den Lego-Steinen baute das Team zunächst schnell und einfach ein grundlegendes Modell für die Federung des Demo. Damit konnte das ganze Team herum spielen, es drehen und wenden und überdenken, bis Super-Ingenieur Jason Chamberlin alles in die Tasten seines Computers klopfte, um das ganze auch produktionsfähig zu gestalten.

Man braucht nicht Albert Einstein zu sein, um zu erkennen, dass der Teil mit den Lego-Steinen der leichteste war. Eine wirklich funktionierende Konstruktion mit der PRO/E 3-D Software zu erstellen, erste Prototypen aus der Spezialwerkstatt in Morgan Hill und das Demo-Design dann auch noch gnadenlos zu testen, dauerte Jahre. Um genau zu sein, zwei Jahre, und es verschlang hunderttausende von Dollars.

Das Ergebnis aus dem genialen Chamberlin-Computer und zahlreicher Ausflüge von Produktmanager Brandon Sloan an die North Shore, erbrachten einen Viergelenker-Federungsrahmen mit 230mm Federweg, ausgestattet mit einer normalen Schwinge, unterstützt von einer zweiten Schwinge und sechs Lagern. Um das Demo steif und stabil zu machen, entwarfen Chamberlin und Co. die teuerste Art des Kaltschmiedens, die je für ein Bike gebaut wurde und die den kompliziertesten Vorgang überhaupt enthielt: Die zentrale Stützenkonstruktion, die den Dämpfer aufnimmt, muss mit einer 2-Millionen-Kilo-Presse hergestellt werden.

Wer hätte gedacht, dass ein Bike für die höchsten Drops, fiesesten Sprünge und brutalsten Lines aus einem Haufen Lego-Steine entstand.

88 & 89

30 JAHRE SCHNELL UND IMMER AUF DEM SPRUNG

Wer ist hier alt?

Die fette Drei mit der runden Null dran. Das war früher eher ein Alarmsignal als ein Grund zum Feiern: Schluss mit den Kindereien, jetzt beginnt der Ernst des Lebens. Heutzutage kauft man sich ab 30 neue Flip-Flops und trinkt ein bisschen weniger Bier vor dem nächsten Mittag (zumindest an den Werktagen). Trotzdem traute sich keiner, es anzusprechen. Das kleine Kerlchen, das aus einem lumpigen Wohnwagen in San Jose Vorbauten und andere Teile verhökert hatte, wurde 30 Jahre alt. In Worten: Drei (!!!) -ßig. Die fette Drei mit der runden Null dran.

Macht ja nichts. Heute geht's mit 30 erst richtig los, oder? Eigentlich sind 30 die neuen 25.

Dabei muss man wirklich zugeben, dass der Stumpjumper beim 30. Geburtstag (der Gründung von Specialized) besser denn je aussah. Zeitlos schick und immer noch ein Bike, von dem jeder mit einem dicken Grinsen absteigen würde, egal wo und wie lange er darauf gesessen war. Die Karosse? Ist sie nicht ein Traum in Silber? Wie der legendäre Oberdesigner von Specialized, Robert Egger, zu sagen pflegt: „Wenn es gut aussieht, ist es auch gut." Und er sieht immer gut aus, egal ob mit den Dolomiten oder den Rocky Mountains im Hintergrund. „Die Teile des Bikes wurden so gut gebaut, dass es als Einheit noch besser aussieht als die Summe der Teile", sagt Egger, der Kunstwerke wie das Enduro, das Hemi und das Tarmac entworfen hat.

90 & 91

RIDE ON CAPTAIN

Eine Position vor der Meute gibt man einfach nicht auf.

Wieder beginnt für den „Captain" eine dieser Nächte am Samstag. In einem kleinen Zimmer in einem Billig-Hotel, mit einer Eispackung auf seinem verletzten rechten Fuß, liegt er auf dem Bett. Er schlürft seinen Energie-Zaubertrank nach geheimer Rezeptur, und zieht sich die Spätnachrichten im Fernsehen rein, obwohl er am nächsten Morgen um 7 Uhr früh am Start stehen muss. So hat es der Captain schon immer gemacht.

Offiziell hat sich Ned 1996 aus dem Renngeschehen verabschiedet, aber anscheinend hat er das vergessen. Seit Specialized im Herbst in diesem Jahr eine rauschende Abschiedsparty für ihn schmiss, hat der Captain an Worldcups, NORBA-Rennen, Straßenrennen, Bergrennen, Downhills (wo er schneller als sein eigener Sohn war), Duathlons, Triathlons, X-Terra-Wettbewerben, Marathons, Geländeläufen, Adventure-Rennen und allen möglichen anderen Wettbewerben teilgenommen. Wenn es irgendwie um erhöhte Laktat- und Adrenalinausschüttung geht, ist der „Captain" dabei. Genau an seinem 50. Geburtstag wurde Ned 4. beim brutalen Mount Washington Berglauf.

Eine Menge der Kids, die Neds Staub schlucken müssen, waren noch nicht einmal auf der Welt, als Ned 1980 beim Ironman auf Hawaii als 24. Ins Ziel kam, oder 1983 sein allererstes Mountainbike-Rennen gewann oder das Coors Classic-Straßenrennen mit dem legendären Ti-Raleigh-Team (mit Andy Hampsten, Roy Knickman und Steve Tilford) fuhr, oder sogar als er 1987 sowohl den Europameister- wie den NORBA-Weltmeistertitel gewann.

Ned legt keinen Wert auf eine Sonderbehandlung oder Extra-Lob. Für Ned gibt es Schlimmeres in seinem Wettkampfleben als miese Hotels, kaputte Knöchel und Startzeiten früh um 7. „Ich mache das nicht, um zu beweisen, dass ich schneller als die Jüngeren bin", sagt er, „ich mache mit, weil ich die Jungs vorne an der Spitze einfach gerne aufmische – ich liebe den Wettkampf."

92 & 93

STUMPJUMPER FIELD GUIDE/2006 S-WORKS STUMPJUMPER CARBON

Für den Flow auf dem genialsten Carbonbike, das je hergestellt wurde.

Rahmen Aus FACT Y570 composite, das stärkste Carbon, aus dem Rahmen hergestellt werden. Der S-Works Carbon Stumpjumper wird gelobt für seine Effizienz und sein rasiermesserscharfes Handling.

Dämpfer Brain mit Brain Fade, der erste Dämpfer, der weiß, wann er maximal aktiv zu sein hat und wann er hart für die Kraftumsetzung sein muss. Die 2006 vorgestellte Brain Fade-Technik ermöglicht dem Fahrer eine Abstimmung des Brain Shocks auf die persönlichen Bedürfnisse und die des Trails.

Reifen Exakt für ein schnelles Fullsuspension-Bike wie den Carbon Stumpjumper entwickelt: Die Adrenaline Pro 26x2.0 Reifen werden mit einem 120 Tpi-Gewebe gebaut, um das Gewicht niedrig zu halten und besitzen eine Zwei-Komponenten-Mischung für beste Traktion bei niedrigem Rollwiderstand.

Lenker Die perfekte Ergänzung zum Verbundrahmen des Carbon Stumpjumpers. Der Specialized OS Carbon-Lenker ist mit 175 Gramm leicht und besitzt die optimale Form mit 6 Grad Aufbiegung und 8 Grad Kröpfung.

Sattel Neu im Modelljahr 2006 kommt der Rival mit Specializeds exklusiver Body-Geometry-Ausstattung, der nach Labortests die Blutzufuhr zu empfindlichen Teilen verbessert.

94 & 95

DIE ZUKUNFT?

Schwer zu sagen, was die Zukunft bringt, oder wo alles hinführen wird.
Größere Leute als wir haben sich schon an Prophezeiungen versucht, und man hat ja an Y2K gesehen, was herauskam.
Was ziemlich sicher ist, dass sowohl die verunglückten wie die geglückten Versuche des Aufbaus der Mountainbike-Kultur bewahrt werden müssen. Deshalb werden 100 Prozent des Gewinns aus diesem Buch an die IMBA und die Mountain Bike Hall of Fame gespendet.

ITALIAN/Translation

6 & 7

DEDICA

20 anni, 20 giorni o solo 20 ore fa - È difficile non ricordare la prima volta che si è saliti su di una mountain bike. Le foglie scricchiolanti ed il crepitio delle cortecce sotto le ruote. La gomma anteriore che schizza fango e schiaccia quasi ogni cosa che trova sul suo cammino. Muoversi tra le zone selvagge con quella facilità e con quella grazia tipica di un grande felino. Percorrere terreni come con una XR-250. Quella prima storica enduro "spaccastinchi" che richiedeva un pizzico di accortezza all'accensione, ma che quando scalciava era quasi sempre un dolore eccitante. Troppo bello per essere vero - un improbabile primo dolce bacio, un preludio ad uno meraviglioso forma di dipendenza!

La mountain bike ha fatto tutto questo. Ha questo tipo di potere. Vivace, ma accessibile; pericolosa, ma selvaggia, con manubrio rialzato, sella morbida e telaio ben ammortizzato, adorabile nel suo insieme. Non è, semplicemente, un toccasana per il morale, ma suscita nuove emozioni e pensieri. La mountain bike riunisce le persone: medici dalle periferie, idraulici dalle città, insegnanti dalle campagne, e li conduce in luoghi di cui ignoravano l'esistenza, anche se erano proprio dietro casa. La mountain bike fa sì che le persone – persone come noi – tornino a casa entusiaste e soddisfatte dell'avventura trascorsa.

La storia narrata in queste pagine sarebbe potuta essere un semplice trattato sulla tecnologia, ma la mountain bike non è mai stata caratterizzata semplicemente dalla tecnologia. Sicuramente daremo un'occhiata per vedere che tipo di deragliatore o forcella si trova sulla nostra bici, ma in questo vi è molto di più: cultura e passione. Grazie alla passione, all'ispirazione ed all'intuizione, la Stumpjumper è stata originariamente immaginata come un modo semplice per portare il sorriso ad un numero sempre maggiore di persone. Per fortuna le persone lo hanno capito e da oltre 25 anni mantengono vivi la Stumpjumper, questo sport e la sua cultura. Per questo, noi ringraziamo chiunque si sia lasciato sedurre da una Stumpjumper. Siete voi che avete reso possibili questo libro, questa cultura e stile di vita.

8 & 9

I PRIMI PASSI DELLE RUOTE GRASSE

Da dove è iniziato tutto?
Un momento. Questi ragazzi sono forse dei bikers? Pare proprio di sì, sebbene dovranno ancora trascorre circa 20 anni prima dell'invenzione della mountain bike. Dopotutto, stanno pedalando nel fango, hanno 'ruote grasse' ed un sorriso 'stampato' da un orecchio all'altro.

Che ne dite di John Finley Scott e della sua Schwinn Varsity del 1953 che utilizzava negli anni '60 per macinare migliaia di miglia off-road, inclusa l'ascesa della White Mountain di 14260 piedi (4321 m) della Sierra Mountain Californiana? Poteva già essere considerato un biker?

E se ritornassimo indietro nel tempo, all'epoca dei 20 soldati di Buffalo che, nel 1897, percorsero un circuito di 1900 miglia (3058 km) attraverso il west, incluso il passaggio in quello che oggi è il Parco Nazionale di Yellowstone? Certo è che non si trattò di un'allegra e facile gita su asfalto attraverso il Selvaggio West. Del resto non è che lo facessero per spirito sportivo.

Ed allora? Esattamente quando si smise 'semplicemente di pedalare off-road' ed iniziò il fenomeno 'mountain bike'? Fu forse il 1 dicembre 1974 quando Russ Mahon, della Bay Area di San Francisco per la prima volta piazzò un cambio su una clunker? Oppure fu nell'ottobre 1977, quando Joe Breeze con una bicicletta plurivelocità a 'ruote grasse' di sua creazione, realizzata su misura, partecipò alla leggendaria Repack Downhill? Od ancora fu diversi anni dopo, quando Tim Neenan, progettista della primissima Stumpjumper, in sella ad uno dei primi prototipi si era arrampicato sulle colline dietro la sede di Specialized a San Jose?

Scoprire dove sia nata effettivamente la mountain bike è un compito che sarebbe meglio demandare agli accademici o magari alla banda di amici della MTB che si può trovare in un qualsiasi pomeriggio al Saloon Zeitgeist di San Francisco.

10 & 11

CRESTED BUTTE

Quando i primi outsider, una banda di cinque fanatici del clunker di Marin, confluirono a Crested Butte nel 1978 per il 'terzo, ma in realtà secondo' Tour di Pearl Pass, scoprirono, come la descrisse Joe Breeze, "Una corsa lungo la vecchia città di miniere di carbone, con gli ultimi minatori dai polmoni anneriti rimasti sulle panchine, mentre i giovani danzavano a piedi o in bicicletta lungo le strade". Città di minatori all'epoca della Febbre dell'Oro in Colorado del 1859, alla fine degli anni '70, Crested Butte aveva un aspetto piuttosto trasandato, ma avendo accolto i primi appassionati di telemark e di terapie alternative come la wheatgrass, era considerata all'avanguardia nel mondo hippie. I nuovi abitanti del posto, spesso temuti e non di rado scarsamente attenti all'igiene personale, amavano nomi come Cloud, Star, Plank e Suitcase.

Grazie alla sua lunga tradizione negli sport all'aperto - la città si ricorda per essere stata la patria del primo ski lift in Colorado - sia gli hippie che i nostalgici mostravano una chiara predilezione per il divertimento all' aria aperta, inclusa la vecchia passione per la bicicletta. Naturalmente quelli che andavano in bicicletta prima del 1978 non erano ciclisti veri e propri: andavano semplicemente in bicicletta. Di solito erano biciclette malconce del tipo Denver, vecchie Schwinn, Hawthorne e clunker BF Goodrich di seconda od addirittura terza mano. Anche senza la coltre di neve e di ghiaccio che copriva la città per 8 mesi all'anno, le strade di Crested Butte erano quasi tutte fangose, pertanto le ruote grasse si erano sempre dimostrate come le più adatte per girare in città.

In una notte dell'estate del 1976, nel Grubstake Saloon di Crested Butte fu deciso che i clunker sarebbero stati perfetti per una salita attraverso il Pearl Pass (12692 ft - 3878 m) per poi ridiscendere fino al bar del Jerome Hotel di Aspen. Nel settembre di quell'anno un gruppo di 15 ragazzi dall'aria goliardica e piuttosto ebbri si misero in sella alle loro clunkers dirigendosi a nord verso Aspen. Dopo aver fatto bagordi per una notte al Pearl Pass - secondo le cronache del Crested Butte Pilot, i corridori e lo staff di supporto consumarono un fusto di birra, tre bottiglie di grappa, 9 litri di vino e tre bottiglie di champagne - il gruppo si precipitò giù, procedendo, non senza farsi in parte guidare dall'alcool, verso il Jerome Hotel dove li attendevano altri drinks e nuove leggende.

14 & 15

IL RE DELLE CLUNKER

Chiunque possieda una mountain bike, uomo, donna o bambino, dovrebbe brindare, cantare una canzone, gridare in riva al mare o recitare una preghiera in onore di Charles R. Kelly. Nascosto nella burbera comunità di Fairfax, California, Sir Charles diede vita al 'Fat Tire Flyer', la prima rivista specializzata di mountain bike, prima ancora della loro comparsa. Se da un lato molti possono rivendicare di avere inventato qualcosa che avesse a che fare con la MTB – il primo telaio, la prima bicicletta, la prima gara – Charlie fu quello che teorizzò la filosofia portante degli amanti della 'clunker'. Fu lui che spiegò al mondo cosa significasse esattamente 'Clunking'.

"Se è vero che le Clunker per certi versi assomigliano a motociclette leggere e polverose, la somiglianza è solo nell'aspetto: curvare ad alta velocità con questi mezzi è una forma esclusiva di arte corporea. Una motocicletta possiede ruote larghe ed ammortizzatori, una Clunker no. Di conseguenza tende a perdere l'aderenza con il suolo quando urta anche gli ostacoli più lievi. In presenza di una curva stretta, una Clunker non dispone dell'accelerazione istantanea di cui si serve una motocicletta per tenere in traiettoria la ruota posteriore, ed essendo priva di ammortizzatori, tende a saltellare. Ciononostante, i corridori più esperti prendono le curve molto più velocemente di quanto si possa immaginare.

"Scivolare in derapata su una curva già segnata dai passaggi precedenti ti trae in inganno. Senza più controllo, devi prendere una decisione rapidamente: uscire dalla traiettoria o lasciare cadere la bici. Lasciarla cadere.... accidenti... camicia strappata, gomito sanguinante. Ora non c'è tempo di stare a guardare queste cose, tanto la camicia era vecchia ed anche il gomito; in che condizioni è la bici? OK...in sella e con la mano rimetti in tensione la catena via via che percorri i primi metri. Di nuovo sul rapporto giusto, in fuorisella, per recuperare il tempo perso".
--Charles Kelly
Bicycling Magazine 1979

16 & 17

SPECIALIZED PROTAGONISTA PER ECCELLENZA NELLA RIVOLUZIONE DELLE RUOTE GRASSE

Il primo anno le vendite ammontarono a $ 60.000
L'anno successivo erano salite a $128.000
L'anno seguente avevano superato i $ 200.000
"Ripensando a quel passato con gli occhi di oggi le cose si muovevano lentamente, ma allora mi sembrava accadesse tutto così rapidamente", ha dichiarato Mike Sinyard, fondatore e presidente di Specialized, parlando dei primi anni immediatamente successivi all'avvio dell'attività dell'azienda.

Molto prima che gli appassionati di mountain bike creassero siti web dedicati alle loro collezioni di tatuaggi realizzati con la riproduzione della guarnitura come soggetto, essere talmente ossessionati dalle biciclette a tal punto da vendere gli unici oggetti di valore in proprio possesso (un Volkswagen Microbus nel caso di Mike) ed utilizzare il ricavato per finanziare un viaggio in un altro continente significava essere da matti da legare. A dire la verità ciò è inconsueto anche oggi, ma nel 1973, quando Mike impacchettò la sua bicicletta Bob Jackson blu e bianca e partì per l'Europa, fu un'autentica pazzia.

Dopo aver pedalato per il Regno Unito, Amsterdam (toccata e fuga) e Barcellona, Mike percorse in Italia la pianura Padana, sentendosi spaesato così come si sarebbe sentito chiunque altro senza alcuna idea di cosa stesse facendo, ma con una sensazione istintiva che qualcosa di grande sarebbe potuto accadere in qualsiasi momento. E così fu, grazie ad una ragazza che Mike ebbe occasione di incontrare all' Ostello Della Gioventù di Milano. La ragazza conosceva Cino Cinelli, il 'guru' del mondo italiano della bicicletta, fondatore dell' omonima azienda di telai e componenti per biciclette di cui Mike aveva grande stima.

Da lì ad un mese Mike era di nuovo nella sua casa mobile di San Jose con un carico di componenti Cinelli: aveva speso ogni centesimo per attacchi, curve manubrio e telai firmati Cinelli. A quel punto, senza auto, né alcun supporto tipo eBay che potesse aiutarlo a vendere i suoi 'articoli Milanesi', Mike si recò in bicicletta dai commercianti della zona, trainando un rimorchio pieno di componenti e vendendo i suoi articoli lungo il percorso.

Nell'anno del bicentenario della fondazione degli Stati Uniti d'America, Specialized era ormai diventata un'azienda dedita all'importazione di biciclette e componenti totalmente affermata, la cui offerta era costituita da articoli di nicchia e pezzi difficili da reperire, particolarmente ricercati dai corridori delle ruote grasse: oggetti moda come i cambi Huret DuoPar, i freni Macfac ed i set di tubazioni Columbus. Con una clientela che includeva la maggior parte dei costruttori di telai della west coast, Specialized era al centro del boom del fenomeno mountain bike. Artigiani costruttori di telai come Joe Breeze, Albert Eisentraut e Tom Ritchey (che eseguivano lavori a contratto per Specialized, come ad esempio mozzi su misura per ruote rinforzate da tandem), erano tra i clienti regolari e via via che i loro ordini di componenti particolari, quali le guarniture TA ed i supporti per cantilever, aumentavano vertiginosamente, Mike si domandava fin dove volessero arrivare. Ciò che avevano in mente era reinventare la bicicletta e Mike era pronto a fare la sua parte.

20 & 21

STUMPJUMPER FIELD GUIDE/1981 STUMPJUMPER

Telaio. Progettato da Tim Neenan di Lighthouse Bikes, Santa Cruz, il telaio originale della Stumpjumper era dotato di saldature in TIG. Se il vostro telaio 1981 possiede delle congiunzioni significa che è della fine dell' 81. E la vernice blu? Il colore venne scelto perché era simile al blu già utilizzato per la Sequoia touring.

Attacco manubrio. Il leggendario attacco manubrio 'Golf Club'; questo gioiello era la versione modificata di un attacco manubrio per BMX realizzato a quell'epoca. La curva manubrio in acciaio originale della Stumpjumper era derivata dal manubrio Magura per motocicletta.

Leve freno. Standard su tutte le prime Stumpjumper, le leve freno Tommaselli Racer furono progettate per essere usate sulle motociclette leggere da turismo degli ultimi anni '70. Erano accompagnate da cavi di comando ad alta resistenza che ne miglioravano la frenata e le prestazioni.

Coperture. Specialized utilizzò le conoscenze acquisite nella creazione della sua linea di successo di ruote da strada per creare il primo pneumatico leggero da MTB con scolpitura specifica, lo Stumpjumper. Se ne avete ancora un paio, teneteveli stretti: i copertoni delle mountain bike di 25 anni fa sono molto difficili da trovare!

Guarnitura: Un componente che Specialized importava in America per le touring bikes, la guarnitura TA Cyclotourist, aveva una finitura lucidissima e permetteva di utilizzare rapporti ultra-corti. I guasti erano frequenti in quanto la progettazione di questa guarnitura non ne contemplava l'uso off-road.

22 & 23

LA PRIMA VOLTA CHE VIDI UNA STUMPJUMPER

JOE BREEZE: Pioniere della mountain bike, costruttore di telai, scrittore
La vidi al Bike Odyssey a Sausalito, California, vicino a casa mia. "Ho pensato: che cosa diavolo è quell'attacco manubrio a forma di mazza da golf?" e mi sono anche chiesto perché avessero usato le leve freno Tommaselli anziché le Magura, ma al prezzo di 750 dollari, ho poi pensato che ne avrebbero vendute molte".

TOM RITCHEY: Pioniere della mountain bike, costruttore di telai, inventore, atleta di calibro nazionale
La Stumpjumper era rozza e rispecchiava semplicemente il livello di tecnologia disponibile in Giappone in quel periodo. Le nostre bici costavano il doppio (ed erano più leggere), ma la Stumpjumper aveva un prezzo ragionevole ed era costruita con pezzi interessanti per quel tempo.

RICHARD CUNNINGHAM: Fondatore di Mantis Cycles e redattore di Mountain Bike Action.
La Stumpjumper era pesante, poco maneggevole e non curvava affatto bene, ma, vedendone una per la prima volta, rimasi sbalordito ed ho esultato: "Questa mountain bike è davvero un affare...proviamola!" Di lì a poco costruii la mia prima mountain bike.

DON COOK: Pioniere della mountain bike, co-direttore della Mountain Bike Hall of Fame.
In quel periodo il solo telaio di una Ritchey artigianale costava dai 1.200 ai 1.500 Dollari. Abbiamo visto la Stumpjumper ed abbiamo pensato 'Ora ne possiamo parlare.' Improvvisamente non bisognava più aspettare tre o quattro mesi per avere una mountain bike di Tom (Ritchey) e Gary (Fisher).

GARY FISHER: Un giorno andai ad acquistare alcuni componenti da Mike, quando mi disse "Vieni, ti voglio mostrare una cosa". Così mi portò nel retro del negozio. Rimasi folgorato. Aveva la prima Stumpjumper ed era quasi identica a quella che stavamo producendo al costo di $ 1.320, con la differenza che la sua costava solo $ 750. Doveva essere il novembre del 1981. Subito dopo mi recai in Giappone perché mi resi conto che si potevano importare container di buone biciclette a prezzi ragionevoli.

JACQUIE PHELAN: Pioniera della mountain bike; fondatrice dell'associazione WOMBATS, scrittrice. Ho visto le Stumpjumper, ma non sapevo cosa fossero. All'epoca stavo con Gary Fisher, che le definiva "imitazioni".

VICTOR VINCENTE OF AMERICA: Pioniere della mountain bike, corridore su strada ai Giochi Olimpici, promotore di competizioni, artista.
Non ho un ricordo molto chiaro, ma credo che reagii riconoscendone il design standard, funzionale, che avrebbe conquistato le masse, diverso dalle mountain bike convenzionali già presenti sul mercato.

RICHARD HEMINGTON, GB: Il primo a vendere una Stumpjumper fuori dai confini dagli Stati Uniti.
La Stumpjumper arrivò tutta smontata dentro ad uno scatolone e dovetti montarla partendo quasi da zero. Mi sembra ancora di vederne i pezzi sparpagliati sul pavimento; mi ci volle una vita per metterli assieme. Ricordo che pensai al guaio in cui ci saremmo trovati se avessimo davvero cominciato a venderla! E naturalmente fu esattamente ciò che accadde.

JOE MURRAY: Uno dei primi corridori, progettista di biciclette, collaudatore
La mia Stump del 1981 sembrava una slitta, ma ricordo che mi piaceva, anche se ci voleva un certo stile per farla scendere dalla strade piene di curve delle colline di Marin. Dopo aver iniziato a gareggiare per Fisher, Gary mi regalò una mountain bike e vendetti la Stumpjumper. Vorrei non averlo fatto.

MERT LAWWILL: Leggenda del motociclismo, uno dei primi progettisti di biciclette
"Quando vidi a quanto veniva venduta (la Stumpjumper) e quanto fosse migliore della mia, immaginai che il gioco fosse finito e che fosse ora di tornare alle moto."

24 & 25

UN MODELLO PER LA PUBBLICITÀ

Il nuovo tipo di bicicletta esigeva un nuovo modo di fare pubblicità... Una strategia che dura da 25 anni.

Non molto tempo fa, Mike viveva in una roulotte , scrivendo il suo catalogo su fogli gialli standard e persuadendo i dipendenti a dormire la notte raggomitolati su pile di gomme, tanto era piccolo il magazzino di cui disponeva. Il momento era propizio per cavalcare la tigre, altrimenti nota come Stumpjumper.

Con una bicicletta di produzione di serie, diversa da tutte quelle mai realizzate prima di allora da Specialized o da qualsiasi altra azienda, le vecchie strategie promozionali non avrebbero mai funzionato. Prima della campagna 'Uno sport completamente nuovo', come è conosciuta nella sede centrale di Specialized, la pubblicità dell'azienda era realizzata perlopiù in bianco e nero e si limitava ad occupare al massimo mezza pagina. Tutto cambiò con la Stumpjumper, il nuovo gioiello scuro e fiammante che divenne il prototipo della pubblicità Specialized sulla carta stampata per i successivi 25 anni. Realizzata da Jack Christensen nello stesso garage in cui stampò la prima brochure di Apple Computer e progettata da Patrick Mountain, collaboratore veterano di Specialized, 'Whole New Sport' non poteva passare inosservata sulle riviste in bianco e nero dell'epoca.

Senza dubbio è fantastica, perfetta, ma perché il tipo della pubblicità è immortalato - nel momento in cui è pronto a farsi una pedalata - con indosso calzini tubolari ed una tuta da lavoro? Il ragazzo in questione è proprio il progettista di Stumpjumper Tim Neenan ed è così che ricorda quel momento: "A quell'epoca non esisteva un abbigliamento specifico per la mountain bike, nulla che si presupponeva si dovesse indossare". Avevo una tuta che indossavo quando lavoravo, così sono andato a fare le riprese esattamente com'ero vestito."

26 & 27

METTI IN MOTO

Nella prima metà degli anni '80, le competizioni erano molto simili alla situazione delle corse NASCAR (National Association for Stock Car Auto Racing) nella seconda metà degli anni '40: bastava delimitare con dei picchetti un percorso in un terreno preso a caso, mettere in fila i corridori ed abbassare la bandiera di partenza. I corridori erano conosciuti per essere tipi che dormivano in macchina, emettevano assegni a vuoto per pagare le quote di iscrizione e divoravano barrette energetiche. Era naturale, autentica, una competizione su due ruote con una purezza che non si vedeva da cent'anni. Ed era anche troppo bello perché rimanesse un segreto. Tra il primo raduno tenutosi in una casa di Danville, California, nel 1983 ed il 1989, la NORBA passò da zero a oltre 20.000 soci. "Nel giro di qualche anno, da un appuntamento segreto tra amici si giunse ad un fenomeno planetario," afferma il fondatore di Ibis Bicycles Scot Nicol. "Nessuno avrebbe mai potuto trovarsi preparato per affrontare questa situazione."

28 & 29

SPAVALDERIA — IL TEAM STUMPJUMPER NE AVEVA DA VENDERE

Del resto l'avresti mostrata anche tu, se ti fossi presentato alla linea di partenza su una mountain bike rosa.

Nel 1984 non esisteva un 'normale' team di mountain bike e, anche se fosse esistito, comunque non sarebbe stato il Team Stumpjumper, che fu il primo team in assoluto a livello professionale; gli atleti correvano su mountain bike rosa con manubri stradali ed indossavano vere scarpette da ciclista in un'epoca in cui molti dei migliori corridori di mountain bike divoravano barrette energetiche e se la cavavano con semplici scarpe da tennis, tipo le Nike Lava Dome. Organizzato dal guru delle corse su strada di Specialized, Bill Woodul, il Team Stump fu un vero e proprio esperimento per l'off-road. "Woody (Woodul) mise insieme un gruppetto di corridori Categoria 1 su strada ed alcuni biker ed applicò le stesse idee e gli stessi metodi che aveva sviluppato nelle corse su strada," ricorda l'ex-corridore del Team Stumpjumper Dave McLaughlin. "Ci allenavamo, eravamo organizzati e usavamo strategie di gara durante le competizioni."

Durante il primo anno di vita del team, Woodul scoprì talenti come la rivelazione del ciclo-cross McLaughlin, Gavin Chilcot (che in seguito gareggiò su strada per il celebre team 7-Eleven), i californiani del nord Mark Michelle e Alan Ott ed il padre del cross americano, Laurence Malone. Stipati in un furgone Specialized, girarono gli Stati Uniti, partecipando all'esiguo numero di grandi competizioni allora esistenti: le Suntour Pacific States Challenge Series, le Gant Challenge Series (competizioni urbane a Seattle, Washington; Chicago, Illinois; Golden, Colorado; Tampa e Miami, Florida), la Ross Stage Race e le classiche corse one-day, come la Rockhopper, la Rumpstomper ed i Norba National Championship. "Allora le competizioni erano un po' discontinue. Soprattutto, non vi era lo stesso livello di competitività di oggi, ma quando fecero la loro comparsa Joe Murray od alcuni corridori professionisti su strada come Andy Hampsten e Steve Tilford, le cose cominciarono a farsi piuttosto serie," così Maclaughlin ricorda il periodo in cui le competizioni muovevano ancora i primi passi.

Nel giro di alcune stagioni, caratterizzate da competizioni su terreni accidentati e costellate di cadute, il Team Stumpjumper si era trasformato nel Team Specialized, il migliore ed il meglio equipaggiato team di mountain bike del mondo. Nelle sue prime stagioni il Team Specialized schierò i campioni del mondo Ned Overend, Lisa Muhich e Sara Ballantyne ma anche il fenomeno del cross-country Daryl Price ed i diavoli dei pendii Elladee Brown e Paul Thomasberg. Quella e le successive formazioni della squadra delle 'gomme grasse' di Specialized fecero a meno delle mountain bikes di colore rosa, ma non della spavalderia.

30 & 31

STUMPJUMPER FIELD GUIDE/1984 STUMPJUMPER TEAM

Se pedali su di una bici rosa, è bene che tu sia uno che va forte!

Telaio. Progettato da Jem Merz in tubi realizzati dalla giapponese Tange Prestige, il telaio della Team Stumpjumper 1984 era il più leggero che Specialized avesse mai realizzato fino a quel momento.
Forcella. La Stumpjumper Team rosa era altresì dotata della prima forcella con testa uni-crown, molto più leggera e semplice da realizzare rispetto alle forcelle utilizzate a quell'epoca.

Freni posteriori. Fortunatamente, i freni U-brakes montati sotto la scatola del movimento centrale, come i Suntour Rollercam, furono una moda di breve durata. Una vera e propria calamita per il fango, questi U-brakes sono ricordati come uno dei più grandi errori collettivi nel mondo della bicicletta.

Coperture. Nel 1984 le coperture TriCross si affermarono come il battistrada di scelta per le mountain bike di alta gamma, soppiantando le Stumpjumper. Note soprattutto per i tasselli a basso profilo e la grande tenuta di strada in condizioni di secco e polvere.

Ruota libera. Una macchina da competizione a tutti gli effetti, la Stumpjumper Team era dotata di ruota libera da strada Shimano 600 con un pignone maggiore di soli 26 denti, nulla a che vedere con i pignoni a 30 denti preferiti dalla maggior parte degli off-roader di quell'epoca.

32

MBHOF

Se gli streaker e i suonatori di ukulele possono averne uno, perché non potremmo averne uno anche noi?
Cercate su Google l'espressione 'Hall of Fame' ed otterrete 47.400.000 risposte: sì, 47 milioni di risposte! Certo, c'è una "Hall of fame" dei minatori, delle cowgirl, dei PC, degli streaker (nudisti per protesta), dell'ukulele. Una "Hall of fame" dell'ukulele! Santo Cielo, cosa mai potrà esservi nella "hall of fame" dell'ukulele? Probabilmente più di quanto vi sarà nella "hall of fame" degli streaker, questo è poco ma sicuro.

Vi è qualcosa di innegabilmente universale nel fatto di voler onorare coloro che hanno contribuito alla diffusione di una cultura ed i fanatici delle gomme grasse non sono diversi dalle cowgirl, dagli streaker o dagli appassionati di ukulele. Ospitata in maniera abbastanza comoda, presso un vecchio distributore di benzina sulla Crested Butte's Elk Avenue, la "hall of fame" della Mountain Bike fu concepita dall'ispirazione di Carole Bauer. Nella metà degli anni '80 la Bauer, da tempo residente in città, temeva che gli inventori della cultura della mountain bike fossero destinati ad essere dimenticati senza un'istituzione che onorasse i loro risultati e lo sport che essi avevano contribuito a creare.

Nel 1988 la "MBHoF" (Mountain Bike Hall of Fame) era pronta ad accogliere il primo gruppo di appassionati. Non sorprende che i pionieri delle gomme grasse, con nomi come Breeze, Fisher, Kelly, Cunningham, Ritchey e Murray, fossero presenti in quella prima classe. E così fu anche per Mr. Specialized, che era emozionato, sbalordito e profondamente onorato per il fatto di essere tenuto nella medesima considerazione di questo selezionato gruppo di compagni. Dopo Mr. Specialized almeno altri tre biker con una "S" sul petto ebbero l'onore di essere presenti nella MBHoF: "The Captain", il progettista di telai Jim Merz, ed il guru Tom Hillard, sostenitore dell'aspetto agonistico della mountain bike.

Oggi la MBHoF continua ad esistere, così come la cultura della mountain bike, grazie al sostegno dell'industria ciclistica e dei fans della mountain bike di tutto il mondo. (www.mtnbikehalloffame.com)

33

LA MIA STUMPJUMPER N.1

Bill Hennion
TITOLO: 2 Stumpjumper, un giovanotto di 65 anni che percorre 150 miglia alla settimana
Bill si sposta quasi ogni giorno su una delle sue due Stumpjumper (due Stumpjumper! Quanto è caro Bill?), per un totale di circa 150 miglia alla settimana. Non male per un vecchietto di 65 anni, o no?

Qualche anno fa il nipote di Bill (un adolescente) cominciò a dedicarsi ai singletrack. Bill sapeva di dover rinnovare la sua vecchia Stump se voleva stare al passo con il nipote. Bill non impiegò molto tempo per rendersi conto che la sua moderna FSRxc biammortizzata lo aiutava a stare al passo con il suo piccolo sbarbatello. Bill dichiara che, grazie al carro ammortizzato posteriore a parallelogramma brevettato, oggi è in grado di cavarsela meglio di prima.

La bicicletta che Bill usa tutti i giorni è una Stumpjumper in acciaio del 1982 (quella con testa forcella "ad ala di biplano") che ha acquistato, di seconda mano, alcuni anni fa. "E' una delle mie biciclette preferite per andare in giro", dice Bill "E' eccezionale per i tracciati che devo percorrere quando vado a pescare nei dintorni".

Per quanto vorremmo poter affermare diversamente, Bill non sta diventando più giovane, ma può ancora fare tutte le cose che ama – ad esempio uno "short stop" – grazie alla sua forma fisica che riesce ad mantenere grazie alle due ruote. "In breve", dice Bill, "le mie bici sono la mia vita".

34 & 35

SUPPORTO TECNICO GRATUITO?

Specialized è impazzita?
"Backindaze", prima ancora che si dicesse back in the day (a quel tempo) – intorno al 1985 – il fenomeno mountain bike stava appena cominciando a prendere piede. Non vi erano molti eventi, ma ogni anno vi erano organizzatori sempre più eccitati, corridori sempre più determinati e molto spazio per commettere errori. Così Specialized, che aveva già venduto un mucchio di Stumpjumper ed aveva partecipato ad un bel numero di gare, decise di dare una mano per aiutare gli organizzatori a promuovere le gare ed i corridori a gareggiare. Come veniva fatto per le gare su strada almeno fin dal 1982, Specialized decise di fornire un supporto tecnico ad ogni corridore, con qualsiasi tipo di bicicletta, gratuitamente. Inoltre decise di aiutare gli organizzatori ogni qualvolta fosse possibile, tracciando un percorso, preparandolo per la gara, montando una tenda, guidando una motocicletta apripista in testa alla gara, effettuando la registrazione dei concorrenti. Qualsiasi cosa si rendesse necessario, la banda di Morgan Hill era pronta a farlo.

Per garantire il successo, assunsero uno fra i più autorevoli ed esperti tecnici di gara presenti sul territorio nazionale, Tom Hillard della Contea di Sonoma in California, autore del regolamento di gara NORBA e promotore del Punk Bike Enduro. Tom afferma di essere stato il primo ad avere tracciato un percorso per le mountain bike "in quei giorni ormai lontani" (1961). Così, Mr. Specialized gli affidò le chiavi di un furgone e Tom si dedicò alle gare dai nomi oggi leggendari come 'Rockhopper', 'Rumpstomper', 'Reseda-To-The-Sea', 'Kamikaze' e 'Whiskeytown'.

Sia che si trattasse di una gara NORBA National, Cactus Cup o Tuesday night club in Texas, i corridori sembravano sempre caricati quando uno dei meccanici di Specialized, tipi cortesi che lavoravano sodo, come Tom Hillard o Dave Meyers, Steve Mosher o Joe Buckley, scendevano dalle loro mountain bike superaccessoriate per una rapida riparazione (nella maggior parte dei casi gratuita). Credeteci! Gli stessi organizzatori, sempre indaffarati e con poco personale nel loro staff, mostravano di apprezzare molto la cosa. "Le cose iniziano ad andare per il verso giusto quando cominciarono ad apparire i camion Specialized," disse un vecchio direttore di gara.

Ovviamente il fatto di avere dei camion e dei meccanici sulla strada comporta dei costi non indifferenti, ma Specialized non ha mai pensato che si trattasse di una strada a senso unico. Naturalmente il fatto di organizzare delle buone gare ha contribuito a far crescere questo sport, ma essere sul campo, riparare biciclette sulle quali i corridori pedalavano con forza e spingevano al limite, spesso era meglio che avere 1.000 tecnici chiusi in un laboratorio nel tentativo di indovinare a che tipo di "maltrattamenti" potesse essere sottoposta una bicicletta nell'utilizzo off-road.

Supporto tecnico e di gara gratuito? Ricerca e sviluppo a buon mercato? Chi non sarebbe d'accordo sul fatto che la strategia di supporto tecnico adottata da Specialized non fosse una buona soluzione?

36 & 37

L'ARRIVO

Non molte persone al mondo sono state a 7.275 di latitudine Nord – 107.879 di longitudine Ovest, luogo altrimenti noto come Durango, Colorado, che non a caso si chiama così. In mezzo al deserto, a sud-ovest, nella regione dei Four Corners, tra i boschi, in una riserva circondata da montagne e valichi. 'In the middle of nowhere', nel bel mezzo del nulla, appunto. Anche con una scorta gigante di snacks ed una cassa di coca cola, Durango si trova comunque a 14 ore di strada da Los Angeles ed a quasi 7 ore da Denver. Già, proprio in mezzo al nulla.

Sebbene fosse il 1 aprile 1989 non era affatto un pesce d'aprile; Ned stava lasciando il sole della sua San Diego alla volta di Durango con il suo pick-up Datsun del 1965. Nel cuore della notte trainando un rimorchio realizzato artigianalmente che, come lui stesso diceva, era "proprio come quello dei Clampett", fu costretto a tornare indietro a causa di una tempesta. Avrebbe dovuto servigli di lezione. Ma dopo una notte ad Aztec, New Mexico (circa 35 miglia a sud e alcune migliaia di piedi più in basso rispetto alla quota di Durango), si inoltrò attraverso le montagne per scoprire il suo Nirvana. Una roulotte in affitto da 8 X 35 piedi (2,4 X 10,5 m) nel Junction Creek Trailer Park. Sì. Ned Overend era arrivato.

Per pagare l'affitto Ned aveva lavorato come meccanico riparando tutte le auto che circolavano nella Contea di Animas. Per mettere a punto il suo mezzo fece memorabili pedalate sui tracciati fuoristrada ed in asfalto del vecchio anello di Elmore Store. In pochi anni iniziò a praticare il ciclismo su strada, partendo dall'essere nessuno fino a correre alla Coors Classic nella migliore squadra d'America in poco più di un anno. Un giorno, dopo l'edizione 1983 della Coors Classic un trio di residenti locali di Durango, incluso Bob Gregorio, detto 'Bicycle' presentarono a Ned le loro clunker a 5 velocità. Era stato catturato. "Ero come un bambino in mezzo alla vasca di sabbia dello spazio giochi", dichiara The Captain. "Capii immediatamente che lì c'era qualcosa da fare".

Era possibile ottenere dei risultati? Pochi anni dopo Ned poteva vantare il miglior curriculum nella storia delle ruote grasse: quattro campionati Nazionali NORBA, Campionati Mondiali NORBA ed i primi Campionati Mondiali UCI. Sì, Ned Overend era arrivato. Ce l'aveva fatta.

40 & 41

MISSIONE IMPOSSIBILE

La parola d'ordine è "organizzarsi."
Amici in prima linea. Sulla prima pagina della prima edizione della prima rivista di mountain bike, il 'Fat Tire Flyer' di Charlie Kelly dell'agosto 1980, ci fu un chiaro invito all'azione. "Senza un'organizzazione che protegga i nostri interessi non avremo interessi da proteggere", supplicò Charlie Kelly. Addirittura prima ancora di riuscire a trovare una mountain bike nel negozio sottocasa, riuscire a mettere le ruote su un tracciato fuoristrada si prospettava come una missione impossibile.

Facciamo un salto all'estate del 1987. Mentre la maggior parte del paese stava da poco scoprendo i piaceri del mountain biking, nella patria del clunker i toni del dibattito sul tema dell'accesso ai percorsi diventavano sempre più accesi. "Terrore a due ruote", nello strillo del Newsweek del 28 settembre 1987. Dall'American River Parkway vicino a Sacramento alle montagne di Santa Monica a Los Angeles, le biciclette venivano bandite dai singletrack o letteralmente sbattute fuori dai parchi. Il National Park Service aveva chiuso tutti i suoi sentieri e il Bureau of Land Management stava vietando alle biciclette l'accesso alle foreste. Se si voleva un futuro per la mountain bike, gli appassionati dovevano unirsi ed organizzarsi. E senza perdere tempo.

Quell'autunno i rappresentanti di cinque gruppi di attivisti della MTB con sede in California – Bicycle Trails Council di Marin, Bicycle Trails Council di East Bay, Sacramento Rough Riders, la Concerned Off-Road Bikers Association di Los Angeles e Responsible Off-Road mountain Pedalers di San Jose – si riunirono alla fiera annuale della bicicletta a Long Beach. Nell'arco di sei mesi, l'International Mountain Bike Association (IMBA) si era creata uno statuto e lottava affinché la mountain bike avesse accesso su tutti i tracciati.

Grazie alla visione di Linda DuPriest ed Eric Eidsmo, allora membri dello staff di Specialized, alla IMBA fu concesso uno stanziamento di 1.000 dollari a nome della società. Fu il primo passo importante che Specialized (o qualsiasi altra grande società) avrebbe fatto per difendere la libertà di accesso delle mountain bike sui sentieri. Di lì a poco Linda convinse la società a sponsorizzare una conferenza, aperta all'industria, al salone di Interbike del 1989, che avrebbe incoraggiato altre aziende ad aderire all'iniziativa di sostegno per la difesa dell'obbiettivo comune. Una svolta nello sviluppo della IMBA, la conferenza contribuì a sensibilizzare l'opinione pubblica ed a raccogliere fondi per la difesa dei singletracks; inoltre, servì ad avviare una serie di iniziative, tra cui le prime importanti conferenze per la difesa della mountain bike a Washington D.C. ed a Durango. Linda DuPriest fu membro del consiglio della IMBA per dieci anni, patrocinando i primi gruppi di attivisti, aiutandoli a rivedere le loro presentazioni ed i loro programmi ed a servire da collegamento tra IMBA e l'industria della bicicletta.

Sorretta dai fondi e dal sostegno di tutti i principali operatori dell'industria della bicicletta e degli oltre 35.000 membri attuali, l'IMBA da allora promuove l'informazione e il libero accesso ai percorsi in tutte le regioni degli Stati Uniti e del resto del mondo. Senza l'IMBA oggi non avremmo percorsi da proteggere.

Bene, avete sentito la predica, ora mettete le mani al portafoglio (www.imba.com)

42

LA MIA STUMPJUMPER N.2

Denise Weber
Dopo i 30 anni ha scoperto nuovi orizzonti ed iniziato una carriera da corridore
Denise, una donna di 36 anni, veterinaria libera professionista, iniziò ad andare in bicicletta su suggerimento del medico. Un ginocchio malconcio le impediva di correre o persino di salire sul "tapis roulant", così il medico le suggerì di iniziare ad andare in bicicletta per ridurre il carico sul ginocchio e rimettersi in forma. Dopo essere salita in sella a una "due ruote" la sua vita cambiò per sempre.

Cercando una motivazione in più, Denise cominciò a gareggiare 6 mesi dopo il primo fatidico giro in bicicletta. Le ci vollero pochi minuti nel corso di una gara concitata, perché Denise si rendesse conto che aveva bisogno di un mezzo più leggero ed affidabile se voleva essere competitiva. Così acquistò una Rockhopper e, dopo averla usata per alcune stagioni, la sostituì con una Stumpjumper usata. "Si adatta perfettamente alle mie esigenze e me ne sono proprio innamorata," ha dichiarato. "Improvvisamente ho preso velocità, senza rendermene conto ho preso confidenza come non mai." Denise, che partecipa ad alcune corse su strada per mantenere una buona forma di base, ammette che non vi è niente di meglio che stare in sella alla sua Stumpjumper e vagare nei boschi la mattina presto.

Ora il suo ginocchio si è talmente rinforzato da non aver più bisogno di portare il tutore anche quando si allena correndo sui percorsi fuoristrada. Non che ora corra a piedi di sovente, "Preferisco stare molto di più sulla mia Stumpjumper, dopo tutto ora sono un corridore di mountain bike."

43
STUMPJUMPER EPIC
Riscrivere il libro delle regole una pagina alla volta
Nell'arco di cinque anni, Specialized riscrisse completamente la storia della mountain bike. Tra il 1988 ed il 1993 Specialized divenne la prima azienda ad assemblare telai di serie in acciaio/carbonio, titanio/carbonio e metal/matrix (per non parlare delle prime forcelle ammortizzate con foderi in fibra di carbonio ed il primo telaio di serie progettato interamente al computer). Molte regole tradizionali, con la fine del periodo legato alla Guerra Fredda, vennero abbandonate e se c'era qualcuno che non vedeva l'ora che ciò accadesse era proprio Jim Merz ingegnere di Specialized e nella "hall of fame" della mountain bike.

Quando Reagan chiese a Gorby di 'abbattere il muro', un'ondata di materiali e tecnologie rimasti rinchiusi nelle 'stanze segrete' dell'esercito si rese disponibile. Grazie alla sua passione per una buona rivista scientifica ed alla sua esperienza di lavoro con l'allora innovativo software di progettazione a 3D (per il quale Specialized dovette sborsare ben $ 250.000 nel 1985), Merz era nella posizione perfetta per recepire le nuove opportunità che si offrivano grazie all' utilizzo dei nuovi materiali e tecnologie legate alle loro applicazioni.

Dopo aver fatto conoscenza con la fibra di carbonio, grazie a un gruppo di ingegneri che stavano lavorando con i materiali compositi presso una filiale della Prince racchette da tennis a El Cajon, California, Merz si mise al lavoro per ottimizzare i tubi in materiale composito e progettare una serie di congiunzioni per unirli in un telaio. "Ho sudato sette camicie per riuscire a trovare una soluzione", ha commentato Merz. Dopo diverse prove ed un duro lavoro alla sua stazione di lavoro Applicon, Merz riuscì ad ottenere un set di congiunzioni in chromoly saldate con alta precisione dal partner giapponese di Specialized, peraltro anche validissimo costruttore di telai. Richiedendo tanto lavoro quanto la costruzione di un'intera bicicletta, le congiunzioni e la progettazione personalizzata dei tubi portarono ad un costo di 2.400 dollari per la realizzazione del telaio e delle forcelle del modello Epic . Le congiunzioni furono quindi spedite alla sede generale di Specialized dove furono assemblate con una serie di tubazioni in fibra di carbonio utilizzando un'apposita dima. Con sole due dime, una per taglia, costruire le circa 2.000 Epic che furono prodotte si dimostrò effettivamente un'impresa colossale.

Mai soddisfatto, Merz passò presto dalle congiunzioni in chromoly a quelle in titanio e non ad un titanio qualsiasi, ma al titanio lavorato dagli esperti della Merlin Metalworks di Cambridge, Massachussetts. Questa, comunque è tutta un'altra storia.

46 & 47
MR. AMERICA
L'impresa di The Captain a Durango.*
Se vi foste trovati nella regione dei Four Corners in Colorado e vi fosse capitato di accendere la radio o la TV nei primi giorni di settembre di quell'anno, probabilmente avreste sentito il nome di Ned o visto il suo volto baffuto sullo schermo. Era il tema principale degli articoli del Durango Herald e compariva sulla copertina del programma ufficiale della gara. Qualcuno si era addirittura preso la briga di stampare delle T-shirt con The Captain, vincitore dell'imminente Campionato del Mondo. Durango non si accontentava di essere la patria dei primi Campionati del Mondo, voleva che il 'suo' ragazzo vincesse.
The Captain avrebbe potuto fare un sacco di quattrini gareggiando come corridore professionista su strada o nel triathlon, ma scelse il fango della mountain bike, semplicemente perchè pensava che tra le discipline del pedale questa fosse la più divertente. Tuttavia, una settimana prima dei primi Campionati del Mondo 'unificati' UCI del 1990, il re del cross-country americano comprese di non avere scelto la strada più semplice. La pressione dovuta al fatto di ospitare il primo Campionato del Mondo UCI della storia pesava come un macigno sulle spalle degli abitanti di Durango.

Poi accadde. Il trentacinquenne Ned, che gareggiava su un prototipo Stumpjumper Epic Ultimate con congiunzioni in titanio ed una forcella ammortizzata Rock Shox nera antracite, aveva sganciato Tim Gould (Gran Bretagna) e Thomas Frischknecht (Svizzera), unici veri avversari su un campo di 130 corridori, e si stava dirigendo a tutta velocità verso il traguardo della pista di sci di Purgatory. Salvo i quasi 10.000 spettatori in delirio, The Captain era solo. "E' stato più che altro un sollievo", direbbe oggi Ned se glielo domandaste, ma come disse Greg Herbold, un altro abitante di Durango e vincitore del primo campionato mondiale di donwhill: "Stare lassù e ricevere la medaglia per la quale avevo lavorato così duramente... mi sentivo come Miss America" - anche se, certamente, è più corretto considerare Ned, come Mr.America!

*The Captain non fu l'unico campione iridato di Specialized a Durango — anche Lisa Muhich guadagnò la vittoria nella categoria Veterani Donne mentre Sara Ballantyne si fece sfuggire per poco la vittoria nella gara Elite Donne.

48 & 49
STUMPJUMPER M2
Il dipartimento della difesa svela alcuni dei suoi segreti.
"Chi ha mai sentito parlare di compositi metal/matrix?" Era questa la domanda comparsa il 1 aprile 1991 in un articolo del San Francisco Chronicle. Poiché questi materiali erano stati tenuti segreti grazie al Munitions Control Act (che limitava lo scambio di informazioni sui materiali ibridi alluminio/ossido di alluminio), non molte persone senza un'autorizzazione espressa da parte della sicurezza nazionale erano informate al riguardo. A quel tempo non vi era un singolo prodotto di consumo al mondo realizzato in matrice metallica ed alla tecnologia di quel tempo quasi non era permesso lavorarlo o saldarlo; ma Jim Merz, Mark Winter, Mark DiNucci ed il resto del team di Specialized, scoprirono il segreto di quel materiale da 'corsa allo spazio'. Il risultato fu la Stumpjumper M2, il primo prodotto in assoluto non 'puntato verso Mosca', realizzato in composito metal/matrix.

Concepito originariamente per le parti anteriori dei satelliti e gli alberi di trasmissione dei carri armati, l'M2 era considerato 10% più resistente e 20% più duro dell'alluminio convenzionale. Secondo i 'cervelloni' del Pentagono, la sua robustezza derivava dai cristalli di ossido di alluminio, un materiale ceramico, intrappolato nella struttura reticolare microscopica della base di alluminio serie 6000 del materiale. Leggero e resistente come si pensava che fosse, trasformarlo in un telaio di bicicletta non sarebbe stata un'impresa tanto semplice.

Così, proprio come per le ruote in fibra di carbonio a tre razze (sì, quello stesso design che un tal americano utilizzò ad un certo punto della sua carriera, carriera che culminerà con sette vittorie del Tour de France) che il team di Specialized aveva creato in collaborazione con DuPont l'anno precedente, venne chiesto aiuto ad un altro gigante dell'industria. Il partner per il progetto del materiale MMC della Stumpjumper M2 fu Duralcan, una delle società controllate della seconda azienda di alluminio più grande al mondo. Gli scienziati dell'MMC presso la Duralcan di San Diego misero a punto la formula giusta per le tubazioni, mentre il team di Morgan Hill realizzò il progetto (incluso il compito di realizzare le estremità a spessori differenziati dei tubi in questo materiale durissimo) e pensò a come saldare i componenti. Infine, Specialized si unì con un altro partner, Anodizing Inc, per realizzare un nuovo impianto di produzione a Portland, creato appositamente per estrudere i tubi in M2 e saldarli in una struttura telaistica. I due partners riuscirono a reinventare i processi di estrusione e spessorazione differenziata, grazie ai quali, con il tempo i telai in M2 divennero sempre più leggeri.

Certamente per realizzare un telaio più leggero e resistente, Specialized non scelse la strada più rapida ed economica, ma quando mai Mike ha detto a qualcuno di scegliere la strada più facile?

50 & 51
PASSIONE
C'è solo una cosa che Mike vi dirà di avere imparato in tutti questi anni: "Se volete vincere, fate un gioco per il quale sentite di avere sentimento, un gioco per il quale sentite di aver un'autentica passione."

Così torniamo al 1989, quando Specialized aveva la necessità di un supporto pubblicitario e cercava qualcuno che fosse un appassionato narratore, perché stava iniziando la produzione delle mountain bike. Un pizzico di fortuna ne porta dell'altra e... voilà, come per magia riuscì ad agganciare una delle migliori agenzie: Goodby, Silverstein e Partners. Sapete chi è GSP? E' l'agenzia che ha curato i più popolari spot americani, la stessa che in questi ultimi anni ha curato il rilancio del consumo del latte con la famosa campagna 'Got milk?' Poi la sorpresa. Specialized scoprì che la 'S' di GSP, Rich Silverstein, era un appassionato ciclista, un tipo asciutto che si vedeva spesso partire da casa sua, nella Contea di Marin, in mountain bike per proseguire oltre il "Golden Gate Bridge" fino ad arrivare alla sede generale di GSP a San Francisco.

Il resto è una bella storia. Sebbene impegnati con alcuni clienti come Anheuser-Busch, Morgan Stanley, Haagen-Dazs, Saturn e Hewlett—Packard, i creativi di GSP interpretarono quasi tutte le migliori campagne promozionali che si rammentino sull'attività di Specialized.

La lezione che si può trarre in questo caso? Sia che si tratti di mountain bike, di pubblicità per la birra BudLight o di una catena di panetterie, sarà comunque un'impresa difficile da realizzare se non ci si mette passione.

52 & 53
STUMPJUMPER FIELD GUIDE/1992 S-WORKS EPIC ULTIMATE*
*La bicicletta qui illustrata rappresenta un raro prototipo sperimentale mai commercializzato con questo montaggio.

Telaio. Dal 1990 al 1995 Specialized ha costruito nella sua sede centrale di Morgan Hill, California, circa 1.500 telai titanio/carbonio Epic Ultimate di peso inferiore alle 3 libbre (1360 g). La costruzione di Stumpjumper Epic Ultimate in titanio/carbonio, la prima a quel tempo, fu in seguito imitata dai costruttori di prodotti di alta gamma per oltre un decennio.

Congiunzioni. Versione ulteriormente migliorata della Stumpjumper Epic standard, la Stumpjumper Epic Ultimate utilizzava congiunzioni in titanio realizzate dalla Merlin Metalworks di Cambridge, Massachussetts. A causa degli elevati costi delle materie prime ed al lavoro di sub-appalto, questi telai si rivelarono un investimento particolarmente oneroso per l'azienda.

I tubi dei telai delle prime Epic Ultimate erano realizzati in materiale composito ad altissimo modulo che si rivelò troppo fragile per essere utilizzato con profitto; per la maggior parte dei telai Epic Ultimate si decise quindi di ricorrere a tubi con modulo elastico più basso prodotti dalla Maclean Quality Composites di Salt Lake City, Utah. Forcella. Sebbene presentata con una Future Shock FSX Specialized, progettata in carbonio/titanio, la Stumpjumper Epic Ultimate, prodotta fino al 1995, non fu mai venduta dotata di forcella ammortizzata. Fu invece commercializzata con una forcella Direct Drive in chromoly dal comportamente abbastanza elastico.

Edizione limitata. Nel 1995 furono realizzati gli ultimi telai della Stumpjumper Epic Ultimate, tutti costruiti da Brian Lucas a Morgan Hill. Ognuno dei 60 telai possiede un numero di serie esclusivo, apposto su una targhetta applicata sul tubo orizzontale del telaio. A Ned Overend fu assegnato il N. 1 per commemorare la sua vittoria dei Campionati del Mondo del 1990 in sella ad una Ultimate.

54 & 55
SMITHSONIAN
Musei e mountain bike? Probabilmente vi chiederete quanto hanno in comune tra loro una vera e propria istituzione culturale fondata a Washington D.C. oltre 100 anni fa grazie ad una donazione di un aristocratico inglese ed i bikers sui singletracks. Come vedremo a breve, qualche punto di collegamento esiste!

James Smithson, scienziato ed esploratore che lasciò in donazione poco più di mezzo milione di dollari al popolo statunitense per costruire un'istituzione che promuovesse "la crescita e la diffusione della conoscenza", era stato da giovane uno studente brillante, quindi un appassionato ricercatore scientifico e, soprattutto, un ragazzo amante dell'avventura. Era conosciuto per aver rischiato la vita, incluso un mezzo annegamento mentre stava raccogliendo materiale per osservazioni geologiche in un tour delle Isole Ebridi al largo della costa nord-occidentale della Scozia, ed avrebbe apprezzato l'energia e l'inventiva dei primi pionieri della mountain bike.

Oggi, l'istituzione dello Smithsonian si è trasformata nel più grande complesso di musei del mondo ed ospita i musei nazionali ed i centri di ricerca più importanti d'America, come il Museo della Storia Naturale, il Museo della Storia Americana, lo Zoo Nazionale, il Museo Nazionale Aeronautico e Aerospaziale, il Museo Nazionale delle Arti e dell'Industria, la rivista Smithsonian e, in un piccolo angolo del Museo Nazionale di Storia Americana, la Specialized Stumpjumper.

Un giorno, intorno al 1989, lo Smithsonian scoprì la mountain bike e, con l'incarico di catalogare i migliori esempi di trasporto che avevano cambiato l'America, contattò telefonicamente l'ufficio di Specialized a Morgan Hill. 'Potreste inviarci una bici?' 'Certamente' rispose Mike. Ora allo Smithsonian, a far polvere insieme a tutti gli altri oggetti, dalle navi a vapore alle navicelle spaziali, c'è anche una Stumpjumper. Speriamo che almeno mantengano le gomme in pressione!

56 & 57
COME RIUSCIRE A VENDERE UN'OSSESSIONE?
Porsche sembra riuscirci piuttosto bene.
L'invito giunse dallo stesso Harm Lagaay. Essendo olandese con forte accento tedesco, era difficile capire se il capo della divisione progettazione della Porsche stesse facendo sul serio o scherzasse. Specialized poteva inviare alcuni ingegneri nel laboratorio super segreto di Weissach per discutere della realizzazione del telaio in titanio/carbonio da 2,7 libbre (1224 g) della Stumpjumper Epic Ultimate in versione Porsche Design. Difficile rifiutare un'offerta del genere.

Così, alcuni membri del team Specialized fecero i bagagli, prepararono i passaporti e si recarono nel laboratorio che il buon Dottor Lagaay aveva costruito. Ciò che li attendeva a Weissach era un atelier con oltre mille tra i migliori ingegneri del mondo, tutti ossessionati da un unico glorioso obiettivo: progettare e realizzare il meglio. Auto costruite esclusivamente per le gare, vetture progettate per testare e verificare carburanti alternativi o sperimentare l'utilizzo di nuovi materiali, oppure ancora realizzate esclusivamente come studi di design. Il budget sembrava infinito, esattamente come la produzione di magnifiche idee, e sebbene da Weissach uscissero regolarmente auto leggendarie ed altri prodotti di consumo, non vi era alcuna direttiva per cui dalla fabbrica dovesse scaturire sempre qualcosa di immediatamente commerciabile. Si trattava di Ricerca e Sviluppo allo stato puro. Alla fine, la bicicletta in versione Porsche Spider non fu mai realizzata, ma il tempo trascorso nella Foresta Nera diede il suoi frutti: il laboratorio di Weissach riprodotto in versione Specialized, proprio a Morgan Hill.

Fin dall'inizio, il programma prevedeva di concedere agli ingegneri ed ai progettisti più quotati di Specialized la massima libertà nel condurre il lavoro, ovvero eliminare ogni tipo di restrizione ed abbandonare tutti i preconcetti. Ignorare questioni economiche, tradizioni e tempistica per perseguire un unico semplice obiettivo: realizzare le migliori biciclette del mondo. E' stato un successo? Le biciclette S-Works hanno portato sul podio i corridori nei Campionati Mondiali su asfalto ed in fuoristrada, atleti che hanno vinto tappe ed indossato la tanto ambita Maglia Gialla nel Tour de France, atleti che hanno conquistato medaglie agli X Games e vinto l'Ironman. C'è anche una grande quantità di biciclette e componenti che non hanno mai lasciato il laboratorio; esse contenevano alcune idee buone e molte probabilmente finiranno per essere applicate in altre biciclette ed in altri tempi, ma non è questo lo scopo delle S-Works: il concetto fondamentale è realizzare il meglio, indipendentemente da tutto il resto.

58 & 59

SOSPENSIONI SPECIALIZED?

L'ammortizzatore del futuro?
Quando The Captain vinse i Campionati del Mondo del 1990 a Durango, sulla sua Specialized Epic Ultimate aveva montato una forcella ammortizzata prototipo RockShox RS-1. Il fatto che Ned ed altri corridori di primo piano (come Greg Herbold) usassero il nuovo componente per questa importantissima competizione fu un chiaro messaggio: le forcelle ammortizzate rappresentavano il futuro.

Cogliendo questa opportunità, Specialized si mise a lavorare ad una forcella ammortizzata di propria progettazione. Dopo aver testato alcuni modelli di RS-1, facendoli correre e strapazzandoli, non ci volle molto perché la squadra di progettisti di Morgan Hill si rendesse conto che sarebbe stata un'impresa tutt'altro che facile riuscire a progettare qualcosa che fosse migliore dei modelli con meccanismo interno ad aria/olio creati dal fondatore di RockShox Paul Turner. Così, si recarono al quartier generale di Turner a Mountain View, California e conclusero un accordo con lui: i tecnici Specialized, guidati da Mark Winter, avrebbero realizzato le parti esterne della forcella mentre RockShox avrebbe fornito i più complessi componenti idraulici interni e la mano d'opera.

Nel 1992 una linea di forcelle Future Shock venne montata sulle mountain bike Specialized, ma, a onor del vero, bisogna ammettere che le prime forcelle erano molto simili a quelle che RockShox produceva con il suo marchio. Poi arrivò la Future Shock FSX. Progettata da Winter, la FSX era un modello studiato senza vincoli di tipo economico ed analogo a quello di cui era dotato il telaio in carbonio e titanio della Specialized Epic Ultimate (sebbene le due parti non siano mai state vendute assieme). Analizzando la forcella, equipaggiata di componenti interne aria/olio della RockShox Mag21, la FSX fu la prima ad usare foderi in carbonio che dovettero essere messi a punto, progettati e prodotti proprio per quel preciso scopo. Detta così ha tutta l'aria di essere un operazione costosa, ed infatti lo fu; si dice che ciascun fodero in carbonio costasse più di 100 dollari. I tubi in materiale composito, la struttura ed i supporti in lega di alluminio lavorati su macchine CNC rendevano la FSX tanto più leggera quanto più costosa di qualsiasi altra forcella in commercio. "A quel punto fummo consapevoli che la forcella Specialized era effettivamente migliore della nostra", ha commentato Mike McAndrews, il guru delle sospensioni presso Specialized, che a quel tempo lavorava alla RockShox con l'amico d'infanzia Turner. "Ma era anche qualcosa che non potevano permetterci di produrre."

Alla fine, tuttavia, la competizione fra i produttori di sospensioni fece comprendere che, per Morgan Hill, continuare ad operare nel settore delle forcelle non era conveniente. Così, come per i deragliatori, i cerchi ed i pedali, Specialized tornò a selezionare i modelli più idonei tra una serie di ottimi marchi del settore. Significa forse che Specialized sia fuori dal gioco per sempre? Difficile rispondere, per certo Specialized è sempre stata capace di cogliere le opportunità.

62 & 63

FUTURE SHOCK REAR

Cosa accade quando gli ingegneri di Specialized mettono mano su di un carro posteriore austriaco?

Noi la chiamiamo "quella del '91". Nei dieci anni successivi al lancio della prima Stumpjumper, il mondo off-road era esploso in un modo che nessuno avrebbe mai previsto. I modelli full-suspended spuntavano ovunque come funghi. Il problema era che la maggior parte di loro erano vere e proprie mostruosità inefficienti. A quel tempo le sospensioni delle biciclette erano così complesse ed inaffidabili che molti, nella sede generale di Specialized, non erano neanche convinti che fossero una trovata efficace.

Tuttavia, avendo ben presente non cosa fossero ma cosa sarebbero potute diventare, Mike affidò al suo team l'incarico di progettare una bicicletta biammortizzata senza compromessi. Una che si pedalasse adeguatamente anche quando si trasmette la potenza della pedalata alla catena, che mantenesse il controllo ed il comfort in ogni momento, che fosse leggera (peso ipotizzato inferiore alle 27 libbre - 12,25 Kg), che fosse affidabile e di facile manutenzione. Anche oggi sarebbe un BHAG (Big, Hairy, Audacious Goal – obiettivo audace, ambizioso e difficile), e nel '91 gran parte della tecnologia che avrebbe reso possibile una full-suspended di quel tipo non esisteva nemmeno.

Lavorando oltre un anno al progetto, gli ingegneri John O'Neil, Mark Winter e Mark DiNucci prepararono svariati prototipi ed analizzarono minuziosamente ogni progetto su cui riuscirono a mettere le mani. Alcuni erano buoni, ma nessuno era perfetto. Così continuarono a costruire Bici-Frankenstein ed ad ascoltare qualsiasi Frankenstein-Biker che bussasse alla loro porta (del resto è proprio così che Nike scoprì Air). Finalmente, l'ingegnere austriaco Horst Leitner, che negli anni '70 aveva lavorato per i giganti europei dell'auto e dei motocicli, illuminò i cervelli del gruppo con un progetto multi-link che sarebbe poi diventato la FSR. Per DiNucci e gli altri progettisti, Horst era un guru della progettazione di motociclette in possesso di una sfilza di brevetti a suo nome; per Horst, Specialized disponeva delle risorse necessarie per mettere a punto il suo progetto e ripetere il successo ottenuto con la Stumpjumper.

Con i primi prototipi di carro posteriore con articolazione multi-link alla mano, DiNucci e Co. realizzarono le prime FSR amputando il carro posteriore dai telai già esistenti della Stumpjumper, sostituendolo con uno degli swing-arms di Horst. Con un cumulo di bici da rottamare grande come uno stadio (e un nuovo team di tester creato appositamente per il progetto), alla fine dalla progettazione si passò alla produzione. Forse un po' troppo rapidamente. Nell'estate del 1993 le prime centinaia di biciclette prodotte dovettero essere rottamate, allorché si scoprì che l'originario supporto dell'ammortizzatore presente sul tubo verticale non si era dimostrato abbastanza robusto. Come ha dichiarato DiNucci "Abbiamo fatto un'esperienza abbastanza comune, quella di esserci lanciati a capofitto in un progetto e prendere delle decisioni istintivamente. Non disponevamo dei sistemi di prova e di sviluppo necessari per una bici così complessa come la FSR". Ed è qui che risiede l'importanza della FSR per il mondo di Specialized: fu una bicicletta che fece inceppare tutto l'apparato e costrinse Morgan Hill a ripensare al modo di condurre le attività di ricerca e sviluppo. "Improvvisamente il piccolo apparato non era più sufficiente: era necessario creare una vera struttura di prova e progettazione", ha commentato Chris Murphy, da anni nella divisione Marketing e Ricerca e Sviluppo di Specialized.

64 & 65

CACTUS CUP

L'apertura di stagione sponsorizzata da Specialized.
Il fascino della Cactus Cup, per gran parte degli anni '90 gran classica non ufficiale di apertura della stagione, era innegabile: trascorrere alcuni giorni (o qualcuno in più se si riusciva a trovarne il tempo) correndo e gareggiando nel caldo deserto di Sonora con cinque o sei mila amici? Non sarebbe stato affatto male. "Della Cactus Cup, non ricordo molto delle singole gare, ma ricordo di essermi divertito moltissimo in ognuna di loro" ha commentato Richard Cunningham, giornalista, veterano della mountain bike ed uno dei primi costruttori di telai.

Come per Lago di Havasu o Daytona, la localizzazione temporale della Cactus Cup era importantissima. La data di metà marzo, non solo dava ai corridori una rapida ed efficace possibilità di verificare il livello di allenamento invernale senza sottostare alla pressione della Coppa del Mondo, ma offriva anche al mondo del business del ciclismo l'opportunità di poter avere un primo approccio all'imminente stagione. Nel suo periodo di maggior successo, la Cactus Cup era il luogo, lontano dai saloni dell'industria - che si svolgevano ogni anno in autunno - dove la frenesia degli affari, di azioni promozionali e vendite di biciclette, raggiungeva il culmine.

Con gli anni i percorsi variarono via via che il corpo urbano di Scottsdale si espandeva verso nord, inghiottendo i sentieri e lasciando dietro di sè solo parti e pezzi di tracciato, ma due cose rimasero una costante della Cactus Cup: le rocce ed il salto dei cactus cholla. Con una pressione di esercizio adeguata ed un po' di 'Slime' nelle camere d'aria, si riusciva a tamponare le forature, ma la tortuosità del percorso, che neanche un romanzo di Umberto Eco riusciva ad immaginare, rendeva praticamente impossibile evitare le spine dei cactus.

Per i corridori, sia professionisti che dilettanti, la struttura dell'evento era assolutamente unica nel suo genere: quattro tappe, inclusi un percorso a cronometro, il dirt criterium, il Fatboy criterium sotto le luci di Scottsdale downtown ed una gara di cross-country atipica che, negli ultimi anni, includeva perfino curve in appoggio e table-top jumps per chiudere la festa. I corridori con la 'S' sul petto conquistarono un bel po' di trofei a Scottsdale; Steve Tilford, da tempo corridore Specialized, fu quasi imbattibile nella specialità Fatboy criterium, vincendo ben 21 gare.

L'atmosfera che si respirava sotto il grande tendone da circo ed il programma multispecialistico della competizione era così ben strutturato che intorno alla metà degli anni '90, la Cactus Cup fece i bagagli e iniziò la sua tournée per il mondo. Si tennero edizioni della Cactus Cup nell'Illinois, nell'Ohio, in Canada, in Francia, in Germania ed in Giappone (dove continua a vivere), località che non erano abituate ad eventi di un certo spessore ma che li sapevano riconoscere al volo quando ne vedevano uno.

66 & 67

STUMPJUMPER FIELD GUIDE/1994 S-WORKS FSR

Telaio. Progettato da Mark DiNucci e Mark Winter, il triangolo anteriore Direct Drive, leggero ma ancora rigido utilizzato sulla FSR del 1994 rappresenta l'apice del lavoro di Specialized sui telai in materiali ferrosi.

Carro ammortizzato. Sviluppato in collaborazione con il fondatore di Amp Research, Horst Leitner, il sistema di sospensione FSR fu progettato per essere completamente attivo e completamente indipendente dalla pedalata per migliorarne comfort, controllo ed efficienza. Nel corso degli anni il modello FSR si è dimostrato sorprendentemente versatile.

Forcella. Sviluppata in collaborazione con Rock Shox, la forcella della FSX utilizza i componenti idraulici interni della Rock Shox Mag 21 modificati in combinazione con dei foderi in fibra di carbonio Specialized ed un archetto di rinforzo in lega M2.

Comandi cambio. Prodotti per la prima volta nel 1993, i comandi rotativi SRAM SRT 500 8 velocità furono i primi cambi di alta gamma realizzati dall'azienda di Chicago costruiti specificatamente per la competizione.

Coperture. Battezzata con il nome di un album dei Pink Floyd, Umma Gumma fu la prima gomma a mescola morbida ad essere introdotta sul mercato. Forse troppo all'avanguardia per il suo tempo, questa copertura non trovò mai molto seguito, pertanto ad un certo punto si decise di interromperne la produzione.

70 & 71

NON SOLO GAREGGIARE, MA VINCERE

È facile volare quando si ha una 'S' sul petto.

Biglietti aerei? Volete parlare dell'acquisto di biglietti aerei? Da che Mike affidò a Laurence Malone, il nostro primo corridore sponsorizzato, le chiavi del nostro furgone, Specialized ha speso milioni di dollari per mandare centinaia di atleti e squadre di supporto tecnico in giro per il mondo alla ricerca di una sola cosa: il gradino più alto del podio.

Aprite la copertina dell'albo d'oro delle competizioni e vedrete che gli uomini e le donne con la 'S' sul petto hanno lasciato il loro segno con la stessa ferocia di un pit bull di Detroit e l'efficienza di una Lexus. I risultati? I corridori di mountain bike sponsorizzati da Specialized, hanno vinto 5 campionati mondiali Elite UCI, decine di gare della Coppa del Mondo UCI e titoli di Coppa del Mondo; e così tanti Campionati Nazionali NORBA e Campionati Nazionali che ne abbiamo perso il conto.

Se da una lato per i corridori con la maglia rossa, vincere era l'unica cosa importante, per Specialized, l'obiettivo era offrire ai migliori corridori esistenti al mondo il materiale tecnico progettato specificamente per aiutarli ad andare veloci. Una vera e propria ossessione. Risulta chiaro che senza il team di agonisti non vi sarebbe stata nessuna S-Works e senza S-Works non ci sarebbe stata alcuna Stumpjumper in fibra di carbonio, o nessun ammortizzatore Brain in grado di riconoscere la differenza tra una sollecitazione indotta dal terreno e l'azione dei muscoli sui pedali.

72

LA MIA STUMPJUMPER N.3

Vedran Novak
Da ex-rifugiato politico è tornato alla vita normale su una Stumpjumper.
30 anni, Verdan viveva a Zagabria, Croazia. Quando la guerra civile devastò il suo paese negli anni '90, divenne uno delle migliaia di rifugiati che trovarono un rifugio sicuro in Serbia. Non si vedono molte biciclette da corsa nei campi profughi per il semplice motivo che la gente che abbandona le proprie case portandosi via tutto sulle proprie spalle non ha posto per le due ruote. In Serbia, Verdan ed il resto della popolazione croata era sotto il regime repressivo di Slobodan Milosevic. Quando è difficile soddisfare le necessità primarie, la vita non è affatto semplice ed una mountain bike è un lusso che nessuno può permettersi. "Le cose andavano talmente male che non avrei neppure potuto immaginare il giorno in cui sarei andato di nuovo in bicicletta," commenta Vedran ricordando il tempo trascorso in Serbia.

Fortunatamente per Vedran (e per il resto del mondo), Milosevic è stato destituito e la vita nei Balcani è tornata lentamente alla normalità. Vedran ha messo da parte i soldi ed è riuscito a comprarsi una Stumpjumper Pro usata in ottime condizioni. Da allora va in bicicletta tutti i giorni e dice che non vorrebbe mai fermarsi. "Prima di avere la mia nuova Stumpjumper, mai pensavo che mi sarei potuto divertire così tanto con una due ruote! La mia mountain bike mi aiuta a ricordare in ogni istante quanto può essere bella la vita".

73

IL DECOLLO

Il cortometraggio Pulp Traction consegna alla storia la nascita del 'freeride'.
Un tipo vestito di Lycra che si precipita giu' da una discesa da incubo su di una hardtail con forcella da due pollici di corsa, ben prima dell'arrivo della Marzocchi Bomber a singola piastra? Non sembrerebbe poi tanto 'freeride'. Di sicuro in quegli anni non si vedevano in giro "numeri" sui pedali come il "tailwhip" od il "back flip" od ancora il "suicide drop", ma quello era freeride. Le radici del freeride. Grazie al regista di Pulp Traction, Greg Stump, nativo della British Columbia nonché leggenda dello sci, Pulp Traction fu il primo cortometraggio sulla mountain bike a puntare l'obbiettivo sul North Shore e sul nuovo scenario che in seguito avrebbe segnato la nascita del fenomeno 'freeride'.
Pulp Traction è un documentario che ha reso popolari i pionieri Ritchie Schley e Brett Tippie e che ha fissato nel tempo un pezzo della nostra storia, quando gli unici pantaloncini sportivi comodi conosciuti erano quelli per il basket e la parola "long travel" significava al massimo un viaggio senza scalo fino in Cina.

Dato che allora non vi erano dei registi specializzati nelle riprese d'azione aventi come soggetto le mountain bikes, il reparto marketing di Specialized si rivolse a Stump, regista specializzato in pellicole dedicate allo sci ed autore di 'P-Tex', 'Lies' e 'DuctTape', nonché di altri classici sugli sport invernali, per produrre un film che catturasse l'essenza delle corse sui pendii vertiginosi, dei paesaggi stupendi e con uno sguardo rivolto allo stile di vita dei biker. "La maggior parte di noi aveva già interpretato film sullo sci e lo snowboard. Così, quando vennero per girare le riprese non facemmo altro che riproporre le stesse cose che già avevamo fatto sulla neve, con la differenza che avremmo dovuto farle su ripidi pendii inframmezzati da salti", ha commentato Schley. "L'altro giorno eravamo di nuovo in uno dei luoghi in cui erano state effettuate le riprese di 'Pulp Traction' e ci siamo messi a ridere ricordando quello che eravamo riusciti a fare con una hardtail con forcella di soli due pollici di escursione".

Certo non è stato facile, ma abbiamo fissato per sempre sulla pellicola l'atto di nascita di un nuovo sport.

74 & 75

NIENTE DI PIÙ. NULLA

Il colpo di grazia alla hardtail.

Allenarsi ed allenarsi, allenarsi ed allenarsi ancora per essere il più veloce nel cross-country e scoprire che, oltre ad un paio di quadricipiti formato maxi, ti ritrovi tirato come una top model. Questa è l'idea che sta alla base della FSRxc: spogliare una bicicletta ammortizzata di tutto tranne che dell' indispensabile, proprio come il fisico di un corridore di XC.

Il tempo, comunque, ha portato i suoi frutti: nel 1996 le mountain bike con le sospensioni acquistavano progressivamente popolarità e diffusione sul mercato, ma con esse guadagnavano anche peso. Con questa implicazione persero molto del loro fascino agli occhi delle persone che erano più interessate alla velocità ed all'efficienza che non alla robustezza.

Così, mente tutti andavano in una direzione, il team di Specialized, composto da Ben Capron, Mark Norris, Mike Ducahrme e Jeff Pint decise di andare controcorrente. Essi, ottimizzarono, tagliarono e curarono ogni minimo dettaglio del telaio con maniacale attenzione al peso fino ad arrivare alla creazione della FSRxc da 3 pollici di corsa (76 mm), un telaio che aveva sì una corsa inferiore di un pollice rispetto alla FSR originaria, ma pesava meno ed aveva un'estrema maneggevolezza e precisione di guida. Ducharme, Capron e compagni studiarono ogni millimetro quadrato del telaio, affinandone i diametri e gli spessori dei tubi, accorciandone le estremità rinforzate ed rendendo minimale il design del telaietto di supporto sella. Tuttavia, il principale segreto che si celava dietro la leggerezza della FSRxc era che l'ammortizzatore, la biella ed i foderi obliqui si articolavano tutti su di un solo perno: erano così necessarie solo la metà delle parti meccaniche solitamente impiegate.

Il risultato fu una delle più leggere mountain bike con carro a parallelogramma articolato mai costruite; equipaggiata con un gruppo di componenti di alta gamma, la FSRxc fermava l'ago della bilancia ben al di sotto delle 25 libbre (11.3 kg). Di questa bicicletta un esemplare perfettamente utilizzabile in gara, del peso di soli 20,6 libbre (9.3 kg), fu esposto al salone di "Interbike" del 1998.

Ma perché mai dovreste solo credere alle mie parole? Verificate quanto è stato citato da un biker nel sito MTBR.com nel 1999, "Non tornerò mai più indietro ad una hardtail. Provate a salire su questa mountain bike e sarete d'accordo con me: non desidererete nient'altro."

78 & 79

NAPALM!

Quando Shaun Palmer, l'atleta più famoso al mondo, comparve sulla scena della mountain bike, lasciò dietro di sé terra bruciata e multe non pagate.

Il fatto è che non era un mountain biker. Veramente non si considerò mai un biker, semplicemente iniziò per caso, provò a salire su di una mountain bike esattamente come avrebbe fatto su di uno snowboard o su di una moto o in una delle sue numerose Cadillac.

Non era un mountain biker, era una rock star, quel genere di persona che non ci si sarebbe mai nemmeno immaginati poter esistere nel mondo dei biker. Fin dal suo primo giorno su di una tavola da snowboard, al Donner Ski Ranch, l'uomo che chiamavano "Mini-Shred" (qualcosa come il Piccolo Petardo) conquistò il mondo degli sport sulla neve. Poi un giorno esplose la rabbia. "Nel 1992 mia nonna morì, così diventai un vero e proprio idiota: litigavo nei bar, bevevo, non andavo da nessuna parte. Poi mi rimisi in sesto, iniziai a riversare tutta la mia rabbia per la sua morte dedicandomi completamente allo sport. Per me fu come… Al diavolo! Ho intenzione di vincere tutto'." Così "Mini-Shred" si trasformò in puro Napalm e si mise a battere chiunque incontrasse al suo stesso gioco. "Mi fa sentire bene", fu il suo lapidario commento.

Nel 1996 era passato alla mountain bike e con le Olimpiadi alle porte ed il denaro investito in tecnologia nel settore dello sport, non avrebbe potuto scegliere momento migliore. Palmer accolse gli elogi e la luce dei riflettori: era al centro dell'attenzione ed è per questo che le gare di mountain bike di fine millennio saranno ricordate. Abito di lamè d'oro, Motor-Home Prevost dipinto da Troy Lee ed un contratto a sei cifre (anche se Mike e quasi tutti gli altri dell'ambiente sostengono che tali cifre fossero piu' che sovrastimate). "Il ragazzo non ha mai preso la cosa abbastanza seriamente per poter vincere un titolo di Campione del Mondo, ma sicuramente ha fatto molto parlare di sé", ha commentato l'ex assistente tecnico e garante delle cauzioni delle innumerevoli multe stradali prese da "Mini-Shred", Joe 'Buck' Buckley.

80

ENDURO

Perché si dice "all mountain" e non "easy mountain."

Con l'avvicinarsi della fine del millennio alcuni avevano preannunciato il caos. La crisi dell'anno 2000 era sulla bocca di tutti. "La fine del mondo è vicina", proclamavano certe sette religiose. Di fatto non fu così, ma questa è tutta un'altra storia.

Per i corridori off-road il caos si rifletteva nel modo in cui venivano considerate le mountain bikes in rapporto ai percorsi e di come le due cose si potessero coniugare al meglio. Grazie alla popolarità guadagnata dalle mountain bikes, i luoghi facilmente raggiungibili (quelli con parcheggi in prossimità dell'inizio dei percorsi) erano al limite della capienza e talvolta venivano anche chiusi perché troppo frequentati. I veri appassionati di mountain bike volevano stare lontano dalla massa e chiedevano all'industria del settore delle MTB di essere messi in grado di percorrere piste più impegnative, tracciati che la maggior parte della gente avrebbe evitato; ma poiché quel tipo di percorsi si trova generalmente in luoghi impervi e difficilmente raggiungibili, aumentare il peso o ridurre l'efficienza delle biciclette era un concetto fuori discussione.

L'esperienza ed il molto tempo trascorso sui percorsi – fortunatamente, in Specialized, andare in mountain bike è sinonimo di ricerca - ed una rivisitazione del ben collaudato design del carro posteriore a parallelogramma, che gli ingegneri avevano messo a punto con il 'guru' delle sospensioni Horst Leithner nel 1991, diede come risultato la prima Enduro. Creata nell'estate del 1999 per l'utilizzo sui percorsi piu' tecnici ed ostici, la struttura originaria della Enduro Pro era caratterizzata dal robusto telaio MAX (Manipulated Aluminum eXtrusion) Backbone con 4,6 pollici di corsa regolabile, solo 250 grammi più pesante di un FSR a corsa più corta dell'anno precedente. L'Enduro aveva inoltre un tubo orizzontale ribassato con un design 'a V' che garantiva all' utilizzatore un eccezionale valore di standover per una bicicletta con così tanta escursione. Nel modello commercializzato nell'anno 2000 il telaio venne ulteriormente alleggerito e rifinito, con l'aggiunta di parafanghi per conferire alla bicicletta lo stesso unico ed inconfondibile richiamo estetico che possiede una moto.

81

LA MIA STUMPJUMPER N.4

Bob Brewer

Da difensore a peso mosca, Bob ha perso 90 libbre (41 kg) sulla sua Stumpjumper Due anni fa, la salute di Bob Brewer non poteva essere peggiore. L'ago della bilancia indicava ben 250 libbre (113 kg) ed inoltre era iperteso; a peggiorare la situazione una malattia renale congenita. Il medico disse a Bob, 40 anni, senior account presso MSM, Inc. e padre di due bambini, che doveva perdere peso e rimettersi in forma altrimenti non sarebbe rimasto a lungo in questo mondo.

A Bob era sempre piaciuto andare in bicicletta, ma per lui non era mai stata una priorità: andava in bicicletta sperando che ciò l'avrebbe aiutato a mantenersi in buona salute, ma la sua vecchia bici era scomoda e pesante ed in generale non si divertiva un gran che. Bob ripose quindi le sue speranze sul web; fece alcune ricerche e ben presto venne a conoscenza della fama indiscussa che Specialized aveva ottenuto presso i ciclisti più appassionati e competenti. Fortunatamente Bob fece un buon affare acquistando una Stumpjumper Comp del 2004. "La differenza è sbalorditiva", ha dichiarato. "Non lascerò più la mountain bike: ora è diventata la mia nuova passione."

Oggi Bob non va più in bicicletta perché deve o perché fa bene alla salute, ma va in bicicletta perché è qualcosa di cui non può più fare a meno. "Ora mi trovo nella mia forma fisica migliore . Ho perso 90 libbre (41 Kg) ed esco con la mia mountain bike per percorrere i singletracks nei dintorni della mia abitazione 4-6 volte alla settimana."

Bob era sempre ammalato, stanco, stressato e demotivato. Oggi è stimolato, pieno di energia ed entusiasta della vita. Inoltre, sta per diventare di nuovo papà. Sembra che la Stumpjumper abbia colpito di nuovo.

82 & 83

COSA SI PUÒ IMPARARE DA UN SOBBALZO?

Abbastanza per far sì che i tuoi ammortizzatori funzionino soltanto quando lo vuoi tu.

Avete mai provato a comprimere le sospensioni di una full da cross country di un 'Pro' spingendo sul manubrio o sulla sella prima che inizi una gara di Coppa del Mondo? La cosiddetta forcella ammortizzata anteriore della loro bici non si muove molto. Infatti, la maggior parte degli atleti hanno le forcelle così precaricate, che non vi è quasi corsa. Beh', se a loro piace così e se riescono a vincere, che male c'è?

Chiedete a Mike McAndrews, da sempre appassionato di ammortizzatori ed ingegnere presso Specialized e lui vi dirà cosa c'è di male: ha trascorso anni ed anni a realizzare ammortizzatori in grado di funzionare davvero bene. Quindi, quando un gruppo di corridori del team Specialized disse di volere degli ammortizzatori che si muovessero solo quando sollecitati da un urto di una certa entità, Mick, con un approccio positivo verso qualsiasi tipo di innovazione nel campo delle sospensioni, ebbe l'intuizione che faceva al caso loro.

Un amico ingegnere alla FoMoCo, una volta, aveva parlato a Mick di un ammortizzatore che aveva progettato e che si comprimeva solo quando la ruota dell'auto colpiva un grosso dosso. A Detroit lo avevano battezzato "ammortizzatore Jerk shock", proprio perché era necessario un forte impatto per attivarlo. Così Mick iniziò a trafficare con la sua versione di "ammortizzatore d'urto" che a Morgan Hill chiamavano scherzosamente "l'ammortizzatore di Jerk".

Mick pensava che fosse un'idea brillante e poiché l'ammortizzatore riconosceva la differenza tra una spinta proveniente da un impatto con il terreno rispetto a quella provocata dai muscoli sui pedali, battezzò il progetto 'Brain' (letteralmente 'Cervello'). Quindi mise immediatamente a punto un prototipo in grado di funzionare, ma non in maniera così affidabile come lui avrebbe desiderato. Alla fine, ebbe un lampo di genio: se il cuore dell'ammortizzatore d'urto, la valvola inerziale, fosse stata spostata il più vicino possibile all'asse della ruota posteriore, tutto avrebbe funzionato meglio, più rapidamente ed in modo più affidabile. Provò e riprovò ed, alla fine, quella camera ausiliaria divenne il "Brain". Con l'aiuto di Fox per il perfezionamento dei punti più delicati e per la produzione, l'impresa venne finalmente realizzata.

Un altro fatto noto è che Filip Meirhaeghe — uno di quelli atleti che era solito gareggiare con la hardtail mantenendo la forcella precaricata al massimo - vinse un Campionato Mondiale su una Epic dotata di ammortizzatore Brain (è anche vero che Meirhaeghe fu sconfitto la stagione successiva a causa di un certo "squilibrio chimico" nel suo organismo, ma la Epic certamente non era stata 'gonfiata' con sostanze illegali!)

Oggi l'ammortizzatore Brain di Mick, dotato di una tecnologia che consente la regolazione fine in base alle caratteristiche del percorso, è così evoluto da poter essere utilizzato sia nelle competizioni che su qualsiasi altro tipo di tracciato.

86 & 87

DEMO

Una bici costruita per interpretare le acrobazie più incredibili ed 'insane' – E tutto incominciò con dei mattoncini LEGO!

Darren Barrecloth. Il signore della nuova scuola di freeride. Darren aveva bisogno di un'arma nella sua battaglia contro limiti, regole della fisica e preconcetti. Così Mike decise di commissionare la Demo, una mountain bike che, secondo le esigenze di "Bear Claw" - questo il soprannome di Darren - doveva essere caratterizzata da una escursione morbida, progressiva e molto sensibile alle asperità, una geometria sufficientemente bilanciata per i passaggi super ripidi e super stretti, un baricentro molto basso, un tubo orizzontale realizzato per consentire una grande manovrabilità ed un ottimo sistema di trasmissione della cambiata, inclusa la possibilità di ospitare un deragliatore anteriore. "Nessun problema," disse Mike, "la possiamo realizzare".

Così un gruppo di ingegneri, progettisti e product managers di Specialized, tra cui Jason Chamberlain, Brandon Sloan e Rober Egger, si buttarono nel progetto giocando con una pila di mattoncini delle costruzioni LEGO. Assemblando i mattoncini LEGO il team riuscì a costruire un modello semplice ed efficace del concetto dell'ammortizzatore alla base della Demo, che fu poi messo a punto, regolato e riesaminato prima che il mago dell'ingegneria Jason Chamberlin, si cimentasse con il suo computer per dare forma al complesso lavoro di ingegnerizzazione.

Non è necessario uno scienziato specialista in razzi spaziali per capire che giocare con i LEGO era la parte facile del progetto. Realizzare un progetto funzionale con un software per la creazione di modelli Pro/E a 3-D, costruire i prototipi nell'officina della sede centrale di Specialized a Morgan Hill e sottoporre a test continui la Demo, ha richiesto anni – due per la precisione - e centinaia di migliaia di dollari

Il risultato della maestria di Chamberlin al computer e dei numerosi collaudi e test effettuati nel North Shore dal product manager Brandon Sloan, fu un telaio ammortizzato con carro a quadrilatero con 9 pollici di corsa (228 mm) ed uno swingarm sì tradizionale, ma corredato di una sub-struttura per un totale di 6 punti di infulcro. Per rendere la Demo più rigida e robusta, Chamberlin ed i suoi collaboratori progettarono una serie di particolari forgiati a freddo, i più costosi che mai una mountain bike avesse utilizzato, compresa la forgiatura individuale più complessa mai prodotta – il monoblocco centrale che ospita l'ammortizzatore che, per la sua realizzazione richiede una pressa da 5 milioni di libbre (2.267 tonnellate!).

Chi avrebbe mai immaginato che una mountain bike creata per poter affrontare i pendii più ripidi ed i salti più lunghi sarebbe stata concepita partendo da dei mattoncini LEGO?

88 & 89

TRENT'ANNI DI PEDALATE E DI OPPORTUNITÀ

Ehi, a chi dite vecchietto?

Il grande traguardo dei 30 anni. Un tempo era una consuetudine più che una vera celebrazione; fine dell'infanzia e via con la vita nell'età adulta. E' giunto il momento di eliminare le infradito e ridurre il numero di birre tracannate prima di mezzogiorno (perlomeno nei giorni lavorativi). Comunque, nessuno voleva dirlo. L'attività che il ragazzino aveva iniziato in maniera disorganizzata vendendo attacchi manubrio e simili dalla sua roulotte a San Josè, compiva 30 anni. Il grande traguardo dei 30.

Una cosa che non si può assolutamente negare è che, nell'anno del suo 30° anniversario (della fondazione di Specialized), la Stumpjumper sia più in forma che mai. Intramontabile, ti porta ovunque desideri andare con il con il sorriso intatto. Ed il fisico? Basta dare un'occhiata alle particolarità della struttura del suo telaio color Dream Silver. Come piace dire al leggendario capo progettista di Specialized, Robert Egger, "Se è bella, allora significa anche che va bene". E con le Dolomiti a fare da sfondo è il massimo. "La bicicletta aveva bisogno di molte parti resistenti che, una volta assemblate, risultassero persino più robuste della somma delle singole parti" ha commentato Egger, il progettista che sta dietro ai gioielli Specialized che vanno sotto il nome di Enduro, Hemi e Tarmac.

90 & 91

CONTINUA A PEDALARE MR.CAPTAIN

Non si può fermare una vita vissuta sempre nelle prime posizioni del plotone.

Ancora un altro sabato notte per The Captain. Chiuso nella stanza a $99 per notte di uno dei nuovissimi hotel di una catena mondiale di alberghi. Un po' di ghiaccio sul piede destro contuso per via di un'infida caduta sullo scendiletto. Vedrà in TV le ultime notizie locali e berrà l'ultimo sorso dell'elisir di energia segreta, anche se dovrà alzarsi alle 7 del mattino. Questo è lo stile di vita di The Captain.

Ufficialmente Ned è in pensione dal 1996, ma non sembra ricordarsene. Da quando Specialized gli ha organizzato una festa di addio all'attività nell'autunno di quell'anno, Ned ha continuato a partecipare alle "World Cup" ed ai "NORBA Nationals", alle gare su strada, alle gare di hill climb, downhill (ha perfino battuto il figlio adolescente), alle gare di duathlon, triathlon, X-terra, maratone, trail races, corse adventure e quant'altro si possa immaginare. Se la gara prospetta livelli elevati di acido lattico ed un eccessivo accumulo di endorfine, The Captain sarà presente. Diavolo, proprio il giorno del suo 50° compleanno è arrivato 4° nella tremenda gara di Hillclimb sul monte Washington.

Molti dei ragazzini che di regola si lascia alle spalle non erano neppure nati quando nel 1980, Ned concluse l'"Ironman" piazzandosi al 24° posto, o nel 1983 quando vinse la sua primissima gara di mountain bike gareggiando alla "Coors Classic" con il leggendario team Ti-Raleigh (quello di Andy Hampsten, Roy Knickman e Steve Tilford) o, ancora, quando vinse sia i Campionati Europei che i Campionati Mondiali NORBA nel 1987.

Ma Ned non vuole nessun trattamento speciale né elogi extra. Al Captain non interessa avere appartamenti speciali, ha le membra indolenzite ed alle 7.00 del mattino inizia ad allenarsi come ha fatto per la maggior parte della sua vita di corridore. "Non lo faccio per cercare di dimostrare che sono più veloce dei giovani," dice "Lo faccio perché mi piace misurarmi sul campo – amo la competizione."

92 & 93

STUMPJUMPER FIELD GUIDE/2006 S-WORKS STUMPJUMPER CARBON

Per trovare il ritmo sulla bici in fibra di carbonio più confortevole che sia mai stata prodotta.

Telaio. Realizzato in materiale composito brevettato FACT Y570, ad oggi la fibra di carbonio più resistente utilizzata per costruire telai per mountain bike. La Stumpjumper S-Works in fibra di carbonio è apprezzata per il suo insieme di efficienza e grande guidabilità.

Ammortizzatore posteriore Brain con dispositivo Brain Fade. Il primo ammortizzatore che sa quando essere attivo per garantire la massima aderenza e quando rimanere rigido per migliorare l'efficienza. Il modello 2006 presenta la tecnologia Brain Fade che consente ai bikers di personalizzare ulteriormente il comportamento dell'ammortizzatore Brain.

Pneumatici. Messi a punto espressamente per una MTB da competizione come la Stumpjumper FSR Carbon, gli pneumatici Adrenaline Pro 26 x 2.0 adottano una carcassa da 120 Tpi per mantenere il peso al minimo ed un battistrada con gomma a doppia mescola per la miglior combinazione possibile di aderenza in curva e bassa resistenza offerta al rotolamento.

Manubrio. Complemento perfetto del telaio in composito della Stumpjumper FSR Carbon, la curva manubrio 'Oversize' Carbon Rise di Specialized pesa solo 175 grammi ed offre una perfetta combinazione ergonomica, con una inclinazione delle estremità di 6° verso l'alto ed 8° all'indietro.

Sella. Nuovo modello per l'anno 2006, la Rival è caratterizzata dall'esclusiva tecnologia Body Geometry di Specialized che nei test di laboratorio ha dimostrato di migliorare il flusso sanguigno nelle aree del soprassella più sensibili.

94 & 95

IL FUTURO?

Difficile dire in quale direzione ci stimo muovendo.
Persone più importanti hanno cercato di indovinare il futuro e, beh, sapete bene come è andata a finire con le previsioni circa la crisi dell'anno 2000.
Una cosa di cui siamo certi è che sia gli sperimentatori che gli ideatori di questa cultura hanno bisogno di essere tutelati. Pertanto devolveremo il 100% dei guadagni di questo libro all'IMBA ed alla Mountain Bike Hall of Fame.

SPANISH/Translation

6 & 7

DEDICACIÓN

20 horas, 20 días, hace 20 años—es difícil no recordar aquella primera salida en mountain bike. Los crujidos de las hojas y cortezas de los árboles. Le rueda delantera levantando agua y pasando por encima de todo, de casi todo lo que se encuentra en su camino. Moviéndose por el terreno inexplorado con la soltura y donaire de un gran gato. Avanzando como una XR-250. Esas primeras sensaciones o el primer golpe del pedal en la espinilla, una pequeña advertencia, pero principalmente un dolor sin importancia. Era demasiado bueno para ser verdad—el primer dulce beso imposible, el preludio de una hermosa adicción.

El mountain bike hacía esto. Tiene esta clase de poder. Descarado, pero accesible; peligroso pero con manillar ancho y elevado, sillín blando con un cuadro delgado, todo adorable al mismo tiempo. Y no contento con introducir nuevos sentimientos y pensamientos, el mountain bike atrae e iguala a la gente—doctores de las zonas residenciales con fontaneros de la ciudad y profesores del mismo país—y les lleva a lugares que ni siguiera sabían que existían. Incluso si están a la vuelta de la esquina. El mountain bike hace que la gente-gente como nosotros-regrese elevando sus endorfinas y garantice la aventura.

La historia de estas páginas hubiera podido ser un simple cuento de tecnología, pero el mountain bike nunca ha sido sólo eso. Claro que siempre miramos de reojo qué cambio u horquilla están montados en una bicicleta, pero también hay pasión y cultura. Gracias a la pasión, inspiración y entendimiento, la Stumpjumper fue originariamente imaginada como un simple modo de aumentar las sonrisas en nuestros rostros. Felizmente la gente se ha percatado y han elevado a la Stumpjumper y al resto del deporte y cultura que ha estado rodando con fuerza durante más de 25 años. Por eso, agradecemos a todo el mundo que alguna vez ha puesto su pierna encima de una mountain bike. Habéis hecho este libro, esta cultura y, en definitiva, esta vida posible.

8 & 9

EL PRÓLOGO DE LAS RUEDAS GORDAS

¿De dónde venimos?
Espera, ¿están haciendo mountain bike? Aunque han pasado algo más de veinte años desde la invención de la bici de montaña lo cierto es que parece que efectivamente eso es lo que están haciendo. Después de todo están montando en el campo, tienen neumáticos gordos y sin duda llevan una sonrisa de oreja a oreja.

De acuerdo, entonces, ¿qué decimos sobre John Finley Scott y la Schwinn Varsity de 1953 que utilizó para recorrer miles y miles de kilómetros todo terreno incluyendo la ascensión de 3.450 metros del Monte Blanco en la Sierra Mountains de California en los años sesenta? ¿Podemos considerar que estaba haciendo mountain bike?

¿Y si nos remontamos a los veinte soldados americanos que en 1.897 recorrieron algo más de 3.000 kilómetros a través del oeste de los Estados Unidos incluyendo una excursión por el Parque Nacional de Yellowstone? Sin duda alguna no estaban montando en las carreteras a través del más puro, antiguo y salvaje Oeste. En este caso ellos tampoco estaban buscando hacer algo así para darse a conocer.

Así que, ¿exactamente en qué momento simplemente se abandonó el hecho de montar por fuera de carretera y se comenzó a hacer mountain bike? ¿Fue el 1 de diciembre de 1974 en la zona de la Bahía de San Francisco cuando Russ Mahon enganchó un cambio trasero en su antigua bici tradicional que por aquel entonces se denominaban cordialmente Clunkers? ¿O fue cuando Joe Breeze por vez primera compitió con una bicicleta a medida de múltiples velocidades y neumáticos anchos en la carrera legendaria del Repack que él mismo popularizó en octubre de 1977? ¿O pudo haber sido unos años más tarde, cuando Neil Teenan, el diseñador de la primera Stumpjumper de la historia, montó con uno de los primeros prototipos por las colinas detrás de las oficinas de Specialized en San José?

Mejor que dejemos la respuesta a la pregunta de dónde exactamente comenzó el mountain bike en manos de los profesores de universidad, o a la pandilla de demonios del mountain bike que encontrarás en la taberna Zeitgeist de San Francisco una tarde cualquiera.

10 &11

CRESTED BUTTE, COLORADO

Cuando los primeros forasteros, una pandilla de cinco clunkers endemoniados de Marin se marcharon hasta Crested Butte en 1978 para "el tercer anual, segundo vigente" Pearl Pass Tour, se encontraron con las palabras de Joe Breeze, "una ciudad extractora de carbón acabada, con sus últimos mineros de pulmones negros apalancados en sus bancos entre los que la juventud bailoteaba a pie o montando en bici. Una ciudad extractora de carbón desde la "fiebre del oro" de Colorado en 1859, el Crested Butte de finales de los '70, más bien parecía bastante ensuciada, pero con su pronto acercamiento hacia el ski telemark y la terapia de la marihuana, se pensaba que era la referencia del movimiento hippy más actual. Los frecuentemente temidos y a menudo sucios residentes preferían nombres como Nube, Estrella, Tablón y Maleta (cuyo hijo es el maletín).

Gracias a la larga historia de deportes al aire libre- la ciudad tiene la distinción de ser la primera en contar con los primeros remontes para esquiar de Colorado- tanto los hippies como los más viejos mostraban una tendencia aparente hacia la euforia por los deportes al aire libre, incluida una larga aventura amorosa por la bicicleta. Por supuesto, quienes montaban en bici con anterioridad a 1978 no eran ciclistas de por sí, simplemente montaban en bici. Generalmente bicis de la variedad del depósito de basura de Denver, como viejas Schwinn, clunkers de Hawthorne y BF Goodrich, en su segunda o incluso tercera vida. Incluso sin la manta de nieve y hielo de 8 meses de duración, las calles de Crested Butte estaban prácticamente llenas de suciedad, por lo que las ruedas de gran balón siempre demostraban ser las mejores para recorrer la ciudad.

En el verano de 1976, de madrugada en el pub de la Banda Civil de Grubstake se decidió que las clunkers serían perfectas para subir empujando los 3.878 metros de altitud del Pearl Pass y bajar hasta el bar del Hotel Jerome en Aspen. En septiembre de ese mismo año, 15 compañeros y almas bien lubricadas se subieron al sillín de sus clunkers y se dirigieron hacia el norte, dirección a Aspen. Después de montar una fiesta en el Pearl Pass durante una noche entera – de acuerdo a un informe en Crested Butte, los ciclistas y personal de apoyo consumieron un barril de cerveza, tres botellas de aguardiente, nueve litros de vino y tres botellas de champagne- montaron de nuevo en sus clunkers para descender a golpes y arrastras en dirección al Hotel Jerome donde se bebieron más cervezas y siguieron prodigando la leyenda.

14 & 15

EL REY DE LAS CLUNKERS

Cada hombre, mujer o niño que tenga una mountain bike debería hacer un brindis, dedicar una canción, gritar al mar o rezar una oración en el nombre de Charles R. Kelly (también conocido como SeeKay). Desde lo más profundo de la soberanamente dura comunidad de Fairfax, en California, el señor Charles creó la primera revista del mundo sobre el mountain bike – Fat Tire Flyer - incluso mucho antes de que hubiese mountain bikes. Aunque algunos puedan atribuirse el haber inventado algo que tenga que ver con gordo -el primer cuadro, la primera bici, la primera carrera- Charlie fue el que definió el particular punto de vista de toda la pandilla de clunkers. Fue él mismo quien explicó minuciosamente al mundo lo que el término Clunking quería decir exactamente.

"Mientras las Clunkers puedan asemejarse un poco a una moto de campo ligera, su similitud se encuentra simplemente en su aspecto y el hecho de dar las curvas a alta velocidad es una experiencia única de arte y destreza. Una motocicleta tiene neumáticos grandes y amortiguadores, pero una Clunker no. Por lo tanto en cualquier imperfección de la superficie de la carretera en seguida tiende a despegar del suelo. En una curva cerrada una Clunker no tiene la aceleración instantánea que la moto utiliza para enderezarse y sin amortiguadores va todo el rato dando pequeños botes. A pesar de todo, los ciclistas más expertos toman las curvas mucho más rápido de lo que puedas llegar a imaginar."

"Derrapando a la entrada de una curva de piedra suelta en contra-peralte calculas mal. Sin control, tienes que tomar una rápida decisión: caerte por el precipicio o tirarte al suelo. Tirarte al suelo...maldita sea...camisa rota, codo ensangrentado. No hay tiempo ahora para preocuparse por ello (la camisa era vieja, como lo es el codo), ¿cómo está la bici? Ok... Monta de nuevo en ella y mete la cadena con tu mano mientras la llevas arrastrando los primeros metros. Otra vez todo en orden te pones de pie para intentar recuperar el tiempo perdido."
--Charles Kelly
Bicycling Magazine 1979

16 & 17

SPECIALIZED LOS PRIMEROS CINCO AÑOS DE EXPANSIÓN

Specialized precursora de la revolución de las ruedas gordas con toda clase de objetos.
Las ventas del primer año fueron: 60,000 $
Al año siguiente: $128,000
Al siguiente: más de 200,000 $.

"Mirando hacia el pasado las cosas avanzaban de un modo lento, pero a mí me daba la impresión de ser bastante rápido" dice Mike Sinyard, fundador y presidente de Specialized, sobre los primeros años tras comenzar a colocar los primeros ladrillos de Specialized.

Mucho antes de que la gente hiciese páginas web dedicadas a su colección de tatuajes de platos de bicicleta (es cierto, blackbirdsf.org), estando tan obsesionados por las bicis que vendieses tu única cosa de valor (un Volkswagen Microbús en el caso de Mike) y utilizar el beneficio para financiar un viaje en bicicleta por otro continente era certificablemente para echar la llave. Demonios, es todavía extraño, pero atrás en 1973 cuando Mike empaquetó su bici de paseo Bob Jackson y se marchó enseguida a Europa era verdaderamente una locura.

Tras pedalear a través del Reino Unido, Ámsterdam (en un pestañeo de ojos) y Barcelona, Mike llegó a las planas llanuras del Norte de Italia en el valle del Po, sintiéndose como cualquiera de nosotros lo haría, sin tener idea alguna de lo que estaba haciendo, pero con un sentimiento en el estómago de que algo grandioso podría suceder en cualquier momento. Y sucedió. En la forma de una chica joven que Mike conoció por casualidad en un albergue juvenil en Milán. Ella tenía conexión con el gran hombre del universo del ciclismo italiano, el señor Cino Cinelli, fundador de la empresa de cuadros y componentes que lleva su marca y que Mike le tenía considerado como una de las personas de mayor aprecio.

En el plazo de un mes Mike ya estaba de vuelta en San José en solitario pero con un enorme cargamento de componentes Cinelli. Se había gastado cada centavo que tenía en los famosos manillares, potencias y cuadros de Cino. Ahora, sin coche y sin algo como Ebay que le ayudase a mover su mercancía Milanesa, pedaleó hasta los distribuidores de bicicletas en los pueblos costeros, arrastrando un remolque lleno de componentes y vendiendo todo el equipamiento mientras proseguía su camino.

Para el bicentenario, Specialized era ya un importador de bicicletas y componentes hecho y derecho, cuya cualidad era el comercio de mercaderías favorecido por la demanda de los ciclistas de neumáticos gordos. Los cambios Huret Duopar pasados de moda, los frenos Mafac y los tubos del cuadro de Columbus. Con una clientela que incluía a la mayoría de los fabricantes de cuadros de bicicleta de la costa oeste de los Estados Unidos, Specialized era el centro del auge del negocio del ciclismo. Artesanos constructores de cuadros como Joe Breeze, Albert Eisentraut y Tom Ritchey (quien trabajaría contratado por Specialized para taladrar a mano los bujes para los Tandems), se contaban como clientes regulares y, como sus pedidos por material extraño como los pedalieres TA y tornillos de cantilever crecían sin parar, Mike se preguntaba qué es lo que estarían tramando. Lo que estaban tramando era reinventar la bicicleta y Mike estaba dispuesto a colaborar con su labor para ayudar.

20 & 21

STUMPJUMPER FIELD GUIDE/1981 STUMPJUMPER

Cuadro Diseñado por Tim Neenan de Lighthouse Bikes en Santa Cruz, la Stumpjumper original estaba soldada a TIG. Si tu cuadro tiene parrillas es de finales del '81. ¿La pintura de color azul? Se eligió porque era similar al azul ya existente en la bici de paseo Sequoia.

Potencia La legendaria potencia Palo de Golf, esta joya se modificó respecto de la versión de la potencia de BMX de aquella época. El original manillar de acero de la Stumpjumper estaba basado en el modelo Magura de manillar para motos.

Manetas de freno De serie en todas las primeras Stumpjumpers, las manetas de freno Tomaselli Racer estaban diseñadas para utilizarse con las motos de carreras de café de finales de los '70. De serie contaban con cables reforzados que mejoraban el tacto y el funcionamiento.

Neumáticos Specialized utilizó el conocimiento ganado en la creación de su exitosa línea de neumáticos de carretera para troquelar los primeros dibujos específicos para bicicleta de montaña, el Stumpjumper. Si aún tienes un par de ellos guárdalos; cubiertas de montaña de hace 25 años son difíciles de encontrar.

Bielas Un artículo que Specialized había importado a América para utilizar en bicicletas de paseo, las bielas TA Cicloturista tenía un acabado pulido y contaba con unos desarrollos muy cortos. Los fallos fueron muy comunes ya que no estaban pensadas para utilizarse en un uso todo terreno.

22 & 23

LA PRIMERA VEZ QUE VÍ LA PROPAGACIÓN DE LA STUMPJUMPER

JOE BREEZE; pionero del mountain bike, fabricante de cuadros, autor.
La ví por primera vez en Bike Odyssey en Sausalito, California cerca de mi casa. "Pensé, qué es ese pedazo de potencia de palo de golf" y también me pregunté por el uso de las manetas de freno Tomaselli en vez de Magura, aunque por 750 $, pensé que probablemente venderían muchas de ellas.

TOM RITCHEY; pionero de moutain bike, fabricante de cuadros, inventor, corredor de calibre nacional.
Era (la Stumpjumper) tosca y básicamente era algo que representaba el nivel de tecnología al que podíamos acceder a través de Japón en aquella época. Nuestras bicicletas eran el doble de caras (y de ligeras), pero la Stumpjumper contaba con un precio razonable y unos componentes muy interesantes en esos tiempos.

RICHARD CUNNINGHAM; fundador de Mantis Cycles y director de la revista Mountain Bike Action.
La Stumpjumper era pesada, rebotona y no tomaba las curves muy bien, pero cuando la ví por primera vez me di una bofetada y exclamé: "Esto de la mountain bike es realmente lo que mola... ¡a por ello!" Construí mi primera mountain bike poco tiempo después de aquello.

DON COOK; pionero del mountain bike, co-director del Salón de la Fama del Mountain bike.
En aquella época, un cuadro Ritchey hecho a mano costaba de 1.200 a 1.500 $ simplemente el cuadro. Vimos el Stumpjumper y pensamos, "Ahora sí que empezamos a hablar". De repente dejamos de esperar entre 3 y 4 meses para conseguir una bici de Tom (Ritchey) y Gary (Fisher).

JACQUIE PHALEN; pionero del mountain bike; fundador de WOMBATS, author.
Ví las Stumpjumpers, pero no sabía lo que eran. En aquella época yo iba con Gary Fisher y él las describía como "copias". No podría mirar a nadie si permitís poner eso en el libro.

VICTOR VINCENTE DE AMERICA; pionero del mountain bike, corredor Olímpico de carretera, promotor de carreras, artista.
Mis recuerdos están un poco desvanecidos aquí, pero creo que mi reacción fue reconocerlo como el estándar, el diseño funcional que atraería a las masas, de modo diferente a las bicicletas artesanales que se habían estado haciendo con anterioridad.

RICHARD HEMINGTON, Reino Unido; La primera persona en vender una Stumpjumper fuera de los Estados Unidos.
La Stumpjumper venía en una caja y la teníamos que montar comenzando prácticamente de cero. Todavía puedo ver todas las piezas esparcidas por el suelo y llevándonos una eternidad para montarla. ¡Recuerdo el pensar en qué problema estaríamos si en realidad si se comenzase a vender en serio! Por supuesto ocurrió y nos metimos en más problemas.

JOE MURRAY; antiguo corredor, diseñador, probador de bicicletas
La Stump de 1981 que yo tenía era un poco como un trineo, pero recuerdo que me gustaba incluso necesitando un estilo especial para poder bajar por las pistas llenas de curvas en las colinas del condado de Marin. Una vez que comencé a competir para Gary Fisher él me dio una bicicleta, así que vendí la Stumpjumper. Ojalá la tuviera en estos momentos.

MERT LAWWILL; leyenda del motociclismo, antiguo diseñador de mountain bikes
"Cuando ví (la Stumpjumper) por cuánto se vendía y cuánto mejor era respecto de la mía, me supuse que el juego había terminado y debía volver a las motos."

24 & 25

REFERIDO A ARQUETIPO

Un nuevo tipo de bicicleta que requiere un nuevo tipo de publicidad; una que ha durado al menos 25 años.

No hace muchos años atrás, Mike estaba viviendo en un trailer, escribiendo en su catálogo de papel legal de color amarillo y rogando a sus empleados para que se quedaran a dormir por la noche junto a un montón de neumáticos que no podían ser guardados en el pequeño almacén que tenía por aquel entonces. Ahora estaba colgado de la cola de tigre que de otro modo también era conocida como la Stumpjumper.

Una bici de producción a diferencia de cualquier otra cosa que Specialized o cualquier otro hubiera hecho, con los antiguos métodos para venderla simple y llanamente no iba a funcionar. Antes de que la campaña sobre "El Totalmente Nuevo Deporte" como se conocía alrededor del cuartel general de la S, los anuncios de Specialized eran la mayoría en blanco y negro y a media página o incluso menos. Todo eso cambió con esta oscura, reluciente belleza que se convirtió en el arquetipo para los anuncios impresos de Specialized para los siguientes 25 años. Fotografiado por Jack Christensen en el mismo garaje donde tomó la primera fotografía del primer catálogo sobre los ordenadores Apple, y diseñado por el tanto tiempo colaborador de Specialized Patrick Mountain, El Totalmente Nuevo Deporte – Whole New Sport – nunca podía faltar en las grandes revistas en blanco y negro de la época.

Cierto, es grandioso y todo, pero por qué el chico que sale en el anuncio lleva puestos esos calcetines altos y ese mono? El chico en cuestión es el diseñador original de la Stumpjumper, Tin Neenan y lo recuerda de este modo: "En aquella época no existían prendas específicas para mountain bike, nada que se suponía que te tenías que poner para montar en bici. Tenía unos monos que utilizaba para trabajar así que fui con ellos puestos"

26 & 27

ARRANCA EL MOTOR

Competir en la primera mitad de los '80 era muy parecido a las carreras de la NASCAR en la segunda mitad de los '40: Supervisión de un circuito en un terreno al azar, alinéalos y deja caer la bandera. Los corredores solían dormir en sus coches, saltarse los controles de acceso a las carreras y ahumar sus barritas energéticas. Era natural, era real, era una carrera en dos ruedas con la pureza que no se había visto en más de cien años. Era también demasiado bueno como para mantener en secreto. Desde su reunión inicial en una casa de Danville, California de 1983 a 19990 la NORBA creció de cero a más de 20.000 miembros.

28 & 29

ARROGANCIA—EL EQUIPO STUMPJUMPER TENÍA UN MONTÓN

Tú también lo tendrías si aparecieses en la línea de salida con una bici de color rosa.

En 1984 no existía algo así como un equipo de mountain bike normal, pero incluso si lo hubiese habido, el equipo Stumpjumper no habría sido considerado normal. Ellos fueron el primer equipo pro de la historia, llevaban bicicletas de color rosa con manillares de carretera y utilizaban calzado adecuado en una época cuando muchos de los mejores ciclistas de montaña ahumaban sus barritas energéticas y montaban con zapatillas de deporte como las Nike Lava Dome. Organizado por Bill Woodul, el guru de las carreras de carretera de Specialized, el equipo Stump era un experimento todo-terreno. "Woody (Woodul) nos juntó a unos cuantos de nosotros de primer nivel de carretera y ciclocross y aplicó las mismas ideas y métodos que había desarrollado en el asfalto," dice Dave McLaughlin, antiguo corredor del equipo Stumpjumper. "En realidad entrenábamos y nos organizábamos utilizando estrategias durante las carreras".

En el primer año del equipo, Woodul eligió a los talentos del ciclocross McLaughlin, Gavin Chilcot (quien más tarde correría para el afamado equipo de carretera 7-11), Mark Michelle y Alan Ott residentes en el norte de California, y el padrino del ciclocross americano, Laurence Malone. Empaquetados dentro de una furgoneta de Specialized, recorrieron todo Estados Unidos compitiendo en el puñado de grandes carreras que había en aquella época: Las series Suntour Pacific States Challenge, las series Gant Challenge (carreras urbanas en Seattle, Washington; Chicago, Illinois; Golden, Colorado; Tampa y Miami, Florida), la carrera por etapas de Ross, y las clásicas de un día como la Rockhopper, Rumpstomper y los Campeonatos Nacionales NORBA. "Las carreras estaban un poco descompensadas en aquella época. Sobre todo es que no eran lo competitivas que lo son hoy, pero cuando aparecían Joe Murray o los selectos pros de carretera como Andy Hampsten y Steve Tilford, las cosas entonces sí que se ponían serias," dice McLaughing del periodo de competición gateando-antes-de-que-pueda-caminar.

Sólo unas pocas temporadas de competición puras-y-duras transcurridas, el equipo Stumpjumper había evolucionado para convertirse en el equipo Specialized, el mejor del mundo, el que estaba mejor equipado. Las primeras ediciones del Team Specialized contaban con Campeones del Mundo como Ned Overend, Lisa Muhich y Sara Ballantyne, además del fenómeno del cross-country Daryl Price y los demonios del descenso Elladee Brown y Paul Thomasberg. Eso, y las posteriores versiones del equipo Specialized de ruedas gordas acabaron con las bicicletas de color rosa, pero ellos siguieron manteniendo la misma arrogancia en su comportamiento.

30 & 31

STUMPJUMPER FIELD GUIDE/1984 STUMPJUMPER TEAM

Si vas en una bici de color rosa, ¡ya puedes ir deprisa!

Cuadro diseñado por Jim Merz, de la marca japonesa Tange Prestige, el Stumpjumper de 1984 era el más ligero que Specialized había hecho hasta la fecha.

Horquilla Stumpjumper Team de color rosa, que se caracterizaba por contar el primer diseño de cabeza única, que era mucho más ligera y fácil de hacer que las de cabezas adelantadas realizadas hasta esa fecha.

Freno trasero Fortunately, U-brakes montados bajo el eje de pedalier, como el Suntour Rollercam del modelo Team, que fueron una moda pasajera. Como un imán para la suciedad, los frenos U-brakes son recordados como uno de los mayores errores colectivos cometidos por todo el mundo de la bicicleta de montaña.

Neumáticos En 1984 el modelo TriCross reemplazó al Stumpjumper como la mejor elección para bicicletas de gama alta. Conocido por sus tacos de perfil bajo y fabuloso agarre en seco y condiciones polvorientas.

Rueda libre Una bicicleta de fábrica en cada sentido de la palabra, la Stumpjumper Team se caracterizaba por un casete trasero Shimano 600 de carretera con un piñón grande de sólo 26 dientes-nada como el piñón de 30 dientes favorito entre la mayoría de los ciclistas de montaña de aquel momento.

32

MBHOF

Si Los Rayadores Y Los Que Tocan Las Guitarras Hawaianas Ukeleles Tienen Uno, ¿Por Qué Nosotros No?

Introduce en el Google la frase 'Hall of Fame' y obtendrás 56,800,000 respuestas. 56 millones. Sí, hay un Salón de la Fama de Minería, un Salón de la Fama de Vaqueras, un Salón de la Fama de Ordenadores Domésticos, un Salón de la Fama de rayadores, de los que tocan las guitarras Ukelele. ¡Un Salón de la Fama de los que tocan las guitarras Ukelele! Por la madre de esta bonita Tierra, ¿qué es lo que probablemente puede haber en un Salón de la Fama de Ukelele? Probablemente más que en el Salón de la Fama de rayadores, eso por supuesto.

Hay algo indiscutiblemente universal sobre querer glorificar a aquellos que han contribuido con una cultura y con unos fanáticos de las ruedas gordas que no son diferentes a las vaqueras, rayadores o amantes del ukelele. Hospedados convenientemente en una vieja gasolinera en Elk Avenue de Crested Butte, el Mountain Bike Hall of Fame fue el proyecto original de Carole Bauer. A mediados de los '80, Bauer, residente en Butte desde hace mucho tiempo, se preocupaba del hecho de que los organizadores de la cultura del mountain bike estaban destinados a ser olvidados sin una institución que les honre sus logros y el deporte que ayudaron a crear.

Para 1988 el MBHoF estaba preparado para aceptar su primer grupo de reclutas. Y no de un modo sorprendente, los pioneros de las ruedas gordas como Breeze, Fisher, Kelly, Cunningham, Ritchey y Murray se encontraban en aquella primera clase. Como lo estaba Mr. S, que estaba agitado, sobrecogido y muy orgulloso de ser convocado con la misma consideración que tal selecto grupo de elegidos. Tras Mr S., al menos otros tres mountain bikers con la S en su pecho fueron homenajeados por el MBHoF, incluido El Capitán, el diseñador de cuadros Jim Merz y el guru de la asistencia en carreras Tom Hillard.

Hoy en día el MBHoF mantiene sus luces encendidas, con una próspera cultura gracias al apoyo de la industria de la bicicleta y los fans del mountain bike de todo el planeta. mtnbikehalloffame.com

33

MI STUMPJUMPER N.1

Bill Hennion

2 Stumpjumpers, 65 Años-De-Juventud & 240-Kilómetros Por-Semana

Bill monta casi todos los días en una de sus dos Stumpjumpers (¡dos Stumpjumpers! ¿Es Bill simpático?), durante un total de 240 kilómetros semanales. No está mal para un tío de 65 años, ¿verdad?

Hace unos cuantos años, el nieto de Bill comenzó a montar por los senderos y él sabía que tendría que mejorar su antigua Stumpjumper si quería mantener el ritmo del Jr. No le llevó más que unas cuantas salidas darse cuenta de que su moderna FSRxc de doble suspensión ayudaba a seguir al pequeño chiquilicuatro. Bill dice que, gracias a su sistema patentado FSR ahora más que nunca puede mantener más velocidad por terreno bacheado.

La de todos los días para Bill es una Stumpjumper de 1982 de acero con racores (la de la horquilla con cabeza bi-plana) que compró de segunda mano hace unos años. "Es una de mis bicis favoritas para salir a dar una vuelta", dice Bill "Es genial para llevármela a los cercanos recintos de pesca".

Sin embargo por mucho que lo queramos decir, Bill ya no se está haciendo más joven. Pero dice que aún puede hacer todas las cosas que a él le gustan -como jugar un poco-gracias al buen nivel físico que ha logrado sobre dos ruedas. "Simplemente", dice Bill, "Mis bicis son mi vida".

34 & 35

¿APOYO TÉCNICO GRATUITO?

¿Está loco Specialized?

En aquella época -alrededor de 1985-, el asunto del mountain bike estaba comenzando a volverse un poco loco. No había muchos eventos, pero cada año había nuevos organizadores entusiasmados, corredores ilusionados y una gran cabida para cometer errores. Así que Specialized, que ya había vendido un montón, un montón de Stumpjumpers, y estado presente en un montón de carreras, decidió prestar su mano para ayudar a los organizadores a hacer las carreras y ayudar a los corredores a correr. De igual modo que hicieron en las carreras de carretera desde al menos 1982, decidieron repartir ayuda técnica a cualquier corredor y para cualquier clase de bicicleta sin cargo alguno. También decidieron ayudar a los organizadores en cualquier cosa que fuese posible, como el marcaje de un circuito, barrerlo, poner las carpas, llevar la moto que abre carrera, hacer las inscripciones. Lo que fuese, los de Morgan Hill estaban preparados para hacerlo.

Para garantizar el éxito, contrataron a uno de los más experimentados técnicos vivientes, Tom Hillard del Condado de Sonoma en California, escritor del libro de normas de la NORBA, organizador del Punk Bike Enduro, y un hombre que afirma haber hecho su primer recorrido en bicicleta de montaña en 1961. Así que, Mr S. le lanzó las llaves de una furgoneta y Tom se dirigió a carreras con nombres tan legendarios como Rockhopper, Rumpstomper, Reseda-To-The-Sea, Kamikaze y Whiskeytown.

Ya fuese para una carrera nacional de la NORBA, Cactus Cup o una carrera el martes por la noche en un club de Texas, los corredores siempre estaban encantados cuando uno de los mecánicos de Specialized, cordiales y trabajadores como Tom Hillard o Dave Meyers, Steve Mosher o Joe Buckley ponían patas arriba sus bicicletas averiadas para una rápida (y en la mayoría de las ocasiones gratuita) reparación. A los organizadores agobiados y siempre faltos de personal les encantaba, "Las cosas iban mucho mejor cuando el camión de Specialized aparecía por las carreras" dice un viejo director de carreras.

Por supuesto que el hecho de tener camiones y mecánicos en la carretera no es barato, pero Mr. S. nunca pensó en ello como una calle de único sentido. Por supuesto que organizar carreras ayudaba a que el deporte creciese, pero estar fuera en el campo arreglando las bicis con las que estaba corriendo la gente era a menudo mejor que tener a 1,000 ingenieros metidos dentro de un laboratorio adivinando que clases de maltrato una bici de todo-terreno puede soportar.
¿Apoyo técnico y asistencia en carrera? ¿I+D barato? Quién no estaría de acuerdo en que el apoyo técnico de Specialized era algo bueno.

36 & 37

LA LLEGADA

No demasiada gente en el mundo ha estado en 37º, 16' latitud norte -- 107º 52' longitud oeste, o de otro modo conocido como Durango, Colorado, por una buena razón. Se encuentra en el medio del desierto al sur-oeste-cuatro esquinas-donde hay una reserva de una hierba especial-paso de montaña a ninguna parte. Incluso con una enorme bolsa de gominolas y una maleta llena de Coca-Colas está a 14 horas en coche desde Los Ángeles y a casi la mitad desde Denver. Sí. En el medio de ninguna parte.

Ahora en serio, era el 1 de abril de 1980 y Ned se estaba mudando del soleado San Diego a Durango en su pick-up Datsun de 1965. En mitad de la noche y arrastrando un carrito artesanal del que decía era "como el de los Clampetts", se vio forzado a dar la vuelta por culpa de una fuerte tormenta de nieve. Tenía que haber aprendido en ese mismo momento. Pero tras pasar la noche en Aztec, Nuevo México, (unos 56 kilómetros al sur y algunos centenares de metros de altitud por debajo de Durango), avanzó a través de las montañas para descubrir su Taj Mahal: Un apartamento en alquiler de 2,5 por 10,5 metros cuadrados en Junction Creek Trailer Park. Sí. Mr. Ned Overend había llegado.

Para pagar la renta Ned trabajó en la VW, en los coches como el Dasher, el Squarback o los Beatles que irían dirigidos a lo más profundo del corazón del condado de Animas. Para ponerse en forma solía salir a correr por los caminos y a montar en carretera por el antiguo Elmore Store Loop. Al cabo de pocos años ya había comenzado a competir en carretera, pasando de la nada a correr la Coors Classic con el mejor equipo de América en poco más de una temporada. Un tiempo después del Coors de 1983, un trío de residentes en Durango incluido "Bicycle" Bob Gregorio, presentaron a Ned a sus cinco clunkers de la velocidad. "Ya se había enganchado. "Era como ser un niño en un solar", decía El Capitán. "Sabía desde el primer momento que esto iba a ser algo grande"

¿Algo grande? En unos cuantos años Ned tenía el mejor currículum en el mundo del mountain bike: Cuatro campeonatos nacionales de Estados Unidos NORBA, el Campeonato del Mundo celebrado en Europa y el primer Campeonato del Mundo oficial UCI. Sí. Mr. Ned Overend había llegado.

40 & 41

¿CÓMO SE DOMESTICA A UN GORILA DE 400 KILOS?

Tienes de organizarte.

Amigos desde el primer momento. En la primera página de la primera edición de la primera revista de mountain bike que se publicó, Charles Kelly en el Fat Tire Flier de agosto de 1980 había una clara llamada para pasar a la acción. "Sin una organización con la que proteger nuestros intereses no tendremos intereses que proteger", alegaba SeeKay. Incluso antes de que pudieras encontrar una bicicleta de montaña en tu tienda de bicicletas más próxima, los accesos a los caminos eran un gorila de 400 kilos.

Pasamos al verano de 1987 y, mientras la mayoría de la gente del país estaba descubriendo las delicias del mountain bike, los problemas de los accesos a determinados caminos estaban comenzando a surgir en el corazón de la comarca de las clunkers. "Las dos ruedas del terror" chillaba la revista Newsweek del 28 de septiembre de 1987. Desde las ramblas de American River Parkway cerca de Sacramento en el norte de California, hasta las montañas de Santa Mónica en Los Ángeles, se prohibió a las bicicletas circular por los senderos o por cualquier Parque Nacional en general. Los responsables de los Parques Nacionales habían cerrado todos sus caminos y el Departamento del Interior del Estado que controla el uso de las tierras públicas expulsaba a cualquier bicicleta de los bosques. Si el mountain bike tiene que tener futuro, los mountain bikers necesitaban agruparse y organizarse. Rápido.

Ese mismo otoño, los representantes de cinco grupos de defensa de California-Bicycle Trails Council de Marin, Bicycle Trails Council de la Bahía Este, Sacramento Rough Riders, la Asociación Concerned Off-Road Bikers de Los Angeles y los responsables Off-Road Mountain Pedalers de San Jose se reunieron en la Feria Anual de la Bicicleta en Long Beach. En el plazo de seis meses, IMBA tenía establecidos sus estatutos y comenzaba a luchar por el acceso a los caminos en todos los frentes.

Gracias a la visión de Linda Dupriest y Eric Eidsmo, por entonces dentro del departamento de marketing de Specialized, se donaron 1.000 $ a IMBA en nombre de la compañía. Fue la primera acción que Specialized (u otra gran marca de bicicletas) hizo a favor de la defensa y el acceso a los caminos. Poco después Linda convenció a la empresa a patrocinar una reunión de responsables de la Industria en la feria de Interbike de 1989, la que animara a otras empresas a subirse al carro de ayudas por la defensa del mountain bike. Fue un hecho determinante en el desarrollo de IMBA, ya que el meeting ayudó a acrecentar el conocimiento y los recursos para la lucha por los senderos y sirvió para comenzar a realizar una serie de esfuerzos incluyendo tempranas conferencias de defensa del mountain bike en Washington D.C. y Durango. Dupriest terminaría en la junta directiva de la IMBA durante una década, ayudando a los defensores iniciales a pulir sus conferencias y planes de negocio y siendo la persona de contacto del IMBA para toda la industria de la bicicleta.

Impulsada por los fondos y el apoyo de cada compañía que lo apoya dentro de la industria de la bicicleta además de los 35.000 miembros actuales, IMBA ha educado y luchado desde entonces por los accesos a los caminos por todo Estados Unidos y el resto del mundo. Sin IMBA no tendríamos caminos que proteger.

Ya has escuchado el evangelio, ahora por favor pasa la bandeja para seguir recaudando fondos. Imba.com

42

MI STUMPJUMPER N.2

Denise Weber

Denise de Treinta Y Tantos Descubre Una Ampliación Del Contrato De Vida & Una Carrera De Competición, con 36 años técnica veterinaria matriculada comenzó a montar en bici tras la recomendación de su doctor. Una rodilla maltrecha por correr o incluso por caminar en la máquina de hacer ejercicio, así que el doctor le sugirió que montase suavemente en bici para suavizar el estrés en su rodilla y que le ayudara a recobrar cierto nivel de forma física. En cuanto se subió a la bicicleta su vida cambió para siempre.

En la búsqueda de un poco de motivación extra, Denise comenzó a correr unos 6 meses más tarde de aquella primera salida fatídica. Sólo necesitó un rato en pleno calor de la batalla para darse cuenta de que necesitaba algo más ligero y fiable si quería llegar a ser competitiva. Así que se compró una Rockhopper y, tras rodarla durante unas cuantas temporadas, la mejoró con una Stumpjumper de segunda mano. "Me queda perfecta y ahora sí que estoy definitivamente enganchada", dice. "De repente me he dado cuenta de la velocidad que no sabía que tenía y mi confianza como nunca hasta ahora." Denise, que también monta en carretera para mantener su nivel de forma física, admite que no hay nada como estar con su Stumpjumper montando por el bosque cada mañana temprano

Hoy en día su rodilla se ha fortalecido hasta el punto de que ya no necesita un aparato ortopédico, incluso cuando practica cross-training. Suele salir a correr a menudo, "preferiría estar con mi Stumpjumper, después de todo ahora soy una mountain biker".

43

EPIC

Reescribiendo el Libro de las Leyes, Una Página En Cada Momento.

En el espacio de cinco años, Specialized reescribió completamente el libro del mountain bike. Entre el '88 y el '93 Specialized se convirtió en la primera empresa en realizar cuadros de bicicleta de serie fabricados en acero-carbono, titanio-carbono y metal matrix (aleación de diferentes materiales con el aluminio como metal primario), sin mencionar la primera horquilla de suspensión con botellas de carbono y el primer cuadro diseñado enteramente en el éter digital. Un montón de normas fueron destrozadas en esos días cuando la Guerra Fría estaba finalizando y el hombre que llevaba la voz cantante durante la mayor parte del tiempo era Jim Merz, perteneciente al Salón de la Fama del Mountain Bike y era ingeniero de Specialized.

Cuando Reagan le pidió a Gorby que tirase la pared, se abrieron un montón de materiales y tecnologías que se habían metido dentro del armario militar. Gracias a su amor por una buena publicación mensual científica y la experiencia trabajando con el nuevo software de modelar en 3D (en el que Specialized se gastó 250.000 $ para adquirirlo en 1985), Merz se encontraba perfectamente colocado para comenzar a trabajar con lo último en materiales y métodos.

Después de que un grupo de ingenieros que habían estado trabajando con composites en una empresa filial de las raquetas de tenis de la marca Prince en El Cajón, California, le dieron a conocer los secretos del carbono, Merz comenzó a optimizar los tubos de composite y diseñar un juego de moldes para juntarlos y formar un cuadro. "Me volví loco trabando para sacar adelante el proyecto", dice Merz. Tras muchas pruebas y trabajo duro en su banco de trabajo Applicon, acabó desarrollando un molde de cromoly que fue soldado con la máxima precisión por los socios de Specialized fabricantes de cuadros en Japón.

Con tanto trabajo como construir una bicicleta completa, los moldes y los tubos realizados a medida hicieron de la Epic una derrochadora de 2.400 $ por cuadro y horquilla. Los moldes fueron entonces enviados a la central mundial de Specialized donde se unieron con un refuerzo de carbono optimizado y embutido en un receptáculo especial para su curación. Con sólo dos guías para cada talla, construir aproximadamente 2.000 Epics probó exactamente ser eso. Épico.

Nunca satisfecho, Merz rápidamente evolucionó de los moldes de cro-mo a titanio, y no sólo titanio, sino titanio mecanizado por los expertos de Merlin MetalWorks en Cambridge, Massachussets. Eso, sin embargo, es otra Epic totalmente diferente.

46 & 47

MR. AMERICA

Cómo se gestó la hazaña del Capitán en Durango.®

Si hubieras sintonizado la radio o la televisión en la región de las Cuatro Esquinas de Colorado durante los primeros días del mes de septiembre de ese mismo año, probablemente hubieses oído el nombre de Ned o visto su cara bigotuda en la pantalla. Él era el sujeto de los artículos diarios en el Durango Herald y se le podía ver en la portada del programa oficial de la carrera. Alguno incluso había ido más lejos y había hecho camisetas impresas con El Capitán ganando los (inminentes) Mundiales. Durango no sólo estaba contenta por albergar los primeros Mundiales oficiales de Mountain Bike, querían que su chico también los ganase.

El Capitán podría haber hecho una buena pasta si hubiera corrido como profesional en carretera o sufriendo de Triatlón en Triatlón pero se decidió por el mountain bike por la simple razón de que era más divertido que el resto de opciones del ciclismo. A pesar de todo, una semana antes de los primeros mundiales UCI "unificados" de 1990, el rey del cross country de América no tenía la sensación de haber elegido una salida fácil. La presión de convertirse en el primer Campeón del Mundo de Mountain Bike la estaba sintiendo sobre sus hombros.

Estaba sucediendo. Ned, de 35 años, compitiendo en un prototipo de Epic Ultimate con racores de titanio y una horquilla de suspensión delantera Rock Shox de color negro, había dejado a sus únicos rivales de los 130 participantes, Tim Gould de gran Bretaña y Thomas Frischknecht de Suiza e iba encaminado hacia la victoria en la base de la subida a la última ascensión en la estación de ski de Purgatory. A salvo para los casi 10.000 espectadores que no paraban de gritar, El Capitán iba en solitario. "Era más que un alivio"- te responderá si se lo preguntas hoy mismo, pero como dijo Greg Herbold, otro residente en Durango ganador del descenso de los primeros Campeonatos del Mundo de mountain bike oficiales, "Estar ahí arriba, lograr esa medalla por la que había trabajado tan duro, me sentía como Miss América". Aunque Ned probablemente se sentiría más como Mr. América en todo caso.

*El Capitán no fue el único maillot arcoiris para Specialized en Durango-Lisa Muhich se llevó la victoria en la categoría de chicas veteranas y Sara Ballantyne se quedó muy cerca de la victoria en la carrera de chicas elite.

48 & 49

STUMPJUMPER M2

El Departamento De Defensa Se Relaja.

¿Quién ha oído hablar alguna vez del compuesto metal matrix? Preguntaba la primera edición del San Francisco Chronicle atrás en 1991. Desde su más pronta existencia se mantuvo en la oscuridad gracias al Acto de Control de Municiones (que limitaba el cambio de información sobre el aluminio y el híbrido de óxido de aluminio), no mucha gente sin permiso de seguridad fueron informadas exactamente de qué se trataba. Por aquel entonces no existía ningún producto de consumo fabricado en metal matrix y era prácticamente imposible de formar o soldar, pero Jim Merz, Mark Winter, Mark DiNucci y el resto del personal de Specialized desmembraron el código del material de la carrera espacial. El resultado fue la primera cosa que no se apuntaba como hecha en Moscú de compuesto metal matrix, el Stumpjumper M2.

Inventado para los morros en forma de cono de los satélites, y ejes primarios de los tanques, el M2 era un 10% más resistente y un 20% más rígido que el aluminio típico. De acuerdo a las mentes pensantes del Pentágono, su fortaleza era derivada por trozos de óxido de aluminio, un material cerámico, que se enlazaba en el entramado microscópico de la base de su aluminio de la serie 6000. Si bien era tan resistente y ligero, crear un cuadro de bicicleta con ello no parecía a priori una tarea fácil.

Así que, del mismo modo que las ruedas de carbono de tres palos (sí, el mismo diseño que cierto americano utilizó en algún momento durante cada uno de sus siete victorias en el Tour de Francia), que el equipo de la S había creado en colaboración con Dupont el año anterior, se dirigieron a un gigante industrial para pedir su ayuda. El compañero de baile para el M2 Metal Matrix Composite fue Duralcan, una filial de la segunda compañía de aluminio más grande del mundo. Los científicos del MMC de Duralcan desde la ciudad de San Diego dieron con la receta exacta para los tubos de bicicleta, mientras los chicos en Morgan Hill diseñaban (incluyendo la tarea de conificar internamente un material tan sumamente duro como el este) y averiguaban cómo soldarlo. Al finalizar la jornada Specialized se alió con su empresa compañera Anodizing Inc. Para crear un nuevo complejo de producción en Portland, para realizar la extrusión de los tubos M2 y soldarlos en forma de cuadros de bicicleta. El dúo al cabo de un tiempo reinventaría los procesos de extrusion y conificado, creando cuadros de M2 crecientemente más ligeros a medida que avanzaba el tiempo.

Sin duda no era el camino más rápido y económico para crear cuadros más ligeros y rígidos, pero ¿cuándo ha dicho Mike a alguien que tome el camino más fácil?

50 & 51

PASIÓN

La historia detrás de los autores de los anuncios de Specialized.

Sólo hay una cosa que Mike te dirá que ha aprendido con el paso de los años: Si quieres ganar, juega en un juego en el que sientas que puedes hacerlo, un juego para el que te sientes apasionado.

Así que, en el '89, cuando Specialized necesitaba un autor para sus anuncios, comenzaron a buscar a alguien que estuviese tan apasionado por contar historias como de hacer bicicletas. Un poco de suerte, tras un poco de suerte y ¡boom! (chasca los dedos mientras das un manotazo con tu puño derecho en tu palma izquierda en forma de un efecto mágico), conectaron con uno de los mejores narradores que puedas encontrarte: Goodby, Silverstein y Partners (Asociados). ¿No has oído nunca sobre el GSP? Dos palabras: ¿Tienes leche? Resulta que la S en GSP resultó ser Rich Silverstein, un ciclista empedernido, un tío alto y delgado que a menudo se le podía ver yendo a trabajar a la central mundial de GSP de San Francisco desde su casa en el Condado de Marin atravesando el puente del Golden Gate.

El resto es una pequeña historia que narrar. Mientras estaba muy ajetreado con clientes como Anheuser-Busch, Morgan Stanley, Haagen-Dazs, Saturn y Hewlett—Packard, GSP también ha realizado la mayoría de las ocurrencias imaginativas de Specialized que puedas llegar a recordar.

¿La lección aquí? Tanto siendo bicicletas, anuncios de cervezas BudLight o pan cocido al horno, lo pasarás realmente mal para hacerlo bien si no lo realizas con pasión.

52 & 53

STUMPJUMPER FIELD GUIDE/S-WORKS EPIC ULTIMATE*

*La bicicleta que se muestra aquí es un extraño modelo de pruebas que nunca llegó a venderse con estos componentes.

Cuadro De 1990 a 1995 Specialized fabricó artesanalmente 1,500 cuadros Epic Ultimate de titanio y carbono con un peso inferior a 1.350 gramos en el cuartel general de Specialized en Morgan Hill, California. La construcción especial del Epic Ultimate de titanio y carbono, el primero de su época, fue imitado por algunos fabricantes artesanales durante algo más de una década.

Racores Una mejora respecto el Epic estándar, el Epic Ultimate utilizaba racores de titanio que eran mecanizados por Merlin MetalWorks de Cambridge, Massachussets. El gasto de la materia prima, el coste de subcontratar el trabajo hicieron que los cuadros supusieran una completa pérdida de dinero para la empresa.

Tubos Los primeros cuadros Epic Ultimate utilizaban un compuesto de materiales (de carbono) de super alto módulo que resultaron ser demasiado frágiles para ser prácticos; un material de menor módulo de Maclean Quality Composites de Salt Lake City, Utah, fue el utilizado para la mayoría de los cuadros Epic Ultimate producidos.

Horquilla Aunque se muestra con la horquilla diseñada por Specialized Future Shock FSX, el Epic Ultimate, que fue fabricado hasta 1995, nunca se vendió con una horquilla de suspensión. En vez de eso se ofrecía de serie con la ligerísima horquilla de cromoly Direct Drive.

Serie Limitada Los últimos cuadros Epic Ultimate fueron realizados en 1995, todos fabricados por Brian Lucas en Morgan Hill. Cada uno de los 60 cuadros contaba con un número de serie especial expuesto en una placa en el tubo superior del cuadro. A Ned Overend se le entregó el número 1 para conmemorar su Mundial de 1990 a lomos de una Ultimate.

54 & 55

LA PROPAGACIÓN DEL MUSEO SMITHSONIAN

¿Museos y bicicletas de montaña? Lo que probablemente estás preguntando lo hace una adecuada institución cultural que comenzó en Washingon D.C. hace más de 100 años gracias a una donación de un aristócrata inglés, ¿tiene eso algo que ver con el destrozo de los senderos? Según parece, lo suficiente.

James Smithson, un científico y explorador que dejó algo más de medio millón de dólares a la gente de los Estados Unidos para construir una institución que promocionase " el incremento y la divulgación del conocimiento", era un estudiante muy trabajador, investigador científico esforzado y, por encima de todo ello, alguien a quien le encantaba la aventura. Era conocido por haber arriesgado su vida y sus extremidades, incluido una vez en la que casi se ahoga en un encuentro sobre observaciones geológicas en las Islas Hebrides alejado de la costa norte de Escocia, y es un hombre que hubiera agradecido la energía e inventiva de los precoces pioneros del mountain bike.

Hoy en día, la institución que fundó el Smithsonian ha evolucionado hasta convertirse en la instalación de museos más grande del mundo, la que alberga los museos nacionales y centros de investigación más importantes de América, como el Museo Natural de Historia, el Museo Americano de Historia, el Zoo Nacional, el Museo Nacional del Aire y el Espacio, el Museo Nacional de las Artes y las Industrias, la revista Smithsonian y, en una pequeña esquina del Museo Nacional de la Historia de América, la Specialized Stumpjumper.

En algún momento de 1989, el Smithsonian descubrió el mountain bike y, con el mandato de catalogar a los mejores ejemplos de transporte que cambiaron a América, levantaron el teléfono y marcaron el teléfono de las oficinas de Specialized en Morgan Hill. ¿Si podemos enviar una bicicleta? – claro, dice Mike. Ahora, junto a todo tipo de cacharros desde barcos de vapor a naves espaciales, hay una Stumpjumper acumulando polvo en el Smithsonian. Esperemos que al menos mantengan hinchados los neumáticos.

56 & 57

¿CÓMO SE VENDE PASIÓN?

Porsche parece que lo hace muy bien.

La llamada llegada del mismísimo Harm Lagaay. Siendo un holandés con el acento alemán era difícil de creer si efectivamente era el jefe del departamento de diseño de Porsche. ¿Puede enviar Specialized a algunos de sus ingenieros al súper secreto taller en Weissach para hablar sobre una versión del Porsche Spider del cuadro de 1.225 gramos de carbono y titanio Epic Ultimate? Difícil declinar una oferta de tal envergadura.

Así, unos cuantos miembros del equipo hicieron sus maletas, sacaron sus pasaportes y se marcharon directos al taller que el buen Dr. había construido. Lo que vieron en Weissach fue un gran estudio de trabajo repleto con más de 1.000 de los mejores ingenieros del mundo, todos obsesionados con una meta gloriosa: diseñar y construir lo mejor. Coches construidos especialmente para las carreras, coches creados para la investigación de combustibles alternativos o nuevos materiales, o coches realizados exclusivamente como estudios de diseño. El presupuesto parecía tan interminable como así lo era el flujo de excelentes ideas y, a pesar de que coches legendarios y otros productos de consumo salían regularmente de la factoría de Weissach, no tenían obligación de desarrollar necesariamente algo para poner a la venta en el mercado. Era un departamento de I+D puro y duro. A fin de cuentas, la bici Porsche Spider nunca fructificó, pero el tiempo y la experiencia sirvió para algo: Crear en Specialized, en Morgan Hill, la propia versión de Weissach.

Desde un pricipio el plan era permitir que los ingenieros de mayor talento de Specialized pudieran trabajar sin restricción alguna. Eliminar todas las trabas y acabar con todos los prejuicios. Ignorar los ahorros de costes, tradiciones y planes cronológicos en busca de un simple objetivo: crear las mejores bicicletas del mundo. ¿Ha tenido éxito? Las bicicletas S-Works han impulsado a sus corredores a victorias en los Campeonatos del Mundo en mountain bike y carretera, ciclistas que han ganado etapas y han vestido el Maillot Amarillo en el Tour de Francia, ciclistas que han ganado medallas en las Olimpiadas y en los X Games así como victorias en los Ironman. También hay una buena montaña de bicicletas y accesorios que nunca han llegado a las tiendas; algunas buenas ideas que y muchas probablemente terminen en otras bicicletas de otras épocas, pero ese no es el objetivo del S-Works. El objetivo es, sin embargo, crear lo mejor.

58 & 59

¿SUSPENSIÓN DE SPECIALIZED?

¿La suspensión del futuro?

Cuando el Capitán ganó los Mundiales de Durango en 1990 tenía montada en su Specialized Epic Ultimate una horquilla de suspensión Rock Shox RS-1 prototipo. El hecho de que Ned, al igual que otros corredores de primer nivel (como Greg Herbold y Juliana Furtado) confiasen en un componente tan significativo para una carrera de tal importancia supuso un claro mensaje: las horquillas de suspensión eran el futuro.

Sospechando la oportunidad, Specialized se puso a trabajar en sus propias horquillas de suspensión. Tras haberlas probado y haber indagado en el interior de unas cuantas RS-1, el equipo de ingenieros de Morgan Hill no tardó mucho en darse cuenta de que sería difícil superar la tecnología interna de aire-aceite que Paul Turner, fundador de Rock Shox, había creado. Así que se dirigieron a la tienda de Turner en Mountain View y cerraron un trato: Los ingenieros de Specialized, dirigidos por Mark Winter, crearían muchas de las piezas externas y Rock Shox suministraría todas las piezas interiores y la necesaria producción a gran escala.

Para 1992 la línea de horquillas Future Shock estaban montadas en las propias bicis de Specialized, pero a decir verdad, las primeras horquillas tenían una pinta demasiado similar a lo que Rock Shox estaba produciendo bajo su propio nombre. Entonces llegó la Future Shock FSX. Diseñada por Winter, la FSX era el-coste-no-es-problema en la onda del cuadro Epic Ultimate de Specialized de carbono y titanio (aunque ambos nunca llegaron a venderse en conjunto). Con el mismo funcionamiento aire-aceite de una Rock Shox Mag21, la FSX fue la primera horquilla de suspensión en utilizar botellas fabricadas en carbono, que tenían que ser desarrolladas, diseñadas y fabricadas sólo para ese propósito. Suena a muy caro y realmente lo fue; cada pata de carbono costaba más de 100 $. Los tubos de composite y el arco de aluminio CNC y demás hizo de la FSX ligera y mucho más cara respecto a cualquier otra horquilla de suspensión del mercado. "Sabíamos por aquel entonces que la horquilla de Specialized era en realidad mejor que la nuestra," dice Mike McAndrews guru de las suspensiones en Specialized por entonces trabajando en Rock Shox con su amigo de la infancia Turner. "Pero también era algo que no nos podíamos permitir el lujo de producir".

Al cabo de un tiempo, sin embargo, la carrera entre los fabricantes de suspensiones dejaba claro que mantenerse dentro del negocio de las suspensiones no estaba en las cartas para Morgan Hill. Así que, como con los cambios, las llantas y los pedales, volvieron a elegir entre los mejores modelos que pudieron encontrar de entre unas cuantas empresas. ¿Eso significa que están fuera de juego para siempre? Difícil de decir, pero Mr S. siempre ha solido aprovechar las oportunidades.

62 & 63

FUTURE SHOCK REAR

¿Qué sucede cuando los ingenieros de Specialized ponen sus manos en el sistema de suspensión trasera de un Austriaco?

Lo llamaremos el hecho de 1991. Cuando se cumplía una década tras el lanzamiento de la original Stumpjumper, el mundo del off-road había explotado en numerosas formas que nadie podría haber imaginado. Los diseños de los sistemas de suspensión trasera estaban siendo detectados por los radares como los OVNIS en el desierto de Nevada. El problema era que la mayoría eran muy pesados e ineficientes monstruosidades alienígenas. En la época, la suspensión para la bicicleta era tan complicada y tan poco fiable que incluso muchos dentro del cuartel general de Morgan Hill no estaban convencidos de si era algo bueno.

A pesar de todo, pensando en lo que no era, sino en lo que podría llegar a ser, Mike envió a su equipo en la búsqueda de la bicicleta de suspensión sin compromisos. Que pedalease adecuadamente y que cuando apretases con fuerza a los pedales tuviese mejores ventajas en el mayor control y confort en cualquier circunstancia, fuese ligera (12,25 kg. fue la cifra que se barajó en el primer momento), fiable y de sencillo mantenimiento. Incluso hoy hubiese sido una GPPA (Gran Propósito, Peligroso y Atrevido), pero atrás en el '91 la mayor parte de la tecnología que hubiese hecho tal suspensión posible ni siquiera existía.

Durante algo más de un año en el proyecto, los ingenieros John O'Neil, Mark Winter y Mark DiNucci se rieron de y desmenuzaron cualquier diseño en el que pudieron poner sus manos encima. Algunos eran buenos, pero ninguno era perfecto. Así que siguieron fabricando Frankenbicis y escuchando a cualquier Frankenciclista que atravesaba su puerta (eh, así es como Nike descubrió las cámaras de Aire). Al cabo de un tiempo, el ingeniero austriaco Horst Leitner, que había trabajado para gigantes de la industria del automóvil y de la motocicleta europeos en la década de los '70, llenó las cabezas de la gente del equipo de Specialized con un diseño multipivote mágico que a la postre se convertiría en el FSR. Para DiNuzzi y el resto de diseñadores, Horst era un guru del diseño de motocicletas con un montón de patentes en su nombre; para Horst, Specialized contaba con los recursos para una excelente puesta a punto de su diseño y repetir lo que años atrás habían hecho con la Stumpjumper.

Con prototipos del sistema de suspensión trasera multipivote en la mano, DiNuzzi y su equipo crearon las primeras FSR cortando por la mitad los cuadros ya existentes del modelo Stumpjumper, reemplazándolos con los basculantes traseros de Horst. Con una acumulación de basura como para llenar un estadio lleno de bicis destrozadas (al igual que un nuevo equipo de probadores de bicis implicados exclusivamente en el proyecto), el desarrollo al cabo de un tiempo se transfirió a la producción. Quizás se hizo demasiado rápido: En el verano de 1993 los primeros centenares de unidades de bicicletas de serie tuvieron que desecharse cuando se descubrió que la sujeción del tubo de sillín original no era lo suficientemente fiable. Como dice DiNuzzi, "Era como meter las experiencias personales de cada uno de nosotros dentro de una olla y tomar decisiones basadas en nuestras sensaciones encima del sillín. No teníamos los sofisticados métodos ni la experiencia para que necesitábamos para crear una bicicleta tan compleja como la FSR." Y el porqué la FSR es una bicicleta tan importante dentro del mundo de Specialized es porque rompió las maquinarias y obligó a Morgan Hill a pensar de nuevo en sus procesos de investigación y desarrollo. "De golpe y porrazo la servilleta del cocktail ya no era suficiente, necesitábamos pruebas y estudios de ingeniería reales". –dice Chris Murphy, el hombre tantos años implicado en el departamento de Marketing e I+D de Specialized.

64 & 65

CACTUS CUP

Pausa en la primavera patrocinada por Specialized.

Patrocinado por Specialized que irrumpió en escena durante la mayor parte de los '90, la solicitud de una carrera por etapas como el Cactus Cup en Arizona era algo incontestable: ¿Pasar unos cuantos días (o más tiempo si podías) montando y compitiendo en el caluroso desierto de Sonora con cinco o seis mil amigos? ¿Puede llegar a ser algo malo? "No recuerdo mucho sobre las carreras del Cactus Cup, en realidad. Pero me lo pasaba genial en cada una de ellas." –dice el experimentado periodista de mountain bike y fabricante de cuadros en sus primeros años Richard Cunningham.

Como llegar a Havasu o a Daytona, la época del Cactus Cup era un hecho decisivo. La fecha de mediados de marzo no sólo otorgaba a los corredores una plana y rápida oportunidad de probar cómo había ido su plan de entrenamiento invernal sin la presión de haber llegado a la Copa del Mundo, sino que también daba la oportunidad al negocio de la bicicleta a dar un pronto empujón en la temporada. En su punto álgido, el Cactus Cup era el evento aparte de la feria anual de otoño donde el negocio de la exageración y las ventas de bicicletas iba a toda máquina.

Con el paso de los años varió el recorrido mientras la ciudad de Scottsdale crecía hacia el norte, comiéndose los senderos y creando subdivisiones en los caminos pero dos cosas fueron constantes en todas las ediciones del Cactus Cup: Las rocas y saltar los pinchos afilados de los cactus. Con la presión adecuada de los neumáticos y la ayuda del líquido antipinchazos Slime los pinchazos podían evitarse, pero con más vueltas y revueltas que una novela de Umberto Ecco, casi no había posibilidad de evitar los pinchazos de las púas de las espinas.

Para los corredores, tanto los pro como los amateur, el formato de la prueba era único: cuatro etapas incluyendo una contrareloj, dirt criterium, Fatboy criterium bajo las luces en el centro de la ciudad de Scottsdale y la rápida y deslizante carrera de cross country, que en los años finales incluía curves peraltadas y saltos en forma de meseta para acabar con las celebraciones. Los corredores que llevaban la S en su pecho se llevaron unos cuantos trofeos desde Scottsdale a sus casas; el tantos años corredor de Specialized Steve Tilford era casi imbatible en la carrera del Fatboy Criterium, ganando 21 Fatboys en el transcurso de los años.

El ambiente de las carpas del gran circo y el formato de varias etapas había sido creado en la mitad de los '90, así que el Cactus Cup hizo las maletas y se marchó a la carretera. Se celebraron Cactus Cups en Illinois, Ohio, Canada, Francia, Alemania y Japón (donde aún perdura), lugares donde quizás no se congrega a tanta gente, pero donde se realizan fantásticas fiestas.

66 & 67

STUMPJUMPER FIELD GUIDE/1994 SPECIALIZED S-WORKS FSR

Cuadro Diseñado por Mark DiNucci y Mark Winter, el ligero, pero a pesar de ello rígido triángulo delantero Direct Drive utilizado en la FSR de 1994 era la culminación del trabajo de Specialized en los cuadros ferrosos.

Suspensión Co-desarrollada con el fundador de Amp Research, Horst Leitner, la suspensión FSR había sido diseñada para ser totalmente activa y totalmente independiente para maximizar el confort, el control y la eficacia de pedaleo. A lo largo de los años el diseño FSR ha probado ser increíblemente versátil.

Horquilla Co-desarrollada y fabricada por Rock Shox, la FSX utilizaba la parte interna de una Mag-21 modificada con botellas de carbono diseñadas por Specialized y puente de freno de la horquilla en aluminio M2.

Mandos de cambio Fabricados por vez primera en 1993, los mandos de cambio giratorios SRAM SRT 500 de 8-velocidades eran los primeros mandos de gama alta, específicos para la competición de la empresa de Chicago.

Neumáticos Llamados así tras un album de Pink Floyd, el Umma Gumma fue el primer compuesto de la historia presentado de goma blanda. Quizás adelantados a su tiempo, no tuvieron demasiada continuidad y al cabo de un tiempo se dejaron de fabricar.

70 & 71

NO SÓLO COMPETIR. GANAR

Volar es fácil cuando llevas una S en tu pecho.

¿Billetes de avión? ¿Quieres hablar sobre la compra de algunos billetes de avión? Desde que Mike contrató al primer ciclista de off-road Laurence Malone, las llaves para nuestra furgoneta, Specialized ha gastado millones de dólares en enviar centenares de corredores y personal de apoyo por todo el mundo en busca de una única cosa. El escalón más alto del podium.

Echa un vistazo a la portada del libro de los records y verás que los hombres y mujeres con la S en sus pechos han logrado sus objetivos con la ferocidad de un Pit-Bull de Detroit y la eficacia de un Toyota Prius. ¿El recuento? Los ciclistas patrocinados por Specialized han ganado 5 Campeonatos del Mundo UCI en categoría Elite, docenas de carreras de la Copa del Mundo UCI y títulos de la Copa del Mundo; además de otras muchas carreras de la NORBA y Campeonatos Nacionales de los que perdemos la cuenta desde cuando Ned estaba ganando a corredores oficiales y a todo aquel que se le ponía por delante.

A pesar de que ganar lo es todo para los corredores vestidos de rojo, para Specialized proveer a los corredores más exigentes del mundo con todo el equipo necesario diseñado exclusivamente para ayudarles a ir rápido es una obsesión que merece la pena. Sin el equipo no habría S-Works y sin las S-Works tampoco existirían cuadros tan ligeros como los Stumpjumper rígidos de carbono o el Brain que-conoce-la-diferencia-entre-los-baches-y-el-movimiento-de-la-suspensión.

72

MI STUMPJUMPER N.3

Vedran Novak

El Que Una Vez Fuera Refugiado Vuelve A La Normalidad Con Una Stumpjumper.

Vedran, de 30 años, solía vivir en Zagreb, Croacia. Cuando la guerra civil golpeó el país en los '90 se convirtió en uno de los miles de refugiados que encontraron amparo seguro en Serbia. No se ven muchas bicis de carreras en los campos de refugiados por la simple razón de que la gente cuando se marcha de casa con todo lo que tiene a sus espaldas, generalmente no tienen sitio para una bicicleta. En Serbia, Vedran y el resto de los Croatas se encontraban bajo las leyes opresivas de Slobodan Milosevic. Incluso con las necesidades básicas difíciles de conseguir, la vida era cualquier cosa menos fácil, y una bicicleta era un lujo que nadie se podía permitir. "Las cosas estaban tan mal que ni siquiera podía imaginarme una época donde poder montar en bici de nuevo", dice Vedran de su época en Serbia.

Afortunadamente para Vedran (y para el resto del mundo), Milosevic fue destituido y la vida en los Balcanes poco a poco volvió a la normalidad. Vedran gastó poquísimo dinero y ahorró para poder comprar una Stumpjumper Pro de segunda mano de la que decía estaba en un estado excelente. Desde entonces no ha dejado de montar en ella todos los días y no quiere dejar de hacerlo. "¡Antes de que llegase mi nueva Stumpjumper no me imaginaba que tanta diversión pudiera estar contenida en dos ruedas! Mi bici es un constante recordatorio de lo buena que puede llegar a ser la vida".

73

EL DESPEGUE

Pulp Traction supuso el nacimiento de las películas de freeride para siempre. Un tío vestido de Lycra derrapando en una bajada llena de gravilla en una bici rígida con una suspensión delantera pre-Marzocchi Bomber de 5 cm. de recorrido? No se parece mucho al freeride. Desde luego que no eran unos tail whipps o back flips o suicide drops, pero eso era hacer freeride. Las raíces del freeride. Gracias al director de Pulp Traction, el legendario esquiador y residente en British Columbia Greg Stump, Pulp Traction fue el primer filme sobre bicicletas filmado en North Shore y escenario emergente que daría lugar al nacimiento del freeride. Pulp T capturó a padrinos como Richie Schley y Brett Tippie, cuando los pantalones anchos se utilizaban solo para jugar a baloncesto y largo recorrido significaba un vuelo a China sin escalas.

Ya que en esos días no había productores de películas de mountain bike, el departamento de marketing de Specialized se dirigió al especialista en filmes de ski Stump, el hombre detrás de P-Tex y Mentiras y Cinta Aislante y otros clásicos de los deportes de nieve, para crear una película que incluyese tomas extremas montando en bici, paisajes fantásticos y una visión dentro del estilo de vida del mountain bike. "La mayoría de nosotros ya habíamos participado en videos de ski o snowboard, así que cuando vinieron a filmar procuramos hacer las mismas cosas que hacíamos en la nieve, sólo que en esa clase de cortados y bajadas a las que estábamos acostumbrados por entonces." –dice Schley. "Estuvimos el otro día en uno de los lugares donde grabamos el video Pulp Traction y nos reíamos de por dónde éramos capaces de tirarnos con bicicletas rígidas y horquillas de cinco centímetros de recorrido."

Seguramente no era bonito, pero era el nacimiento de un deporte capturado en video para siempre.

74 & 75

NADA EXTRA. NADA

El ultimo clavo en el féretro de las rígidas.

Entrena y entrena y entrena y entrena para ser rápido en una bici de cross country y te encontrarás tan fino como un supermodelo con los cuádriceps de enorme tamaño. Esa era la idea tras la FSRxc: despojar a una bicicleta de suspensión de todo, salvo lo justo y necesario, exactamente igual que el cuerpo de un corredor de XC.

El momento en el que se pensó fue, en realidad, la verdadera genialidad. En el '96 las bicicletas de suspensión estaban ganando recorrido de sus suspensiones, pero también cargándose de mucho peso extra. En este proceso perdían mucha atracción para la gente que estaba más procupada por la velocidad y eficacia que por lanzarse por rocas tan grandes como una casa.

Así que los miembros de Specialized Ben Capron, Mark Norris, Mike Ducharme y Jeff Pint decidieron hacer zig cuando el resto estaba haciendo zag. Rebajaron, optimizaron y pulieron y el resultado fue la FSRxc de 75 mm. de recorrido, un cuadro con 25 mm. menos recorrido que la FSR estándar, pero que pesaba menos y mantenía el característico manejo tan agresivo. Ducharme, Capron y los demás, obsesionados por cada milímetro cuadrado del cuadro, reduciendo los milímetros de diámetro de cada tubo, rebajando los espesores de los tubos y aligerando el soporte del tubo de sillín. Aunque el gran secreto para ahorrar la mayor cantidad de gramos fue el amortiguador, el punto de giro principal y los tirantes, que giraban en un único eje con la mitad de tornillería respecto a lo que era normal.

El resultado fue una de las bicicletas multipivote más ligeras que jamás se hayan construido; cuando estaba montada con un montón de buenos componentes, la FSRxc se quedaba con holgura por debajo de los 11,35 kg., y una muestra de carreras que sólo pesaba 9.35 kg. flotó por toda la feria de Interbike de 1998.

¿Por qué creerme entonces? Echa un vistazo a la opinión de un ciclista en MTBR.com que fue realizada en 1999, "Nunca volveré a montar en una rígida. Una sola salida con esta bicicleta y tú tampoco lo harás."

78 & 79

¡NAPALM!

Cuando el major atleta del mundo irrumpió en la escena del mountain bike dejó sólo tierras calcinadas y fianzas terminadas en su velatorio.

No era un mountain biker. Ese era el asunto. Nunca se autoconsideró como un biker, simplemente llegó y puso su culo en una bicicleta de montaña del mismo modo que lo hubiese hecho en una tabla de snow, en una moto de cross o en uno de su docena de Cadillacs.

No era un mountain biker, era la estrella de rock del tipo de las que nunca hubieran imaginado que tenía que pedalear en círculos para avanzar. Desde su primer día encima de una tabla en Donner Ski Ranch, el hombre al que llamaron Mini-Destrozo, se hizo propietario de todos los deportes relacionados con la nieve de manera absoluta. Y entonces explotó, "En el año 1992 mi abuela murió y me llevó a ser un peleador idiota, luchando en los bares, bebiendo y yendo hacia ninguna parte. Así que un buen día di la vuelta a la tortilla y comencé a airear toda mi ira sobre su muerte en los deportes. Era como, mierda, voy a ganarlo todo". Así que Mini-Destrozo se convirtió en Napalm y se dispuso a ganar a cualquiera con el que pudiera encontrarse en su propio juego. "Me hace sentir bien", dice.

Para el '96 ya se había pasado al mountain bike y, con el río de las Olimpiadas y el dinero de la tecnología fluyendo en el deporte, su momento desde luego no pudo haber sido más oportuno.

Palmer se llevó todos los elogios y se convirtió en el centro de atención y, a la postre, supuso el comienzo y el final de todo por lo que el mountain bike de finales del milenio será recordado.

Un traje dorado nada sofisticado, un autobus Prevost pintado por Troy Lee y un contrato de seis cifras (aunque Mike y prácticamente el resto de todos quienes lo saben dicen que la cantidad de ese contrato estaba más que ampliamente exagerada) "El chico nunca se lo tomó en serio como para ganar una gran carrera, pero seguramente fue uno de los que más dieron que hablar", dice el antiguo mecánico y persona que pagaba sus fianzas Joe 'Buck' Buckley.

80
ENDURO
Porque se llama "all mountain" y no "easy mountain".

Según se iba acercando el fin del milenio, algunos predecían un caos inminente. El año 2000 estaba en boca de todos. "El fin de los tiempos se acerca", afirmaban varias sectas religiosas. Bien, aparentemente ellos no lo estaban, pero eso es otra historia bien diferente.

Para los ciclistas de off-road el caos se reflejaba en el modo en que pensaban sobre las bicis y los caminos y cómo poder mantenerlos unidos. Gracias a la popularidad del mountain bike, aquellos lugares a los que era más fácil acceder (los que contaban con un parking al lado del camino), estaban bajo una gran presión, si no completamente cerrados debido al uso tan exigente de todos los usuarios. Los mountain bikes más cañeros querían salir de la tónica del resto y reclamaban bicicletas con las que poder defenderse en caminos más exigentes en los que la mayoría no se atrevía, pero como esos caminos estaban bastante más lejos, el peso adicional o la pérdida de eficacia de pedaleo estaba fuera de toda duda.

Un montón de pruebas de campo –si nuestro tiempo lo permite- son realizadas en Specialized y un replanteamiento del modelo FSR con diseño de paralelogramo deformable desarrollado en acuerdo bipartito entre los ingenieros de Specialized y el guru Horst Leitner en 1991 dio como resultado la primera Enduro. Lanzada, literalmente, como lo oyes, lanzada por encima de las rocas y los muelles de carga, en el verano de 1999 el cuadro original Enduro Pro contaba con un chasis en forma de musculosa columna vertebral MAX (Extrusión de Aluminio Manipulada) con 116 mm. de recorrido ajustable que era solamente 250 gramos más pesado que la versión previa del FSR de menor recorrido. La Enduro también contaba con un tubo superior de forma descendiente en forma de V que permitía a los ciclistas una increíble distancia libre respecto del suelo para una bicicleta de enorme recorrido como esta. Para el año 2000 el chasis se aligeró y se refinó mucho más e incluso se añadieron guardabarros delantero y trasero para una atracción inequívoca a las motos.

81
MI STUMPJUMPER N.4
Bob Brewer
De los Pesos Pesados a Peso Mosca, Bob Perdió 40 Kilos En Su Stump
Hace dos años, Bob Brewer estaba en la peor forma de su vida. Con sus 1,64 m. de altura subía la báscula hasta los 113 kilos de peso y tenía hipertensión, los dos casos agravados por una enfermedad del riñón congénita. El doctor, decía Bob de 40 años consultor financiero de la empresa MSM, Inc. y padre de dos hijos, me recomendó que perdiese peso y que comenzase una vida saludable, o no iba a durar mucho en este mundo.

Alguien, a quien siempre le ha atraído montar en bici, pero para el que nunca ha sido una prioridad, se montó en una bici con esperanzas de que le llevase a una salud mejor. Pero su bici antigua era incómoda, pesada, y generalmente no era demasiado divertido montar en ella. Así que Bob comenzó a mirar por internet, hizo algunas investigaciones y rápidamente aprendió sobre la sólida reputación de serios ciclistas. Por suerte, Bob pudo llegar a un acuerdo gracias a la Stumpjumper Comp de 2004. La diferencia, dice, era increíble. "Nada de "dejar la bici a un lado", simplemente una nueva pasión".

Hoy en día Bob no sale a montar en bici porque debe hacerlo, o porque sea bueno para él, monta en bici porque es algo de lo que nunca tiene suficiente. "Estoy en la mejor forma de mi vida. He perdido 40 kilos y aquí estoy dando caña por los senderos de los alrededores de cuatro a seis días a la semana."

Bob solía estar enfermo, cansado, estresado y desmotivado. Ahora se ha vuelto enérgico y entusiasmado de estar vivo. Además él está orgulloso de poder decir que va a ser padre de nuevo. Parece que la Stumpjumper le afectó de nuevo.

82 & 83
¿QUÉ PUEDES APRENDER DE UNA SACUDIDA?
Lo suficiente para hacer que la suspensión trabaje solo cuando tú quieras.

¿Has empujado alguna vez arriba y abajo en el manillar o en el sillín de una bici de un corredor de cross country justo antes de comenzar una carrera de Copa del Mundo? A decir verdad, la tan llamada suspensión delantera en la parte delantera de sus bicicletas no se mueve mucho. De hecho, la mayoría de ellos las llevan tan hinchadas que prácticamente no tienen recorrido útil. Eh, si así es como les gusta, y pueden ganar, ¿quién dice que sea dañino? ¿verdad?

Pregúntale a Mike McAndrews, obsesionado toda su vida por las suspensiones e ingeniero en Specialized, él te contará sobre si son dañinas. Se ha pasado años y años y años fabricando suspensiones que funcionan realmente bien. Así que, cuando un grupo de corredores de Specialized dijeron que deseaban crear una suspensión que sólo se moviese cuando golpease con un impacto de determinada envergadura, Mick, con su cráneo repleto de soluciones para crear suspensiones, tuvo justo la idea correcta.

Un amigo que era ingeniero en FoMoCo le contó una vez a Mick sobre un amortiguador que había diseñado y que sólo se comprimía cuando las ruedas del coche golpeaban con un bache de grandes dimensiones. En su originario Detroit lo llamaron el amortiguador de la Sacudida, ya que se necesitaba un empujón para activarlo. Así que Mick comenzó a currelar en su propia version de un amortiguador de estas características , pero en Morgan Hill lo llamaron de broma el Amortiguador de la Sacudida.

Mick pensaba que era una idea muy perspicaz y ya que el amortiguador sabía diferenciar los diferentes impactos dependiendo de su origen, apodó el proyecto como "Brain". Desarrolló un prototipo que inmediatamente funcionó, pero no de un modo tan seguro como tenía que ser. Entonces tuvo el momento ¡Eureka!: Si el corazón del Amortiguador de las Sacudidas –la válvula de inercia- se moviese tan cerca como fuese posible del eje de la rueda trasera, la cosa tendría un mejor funcionamiento, trabajaría más rápido y sería más seguro. Así lo hizo y la cámara auxiliary se convirtió en el Brain. Con la ayuda de Fox en los apartados más delicados así como en la producción, era trato hecho.

La siguiente cosa que ya sabrás, Filip Meirhaeghe —uno de los tíos que solía correr con bicicletas de cuadro rígido y llevaba su horquilla tan dura como podía- ganó un Campeonato del Mundo en una Epic equipada con el amortiguador Brain. (OK, Meirhaeghe iba como un tiro la temporada siguiente por un cierto desequilibrio químico, pero la Epic no iba como un tiro por contener nada ilegal).

En estos días, el amortiguador Brain de Mick con tecnología de ajuste de su funcionamiento TrailTune es tan listo como para que te lo encuentres en una carrera o incluso en la gama de dobles suspensiones todo-terreno Stumpjumper.

86 & 87
DEMO
La bici construida para hacer los trucos más impresionantes del mundo comenzó con un montón de Legos.

El chico de mayor auge justo antes de esta. Darren Berrecloth. El señor del freeride de nueva generación. Necesitaba un arma en esta batalla en contra de los límites, las leyes y las ideas preconcebidas. Así que Specialized autorizó a crear la Demo, una bici de la que Bearclaw decía que tenía que ser un verdadero colchón, con una suspensión activa, geometría lo suficientemente equilibrada como para bajar los descensos más empinados o los delgados más delgados, un centro de gravedad super bajo y un tubo superior con mucho slooping para mejorar su manejo y, oh sí, unos fabulosos cambios que incluyan hueco para un desviador delantero. "Ningún problema" –dice Specialized- "podemos hacerlo".

Así que un equipo de ingenieros de Specialized, diseñadores y jefes de producto que incluía a Jason Chamberlain, Brandon Sloan y Robert Egger se metieron de lleno en el proyecto jugando con un montón de piezas del Lego. Juntando todas las piezas del Lego permitió al equipo construir el concepto básico de la suspensión de la Demo en un modelo rápido y fácil de entender en el que poder realizar modificaciones antes que el ingeniero superestrella Jason Chamberlain lo introdujese dentro de su ordenador y comenzase a realizar todo el pesado trabajo de ingeniería.

No hace falta ser un genio para saber que jugar con los Legos iba a ser una cosa sencilla. Crear un diseño que funcionase con el Programa de diseño 3-D Pro Engineering, construir prototipos con las máquinas en el cuartel general de Morgan Hill y someter a pruebas exigentes a la Demo llevó unos años, exactamente dos, y centenares de miles de dólares.

El resultado del genial ordenador de Chamberlain y los múltiples viajes a North Shore por parte del Jefe de Producto Brandon Sloan era una bici de 225 mm. de recorrido de suspensión trasera, con sistema de paralelogramo deformable y basculante tradicional aumentado por un basculante y seis puntos de giro. Para hacer de la Demo una bici resistente y robusta, Chamberlain y compañía diseñaron los juegos de forjados más caros jamás creados para una bicicleta, incluyendo el único y más complejo forjado de todos, la estructura central que da cabida al amortiguador para cuya fabricación era necesita de una presión de más de 2.000.000 de kilos.

Quién hubiese imaginado que una bicicleta realizada para lanzarse por los cortados más altos, los saltos más bestias y los impactos más bruscos hubiera comenzado con un montón de Legos.

88 & 89
30 AÑOS DE RODAR A TODA VELOCIDAD Y TOMAR RIESGOS
¿A quién estás llamando viejo?

La gran Tres-O. Solía ser más un despertar que una celebración; kaput con el niño y adelante con las cosas de los adultos. Ahora, es el momento preciso para refrescar tus flips-flops y reducir el número de cervezas antes del mediodía (entre semana, de todos modos). A pesar de todo nadie quería mencionarlo. El chico pequeño vestido con un mono remendado que comenzó vendiendo potencias y cosas así desde un pequeño almacén en San José estaba llegando a los 30. El gran Tres-O.

No pasa nada. En estos días se dice que estás progresando a los 30. ¿Verdad? Los 30 son los nuevos 25.

Una cosa absolutamente innegable es que la Stumpjumper 30° aniversario (de la fundación de Specialized) parecía mejor que nunca. Su eterna sonrisa intacta llévame-a-cualquier-parte-a-la-que-iría-una-persona-racional. ¿Y su "cuerpo"? Simplemente echa un vistazo a su cuadro de estructura plateada de ensueño. Como el legendario líder de ingenieros de Specialized Robert Egger le gusta decir, "Si tiene buen aspecto, está bien". Y con los Dolomitas italianos como telón de fondo, más que nunca. "La bici necesitaba multitud de formas robustas, que cuando se combinan parecen más fuertes y resistentes que la suma de todos los tubos por separado." Dice Egger, el diseñador detrás de las piedras preciosas de Specialized como la Enduro, la Hemi y la Tarmac.

90 & 91
SIGUE MONTANDO CAPITÁN
No hay detenimiento para una vida vivida en cabeza de carrera.

Sin embargo otro sábado noche para El Capitán. Escondido en el más reciente de la cadena de hoteles de 99$-por-noche de calidad mundial. Hielo en su pie derecho herido y un episodio de parpadeo a Speedvision delante de la cama. Verá las últimas noticias locales y se beberá el ultimo trago de su elixir energético secreto, incluso teniendo que estar en la salida a las 7 de la mañana. Así lo hace El Capitán.

Ned se retiró oficialmente en 1996, pero parece no recordarlo. Desde Specialized se le dedicó una fiesta honorífica de su retirada aquel otoño, pero él ha continuado compitiendo en las Copas del Mundo y NORBAs, carreras de carretera, subidas a pie, descensos (sí, e incluso le gana a su hijo adolescente), duatlones, triatlones, X-Terras, maratones, carreras de campo, carreras de aventura y todo lo demás que puedas llegar a imaginar. Si implica elevados niveles de ácido láctico y un exceso de endorfinas, El Capitán estará allí. Demonios, en el mismo día de su 50th Cumpleaños terminó 4° en la brutal ascensión a Mt. Washington.

Muchos de los chicos a los que normalmente les deja a vista de sus retrovisores ni siquiera habían nacido cuando Ned finalizó el Ironman de 1980 en 24° posición, o en 1983 cuando consiguió la victoria en su primera carrera de mountain bike y corrió la Coors Classic con el legendario equipo Ti-Raleigh (el mismo de Andy Hampsten, Roy Knickman y Steve Tilford) o incluso cuando ganó los Europeos y los Campeonatos del Mundo NORBA en 1987.

Pero Ned no quiere ningún tratamiento especial o alabanzas añadidas, El Capitán entiende menos sobre el alojamiento ideal, apéndices lastimados y salidas a las 7 de la mañana como su destino en su vida como corredor "No salgo a competir tratando de demostrar que soy más rápido que los demás chicos jóvenes," dice, "Salgo a competir porque me encanta ir mezclado en cabeza de carrera-me encanta la competición."

92 & 93
STUMPJUMPER FIELD GUIDE/2006 S-WORKS STUMPJUMPER CARBON
Para buscar la progresión en la más refinada bicicleta de montaña de carbono jamás construida.

Cuadro fabricado en carbono exclusivo Y570, en ese momento el carbono más resistente posible para la creación de un cuadro de bicicleta. La Stumpjumper S-Works Carbon fue galardonada por su combinación de eficacia y sensacional manejabilidad.

Amortiguador Brain con Brain Fade, el primer amortiguador que sabe cuando tiene que estar activo para la respuesta más efectiva y cuándo estar firme para una mejorada eficacia de pedaleo. El modelo 2006 contaba con la tecnología Brain Fade que permitía a los ciclistas de montaña ajustar al gusto del usuario el tacto del amortiguador Brain.

Neumáticos Adrenaline 26 x 2,0" desarrollados específicamente para una rápida bicicleta de doble suspension como la Stumpjumper de carbono, utilizaban una carcasa de 120 hilos por pulgada para mantener el peso al mínimo, con un taqueado con goma de doble compuesto para la major combinación de tracción y excelente resistencia a la rodadura.

Manillar El perfecto aliado para el cuadro de composite de la Stumpjumper Carbon, el Specialized OS Carbon de doble altura, era ligero con solo 175 gramos y contaba con una combinación perfecta de angulación hacia arriba (6 grados) y hacia atrás (8 grados).

Sillín Nuevo en 2006, el Rival contaba con la tecnología exclusiva Body Geometry de Specialized que en tests de laboratorio mostraba una mejora en el flujo sanguíneo de las áreas más sensibles.

94 & 95
¿EL FUTURO?

Difícil de decir dónde esto o algo más va dirigido.

Gente de mayor importancia lo han intentado y, bien, ya recuerdas el año 2000.

Una de las cosas de las que estamos seguros es que tenemos que proteger las pruebas y los arquitectos de esta cultura. Así que el 100% de los beneficios de este libro serán donados al IMBA y al Salón de la Fama de Mountain Bike.

6 & 7
はじめに

タイヤのブロックパターンひとつひとつが、大地をしっかりと掴み、ある時は岩塊をものともせず、突き進んでいく。マウンテンバイク…。この乗り物が地球に現れたのが「創造」と言ってもよいだろう。それから20年、あるいは30年の月日が流れたのかがわからないくらい、マウンテンバイクはもはや地球と人との接点として親しまれている。

マウンテンバイクがあれば、どこへだって行ける。それが郊外の医者でも、下町の配管工でも、田舎の教師でも。マウンテンバイクに乗れば誰もが同じ気持ちになり、そして乗っていればアドレナリンが噴出して高揚感に包まれるのだ。そのフィールドはちょっと郊外でありながらも、日常とはまるで別世界。そんな世界へと導いてくれるのがマウンテンバイクなのだ。

マウンテンバイクという乗り物を見つめていると、そこには膨大な技術の結晶があり、集大成であることが分かるに違いない。ヒューマンパワーを最大限に引き出すためのディレイラーやチェーンなどの変速システム、路面からのショックを和らげ、快適さをもたらすショック吸収システムなど、ひとつひとつを見ると、それだけで満たされる人も多い。しかしマウンテンバイクがここまで人々に浸透し、もはや文化、生活の一部となり得たのは人間に多くの笑顔をもたらしたことに尽きるのではないだろうか？　時にそれはインスピレーションとなることもあっただろう。世界で最初の量産型マウンテンバイクであるスタンプジャンパーは、このようにして地球のあらゆるところを駆けてきたのだ。

8 & 9
ファットタイヤの序文
どこでズタズタにちぎれるのか？

マウンテンバイクが発明されてから20年余りが経ち、その姿は確実に本来あるべき形になっている。結局のところ、ファットタイヤを装備し、マウンテンバイクは泥の上を走り、そしてライダーは大きな口を開けて笑っているのである。

それではジョン・フィンレー・スコットはどうだったか？　1960年代にカリフォルニアのシエラ山脈にあるホワイトマウンテン（14,260フィート）を含む多くのオフロードを、1953年製のシュウィン・ヴァシティーで走破した。彼はマウンテンバイクングをしていたと言えるだろうか？

1897年に、もし20人のニューヨークの軍人が、1,900マイルもの距離を、西部のイエローストーン国立公園に向けて旅することになったら、どうするだろうか？　彼らが、自転車を使うことは、ありえなかっただろう。再度言わせてもらうと、彼らはわざわざタイヤがズタズタになるリスクを背負いながら、西部の荒野を自転車で旅するはずがないのだ。

それでは、いったい人々がいつ、めざわざ舗装されていない山道を走る、マウンテンバイキングを始めたのだろうか？　サンフランシスコのライダーであるラス・マホンが、最初にクランカーを壊したリアディレイラーは1974年の12月1日か？　それはジョー・ブリーズが初めてカスタムメイドの、多段ギアのファットタイヤを創って、伝説のリパックダウンヒルに出場した1977年10月のことか？　それともその数年後、最初のスタンプジャンパーのデザイナーであるティム・ニーナンが、初期のプロトタイプに飛び乗りサンゼのスペシャライズド社の後ろにある丘で走り回っていたときのことか？

既存のものを壊すことが、実際にどこで始まったのかという質問の答えを見つけるには、サンフランシスコのZeitgeistサロンで午後になるとやって来る大学教授とバイク乗りの一団に任せるのが一番である。

10 & 11

「荒廃した古い炭鉱町。黒い肺を持った炭鉱夫がベンチに座り込んでいる一方、若者たちは歩きまわり、バイクに乗ってダンスをしている。」カリフォルニア州マリンカウンティーのクランカー狂のひとり、ジョー・ブリーズはこの地をこう表現した。クレステッドビュートからアスペンに向かうパールパスツアーが行われた、1978年のことである。クレステッドビュートは、1859年のコロラドゴールドラッシュ以来、鉱山の町として栄えた。しかし、1970年代後半は、かなり荒廃して見えた。ところが、早い時期からテレマークスキーと麦を使ったセラピーを観光事業として取り入れたことにより、ヒッピーたちにとっては、最先端の地と見なされるようになったのである。

この町はコロラドで最初にスキーリフトを導入したことで知られているし、アウトドアスポーツの長い歴史のおかげで、ヒッピーであろうと古参のオールドタイマーであろうと、両者のバイクに対する好みとかを含め、多様なアウトドアへの趣向の違いが的確に対照している。勿論、1978年以前にバイクに乗っていた人は、本質的にサイクリストではなく、単にバイクに乗っていたのすぎない。通常、中古のシュウィンやハトホンやBF グッドリッチのクランカーを、2人あるいは3人まで、オーナーを変遷させてきた。雪や氷に覆われる8ヶ月が過ぎても、クレステッドビュートの通りは、ほとんど全てが泥で覆われている。そう言うわけで、バルーンタイヤが、この町を走り回るには最高のギアであることが証明された。

1976年の夏、ある遅い夜のこと、クレステッドビュートのステーキハウスで、12,692フィートのパールパスの登頂を行うのにも、アスペンのジェロームホテルのバーに行くのにもクランカーが最適であると見出した者がいた。その年の9月に、15人のメンバーはクランカーにまたがり、アスペンへと向かった。クレステッドビュートパイロットの報告によれば、ライダーとサポーターは、ビール1樽、シュナップス3本、ワイン2ガロン、シャンパン3本を消費し、一晩パールパスで大騒ぎをした後、ジェロームホテルに通うようにして向かった。そこで、また酒を飲み、伝説が生まれたのだ。

14 & 15
みんなが歓喜！
クランカーの王様

マウンテンバイクを所有する全ての人が牧草を育て、歌を歌い、海に向かって叫ぶ、あるいはマウンテンバイクの王様であるチャールズ・R・ケリーの御名により祈るべきである (a.k.a. SeeKay)。カリフォルニア州フェアファックスのコミュニティーに閉じこもり、チャールズ卿が雑誌「ファットタイヤフライヤー」を創刊した。それはマウンテンバイクが生まれる以前のことである。多くの人がバイクや、レースの方法に対して、何か定義づけをしなくてはいけないと考えていた時に、チャールズはクランカーがどのようなものであるかを定義し、世界に知らしめた。

「クランカーは軽いダート用のモーターサイクルにどことなく似ているが、似ているのは表面上のことだけ。モーターサイクルは、大きなタイヤとショックアブソーバーを備えているが、クランカーにはそのようなものは付いていない。そのため路面上のちょっとした突起にもはじかれてしまう。アールのきついコーナーにおいてクランカーは、モーターサイクルが後部を振るような急加速はしないものだ。軽やかに走るためには、ショックアブソーバーをつけるのではなく、スキルによって想像する以上に素早くハンドルをきるのである。」

「逆バンクでスライドしたので、ターンができなかった。計算違いだ。コントロールできなくなったら、瞬時に判断しなければならない。輪からタイヤが外れかかっている。車体を横に倒そう。だめだ、シャツが破れ、ひじが血に染まった。今、そんなことを気にしている暇は無い。最初の2、3ヤードは惰性で進むから自分の手でチェーンを元に戻す。ギアを入れなおせば、時間を取り戻し、もとの競争ラインに立つことができる。」
— チャールズ・ケリー
　　バイシクリングマガジン 1979

16 & 17
ファットタイヤで前進
スペシャライズドはファットタイヤ革命を、ガラクタでかきたてる。

1年目の売り上げは $60,000
2年目は $128,000
3年目は $200,000+

「今、過去を振り返ってみると、物事はゆっくり動いていた。しかし私には早く感じられた。」スペシャライズドの創始者で社長のマイク・シンヤードは、創業後の数年を、そう表現した。

マイクがフォルクスワーゲンのマイクロバスを売り払い、青と白のボブジャクソンのツーリングバイクを持ってヨーロッパに行ったのは、当時は、本当に大冒険であったのである。タトゥーアートのウェブサイトに、チェーンリングのタトゥーが登場するずっと以前の話である。

イギリスからオランダのアムステルダム、そしてスペインのバルセロナへと自転車で旅した後、マイクはイタリアのポ・ヴァレー平原に着いた。何をやっていたのかは忘れたが、次の瞬間に何かすごいことが起こるのではないかという予感がしていた。ミラノのユースホステルで、1人の若い女性に会った。彼女は、イタリアのサイクリング界の重鎮でありフレームとパーツ会社の創始者、シグノア・チノ・チネリ氏とコネクションがあったからだ。

マイクはひと月もたたないうちに、チネリから仕入れた部品を船に積み、サンノゼに戻った。彼は、チネリのハンドルバー、ステム、フレームの仕入れに、手持ちのお金を全て使った。そして、トレーラーを自転車で引いてベイエリアのバイクショップを回り、それらを販売したのだ。

1976年のアメリカ建国200年までには、マウンテンバイカーが好んで使うが入手が難しいコロンバスのフレームチューブやユーレーのディレイラー、マフィックのブレーキなどをアメリカ西海岸に供給し、スペシャライズドはバイクビジネスの中心的存在へと急成長を遂げた。ジョー・ブリーズやアルバート・アイゼントラウト、トム・リッチーのようなフレームビルダーは、パーツにも特殊工作を施していたが、それに使うTAのクランクやカンチレバーブレーキなどの注文も拡大していった。マイクはフレームビルダーたちが新しいタイプのバイクをクリエイトしていることを認識し、その手助けになるようなスタンスをとることに専念した。

20 & 21
Stumpjumper Field Guide/1981 Stumpjumper

全ての検索図鑑の挿絵には、5つの特徴が記されている。各モデルにより、これら5つの特徴も変わってくる。1981年のスタンプジャンパーを例に、見てみよう。

フレーム：　サンタクルーズのライトハウスバイクスのティム・ニーナンにより設計された。最初のスタンプジャンパーフレームはTIG溶接であった。もしあなたの1981年フレームがあるなら、それは81年後半に作られたものである。ブルーのカラーリングは、すでにツーリングバイクのセコイアに使用されていたものだった。

ステム：　当時のBMXのステムをもとに作られたもの。初代スタンプジャンパーのハンドルは、マグラ社のオートバイ用のモーターサイクル用のものとしている。

ブレーキレバー：　初期のスタンプジャンパーに装備されたトマッセリレーサーは、70年代後半のカフェレーサー用モーターサイクルの為に設計されたものだ。これは、ブレーキングのフィーリングと性能を向上させるヘビーデューティーなケーブルとともに、アッセンブルされた。

タイヤ：　かつてロードバイクのタイヤを作り出したときのノウハウを元に、最初の軽量マウンテンバイクのタイヤを作り出していた。

クランク：　スペシャライズドが、ツーリングバイク用に輸入していたTAシクロツーリストは、最高級の研磨仕上げがされ、ウルトラローのギアリングの装着を可能にしている。オフロード用に作られてはいないので、トラブルが多かったことも事実だ。

22 & 23

ジョー・ブリーズ (JOE BREEZE) マウンテンバイクのパイオニアのひとり、フレームビルダー、著述家
「750ドルという安い価格には驚いたね。多くの人がそれでマウンテンバイクの楽しみに目覚めたことだと思う。」

トム・リッチー (TOM RITCHEY) マウンテンバイクのパイオニア、フレームビルダー、ナショナルクラスのマウンテンバイクレーサー
「我々のバイクは、スタンプジャンパーの2倍の価格で、2分の1の重さだったと思う。でも、スタンプジャンパーのリーズナブルな価格と、メイドインジャパンの技術レベルの高いユニークなパーツ構成が印象的だった。」

リチャード・カニンガム (RICHARD CUNNINGHAM) マンティス・サイクルの創始者でマウンテンバイクアクションの編集者
「このマウンテンバイクは、本物だ。これに夢中になろう。」それがスタンプジャンパーの第一印象だった。本当に顔をひっぱたかれたような衝撃だった。その直後にオレは、最初のマウンテンバイクを組み立てたんだ。

ドン・クック (DON COOK) マウンテンバイクのパイオニア、マウンテンバイクの名誉の殿堂

共同管理者
リッチーのフレームが1,200ドルから1,500ドルの時に、完成車で750ドルのスタンプジャンパーが登場。まさにタイムリーだったと驚いた。カスタムメイドのリッチーやフィッシャーのバイクを買うために、3、4ヶ月待つのは、当たり前だったのだ。

ジャッキー・ファレン (JACQUIE PHALEN) マウンテンバイクのパイオニア、WONBATS の創始者、作家
スタンプジャンパーを最初に見た時に、それがどんなバイクであるか解らなかった。ゲーリー・フィッシャーはそれを「コピー」と評していたが、私にとっては十分に斬新なものだった。

リチャード・ヘミングトン (RICHARD HEMINGTON) 英国、最初に米国外でスタンプジャンパーを販売した人物
箱に梱包されて送られてきたスタンプジャンパーのフレームと、全ての部品を床に広げて組み立て始めた時、実際にこれで山の中を走るイメージと同時に、メカトラブルの問題が脳裏をかすめた。もちろん、いろいろな問題は起きたが、それらを改善しながら、現在も進化し続けているのだ。

ジョー・マレイ (JOE MURRAY) 若い頃…　リッチーのスポンサードレーサー
私が所有していた1981年製のスタンプジャンパーにはさんざん乗ったけれど、本当に良いバイクだったね。マリンカウンティのファイヤーロードのスイッチバックを、高速で駆け下りるには、それなりのテクニックが必要だったね。でも、フィッシャーのスポンサードレーサーをしていたので、全く新しいバイクということでは、スタンプジャンパーは人に売ってしまった。いまだに、あれを持っていたらなあと思う。

マート・ローウィル (MERT LAWWILL) モーターサイクルの伝説的人物、初期のマウンテンバイク設計者
完成車としてショップにディスプレイされていたスタンプジャンパーと、それが年々進化していく過程には目を見張るものがあった。それがどのくらい私のデザインしたバイクより良いのかは、よく分かっていた。スタンプジャンパーが、私がモーターサイクルの世界に戻ることを決意させたのだ。

24 & 25
原始的な広告
新しいタイプのバイクは新しいタイプの広告を必要としているが、それは25年も続いているものである。

マイクがトレーラーに住み、カタログを自作し、小さな保管場所に収まりきらないタイヤと一緒に、ひと晩眠ることになった従業員をなだめすかしていたのは、それほど昔の話ではない。

スペシャライズドのバイク、あるいはこれまでに存在しなかったタイプのバイクを量産販売する為には、かつての常識はもはや通用しない。スペシャライズドの広告はほとんどが白黒で、雑誌の半ページかそれ以下のサイズであった。しかし、全く新しいスポーツということを強調するキャンペーンと共に、光沢紙を使った美しい広告に変更された。これは、次の25年間のベース広告にもなったのだ。アップルコンピュータのパンフレットの写真を撮った時と同じガレージで、ジャック・クリステンセンが写真を撮り、長年にわたって共同作業をしてきたパトリック・マウンテン社が企画。マウンテンバイキングという全く新しいスポーツの広告が、誌面の大部分をモノクロの当時の雑誌の中で異彩を放っていた。

もちろん、絵は素晴らしいものだった。しかしながらバイクに乗り飛び出そうとする広告のモデルは、チューブソックスをはきオーバーオールを着ていたのだろう？　広告のモデルは、初代スタンプジャンパーのデザイナーであるティム・ニーナンで、彼は当時こう振り返る。「当時は、マウンテンバイク用のウエアは無かったのだよ。仕事をするときに着ていたオーバーオールを、そのまま着てライディングに飛び出しただけのことさ。」

26 & 27
エンジンをかけなさい
黎明期のマウンテンバイクレース

マウンテンバイクのレースは1980年代半ばから本格化した。それは1940年代後半のNASCARに良く似ていた。コースはフィールドを無作為に杭で仕切って、旗を立てた程度の。レーサー達は、車で寝泊りしながら出場したものだった。このような形で、ピュアなエンスーたちによって支えられ、やがて1983年、NORBA（ナショナル・オフロードレースアソシエーション）がカリフォルニア州ダンビルで最初のミーティングを開催するに至る。それから1989年までにNORBAの会員数は、ゼロから20,000人まで増えた。アイビスバイクルの創業者であるスコット・ニコルは「仲間どうしの秘密のように小さなことが、ほんの2〜3年で世界中に広まる現象に変わってきた。」と言う。

最初のマウンテンバイクのタイヤを作り出していた。

28 & 29
威厳 --- チーム・スタンプジャンパーは大所帯
ピンクバイクでスタートラインに立ったら、貴方も思わず胸を張るでしょう。

最初のマウンテンバイクプロチームである "チーム・スタンプジャンパー" が登場したのは、1984年のことだった。彼らはピンクのフレームにドロップハンドルを装備し、ナイキのラバードームのようなスニーカーを使用したものだ。「スペシャライズドのカリスマロードレーサー、ビル・ウッダルは、カテゴリー1のロードやシクロクロスの選手たちと一緒にトレーニングをして、そこから自分のノウハウを、オフロードトレーニングに融合させていた。まさに、走る実験室だ。」と、前スタンプジャンパーチームのデーブ・マクローリンは話している。

チームの1年目は、シクロクロスで活躍していたマクローリン、ゲービン・チルコット（後にセブンイレブンロードレースチームに加入）、北カリフォルニアのマーク・ミッチェルとアラン・オッター、そしてアメリカのシクロクロスの先輩者でもあるローレンス・マローンなど、一流のレーサーを揃えた。彼らは特別に作られたバンに乗り込み、その当時開催されていたビッグレースに参加するためにアメリカを旅した。他にもサンツアー・パシフィック・ステートシリーズに始まり、ワシントン州シアトル、イリノイ州シカゴ、コロラド州ゴールデン、フロリダ州タンパおよびマイアミ以外でのスタンプジャンパー以外のクラシックレースといわれるガント・チャレンジ・シリーズなど。他にもロス・ステージ・レースやロックホッパー、ランプステンバーやNORBA ナショナル・チャンピオンシップのようなワンデイのクラシックレースをこなした。最初のレースレベルは、今よりばらつきがあり、大会によっては今日のように激しいものではなかった。しかし、ジョー・マーレイやアンディー・ハンプステン、スティーブ・ティルフォードのような有名なプロのロードレーサーが出場する時は、事態は一変し、非常にハイレベルなものになった。

ナショナルクラスのレースが始まった当初は、大会自体のレベルにも差があったが、2〜3シーズンするとよりハイレベルに安定し、またチーム・スタンプジャンパーは、世界で最高のマウンテンバイクを有するチームとして認知された。初期のチーム・スペシャライズドには、1990年にUCIのマウンテンバイククロスカントリーで世界チャンピオンとなったネッド・オーバーエンド、リサ・ミューイック、サラ・バレンタイン、そしてダリル・プライス、ダウンヒルのエラディ・パストー、ポール・トーマスバーグらが参画し、文字通り世界最強を誇っていた。

30 & 31
Stumpjumper Field Guide/1984 Team Stumpjumper
ひとたびピンクバイクに跨ったら、大いに飛ばす！

フレーム： 日本製の有名なタンゲのチュービングを使用してジム・マーズがデザインした。1984年製のチームスタンプジャンパーフレームは、その当時、スペシャライズドが製作した中で最も軽量なものであった。

フォーク： ピンク スタンプジャンパー チームには、当時使用していた荒削りなフォークに代わり、より軽量なユニクラウンフォークが搭載された。

リアブレーキ： 幸いなことに、サンツアー・ローラーカムのような、ボトムブラケットの下に取り付けられたUブレーキは、長い期間流行しなかった。Uブレーキはダートライドでの使用において、幾つかの問題点があったからである。

タイヤ： 1984年にスタンプジャンパーにアッセンブルされたトライクロスは、ハイエンドタイヤの決定版となった。その低いノブとドライな路面での素晴らしいグリップ力は、多くのライダーからの信頼を集めた。

フリーホイール： 世界中の注目を集めるワークマシンとして、スタンプジャンパーチームは、シマノ600のロード用フリーホイールに、歯数26Tのスプロケットを取り付けた。その当時、ほとんどのオフローダーが使用していた30Tとは別のものだった。

32
MBHoF (Mountain Bike Hall of Fame)
もしストリーカーやウクレレ奏者がなれるならば、マウンテンバイカーだって殿堂入りすることができるはずだ。

インターネットの検索エンジン "グーグル" で、「名誉の殿堂」という用語を検索してみると、実に4千700万件のヒットがある。その名誉の殿堂の対象はカウガール、ホームコンピュータ、ストリーカー、ウクレレなど、本当にさまざま。

その中に「MTBの名誉の殿堂」がある。コロラド州クレステッドビュートのエルク通りの古いガソリンスタンドにうまい具合に収容されたマウンテンバイクの名誉の殿堂は、キャロル・バウアーの発案である。クレステッドビュートはアメリカの中でもMTBが盛んなエリアのひとつである。1980年代中頃、この町の住民であったバウアーは、多くのキーマンによって文化として形作られてきたマウンテンバイクを賞賛する機関が何も無かったので、忘れ去られる運命にあるのではないかと危惧したことが始まりだった。

1988年までに、MBHoFは、最初の候補者たちを受け入れる体制を整えた。そしてジョー・ブリーズ、ゲイリー・フィッシャー、チャールズ・ケリー、リチャード・カニンガム、トム・リッチー、ジョー・マレーら、ファットタイヤの先駆者たちが殿堂入りとなった。マイク・シンヤードも、同じく聴衆から選ばれ高い評価と栄誉を与えられた1人であった。彼の後に、スペシャライズドスタッフの中からは、少なくともチームキャプテンのネッド・オーバーエンド、デザイナーのジム・マーズ、レースサポートチームのトム・ヒラードを含む3人がMBHoFからの栄誉を受けている。

今日、MBHoFは世界中のバイク業界とマウンテンバイクファンの支援を受けながら、その文化に光を与え続けている。詳細は、mtnbikehalloffame.com

33
私のスタンプジャンパー その1
デニス・ウェバー（Denise Weber）
2台のスタンプジャンパーを持ち、1週間に150マイルを走る65歳

ビル・ヘニオンはほとんど毎日、2台のスタンプジャンパーのうちの1台に乗り、1週間に約150マイル（約240キロ）を走る。65歳にしては悪くない。

ビルの10代の孫がシングルトラックを走行できるようになった時、ビルは、もし孫と同じペースを保ちたいのなら、自分の古いスタンプジャンパーをアップグレードしなくてはならないと感じた。孫の最新の「SR XC」は、リアの4バーリンケージデザインのおかげで、荒れた路面でもスピードを上げることができるとは、火を見るより明らかだった。

ビルが日常で使用しているバイクは、23年前に購入した1982年製のラグ付きで、スチール製のスタンプジャンパーである。「あちこち走り回る時に使用する、大好きな1台だ。」ビルは続ける、「地元の魚釣りの穴場に行くのにも好都合だよ。」と。

ビルはまだ引退するわけではない。しかし、自転車に乗ることでフィットした身体のおかげで、いまだに自分の好きなことが何でもできる。ビルは語る。「バイクは私の人生そのものなんだ。」

34 & 35
無料のテクニカルサポート
マイク・シンヤードは、気が狂ったのか？

1985年頃、マウンテンバイクのイベントは、好き者の集まりともいわれるほど特化したものだった。そこでマイクは、より多くの人たちにその魅力を知ってもらう為、プロモーターを雇い、一方、スペシャライズド社のスタッフたちは、コースのセッティングや掃除、テント張り、エントリーに関する様々な作業をバックアップした。

レースを確実に運営する為に、カリフォルニア州ソノマカウンティーのトム・ヒラードをスタッフとして迎え入れた。彼は、レース運営がうまる最も現場慣れした人物であり、NORBAルールブックの著者でもある。そういうわけで、マイク・シンヤードはバンの鍵をトムに渡し、トムは今では伝説となったロックホッパー、ランプストンパー、カミカゼダウンヒル、ウィスキータウンなどのレースに出かけて行った。

36 & 37
到着

北緯7.275--西経107.879の地点に行ったことのある人は、それほど多くないだろう。一方、コロラド州デュランゴが有名なのは、ちゃんとした理由があるからだ。そこはユタ、アリゾナ、コロラド、ニューメキシコの4つの州が接する砂漠地帯の南西に位置し、インディアン居住地があり、山に続く道が広がっているからである。車で、ロサンジェルスから14時間、デンバーからはその約半分の所要時間だ。そう、陸の孤島なのだ。

何も馬鹿にしているわけではないが、1980年の4月1日のことだった。ネッドは1965年製ダットサンピックアップトラックで自家製のトレイラーを引っ張り、デュランゴからサンディエゴに向かった。デュランゴより35マイルほど南で、デュランゴより2、3千フィート標高の低いニューメキシコ州アズテックで一夜を明かした後、ネッドにとってのタージマハルを探すために、山々をどんどん進んだ。それは、ジャンクションクリークのトレイラーパークの一区画だった。そこがネッドの最終目的地であった。

2〜3年後、彼はロードレースを始めた。ローカルレベルのレースから始めて、たった1年でアメリカのベストレーサーになるクアークラシックに出場するまでになった。1983年のクアーズが終わったある日、ボブ・グレゴリオらデュランゴのローカルライダーたちが、ネッドに5速のクランカーを見せた途端、ネッドが釘付けになった。「それは、砂場にいる子供のようなものだった」ネッドは言い、直ぐに何かを直感したという。

それが何であったかは、その後のマウンテンバイクの世界での最高のリザルトを見れば明らかだ。4回のNORBA Nationalチャンピオンシップ、欧州世界チャンピオンシップ、UCI世界チャンピオンシップを制覇。これ以上の説明は、もはや必要ないであろう。

40 & 41
800ポンドのゴリラをあなたはどのように手なずけるのか？
心の準備をしなきゃならないよ。

最初に発行されたマウンテンバイク雑誌、チャーリー・ケリーのファットタイヤフライヤー1980年8月号の1ページ目に、明確な呼びかけがあった。「我々の権益を守るための組織無しでは、我々は自分の権益をなくしてしまう。ところが、真夜中に吹き荒れるブリザードのおかげで、彼は引き返さねばならなかった。」地元の店でマウンテンバイクを見つけることができるかどうかという話しり以前に、トレイルへのアクセスは、800ポンドのゴリラを手なずけることと同じくらいの難問だったのだ。

1987年の夏の話になるが、地方で多くの人がマウンテンバイクの楽しさを知り始めた時、トレイルへのアクセス問題が大きく膨らんだ。「二輪の恐怖」と、ニューズウィーク1987年9月28日号で大げさに取り上げられた。サクラメント近くのアメリカンリバーパークウェイからロサンジェルスのサンタモニカ山脈にかけて、自転車のシングルトラックでの乗車が禁止され、公園からも一掃された。国立公園の全てのトレイルを閉め、BLM（土地管理事務局）が森林から自転車を排除しようとした。もし、マウンテンバイクに将来があるならば、マウンテンバイカーは結束して早急に組織作りをしなければならなかった。

この問題は、5つのカリフォルニアにベースを持つ支援団体の代表者たちに向けられ（マリンのバイシクル・トレイルズ・カウンシィル、イーストベイのバイシクル・トレイルズ・カウンシィル、サクラメント・ラフ・ライダーズ、ロサンジェルスのコンセント・オフロード・バイカーズ・アソシエーション、サンノゼのリスポンシブル・オフロード・マウンテン・ペダラー）、彼らは、ロングビーチでの年1回のバイクショーで、話し合いを行った。そして6ヶ月もたいうちにIMBAが認可され、アクセス問題に真っ向から取り組み始めたのだった。

その当時、スペシャライズドの販売スタッフであったリンダ・デュプリーストとエリック・エイズモの熱心な働きかけで、スペシャライズドはIMBAに1,000ドルの助成金を贈った。これは、一企業がアクセスを主張する最初の大きな動きである。1989年のインターバイクで、リンダが会社に産業界への会合を持ちかけるよう説得した。その直後、時流に乗れるように認識させ、その整備や管理の為の資金を獲得し、さらにワシントンDCやデュランゴで初期のマウンテンバイク支援会議などを開催したことが、IMBA発展のターニングポイントになっていった。デュプリーストは、支援者のプレゼンテーション用原稿やビジネスプランを書き上げたり、バイク産業界とIMBAとのパイプ役になりながら、10年あまりIMBAの理事を勤め上げたのだった。

自転車業界のメジャーブランドと35,000名の会員から基金と支援を受け、IMBAは全米および世界中のトレイルへのアクセスができるように知識を深め努力を惜しまなかった。IMBA無しでは、トレイルの存続はありえなかったであろう。

IMBAを理解してくださった皆さん。さあ、IMBAのスローガンを、より多くの人々に伝えようではありませんか。詳細は、imba.com

42
私の相棒、スタンプジャンパー。その2
デニス・ウェバー（Denise Weber）

36歳の獣医師技師であるデニスは、ランニングによる膝の痛みに苦しんでいた。彼女のかかりつけの医師は、膝へのストレスを和らげるため、バイクライディングを勧めた。それが彼女のフィットネスに役立っている。自転車に乗ってから、彼女の人生は一変したのである。

もう少しバイクのモチベーションを高める為に、デニスは6ヶ月後のレースにエントリーすることにした。レースはハードであり、勝つためには、軽量で、もっと信頼性のおけるバイクが必要だと悟った。彼女はロックホッパーを手に入れ、そして2〜3シーズン後には中古のスタンプジャンパーにアップグレードした。「これは私にフィットするし、本当に、はまってしまったわ。」と彼女は言っている。「これまで経験したことのないスピードが出せて、自信が出てきた。」バイクライドはデニスにとって既にデイリーエクササイズとなっており、スタンプジャンパーで早朝の森の中を走ることは至上の楽しみなのだ。

このバイクライドのお陰で膝が強くなってきたが、ランニングはほとんどしていない。「スタンプジャンパーに乗っていたほうが楽しいわ。結局、今、私はマウンテンバイクレーサーなのです。」

43
エピック
それまでの常識を一気に覆す

5年間に、スペシャライズドは、マウンテンバイクの本を完全に書き直してしまった。1988年から1993年の間に、スペシャライズドは、スチールとカーボン、チタンとカーボン、メタル

マトリックス等のマテリアルを自由自在に操りフレームを量産できる最初の会社となった。（カーボンファイバーレッグのサスペンションフォークや完全にカーボンのフレームを実現したという話題を出すまでも無く。）冷戦が終わり名誉の殿堂入りを果たしたスペシャライズドの技術者、ジム・マーズがその新たな技術を記す為にペンを取ったその時、それまでの技術は過去のものになってしまったのだ。

レーガンがゴルバチョフにあの壁を引き倒すように頼んだ時、軍事機密とされていた素材や技術を一気に公開した。素晴らしい科学雑誌を愛し、当時としては洗練された3次元成形ソフトを使っての仕事に従事していたおかげで、マーズは最新の材料と技術を完璧に理解することができたのだ。

カリフォルニア州エルカジョンのプリンステニスラケットの子会社で、合成材作りをしていた技術者の一団がカーボンに着目した。彼らは直ぐにフレームに最適なチュービングとラグの設計に取り掛かった。「私は全てが上手く行くように、本当に頑張った。」マーズは語る。彼の設備の整ったワークステーションで、多種多様なテストと試作を繰り返した結果、スペシャライズドの長年のパートナー（日本のフレームビルダー）に、クロモリ製ラグの精密溶接を依頼することにした。ラグとカスタムデザインのチュービングを作るには、バイク全体を完成させる同様の作業工程を踏むため、2,400ドルという高価なフレーム＆フォークとなった。ラグは、スペシャライズド本社に出荷され、冶具上でカーボンチュービングと繋ぎ合わされた。各サイズにわずか2つの冶具という状況で、約2,000本のエピックが作られたのだった。

決して満足することは無く、マーズはチタン製ラグをこれまでのクロモリ製ラグの代わりに使った。しかしただのチタンではなく、マサチューセッツ州ケンブリッジの金属加工の専門家にチタンの加工を依頼した。こうして、更にグレードアップしたエピックをリリースした。

46 & 47
ミスターアメリカ
ネッドの世界戦参戦顛末とデュランゴ市民の願い*

もしもあなたが、その年の9月にコロラドのフォーコーナーズ・リージョンでラジオかテレビをつけていたなら、多分ネッドの名前を聞き、彼の笑顔を画面で見ただろう。また彼は、デュランゴヘラルドの記事に取り上げられるとともに、スペシャライズドプログラムの表紙をも飾っていたのだ。'The Captain winning the (upcoming) Worlds' とプリントされたTシャツの入手も白熱している勢いである。デュランゴ市民は、単に約束で世界選手権をホストすることのみに満足せず、デュランゴの英雄に優勝してもらいたいと思っていた。

ネッドはプロのロードレーサーあるいはトライアスリートとして、十分な収入を確保できてはいたが、マウンテンバイクが楽しいという単純な理由で、1990年、最初のマウンテンバイク世界選手権への出場を決めたのである。プレッシャーなんて何もなかった。むしろ、本当に最初のUCIワールドチャンピオンをデュランゴから排出しようと願っている市民の方に、プレッシャーが重くのしかかっていた。

デュランゴ市民の夢は、現実のものとなった。チタンラグとRockShoxサスペンションフォークをつけたプロトタイプのエピックアルティメイトに乗って、35歳のネッドは130名のエントリーに潜んでいたライバル、ティム・ゴールド（イギリス）とトーマス・フリシュクネクト（スイス）を引き離し、勝利に向けてスピードを上げた。10,000人の絶叫するファンの夢をかなえる為、ネッドは単独で逃げ切った。もし今日あなたが彼に世界選手権のことを訊ねたら、答えはこうだろう。「それは、本当に安堵以上のものであった」と。しかし、もう1人のデュランゴ市民であり、最初のダウンヒル世界選手権の覇者となったグレッグ・ヘルボルドは、対照的に、こうコメントした。「最大限の努力の末表彰台に立ち、世界チャンピオンのメダルを獲得した。まるでミスアメリカになったような気持ちだ。」ネッドは、おそらくミスターアメリカ以上の人物だろうか。

*ネッドのチームメートたちも健闘した。サラ・ヴァレンタインがエリート女子レースで勝利戦線に加わり、リサ・ミュイックも女子ベテランクラスで優勝した。

48 & 49
スタンプジャンパー M2
国防省が輝きを放つ

「誰がメタルマトリックスの成分を知っているのか？」1991年4月1日のサンフランシスコクロニクルは問いかけている。武器弾薬統制法のために、アルミニウムやアルミニウム酸化混合物についての情報はオープンではなく、秘密事項取扱の許可があるかどうかと、ちょっとした障壁となったのだ。その結果、世界でメタルマトリックスから作られた消費者製品はひとつも無かったし、成型や溶接はほとんど無理だった。しかし、ジム・マーズ、マーク・ウィンター、マーク・ディヤチーとスペシャライズドのスタッフは、宇宙開発競争資材のコードを読み解いた。その結果、モスクワ市では無い最初のメタルマトリックス製品、すなわちスタンプジャンパーM2が誕生した。

衛星のノーズコーンと戦車のドライブシャフトに使われることを予想して、M2は通常のアルミより10パーセント軽く、20パーセントほど硬いと報告されている。ペンタゴンの重要なブレーンの話では、その強さはアルミ酸化物の大きな塊、セラミックによるとのことである。以前にも増して軽量で強靭であることから、それをバイクのフレームにすることが、簡単ではないことは明白である。

前年、スペシャライズドがトライスポークのカーボンホイール（7回のツール・ド・フランス優勝を成し遂げた、かのアメリカ選手が使っていたものと同じデザイン）の開発時にデュポン社と業務提携を結んだ時と同じように、今回もスペシャライズドのスタッフは、産業界の巨人とのパートナーシップをはかった。M2のパートナーは、世界で2番目に大きいアルミニウムの会社であるデュラルカンである。デュラルカンのサンディエゴ駐在のメタルマトリックスコンポジット（合金）担当科学者は、チュービングの正しい調合方法と、溶接の仕方を研究した。そしてアナダイジング社とチームを組んだスペシャライズドは、ポートランドに新しい生産設備を導入。そこでM2チューブを押し出し成型し、溶接によりフレームを作った。2社は押し出し成型と溶接行程のリサーチ＆デデロップメントを繰り返し、M2フレームをさらにいっそう軽いものへと仕上げていった。

確かに、軽くて高硬度を持つフレームを作ることは、時間とコストがかかる。でも、それでいいのだ。マイクが、簡単な方法を選べと言ったことがあるだろうか？

50 & 51
情熱
スペシャライズドの語り部

マイクが長年の経験から学んだ事がある。もしもゲームで勝ちたければ、自らの勝ちたいという気持ちを湧き立たせ、情熱を傾けることができるゲームに参加しなさい。

そこで、スペシャライズドが語り部を必要としていた1989年、バイクを作るのと同様に話をすることについても情熱を持っている人を探していた。ひとつの幸運が次の幸運を呼び起こすように、スペシャライズドは、最高の語り部達（シルバースタインとその仲間達）をパートナーに迎えることができた。GSPを聞いたことがあるのかい？ ヒット作を多く生み出した広告代理店だよ。リッチ・シルバースタインは、熱心なサイクリストで、自転車でマリンカウンティーの自宅からゴールデンゲートブリッジを渡りサンフランシスコのGSPの本社に通っている姿がしばしば目撃されている。

最後は、ちょっとした素晴らしい語り部の話。アンホイザー・ブッシュ、モーガン・スタンレー、ハーゲンダッツ、サターン、ヒューレッド・パッカードなどのクライアントからの仕事をこなしながら、GSPは、独創的で印象深いスペシャライズドの広告を作り上げたのである。

ここで学んだものは？ それがロックバンドであろうとバッドライトのコマーシャルであろうとパンを焼くことであろうと、素晴らしい仕事をするには強い情熱が必要であるということである。

52 & 53
Stumpjumper Field Guide/1992 S-Works Epic Ultimate
フレーム 1990年から1995年にかけて、スペシャライズドはカリフォルニア州モーガンヒルの本社で、約1,500本のエピックアルティメイトチタンカーボンフレームを手がけた。エピックアルティメイトのチタンとカーボンのフレームは、その後、カスタムビルダーのコピー対象となるほどだった。

ラグ アップグレードしたモデルからスタンダードのエピックまで、エピックアルティメイト用ラグは、マサチューセッツ州ケンブリッジのマーリンメタルワークスで作られていた。原料と加工の費用が非常にコスト高であった為、アルティメイトフレームの生産は完全に採算度外視であった。

チュービング 超高モジュラス合成素材を使った初期のエピックアルティメイトフレームは、あまりにもろく実用的ではなかった。そこで、エピックアルティメイトフレームには、ユタ州ソルトレイクシティのマックリーンクオリティコンポジットが生産した、低モジュラス素材が使われていた。

フォーク 羽のように軽いダイレクトドライブクロモリフォークが搭載された。エピックアルティメイトとカーボン・チタンフューチャーショックFSXは同時に発表されたが、この2つが組み合わされて販売されることはなかった。

限定モデル：1995年にモーガンヒルのブライアン・ルーカスにより作られた最後のエピックアルティメイトフレーム。生産された60本のフレームの、トップチューブに、シリアルナンバーが刻印されていた。ネッド・オーバーエンドには1990年世界選手権優勝を記念して、シリアルナンバー1のフレームが贈られた。

54 & 55
博物館とマウンテンバイク？ スミソニアン博物館は、100年以上も前に、英国貴族、スミソニアンの寄付によりワシントンD.C.に設立された。この文化機関と、シングルトラックとの間に何の関係があるのか？ 先に答えを言うなら、十分関係があるということである。

科学者であり探検者であるジェイムズ・スミソニアンは、「知識の増大と普及」を推進するための機関を設立することを目的として、アメリカ合衆国に500万ドルを超える大金を寄付した。青年時代のスミソニアンは、科学の研究に励む若い学生であり、かつ、冒険を好む好青年だった。彼はスコットランド北西沖のヘブライズ諸島へ旅をした時に、地質の観察をしようとして滑れかけ、体の危険をおかしていた。今、彼が生きていれば、マウンテンバイクのパイオニア達のエネルギーと発明力に感心したことであろう。

今日、スミソニアンが創設した機関は、世界で最も大きな総合博物館施設として発展しており、アメリカには国立自然史博物館と研究センター、アメリカ歴史博物館、国立動物園、国立航空宇宙博物館、芸術産業博物館、スミソニアンマガジン、などが含まれている。そしてアメリカ歴史博物館の片隅には、スペシャライズドのスタンプジャンパーが置かれているのだ。

1989年、スミソニアン博物館は、マウンテンバイクに目を向けた。彼らはアメリカの交通手段を変えた革新的な設計例としてマウンテンバイクのスペシャライズド社に電話をかけた。「バイクを送っていただけないでしょうか？」「勿論です」とマイクは答えた。スミソニアン博物館には、蒸気船から宇宙船まで、全ての展示品と並んで、スタンプジャンパーが展示される。少なくとも、タイヤに空気が入っているといいのだけれど。

56 & 57
いかにして商品価値をアピールするか
ポルシェが、かなりうまくやっているようだ。
電話は、ハーム・ラッゲイ彼自身からきた。ドイツ語訛りのあるオランダ人なので、彼が本当にポルシェの設計者なのかは、少しも信じられなかった。「2.7ポンドのカーボン/チタン・エピック アルティメイト（ポルシェで言えばスパイダーにあたるモデル）について話をする為に、スペシャライズドの何人かの技術者をワイザッハの秘密工場に送ることができるか？」そのようなオファーには、なかなかノーとは言えないものだ。

そのプロジェクトでは、スペシャライズドの最も才能あるデザイナーと技術者が、やりたい放題することが許されたのである。最高のバイクを作り出す為に、経済性とか、伝統とか、納期というものを無視した。Sワークスは、遠征中のライダーが、世界選手権で勝利をおさめるべく、ロケットのように飛び出していく。ツアーリーダーの証であるイエロージャージを着るライダーもいれば、オリンピックのメダルやXゲームのメダルを取るライダーもいるし、アイアンマン攻略を行うライダーもいる。スペシャライズド社では、商品化されなかった様々なバイクやパーツも、また大きく山積みにされている。これらの中には素晴らしいアイディアが満載であり、別の機会に何らかの形で商品化されることが多い。しかし、それはSワークスの課題である。課題は、とにかく最高のものを作り出すことだけなのである。

58 & 59
スペシャライズド製のサスペンション？
未来のショック？
チーム・スペシャライズドのキャプテン、ネッド・オーバーエンドは、デュランゴでの1990年世界選手権で勝利をおさめた時、スペシャライズド エピック アルティメイトには、プロトタイプのロックショックスRS-1が装備されていた。ネッドの他にも女子のチャンピオンとなったジュリアナ・フルタド、ダウンヒルチャンピオンのグレッグ・ヘルボルドがサスペンション・フォークを使用していたことは、マウンテンバイクの未来像の明らかな方向性を示していた。

スペシャライズドは、独自にサスペンションフォークの研究を始めた。ロックショックス RS-1のテストライドを重ねた結果、スペシャライズド技術者チームがロックショックのオイル&エア式サスペンションフォークを超えるものを創り出す事ができないことを、理解するのに時間はかからなかった。そこでスペシャライズドは、サンタクルーズ TKストリートのターナーの店に行き交渉。マーク・ウィンター率いるスペシャライズドの技術者は、たくさんの外部部品を製作し、ロックショックスは、複雑なインナーパーツを供給してくれた。

1992年までに、フューチャーショックフォークは、スペシャライズドのオリジナルアイテムとして位置付けられていた。しかし、最初のフォークはロックショックスが自社のラベルで生産していたものと、かなりの部分が似ていることが容易にうかがえる。理解するのに時間がかかった。マーク・ウィンターによりデザインされたFSXは、価格よりも徹底的にクオリティを追求する、スペシャライズドのカーボン・アンド・チタニウム・エピック・アルティメイト・フレームと同一線上のものだった。オイル&エア方式のロックショックス Mag21 インターナルに、FSXはカーボン製のロアレグを初めて使用したサスペンションフォークが登場。そのフォークは高そうに見えたし、実際高かった。カーボンレッグ1本当り100ドル以上と言われた。コンポジットチューブとCNC加工されたアルミブレースとのマッチングも高価なものとなった。「その時点で我々は、スペシャライズドのフォークが、ロックショックスより優れていることを知っていた。」と、マーク・マックブライン（ポール・ターナーの幼なじみで、スペシャライズドのサスペンション開発担当者）は言っている。だがこのようにも付け加えた。「それはまた、我々が生産するには高すぎるしろものであった。」

これを機に、スペシャライズドはフォークを中心に開発を進め、サスペンションを含むパーツの開発や製造競争よりも、ディレイラーやリム、ペダルのように、いろんな会社の中から最良のモデルをチョイスしてコンプリートバイクを作る方法に戻ったのである。だからと言ってスペシャライズドが、永遠にパーツの開発競争から離れることを意味したのではなく、社長のマイク・シンヤードはいつでもその機会を捉えようとしていたのである。

62 & 63
フューチャーショック リア
スペシャライズドとオーストリアの巨匠が作り上げたもの
我々はそれを 1991-ish と呼んでいる。初期のスタンプジャンパーの立ち上げ以来10年間、オフロードの世界は誰もが想像できない勢いでふくらんでいる。リアサスペンションの発想は、レーダーに突然現れるネヴァダ砂漠上のUFOのように、まさに突然の出現であった。当時のサスペンションは、あまりに複雑で信頼性に疑問が残るものだったので、スペシャライズド社のスタッフは、それが良いものだとは思わなかった。

リアサスペンションに関して、どのようなものであったかではなく、どのようにすることができるかを考えながら、マイクは完璧で不安の無いサスペンションバイクを作り出すためのチームを構成した。マイクの求める妥協の無いフルサスペンションバイクとは、ペダリングパワーを無駄なく推進力に替え、ハンドリング操作性と快適さを向上させる（27ポンド以下の軽さ）、メンテナンスが少なくてすむフルサスバイクを意味した。現在でも、それはフルサスペンションの理想の形であるが、1991年当時、そのようなサスペンションを作り出す技術は、存在すらしないのである。

1年以上の歳月をかけて、ジョン・オニール、マーク・ウィンターとマーク・ディヌーチらのエンジニアは、実物大の模型を作り、考えられる全ての試作を行った。良いものもあったが、完璧なものは無かった。試行錯誤を繰り返し、替え、ハンドメイドとコンタクトをとり、彼らの意見に耳を傾けた。そして遂に、1970年代にヨーロッパの中心的な自動車業界で働いていたオーストリアの技術者、ホルスト・ライトナーに、マジカルマルチリンクデザインのアイデアでチームの要求を満たすことができた。ディヌーチとデザイナーにとって、ホルストは多くの特許を持つ、モーターサイクル界の巨匠であった。ホルストにとってスペシャライズドは、これまでの蓄積を表現する場になった。スタンプジャンパーのリアサスペンション開発には、このような背景が存在していたのだ。

マルチリンクリアサスペンションのプロトタイプを手に入れ、ディヌーチとその仲間は、現存するスタンプジャンパーのフレームからリアトライアングルを取り外し、そこに初期のFSRを作った。スタジアムいっぱいになるほどの壊れたバイクの山とともに、遂に生産がスタートしたのだ。しかし、話の進行がちょっと早すぎるかもしれない。実は、シートチューブのマウントが十分に出来上がっていなかったことが判明したので、1993年の夏、最初の数百の量産バイクがスクラップされる運命を辿ったのだ。「FSRの開発は、ほとんど、皆の経験という財産で進められてきたのだが、実際、我々には、FSRの様な複雑なバイクを開発するうえで必要な洗練された試験設備や開発が無かったのだ。」ディヌーチはこのように語っている。スペシャライズドにとって、FSRは特別な存在となっている。彼らの、それまでの研究開発プロセスを考え直させたバイクだからだ。「技術的根拠が無い空想は、もういらない。本当の技術とテストの繰り返しこそが重要なのだ」と、スペシャライズドで長年にわたってR&Dを担当しているクリス・マーフィーは語っている。

64 & 65
カクタスカップ
スペシャライズドがスポンサーした春休み
1990年代、バイクレーシングは、非公式な春休みであった。アリゾナ州で開催されたカクタスカップステージレースの魅力は、誰も否定できないものだった。5,000から6,000人もの友達と孤高のソノラン砂漠で、マウンテンバイクライディングやレーシングに毎日過ごしてみませんか？（時間に余裕があれば、もっと長くいても良いぞ）そんなに悪いものではないだろうか？ 「実際にカクタスカップでレースしたことはあまりはっきりと覚えていないんだよ。しかし、全てのレースで私は燃えていた」と長年のマウンテンバイクジャーナリストで初期のフレームビルダーのリチャード・カンニングハムは語っている。

ハヴァスとかデイトナに行くように、カクタスカップのタイミングは重要であった。その3月中旬の日に、レーサーにとってワールドカップのプレッシャー無しで、冬期トレーニングの成果を検証するチャンスを与えてくれるばかりでなく、バイクビジネスにとってもシーズンに向けてのスタートをきる良い機会を提供していた。その全盛期にはカクタスカップは業界のもう1つのサイクルショーと位置づけられ、バイクをアピールしプロモーションする絶好の場となっていたのだ。

何年かの間に、シングルトラックの数は増え、コーナーに轍ができたりと、そのコースはカクタスカップが北に移動するたびに変化していった。しかし、2つのものが常にカクタスカップには存在した。岩とサボテンのトゲである。適正な空気圧とスライム（パンク防止液）を使って、パンクに対し万全の体制をとるも、アンベルト・エッコの小説よりも多くのトリックキーな要素が含まれるコースでは、サボテンのトゲの一刺しから逃れることができないのである。プロであろうとアマであろうと、イベントのフォーマットは、とてもユニークである。タイムトライアルの4ステージ：ダートクリテリウム、ダウンタウンスコッツデールでのファットボーイクリテリウム、弱肉強食のクロスカントリーレース、そしてエンターテイメント性を多く含むバームとテーブルトップのジャンプで、幕を閉じるのである。スペシャライズドのスポンサーライダーは、スコッツデールから地元に数個のトロフィーを持ち帰った。長年スペシャライズドでライダーをしているスティーブ・ティルフォードは、ほとんどファットボーイでは負け知らずで、数年間で21回の勝利を収めた。

大きなカステントとマルチステージのイベントフォーマットが、1990年代の半ばには上手く軌道に乗った。カクタスカップは拡大路線を辿ることになるのである。カクタスカップは、イリノイ州、オハイオ州、カナダ、フランス、ドイツ、および日本で開催された（現在も継続されている）。多肉植物（サボテンなど）をあまり見かけなくなったが、それを見ることができる最適なイベントになっている。

66 & 67
Stumpjumper Field Guide/1994 S-Works FSR
フレーム スペシャライズドのチタンとカーボンを使用したマルチリンクサスペンションフレームのチュービングは、ダイレクトライブと命名された。このチュービングは、1994年型FSRの前三角にも使用され、スペシャライズドのスチールフレームの頂点を示すものとなった。

サスペンション Ampリサーチの創業者ホルスト・ライトナーと共同で開発したFSRサスペンションは、快適さ、操作性、効率性を最大にするために、フル稼働して、完全に独立するように設計された。何年もの間にFSRのデザインには、驚くほど多様性があることが証明された。

フォーク RockShox と共同で開発し、RockShoxにより製造された。FSXはスペシャライズドが設計したカーボンのローアーレッグと M2合金ブレーキブレースと共に、カスタマイズされたRockShox Mag21 の内部部品を使用した。

シフター 1993年に最初に製造された SRAM SRT 500 8-速 ツイストシフターは、シカゴに拠点を持つメーカーが作った最初のハイエンドレース用シフターである。

タイヤ ピンクフロイドのアルバムの名前にちなんで付けられた Umma Gumma は、自転車用として最初に実用したソフトコンパウンドである。

70 & 71
勝利の為のレース参戦。
胸に「S」の文字をつければ、簡単に飛ぶことができる。

航空券？ 君は航空券を購入する話をしたいのかい？ 我々が最初にスポンサーしたオフロードバイカー、ローレンス・マローンにバンの鍵を渡して以来、スペシャライズドは、たったひとつのこと、表彰台で最上段にあがることを目指して、何百万ドルものお金を使い、多くのライダーとサポートスタッフを世界中に派遣してきた。

記録集の表紙を開いてごらん、そうすれば胸にスペシャライズドロゴをつけた男女が、デトロイトの猛牛や高性能トヨタプリウスを自慢し、そのマークを叩いている姿を見つけることができる。ところで、記録の行方は？ 我々は世界選手権エリートクラスで5回の優勝を飾り、何ダースものUCIワールドカップでの勝利とワールドカップタイトル、そして、多くのノーバナショナルの国内タイトルを獲得した。

赤いチームジャージを身に纏ったスペシャライズドのライダーにとって、優勝することが全てになる。スペシャライズドは彼らの厳しい要求に、例外無く対応する。彼らが勝利をおさめる為のギアを提供しサポートすることに、大きな価値を見出しているからなのである。チーム無しにSワークスは作れなかったであろうし、Sワークス無しでは、スタンプジャンパーカーボンハードテールフレームやバンプと大腿二頭筋からの衝撃を区別できるブレインショックは存在しなかったであろう。

72
私の相棒、スタンプジャンパー。その3
ヴェドラン・ノヴァク（Vedran Novak）
難民の経験を経て、スタンプジャンパーに乗りノルマルシーに戻ってきた。30歳のヴェドランはクロアチアのザグレブに住んでいた。1990年代、クロアチアで国内紛争が起きた時、シベリアに安全な場所を見つけ、何千人もの人々が難民となった。人々は自分で背負うことができるものを抱えて家を離れ、普通は自転車を運ぶ余裕など無いので、難民キャンプではレース用バイクを見ることなど、もちろんない。

「事態は非常に悪化し、再度バイクに乗れる時が来るなどとは考えられなかった。」とシベリアにいた時のことをヴェドランは語る。彼を始めとする他のクロアチア人は、スロボダン・ミロシェヴィッチによりひどく弾圧されていた。基本的な日用品でさえ手に入れるのが難しく、生活は容易ではない。もちろんバイクは、誰もが買おうと思うできないほどの贅沢品であった。幸いにも、ミロシェビッチは投獄され、バルカン半島での生活は少しずつ平穏を取り戻した。ヴェドランは倹約し、お金をためて、中古のスタンプジャンパープロを購入することができた。「新しいスタンプジャンパーが来たよ、自転車にこんなにたくさんの面白みが詰まっているとは本当に思わなかった！ 私にとってバイクはいかに人生を良いものにできるかを、常に知らしめるものである。」彼は連日、バイクに乗り続けている。

73
発射の瞬間
パルプトラクション、永遠のフリーライドムービー
2インチトラベルのマルゾッキ ボンバー シングルクラウンフォーク装備のハードテールに乗って、男が小石が浮いた斜面を降りて来る。「バイクが見えないかい？ フリーライディングのルーツ。バルプトラクシンのディレクターで伝説のスキーヤー、ブリティッシュコロンビア在住のグレッグ・スタンプのおかげで、バルプトラクションはレンズをノースショアに向けた最初のバイク映画となった。これらのシーンは、フリーライドを生んだのである。パルプトラクションは、他でもやっているこのゴッドファーザーであるリッチー・シリーとブレット・トリプルをフリーライドの虜にした。バギーショーツと言えばバスケットボール用、長旅と言えば中国へのノンストップフライトを連想させる時代であった。

その当時、マウンテンバイク映画の制作会社が存在しなかったので、スペシャライズドのマーケティング部門がスノースポーツの人間に着目し、最先端のライディングと美しい風景、ライ

フスタイルの一端を見せる映画を作るための撮影を始した。「我々のほとんどがスキーやスノーボードの映画に出ていたので、この映画を撮る時には雪の上でやっていたのと同じことをやった。そして、ジャンプしたり、飛び下りたり、何回も繰り返す。」とシレーは言う。「その後、以前 Pump Traction を撮影したスポットのひとつに戻り、我々が2インチのトラベルフォークを装備したハードテールでジャンプやライディングをやってのけたことを思い出し、笑いが止まらなくなった。」

勿論、それは洗練されたものではなかった。しかし、永遠にビデオに収められたスポーツ誕生の瞬間である。

74 & 75
余分なものは何も無い。
ハードテイルへの決別

クロスカントリーレースで速くなるには、トレーニングに次ぐトレーニング、さらにトレーニングを重ねなければならない。そうすれば、多くの人々の中から選ばれる、数少ないスーパーモデルのような存在になることができる。FSRxcも、この様な方法で設計された。XC レーサーの身体の様である。まるで、XC レーサーの身体の様である。

しかも、そのタイミングは、完璧であった。1996年、サスペンションバイクにはより大きなトラベルが搭載されたが、その分、重量も加算されることとなってしまった。この傾向は、家屋の高さもある岩を飛び越えるよりも、スピードや効率性を重要視する人々にはアピールしなかった。

そこで、スペシャライズドの開発チームのベン・ケープロン、マーク・ノリス、マイク・ディッシャーム、ジェフ・ピントは、他の競合メーカーとは異なる路線を歩くことに決めたのである。各部の肉厚を削ぎ落とし、形状を最適化し、3インチトラベルのFSRxcを作り上げた。これまでのFSR よりもトラベルが1インチほど小さいフレームは、軽さと剃刀のようなシャープなハンドル操作性を実現した。ディッシャーム、ケープロンとその一団は異なる新しいアイデアを試みた。まず、FSRxcの大幅な軽量化の秘密は、ショックユニット、メインリンク、シートステイが1つのピボットで連結されており、通常の半数のハードウエア（ボルト、ワッシャー等）しか使さなかったからである。

その結果、FSRxcは剃刀で作られたピボット機構のサスペンションバイクで、最も軽いものとなった。最高の部品をアッセンブルすると25ポンド以下となり、さらに、1998年のインターバイクショーには、20.6ポンドのサンプルバイクが展示された。

どうして私を信じるのか？1999年に遡ってMTBR.comに投稿されたライダーレビューをチェックしてごらんなさい。「私は決してハードテイルに戻らない。このバイクに乗ったら、貴方もきっとそうなるでしょう。」

78 & 79
ナパーム爆弾！

デック：世界一のアスリートがマウンテンバイクシーンで炸裂したなら、彼は焦土と化した地球のみを残し、保険保証書をびりびりにやぶき、足元に撒き散らしてしまうことであろう。

彼はマウンテンバイカーではない。それが事実である。彼自身、自分をバイカーとみなしたことは無い。マウンテンバイクで山を走るが、それは彼がスノーボードをしたり、何台も所有しているキャデラックの1台に乗るのと同じことなのである。

彼は、マウンテンバイカーではなかった。彼はロックスターであり、自転車に乗ることなんか想像したこともなかった。ドナースキー場でボードに乗った最初の日から、人々はミニシュレッドがすっかりスノースポーツの世界で有名になってしまったと言った。その後、彼は本当の愛好者だ。「1992年にオレの祖母が亡くなり、オレも飲んだ暮れて、酒場で喧嘩し、何もしない完全な馬鹿になってしまった。しかし、オレは、自分の愚行にも愛想をつかした。オレは全てのエネルギーをスポーツに注ぐことによって、祖母の死に対する己の怒りを吐き出せばいい。そんなの糞らえ、オレは全てに勝つ。」そこで、ミニシュレッドはナパームに形を変え、戦う相手を片っ端から打ち負かすことに決めた。「勝つってことは、気持ちがいいぜ！」

1996年までに、彼はマウンテンバイクに転向した。オリンピックの影響もあり、転向のタイミングとしては、これ以上のものは無かった。パーマーは、数々の賞賛と注目を浴びて、マウンテンバイク史上、伝説の男となったのだ。黄金のラメ入りのスーツを着用、トロイ・リーがペイントした大型マシンで会場入りし、6文字の契約書を書いた。「マイクとその他の状況を知っている者は、その契約が誇張された契約であることを知っていた。「ビッグレースで勝つことを、十分真剣にとらえてはいなかった。彼はいろんなことを頭の中で練っていたに違いない。」と元メカニックのジョー・'バック'・バックレーが言う。

80
エンデューロ
道を選ばない、抜群の走破性

世紀末来、人々はカオス（天地創造の神）を予言していた。Y2Kの話題が皆の口々から出ていた。「この世に終焉は無い」と主張する宗派もあった。しかし、はっきり言って、そんなものは無く、全く別の話なのである。

オフロードライダーにとってカオスというのは、バイクと道路、そしてこの2つがどのように融合するかを考えることである。マウンテンバイクの人気上昇に伴い、トレールの混雑が予想された。アクセスが簡単なトレールは、一定の規則により大混雑を避けるようになった。その反面、コアなマウンテンバイカーたちは、込み合うような所がアクセスが簡単なトレールを避け、より一層の荒れたトレールにチャレンジするようになった。このようなトレールはかなり人里遠く離れているので、コアのライダーたちは、軽さよりも耐久性に優れたバイクを選択したのだ。

長時間のトレールライドは、幸運なことに、スペシャライズド社では研究の一環として位置付けられている。1991年にスペシャライズドの技術者がサスペンションの第一人者、ホルスト・ライスナーと共に長時間のテストライドを繰り返し、フォーバーリンケージ・リアサスペンションを完成させた。このサスペンションシステムが搭載された、荒々しいトレールでのアグレッシブなテストライドを繰り返し、1999年の夏、マックスバックオーン構造によるガッチリとした最初のエンデューロプロファイルが完成した。前年度のFSRよりわずか250グラムの重量増で、耐久性とトラベル（4.6インチ）を大幅に増やすことに成功した。エンデューロのユニークなVシェープのフレームが、十分なスタンドオーバーハイ

トを確保し、驚異的なコントロール性を生み出した。2000年に向けフレームは軽量化され、より洗練された。マシンの確固たるイメージをアピールする為に、マシンにジャストフィットするフェンダーが追加された。

81
私の相棒、スタンプジャンパー。その4
ボブ・ブリューワー（Bob Brewer）

ボブ・ブリューワーは、2年前からスタンプジャンパーに乗り始め、90ポンド（40.5kg）の減量に成功した。それ以前、彼は人生の中で、最悪の状態にあった。たった5フィート7インチ（約168cm）の身長に対し、体重が250ポンド（112.5kg）になり、血圧も腎臓病を悪化させていた。40歳の主任会計責任者で、2人の子どもの父親であるボブに医者は「体重を減らし健康的な生活を送りなさい。さもないと、この世に長くいられないよ。」と言った。

そこで思いついたのがバイクライドであったが、彼の古いバイクは重く、快適ではなく、あまり楽しいものではなかった。そこで、ボブはインターネットで検索をし、熱心なサイクリストからのスペシャライズドバイクについての高い評価を知った。特に2004年のスタンプジャンパー・コンプに大いに注目した。結果、それを入手した。バイクライドを心から楽しめるようになったのだ。

最近のボブは、必要であるからという理由や、それが体に良いからという理由で、バイクに乗っているのではない。彼は今、ただリフレッシュのためにバイクに乗るのである。ボブはかつて非常に病弱で、疲れやすく、ストレスがたまり、何もやる気が起こらなかった。今はエネルギッシュで、生きることに喜びを感じている。

「1週間に4回から6回、地元のシングルトラックでバイクライドをしている。結果的に90ポンド減量できたのだが、何よりもバイクライドが楽しいんだ。私は今、自分の人生の中で1番いい時を過ごしているんじゃないかと、思うことが多い。」と語る。

82 & 83
愚か者から、あなたは何を学ぶことができるのか？
必要な時にのみ作動するサスペンション

ワールドカップのスタート直前に、プロ選手のバイクのハンドルバーを押し、フロントフォークがどれだけ動くのか、チェックしたことがあるかい？彼らのフロントフォークは、ほとんど動かないことを言っておこう。実際、多くの場合、フォーク内の空気圧をぎりぎりまで上げているので、トラベルというものが無い。つまり、彼らがそれを好み、それで勝てれば何も問題は無いのだ。そうでしょう？

長年スペシャライズドでサスペンションに携わってきた技術者のマイク・マックアンドリュース（通称ミック）に聞いてみれば、何が問題であるかを教えてくれるだろう。彼は本当に効果的なサスペンションを作るのに、何年もの歳月を捧げて来た。スペシャライズのチームメンバーたちが、ある一定サイズ以上のギャップを通過する時にのみ作動するサスペンションが欲しいと言ってきた。サスペンションの解決策で頭がいっぱいだったマイクは、その時、閃くものがあった。

FoMoCoの技術者であった友達が、車のタイヤが大きなこぶに当った時にのみ圧縮されるよう設計したショックについて、ミックに話したことがあった。このショックを稼働させる為にはショック自体に衝撃を与える必要があったので、デトロイトでは「愚か者（ジャーク）ショック」と呼んでいたのだ。そういうわけで、ミックは自分版のジャークショックをいじくりまわし始めた。モーガンヒルで、彼らはそれを愚か者のショック（Jerk's Shock）と冗談で呼んだ。

ミックは、それは非常にスマートだと思った。なぜなら、ショックは路面の凸凹とライダーからのインプットの違いがわかるからだ。彼はプロジェクトを「ブレイン（頭脳）」と名づけ、すぐにプロトタイプを作り上げたが、信頼できるものではなかった。その後、彼にはこれだという閃きがあった。もしジャークショックの心臓部（インナーバルブ）を後輪のハブ軸に近づけることができれば、全てがうまくいき、迅速に作動し、信頼性が高くなるのである。彼はそれを実現した。補助チャンバーがブレインになる。より精密な個所と生産に関してフォックス社からの支援を受け、完成に漕ぎ着けたのだった。

次に紹介するのはフィリップ・メイルハーグである。ハードテールでフォークをできる限りポンプアップしてレースをしていたライダーの人だったが、ブレインショックを搭載したエピックに乗り、世界選手権で優勝を飾った。（オーケー、フィリップ・メイルハーグは、何かの化学的不均衡のために次のシーズンは休んでいたが、エピックにはなんの不法もないことはいっている。）

今日、ミックのトレイルサイドチューニングを備えたブレインショックは、レースバイクとトレイルバイクの両方にアッセンブルされている。幅広いライディングスタイルに対応できる、十分に「賢い」ショックなのである。

86 & 87
デモ

世界で最も過激なトリックをこなすバイクは、大量のレゴから始まった。

ダーレン・バルクロス。フリーライディングの新しい「顔」。彼には、限界、常識、先入観を知らない兵器が必要だった。大きなギャップの衝撃を受け止める十分なトラベル、急坂を素早く安定して下ることができるジオメトリー。超低重心と低いスタンドオーバーハイトが生み出す走破性。そして、フロントディレーラーの装着。この要求に対し「問題無いよ、我々はそれができるよ。」とミックは答え、デモを設計した。

そういうわけで、ジェーソン・チェンバレン、ブランドン・スローン、ロバート・エッガーを含むスペシャライズドの技術者、設計者、製造責任者たちのチームは、レゴブロックの山で遊びながら、プロジェクトに没頭した。彼らが共にレゴブロックをパチっとはめ合わせることにより、デモの基本的なサスペンションコンセプトを素早く簡単に作ることができた。つまり、レゴブロックに没頭することで、皆の心が1つになり、素晴らしいチームワークを生み出したのだ。カリスマエンジニアとして名高いジェーソン・チェンバレンが、コンピューターに向かって苦労しながら設計を開始する前に、既に設計の基本は出来上がっていたのだ。

もちろん、レゴで遊んだことが、デモを作り出す過程での最も簡単な部分である。3次元設計ソフトを使い、モーガンヒルのスペシャライズ本社の試作室でプロトタイプを作り、何度も何度もテストを繰り返して商品化することは、時間と、多額の費用が掛かることは言うまでも無いことだ。

チェンバレンがコンピューターを駆使し、ノースショアライドのフィードバックを盛り込んで

設計したデモが、製造部長のブランドン・スローンに渡された。9インチトラベルとサブスイングアームと6つのピボットポイントによって増大されたフォーバーリンケージを装備していた。デモを設計する際に、チェンバレンはこれまでのバイクに使われたことがないほど高価な冷間鍛造法で、非常に複雑な形状のインゴット（フレームの材料）を作ることにした。ショックが取り付けられる中間部は、鍛造時に、何と5百万ポンドの圧力を必要としたのだ。

最も深いドロップや、最も広いギャップ、最も硬いこぶに対応したバイク製造の始まりが、レゴ遊びであったなんて、誰が想像できたであろうか？

88 & 89
30年間走り続けて、チャンスを待っていたのさ。
誰が年寄りだ？

30歳。昔はお祝いというより、自覚をする年齢であった。子供っぽさに別れを告げ、大人らしく振舞う。今は、ちょうどサンダルをリフレッシュして、昼前からビールを飲んで仕事の手を休めてしまう時（平日にかかわらず）。未だ、誰もそれについては言いたがらない。破れかけた服を着た男が、ステムやその他のパーツを、サンノゼのシングルワイドのトレーラーで売り始めてから、30年の月日が経とうとしている。

決して否定できない事実は、（スペシャライズドが設立されて）30周年記念モデルのスタンプジャンパーが、これまでのスタンプジャンパーよりも洗練されているということである。まるで時間を超越し、「誰でも何処にでも連れて行きます。」と微笑みかけているかのようだ。ドリームシルバーのフレームを、ちょっと見て御覧なさい。スペシャライズドの伝説的デザイナー、ロバート・エッガーの「ルックスが良いものは、その性能も良く見えるんだ。」というコメントが理解できるだろう。風景としてのイタリアのドロミテアルプスは永遠である。「バイクには強靭な形が組み込まれた時、より強靭に見えるんだ。」と、エンデューロ、ヘミ、ターマック等のスペシャライズドの宝石をトータルで監修したエッガーは語っている。

90 & 91
キャプテンの走り
集団の先頭で走り続けること

キャプテンの為の土曜の夜がやってきた。一晩99ドルのホテルに泊まり、素敵な弦楽の音色に酔いしれる。傷ついた右足に氷を乗せ、ベッドの足のスピードビジョンがちらちら光っている。翌朝7時スタートであっても、彼は遅いローカルニュース見、秘密のエネルギー源を最後の一滴まで飲み干すのだ。それがキャプテンのやり方である。

1996年、ネッド・オーバーエンドがレースの世界から引退した。スペシャライズドは、その秋に、引退記念パーティーを開いた。だが彼は引き続きワールドカップ、NORBA Nationals、ロードレース、ヒルクライム、ダウンヒル、デュアスロン、トライアスロン、Xテラ、マラソン、トレイルラン、アドベンチャーレースなど、とにかく出場できるであろものは全て出場していている。まるで引退という言葉は、似つかない。もしそれが乳酸値の上昇と、アドレナリンの増加に関与しているのであれば、それがまさにキャプテンの姿だ。そして彼は、50歳の誕生日に、非常に過酷といわれるワシントン山レースで4位に入賞している。

ネッドが1990年に行われた第1回マウンテンバイク世界選手権クロスカントリーのチャンピオンであることはよく知られているが、それ以前の彼の偉業を知っている人は少ない。1980年にトライアスロンのアイアンマンで24位に入る。1983年に初めてマウンテンバイクレースに優勝。伝説のラレーチーム（アンディー・ハンプステン、ロイ・キックマン、スティーブ・ティルフォード）とクアーズクラシックに出場している。1987年には、欧州とNORBA 世界選手権にも優勝しているのだ。

輝かしい過去を持つネッドだが、何も特別扱いや賞賛を求めず、競技者として朝7時に自分の生活を始めるのである。「若者より自分が強いということを証明しようとしているのではない。私は単に先頭集団で皆と競い合うのが好きだから、ここにいるのだ。結局、レースが大好きなんだよ。」ネッドは語る。

92 & 93
Stumpjumper Field Guide/2006 S-Works Stumpjumper Carbon

フレーム　バイクフレームを製作するカーボンとしては最強のFACT Y570から作られたフレーム。Sワークス カーボン スタンプジャンパーは、その機能性と剃刀のように鋭いハンドリング操作性が見事に融合されたマシンに仕上がっている。

ショック　いつも作動し、いつも効率を高める為に硬直するかが予想できる、最初のショックである。2006年はブレインフェードが、ライダーの好みに応じ、ブレインショックのフィーリングを調整できる機構を搭載したのだ。

タイヤ　サスペンションをフル稼働させて高速ライディングを楽しむカーボンスタンプジャンパー用に開発されたタイヤ、アドレナリンプロ（Adrenaline Pro）26 x 2.0は、重量を削ぎ落とすために120TPIケーシングを使用している。優れた回転抵抗性とトラクションのコンビネーションを実現する為、デュアルコンパウンドも使用している。

ハンドルバー　カーボンスタンプジャンパーのコンポジットフレームに、見事にマッチング。オーバーサイズのカーボンバイクは、わずか175グラムと軽量。6度のライズと8度のバックスウィープが、ライダーへのホールディング性をアップする。

サドル　2006年モデルとして、ライバルのデザインが一新された。スイートスポットの血液の流れを妨げない、スペシャライズド特許のボディジオメトリーの技術が生かされている。

94 & 95
未来は？

物事が、どこに向かって進んでいるのかを予想するのは難しい。

偉大な人々は挑戦を続ける。Y2Kを覚えているでしょう。

我々が確信していることの1つは、マウンテンバイクのトレイルとマウンテンバイクという文化を語り継ぐ殿堂を、保護していく必要があるということである。そこで、我々は、この本から得る収益金の全てをIMBAとマウンテンバイクの名誉の殿堂（MBHoF）に寄付するのである。

6 & 7
献辞

20 小时以前、20 天以前、还是 20 年以前—对第一次骑山地车的经历依然记忆犹新。刹车时的刺耳声音。它们几乎以其独有的方式穿过、跨越、经过了一切崎岖与艰险。几乎是一切。它像一只大猫一样轻松而优雅地穿越荒野。就像 XR-250 一样滑过地面。第一次漂亮的腾空而起，虽然有些警戒意味，带给您的却是一种甜蜜的痛苦。这种感觉简直难以置信—无法想象的甜蜜的初吻，一个美丽耽溺的前奏。

山地车能为您带来这种感受。它就是有那种力量。粗犷而又亲切；虽然危险，但是它那宽而高的车把手、柔软的车座和细长的车架，也向时让您感到它的可爱。山地车并不是简单地注入一种新的感情和想法，它还将郊区的医生、城市的水管工人和农村的教师聚集在一起。并带领人们的喜爱集在一起，并带领那些令人无法想象的冒险的又令人激动的领域。哪怕只是在他们所处的街区附近绕行，山地车使像我们一样的人们，在感受快乐和经力冒险的同时得到了情感的回报。

我们花费这么多篇幅讲述的故事可能仅仅是有关技术的故事，但山地车绝非是与技术有关的故事。我们也会关注自行车使用的究竟是哪种前复的变速器。但是，它更多的是一种文化和激情。Stumpjumper 的最初设想完全是出于一种激情、灵感和洞察力，它以一种简单的方式表达了您的青睐。今人高兴的是，人们对 Stumpjumper 的关注，使它和其它同类运动和文化繁荣在 25 年内不断壮大。为此，我们感谢每一位山地车的喜爱者：是你们将它载入史册，使自行车文化得以创新并赋予它生命。

8 & 9
宽胎序言
这项运动的起由？

快看，那些家伙在骑山地自行车吗？尽管山地车发明仅 20 余年，取得今天这样的发展却是其必然趋势。归根结底，在崎岖不平的道路上行驶使宽胎应运而生，并在人群中备受青睐。

那么，在 60 年代 John Finley Scott 和他的 1953 Schwinn Varsity 是如何穿越几千公里的崎岖路面，包括攀登加利福尼亚州西尔瑞山区 (Sierra Mountains) 的 14,260 怀特山 (White Mountain) 的呢？他用的是山地车吗？

如果我们再追溯到 1897 年，20 名布法罗战士骑车 1,900 英里环游西部，行程直达今天的黄石国家公园。当然他们并不当然不是穿越旧的西部荒原进行公路自行车运动。此外，他们的这项运动也完全不是为了荣誉。

那么，人们究竟是从何时开始放弃简单的公路越野，而开始衷情于山地车越野呢？是从 1974 年的 12 月 1 日旧金山湾区的车手 Russ Mahon 首次为一辆破旧的车子安装变速器而说起？是 1977 年 10 月，Joe Breeze 首次用自己自制的多档宽胎自行车，参加著名的 Repack Downhill 开始？或者是从几年之后，最早的 Stumpjumper 设计师 Tim Neenan 跨上早期的原型车，攀登圣荷西专业办公室后面的小山开始？

寻找这种运动究竟源自何处的答案，最好留给那些大学教授或是任何一个下午都出没在旧金山 Zeitgeist 沙龙中的自行车高手。

10 & 11

当第一批户外运动者—五个来自马连郡的 clunker 高手于 1978 年骑克莱斯特德比特，参加"第三度、实际为第二届"的 Pearl Tour 比赛时，他们发现正如 Joe Breeze 所说的："一个停产的老煤矿小镇，它的最后一批患有黑肺尘病的矿工曾陷入煤矿梯段，而如今的步行和骑自行车的年轻人却在工厂跳舞。"70 年代的克莱斯特德比特起源于 1859 年的科罗拉多淘金热，虽然看上去更多的昂贵，但由于其早期的屈膝旋转式滑雪和麦草疗法，而被认为是嬉皮士风格的前沿。当时常其芜和肮脏的新生地才总喜欢被赋予诸如 Cloud、Star、Plank 和 Suitcase（由 Briefcase 演变而来）之类的名字。

由于户外运动的悠久历史--这座小镇因为科罗拉多第一辆滑雪缆车的发源地而享有盛名-嬉皮士和老顽固们对户外运动所有的快乐表现出共同的喜好，这也同样适用对自行车运动经久不衰的热表。当然，1978 年加入前辈队伍的人并不是真正意义上的自行车手，他们只是骑自行车而已。通常，丹佛的自行车类整列、老式的 Schwinn、Hawthorne 和 BF Goodrich Clunkers 山地车引起了新的改装风潮。即使将近 8 个月有冰雪的覆盖，克莱斯特德比特的街道几乎全是泥土，则此宽胎车则被证明是在城市穿行最好的工具。

1976 年夏天的某个深夜，clunkers 以其穿行 12,692 英尺从 Pearl Pass 至阿斯彭杰罗姆酒店 (Jerome Hotel) 的酒吧而证明了其卓越的表现。同年 9 月，15 名充满热情的、极具影响力的灵魂人物登上他们自己的 clunkers 驶向了北部的阿斯彭。在 Pearl Pass 举行了整晚的宴会之后，一如 Crested Butte Pilot 报道，骑手和他们的支持者喝了一桶啤酒、三瓶杜松子酒、两加仑葡萄酒和三瓶香槟酒-他们踉踉跄跄地驶回杰罗姆酒店 (Jerome Hotel)，他们在那里喝了更多的酒并创造了这个传奇故事。

14 & 15
全体欢呼！
Clunker 之王

每一位拥有山地车的男女老少都应当为 Charles R. Kelly (a.k.a. SeeKay) 举杯高歌，为他向大海呼喊祈祷。曾隐居于加利福尼亚州旁尔法克斯的非常封闭地区的 Charles 先生，甚至在为山地车发明之前就创办了第一份山地车杂志-Fat Tire Flyer。当许多人声称发明了与宽胎相关的第一副车架、第一辆山地车和举办第一场比赛时，是 Charlie 确定了旧车改良小组的独特视角。他并展示了究竟什么是"旧车改良"。

"虽然 Clunker 在某种程度上仿造了用于崎岖道路上行驶的轻型摩托车，但它们仅仅是在外观上相似，高速拐弯则是其车身艺术的独特之处。摩托车有大轮胎和避震器，而 Clunker 却没有。这使它在路面上即使遇到很小的障碍物也非常容易离地面。急

转弯时，Clunker 虽然既没有摩托车用来使后轮转动的加速器，也没有避震器。尽管如此，专业骑手的转弯速度要比你想象的要快许多。"

"由于判断错误，您滑入一个久失修的带有斜坡的弯道。身体失去了控制，此时，您必须迅速做出决定：冲出车道或摔倒。摔倒了…可恶…衬衫破了，肘部也流血了。没时间管那些了，肘部破了，自行车怎么样了？还好…跳上车，一边向前滑行，一边弯腰用手把链条搭上。换回原档，继续前进，把浪费的时间补回来。"
--Charles Kelly
《单车杂志》1979

16 & 17
宽胎序言
Specialized 掀起了宽胎零件的革命

第一年的销售额为 $60,000
下一年的销售额为 $128,000
再下一年的销售额超过了 $200,000

"回首过去，一切都在慢慢发展，但对我而言，时光却好似在飞逝，"Specialized 公司的创始人兼总裁 Mike Sinyard 在创立 Specialized 品牌后的第一年这样说。

很久以前，人们为网站以专门展示链轮图片的收藏（这是真的，例如 blackbirdsf.org）。由于对自行车的痴迷，人们卖掉唯一值钱的东西 (Mike 卖掉了一辆大众面包车 (Volkswagen Microbus))，将所得的收益用于投资一次到另一大陆的自行车旅行，这无疑证实为对自行车难以自拔的痴迷。然而当我们回顾 1973 年，Mike 组装一辆蓝白色的 Bob Jackson 旅行自行车驶向欧洲时，发现那才是真正的疯狂。

途经英国、阿姆斯特丹 (wink-wink) 和巴塞罗那，Mike 到达了意大利北部波河流域的人群，他当时的感觉我们可想而知；当您发誓一直要在做什么，但也想象自内心必然感觉到每一分钟都可能在发生奇迹。而且也确实发生了。碰巧，Mike 在米兰的青年旅舍遇到了一位女士。当与意大利自行车业的领导人青 Cino Cinelli 夫人关系密切，此人创建了一家以他的名字命名的车架和零件公司，Mike 对其十分看重。

一个月之后，Mike 带着许多 Cinelli 零件回到了圣荷西。他把自己所有的积蓄都投入到 Cino 著名的车把、车管和车架上。那时，没有汽车，也没有诸如易趣网 (eBay) 等手段帮助他销售从米兰带来的商品，他便骑单车拖着满载的零件到达湾区，向自行车经销商出售他的设备。

二百周年纪念时，Specialized 已经发展成为十分成熟的自行车和零件进口商，其存货已经在专业市场上占有一席之地，且成为宽胎自行车骑手喜爱的各种零部件的经销商。欧洲的业余爱好者们喜欢 Huret DuoPar 的变速器、Mafac 的刹车和 Columbus 的车架管，Specialized 已在西海岸的多数车架制造商为其代理商，进入了急速发展的自行车行业的颠峰时期。自行车工匠们，诸如 Joe Breeze、Albert Eisentraut 和 Tom Ritchey（他们将承包 Specialized 的设计的做双人跨在铁鼓的踏车工作）都是车匠们，他们会定制一些奇怪的设备，如 TA 曲柄和悬臂提升螺栓，这使 Mike 对它们的用途十分好奇。它们的用途是改造自行车，Mike 能够用他的零件帮助他们完成改造。

20 & 21
Stumpjumper Field Guide/1981 Stumpjumper

Stumpjumper 实地指南图包含五个特定的部分。尽管这些说明会随着自行车种类的不同而有所变化，但都会有这五个部分。有关 1981 SJ 的说明如下：

车架：由圣布鲁兹 Lighthouse Bikes 公司的 Tim Neenan 设计，最初的 Stumjumper 车架采用 TIG 焊接方式。如果您的 1981 车架上有接头，则是 81 年下的产品。应该是蓝色的涂漆？选中这种颜色是因为它与 Sequoia 旅行自行车中使用的蓝色相似。

前叉：著名的 Golf Club 前叉，这件珍品是从当时制造的 BMX 前叉改良而来的。最初的钢制 Stumpjumper 把手是在 Magura 摩托车车把的基础上改造的。

刹车握把：以所有最早的 Stumpjumpers 为标准，Tomaselli Racer 刹车握把是为 70 年代末咖啡馆赛车用摩托而设计的。它们采用了能够改善刹车体验和性能的重型刹车线。

轮胎：Specialized 利用其在成功制造公路车系列轮胎方面的丰富知识，制造了第一批轻型山地车专用的轮胎，即 Stumpjumper。如果您的车上还有一对这样的轮胎，这种 25 岁的山地车轮胎则是珍宝之物。

曲柄：Specialized 曾经向美国出口 TA Cyclotourist 曲柄用于旅行自行车，它有精致的抛光表面，且允许极低的传动比。由于并非特为越野使用而制造，因此故障率可能较高。

22 & 23
JOE BREEZE；山地车的先驱、车架制造者、作家

我是在加利福尼亚索萨利托我家附近的 Bike Odyssey 见到它的。"我当时想'那个高尔夫球棒似的树管'能值什么呢？而且，我还对它使用的 Tomeselli 而不是 Magura 刹车握把非常感兴趣，更且它仅售 750 美元。我想它们的销量是不错的，"他这样说。

TOM RITCHEY；山地车先驱、车架制造者、发明家、国家级赛车手

它 (Stumpjumper) 的做工很粗糙，但基本上代表了当时日本的技术水平。虽然我们的自行车价格要高两倍（重量轻两倍），但这个价格对 Stumpjumper 来说却很合理，并且在当时也有其吸引人的地方。

RICHARD CUNNINGHAM；Mantis Cycles 的创始人及《山地车行动》(Mountain Bike Action) 的编辑

Stumpjumper 笨重、颠簸，而且急拐弯不够灵活，但看到它时，我就好像被人在脸上打了一下似的尖叫起来："这才是真正的山地车…就应该骑这种车！"不久之后，我就组装了我的第一辆山地车。

DON COOK；山地车先驱、山地车名人堂副主席

当时，一辆手工制造的 Ritchey 价格为 1,200 美元至 1,500 美元。我们见到了 Stumpjumper，正是它们正在交谈"。突然间，我们不再需要等待三个月或四个月才能从 Tom (Ritchey) 和 Gary (Fisher) 那里购买到一辆自行车。

JACQUIE PHALEN；山地车先驱；WOMBATS 创始人、作家

我曾见过 Stumpjumpers，但不知道它们是什么。当时，正走 Gary Fisher 走在一起，他把它们描述为"复制品"。虽然我并未看到任何人在书中出示这样的叙述。

美国的 VICTOR VINCENTE；山地车先驱、Olympic 公路赛选手、比赛发起人、艺术家。

我对记忆力虽然减退了，但我确信我当时对它的反应是认为它就是一种标准、实用而且能为大众所接受的设计，而不像那些以前的老式自行车。

RICHARD HEMINGTON，英国；将 Stumpjumper 销售到美国的第一人。

对 Stumpjumper 包装在一个盒子中，需要从头开始组装。我仍然记得那些零件散落在地上，我花费了很长时间将它们组装在一起。我记得当时我很恼，如果这种自行车真的开始出售，我们将面临怎样的麻烦！当然，它确已出售，而我们也遇到了这种麻烦。

JOE MURRAY；早期的自行车选手、设计师、试车手

我的 1981 Stump 简直就是一个小雪橇，但我记得尽管我需要以独特的方式从马连郡山上曲折的防火道上直冲而下，我仍然十分喜爱它。我开始参加 Gary Fisher 比赛后，他送给我一辆自制的 Team Stump 山地车，我多么希望我能重新拥有它。

MERT LAWWILL；摩托车传奇人物、早期山地车的设计者

"当我见识到了它 (Stumpjumper) 是以怎样的价格出售，及它要比我的自行车好多少之后，我意识到该结束了，我该回到我的摩托车身边了。"

24 & 25
原型车广告
新型的自行车自然需要新的广告；一中可持续 25 年的广告

在不太遥远的多少年前，Mike 住在一间活动房屋（单宽的）中，在黄色的纸张上写下了他的产品目录，并说想讨好他的雇员整晚睡在那里无法塞入仓库的轮胎上。那时，他简直是骑虎难下了，然而，就是这样才成就了著名的 Stumpjumper。

原厂生产车不同于 Specialized 或其它厂商制造的自行车，旧的销售标准将不再有效。在 Whole New Sport 活动图为 S 总部之前，Specialized 大部分都是黑白的，且有广告占据当页或更小的篇幅。在接下来的 25 年中，Specialized 的这种印刷在光滑纸张上的优雅的暗色调原型车广告发生了全新的变化。拍摄者为 Jack Christensen 在拍摄苹果电脑手册的同一间车库中进行这一广告，其设计者为 Specialized 的长期合作者 Patrick Mountain，Whole New Sport 当然不会错过当时最大的黑白杂志。

当然，这很不错，也很完美，但是，广告中那个人为何要以着装袜和工装裤的形象骑车出现呢？他便是最初的 Stumpjumper 设计者 Tim Neenan，他这样回忆到："在当时，根本没有骑山地车的专用服装，除了那样也不到会穿什么样的衣服了。我正好有一些工作穿的工装裤，所以就那么搭配了。"

26 & 27
发动您的引擎
20 世纪 80 年代前五年的比赛，好像是回到了 40 年代后五年的 NASCAR：在任何一块场地标记当出赛道，让选手排成一列，然后向下挥动旗子。

选手们要睡在车中、交换他们的报套支票并抽大麻烟。这是一百年来并未曾见到过的原始的、真实的、纯粹的两轮竞赛。这种事情是无法悄无声息地发展的。自 1983 年加利福尼亚州内华的首届会议至 1990 年的 NORBA，其成员数从 0 增加到 20,000。

28 & 29
独霸天下的 Stumpjumper 团队
如果您骑着一辆粉色的自行车出现在起跑线上，最好也拥有一台。

追溯到 1984 年，从未有过这样正规的山地车团队，就算有，Stumpjumper 团队不被视为正常。也许这支山地车队很正式与在抽烟，并把希望都在 Nike Lava Dome 之类的运动鞋上时，他们却骑着配有下弯式车把的粉色自行车，脚穿自行车专用鞋。由 Specialized 公路赛领袖 Woodul 组织的 Team Stump 是一次越野尝试。"Woody(Woodul) 将我们这群 1 类公路赛和越野赛选手集结在一起，并把他的想法和方法应用到公路赛中，"前 Team Stumpjumper 骑手 Dave McLaughlin 说。"我们接受训练、组织成队，并在比赛中使用策略。"

在该队成立的第一年，Woodul 曾挑选出一批天才，包括因自行车越野赛而一举成名的 McLaughlin、Gavin Chilcot（后来加入了著名的 7-11 公路团队）、北加利福尼亚州本地的 Mark Michelle 和 Alan Ott 及美国的越野赛"教父"Laurence Malone。搭着 Specialized 的这股东风，这些人们骑遍了美国，赢得了当时水准颇高的大型比赛：Suntour 太平洋国家挑战赛、Gant 挑战赛（华盛顿州西雅图市区赛）、伊利诺州艾加哥市区赛）、科罗拉多州 Golden 市区赛、佛罗里达州坦帕和迈阿密市区赛）、Ross 阶段赛和一日精英赛，如 Rockhopper、Rumpstomper 和 Norba 全国锦标赛。"这些比赛在当时水准还很不平均。大部分不像现在的比赛一样具备竞争性，但是，Joe Murray 或几位职业公路赛选手，如 Andy Hampsten 和 Steve Tilford 的出现，让比赛变得更加精彩，"McLaughlin 在比赛的初期这样说。

在几乎水准一不一的比赛后，Team Stumpjumper 就演变为了 Specialized 队，成为世界上最优秀、装备最精良的山地车团队。早期的专业团队造就了世界冠军 Ned Overend、Lisa Muhich、Sara Ballantyne 和越野"红人"Daryl Price 及山坡赛能手 Elladee Brown 和 Paul Thomasberg。后来的 Specialized 宽胎赛队摒弃了粉色自行车，但他们仍然在业内独霸天下。

30 & 31
1984 年 Stumpjumper 团队
如果您骑着一辆粉红色的自动车，您就会更快！

Jim Merz 采用日本制造的 Tange Prestige 管材设计了车架，1984 Team Stumpjumper 车架是 Specialized 当时生产的最轻的车架。

粉色 Stumpjumper Team 的独特之处还在于其前叉为 Specialized 的第一批有单肩盖的车叉，这要比当时使用的耳状又轻便得多。

幸运的是，车架底部的与 Team 和 Suntour Rollercam 特点相似的 U 形刹车只流行了很短的一段时间。磁铁式的 U 形刹车被认为是自行车界所犯的最大的共同错误。

1984 年 TriCross 轮胎取代了 Stumpjumper，成为高档山地车胎面的首选。它以造型简单的胎纹和在干燥、多尘条件下出色的抓地性能而闻名。

飞轮，一种顾名思义的装置，Stumpjumper Team 配有 26 齿 Shimano 600 公路自行车飞轮—而不再使用当时多数越野选手所喜爱的 30 齿的齿轮。

32
MBHoF (Mountain Bike Hall of Fame)
如果裸跑运动员和四弦琴都有名人堂，为什么我们不能有呢？

如果您搜索"名人堂"这个词，您会得到约 47,400,000 种结果。4700 万。没错，我们有采矿业名人堂、女牛仔名人堂、家用电脑名人堂、裸跑者名人堂和四弦琴名人堂。四弦琴名人堂！天啊，四弦琴名人堂当中有些什么样的人呢？也许比裸跑者名人堂中的成员更多，这是毋庸置疑的。

山地车名人堂设在克雷斯特德比特 Elk Avenue 的某个老加油站内，这是 Carole Bauer 智慧的结晶。80 年代中期很长的一段时间，在 Butte 当地的 Bauer 很担心如果不纪念那些以山地车文化的创造者所取得的成就和在他们的支持下创造的这种运动，他们会渐渐被遗忘的。

到 1988 年，MBHoF 就做好了接收第一批成员的准备。理所当然地，宽胎先驱们，诸如 Breeze、Fisher、Kelly、Cunningham、Ritchey 和 Murray 都在这第一批当中。同时，曾轰动一时，令人大为吃惊的 S 先生也被授予了荣誉。继 S 先生之后，MBHoF 至少有三位胸前有 "S" 标志的山地车选手获得过荣誉，包括 Captain、车架设计师 Jim Merz 和竞赛支持领袖 Tom Hillard。

如今，依赖于自行车行业和全世界山地车迷的支持，MBHoF 继续保持着它的辉煌与该文化的繁荣昌盛。请访问我们的网址 mtnbikehalloffame.com

33
我的 Stumpjumper N.1
Bill Hennion
2 辆 Stumpjumper 车，65 岁，每星期 150 英里

Bill 几乎每天都要骑他的那两辆 Stumpjumper 车（两辆 Stumpjumper 车！Bill 多幸福啊？）每星期大约要骑 150 英里。对一位 65 岁的老人来说并不简单了，对吧？

几年前，当 Bill 十岁的孙子开始接触单轨车时，他就明白如果想赶上 Jr，必须要改进他的旧 Stump。骑了几次之后 Bill 就意识到他最新的 FSRxc 山地车使他赶上了这个自以为是的小家伙。Bill 说，由于他的 FSR 车独特的四杆设计，现在他可以在崎岖的地方比以前骑得更快。

Bill 每天骑的车是一辆几年前买来的 1982 年生产的钢质 Stumpjumper 车（带有小双平面肩盖）。Bill 说："这是我到处游览时最喜欢骑的车之一。它可以带我到当地的鱼塘钓鱼，感觉真是太棒了。"

不过我想，Bill 毕竟不能回到年轻的时候了。但是，他说，多亏了他在山地车上发现的乐趣，他现在仍可以做他想做的事情 -- 如进行短途的登山越野。Bill 说："简单地说，山地车是我生活的全部。"

34 & 35
免费技术支持？
S 先生疯了吗？

甚至有人曾听我们说回首过去之前 - 实际上有些地方大约在 1985 年左右 - 山地车几乎到了疯狂的边缘。当时并没有很多的比赛，但每年都会出现兴奋的赞助商、让人热切期望的选手及很多的 Stumpjumper 并参加过许多大型的竞赛，也决定伸出援手帮助发起人举办比赛和赞助商参加竞赛。就像他们在 1982 年的公路赛中那样，他们决定从各种类型的自行车选手中提供免费技术支持。他们还决定从各个方面帮助发起人安排赛道、清理跑道、搭建摊位、驾驶领航摩托、做记录。无论如何，这些从 Morgan Hill 来的人士都决定着手去做。

为确保成功，他们雇用了加州索诺玛县当时最具实力的技术人员 Tom Hillard，他曾是 NORBA 规则手册的作者之一、Punk Bike Enduro 的发起人，于 1961 年宣称以他自己的方式修建了第一条印山车道，backindaze 车道 (1961)。因此，S 先生也带入这个前卫的领域，而 Tom 从此开始参加比赛，他使用过 Rockhopper、Rumpstomper、Reseda-To-The-Sea、Kamikaze 和 Whiskeytown 等极具传奇色彩的名字。

无论是 NORBA 全国比赛、Cactus 杯或是德克萨斯州的周二晚间俱乐部比赛，当 Specialized 亲切而勤劳的机械工，Tom Hillard、Dave Meyers、Steve Mosher 或 Joe Buckley 等对他们的故障自行车进行紧急修理（通常是免费的）时，车手们似乎总是在吸收能量。您应该知道让人无法抗拒的力量为之减轻膝盖的压力，从而帮助她恢复健康。自从她骑上山地车后，她的生活就永远地改变了。

当然，在公路赛中使用大型车和机械工无疑会增加费用，但 S 先生从不认为这是唯一

36 & 37
成功

世界上并没有很多人到过北纬 7.275 -- 西经 107.879 这个地方，因为这里实在没有什么吸引人的理由，这里是著名的杜兰哥和科罗拉多。这地位于新墨西哥州山口沙漠的中心。即使只带一盒 Costco 大小的 Gummy Bears 旅行包和司机，从洛杉矶驱到这里也要耗 14 小时，从丹佛出发要用近一半的时间。这里就是这么一个前个小村，后有着店的地方。

1980 年 4 月 1 日，Ned 驾着他的 1965 Datsun 小卡车从阳光明媚的圣地亚哥出发前往杜兰哥。在深夜的暴风雪中，拉着被他称为 "酷似 Clampett" 的住宿用拖车，终于不得踏上这程。那时他带了一些自行零件。然而，在阿斯特克和新墨西哥（杜兰哥以南 50 英里，且低于杜兰哥几千英尺）度过一夜之后，他又继续前进，穿过山脉后发现了泰姬陵 (Taj Mahal)：在 Junction Creek 活动房屋停放场租用了一个 8*35 英尺的单篷车位。是的，Ned Overend 先生终于到达了目的地。

为了支付租金，Ned 穿梭于 VW 入时的绅士、Squarbacks 和摩登女性之间，寻匿任何使其成为 Animas County 中入的机会。为调整他的 chi，他骑乘拖着货物往返于旧 Elmore Store。几年后，他开始参加公路赛，一年内从零开始发展为代表美国最好的团队的 Coors Classic 比赛。1983 Coors 之后，杜兰哥当地的三人组中的 "Bicycle" Bob Gregorio 向 Ned 介绍了他们的 5 级变速山地车。他着迷了。"感觉就像是小孩子在沙地上玩多一样，"队长这样说道。"我立刻意识到他会非常出色。"

果真如此。几年之后，Ned 创造了宽胎车的世界最好记录：四次参加 NORBA 国家锦标赛，NORBA 世界锦标赛、欧洲世界锦标赛和首届 UCI 世界锦标赛。不错，Ned Overend 以此为荣。

40 & 41
您如何驯服一辆 800 磅的 "庞然大物"？
您已经准备就绪了。

走在前沿的朋友们。在 1980 年 8 月发表的第一版山地车杂志的首页上，Charlie Kelly 的 Fat Tire Flyer 就开始强烈呼吁采取相关行动。"如果没有一个保护我们的利益的组织，我们的利益将无法受到保护，"SeeKay 申辩道。没有山地车以前，修山间车道简直是不可能的事。

到了 1987 年的夏天，当大多数国家的人们还沉浸在发明山地车的喜悦中时，车道问题开始在山地车发源国萌发。"双轮的力量"，Newsweek 在 1987 年 9 月 28 日这样评价。从美国萨克拉门托河附近的石河河畔的桑塔莫尼卡山脉，自行车被禁止单轨行驶或被逐出河道。国家公园停止了对活动房屋提供的服务，BLM 正在鼓励自行车进入森林地区。如果山地车想要制造奇迹，山地车手们就需要联合起来成立组织。赶快行动吧。

那年秋天，来自加利福尼亚的五个拥护团体 - 马连郡的 Bicycle Trails Council、东海湾的 Bicycle Trails Council、Sacramento Rough Riders、洛杉矶的 Concerned Off-Road Bikers Association 和圣荷西的 Responsible Off-Road Mountain Pedalers - 在长滩市 (Long Beach) 每年一次的自行车贸易展上联合在了一起。六个月内，IMBA 已经制定了规章，并准备好迎接任何最前沿的战斗。

正是由于 Linda DuPriest 和 Eric Eidsmo 的先见之明，以及 Specialized 的市场销售员的努力，IMBA 以自行车的名义获赠了 1,000 美元。这是 Specialized（或其它大型自行车公司）首次做出巨大跨越，从而取得拥护和成功。不久 Linda 说服该公司在 1989 Interbike 会上主办一次业内会议，鼓励其它公司加入拥护者的行列。这是 IMBA 发展的转折点，该会议帮助增长了为早轮运动而热衷于户外的意识，并提高为抗争广泛筹措资金，并提出开展各年的工作，包括在华盛顿和杜兰哥举行的拥护山地车的早期重要会议。DuPriest 在随后的十年内创建 IMBA 委员会，帮助早先的拥护者完善他们的产品展示和商业计划，并成为 IMBA 与自行车行业的纽带。

得到了资金和自行车界的著名选手和 35,000 多名现有成员的支持，IMBA 将在美国和世界的其它地区进行训练并为道路的使用而抗争。没有 IMBA，我们就没有可保护的行车之路。

您已经知道了我们的信条，那就请帮助我们募捐吧。请访问 imba.com

42
我的 Stumpjumper N.2
Denise Weber
30 多岁 -- 找到了有生气的新生活和赛车事业

Denise 是一位 36 岁的注册兽医，她在医生的建议下开始骑车。膝盖的毛病使她不能脱离，且车上不能跑步机上行走了，是的，她的医生建议让用骑车来减轻膝盖的压力，从而帮助她恢复健康。自从她骑上山地车后，她的生活就永远地改变了。

为了寻找一点其它的动力，从第一次开始决定骑车后，Denise 就开始了她长达 6 个月的骑车运动。在进行了一段刻苦的训练后不久，Denise 就意识到如果要参加比赛，就需要一辆更为理想的车了。于是，她买了一辆 Rockhopper，骑了一段时间后，她又换了一辆二手的 Stumpjumper 车。她说："它非常适合我，现在我完全迷上了它。""突然间，我的速度加快了，以往去我不知道自己还会有这么快的速度，而且我以前从没有过的自信。"Denise 是了基本的健康骑车，她说没有比清晨骑车更好地骑她的 Stumpjumper 车畅游在森林里更加惬意的事了。

现在，她的膝盖已经恢复，再也不需要拐杖了，甚至在骑车训练时双腿也是灵活自如。现在她经常跑步，"我很喜欢骑我的 Stumpjumper，毕竟我现在是一名山地车手了。"

43
Epic
改写山地车历史

五年之间，Specialized 完全改写了山地车的历史。1988 至 1993 年间，Specialized 成为了第一家原厂生产碳素纤维、碳素钛合金和金属基（不包括第一批具有磁材的减震前叉和第一批它有利用数字乙醚设计的原厂车架）车架的公司。冷战结束时许多当时的规则就被打破了，在这方面倾注最多精力的是山地车名人之一和 Specialized 的工程师 Jim Merz。

当 Regan 要求 Gorby 打破防冲线时，采用军用材料和技术的想法浮出了水面。正是由于他对科学期刊的热爱和在新奇 3D 模型软设备（Specialized 曾以 1985 年出价 250,000 美元购买）方面的工作经验，Merz 才能找到了埋想的材料和方法。

一批工程师在加利福尼亚埃尔卡洪 Prince 网球附属工厂进行复合物的研究，Merz 认识了碳素。经过他的 Applicon 动力工作站进行了诸多试验与辛勤工作之后，他发明了一种钴合金接头，并用 Specialized 日本的车架制造长期合作伙伴进行精密焊接。这样将整个工作量几乎用去，接头和定制的管材使 Epic 在车架和前叉上花费了 2,400 美元。后来，接头被送到了 S 全球总部，与优化的碳素管材结合在一起，并装入夹具以备不时之需。每种型号有两个夹具，制造大约 2,000 Epics 也不过如此。

Merz 对此并不满意，他很快就突破合金接头到钛合金，但并不完全使用钛合金，而该钛合金是由麻省剑桥的 Merlin Metalworks 的专家制造的。尽管是一个完全不同的 Epic。

46 & 47
美国先生
锦率如何在杜兰哥创建功绩 *

如果您曾在那年的 9 月在科罗拉多的四角地区收听或收看了广播和电视，您肯定听说过 Ned 这个名字或看到过屏幕上那张长满胡须的脸。他曾是杜兰哥 Herald 每日日文章的主角，且官方比赛节日的封面人物。甚至运有人穿上了 S 网印制的带有 "统率（即将）赢得世界" 图案的 T 恤。杜兰哥并不仅仅满足于召开第一次世界会议，他们还想让自己的选手赢得比赛。

Captain 本可以赢得专业自行车公路赛或三项全能运动，但仅由于自行车要其它项目更有趣这个简单的原因，他决定专心在自行车山地车上比赛。然而，在 1990 首届 UCI "标准" 世界锦标赛前一周，美国的越野之王并未意识到他如此简单。成为首届 UCI 世界冠军的压力直接压在这名杜兰哥当地人的肩膀上。

事情就这样发生了。35 岁的 Ned 骑着一辆装有钛合金接头和 bbq 黑色 RockShox 避震前叉的原型 Epic Ultimate 山地车，将 130 名骑手中仅有的几名挑战者 - 英国的 Tim Gould 和瑞士的 Thomas Frischknecht - 甩在了后面，并加速向 Purgatory 滑雪山冲去，赢得了比赛。除了将近 10,000 名尖叫的观众外，Captain 显得如此孤单。如果您今天问他的感受，他会说："那不仅仅是一种信仰"，然而像 Greg Herbold - 另一位首届世界锦标赛下坡赛杜兰哥当地的赢家 - 曾说到："当我站在领奖台上，手捧着为之奋斗已久的奖杯时，我感到自己久像是一位美国小姐。"那么，Ned 就不仅仅是一位美国先生。

*Captain 并不是 Specialized 在杜兰哥唯一的一位绽放异彩的赢家，Lisa Muhich 夺取了山女级别的桂冠，而 Sara Ballantyne 夺在妇女精英赛中险胜。

48 & 49
Stumpjumper M2
国防部露出笑脸

"有人曾听说过金属基复合材料吗？" 1991 年 4 月 1 日版的《旧金山记者报》(San Francisco Chronicle) 提出了这样的问题。由于军需品控制法案 (Munitions Control Act)（该法案限制了有关双铝氧化混合物信息的交流）的规定，这种材料的存在一直被保密中，很少有人通过 "安全检查" 的人听说过。那时世界上这种大空壳类材料的秘密，几乎无法成形成熔焊，然而，Jim Merz、Mark Winter、Mark DiNucci 及 Specialized 的工作人员把这种大空壳类材料制成，结果便产生了第一件由金属基复合材料制成但却不是针对莫斯科的 Stumpjumper M2。

据报道，M2 要比普通铝合金强度大百分之十，硬度大百分之二十，适合制造卫星鼻锥和坦克驱动轴。根据五角大楼大人物的说法，其强度来自于铝氧化物（一种瓷材料）的结合，这种铝氧化物加入到材料的 6000 种铝基微格中。虽然轻巧坚固，然而事实证明，利用这种材料制造自行车架却不是一项简单的工作。

因此，正如三幅各式碳纤维轮鼓（是的，与某位美国人在第七届环法自行车赛中获胜时使用的设计相同），S 团队于前一年与 DuPont 建立了合作伙伴关系，向这个行业巨头寻求帮助。M2 的 MMC 材料的合作伙伴则是 Duralcan，它是世界第三大铝公司的子公司。Duralcan 的圣地亚哥总部 MMC 的科学家们发明了制造管材的正确方法，而在 Morgan Hill 的另一些工作人员用 Anodizing Inc. 成为合作伙伴，在波兰生产新的生产车间以挤压 M2 管材并将其焊接为车架。该车间最终将彻底改造这种挤压和对接程序，使 M2 车架随着时间的推移更加轻便。

当然，这不是获得轻便、坚固车架的快速廉价的方法，但是 Mike 是何时告诉大家简便方法的呢？

50 & 51
热情
Specialized 小说家背后的故事

麦克上可以告诉你他这些年所学到的一件事情：如果您想获胜，就参加一场你有感觉的比赛、一场您充满热情的比赛。

所以在 1989 年，当 Specialized 需要一名小说家时，他们需要一个对讲故事就像他们生产摩托一样充满热情的人。一个接着一个的好运气，最后他们找到了。（当您将右拳放入左掌时按动手指，就会出现不一样的效果），他们联系到一位最优秀的小说家来写一部小说：再见了，Silverstein 和他的伙伴们。你没有听说过 GSP 吗？三个字：有内容？事实证明 GSP 中的"S"，即 Rich Silverstein，是一名敬业的、身材瘦长结实的摩托车手，人们总能看到他从位于 Marin 县的家骑车出发，穿过金门大桥，进入位于旧金山的 GSP 全球总部。

其余的都是一些历史故事。当它于应酬如 Anheuser-Busch、摩根斯坦利、Haagen-Dazs、Saturn 和惠普这样客户的同时，GSP 也制作了了许多你能够回忆的 Specialized 的创造性作品。

这里的教训是什么？无论是骑摩托、做百威啤酒广告或烤面包，如果你没有热情，你想正确的完成却很艰难的。

52 & 53
1992 Specialized S-Works Epic Ultimate*
* 这里展示的自行车是珍贵的极品，且从未以这样的配置售出过。

车架：1990 至 1995 年间，在加利福尼亚总部 Morgan Hill，Specialized 手工制造了大约 1,500 副 sub-3-pound Epic Ultimate 碳钛合金车架。Epic Ultimate 的碳钛合金结构是当时的第一个发明，在其后的十年为高端定制制造商们大力效仿。

接头：为了升级为标准 Epic，Epic Ultimate 使用了由麻省剑桥的 Merlin Metalworks 制造的钛合金接头。原材料的花费和分配的成本使车架的生产对公司造成了损失。

管材：早期的 Epic Ultimate 车架使用的高模量复合纤维管材易碎裂，因此不实用；来自盐湖城的 Maclean Quality Composites 较低模量材料，被用于犹他州大多数 Epic Ultimate 车架的制造。

车叉：尽管与 Specialized 设计的碳素钛合金 Future Shock FSX 共同展示，但直到 1995 年才生产出来的 Epic Ultimate 从未与悬架车叉一同出售。相反，它与轻软的 Direct Drive 铬钼钢模型一同出售。

限量：1995 年，最后一批全部在 Morgan Hill 由 Brian Lucas 制造的 Epic Ultimate 车架被生产了出来。60 个车架中的每一个都有独一无二的序列号，显示在车架顶部的饰板上。Ned Overend 被授予 #1，以纪念他在 Ultimate 的 1990 世界冠军。

54 & 55
博物馆和山地车？什么？您可能会问，一座由英国贵族捐款 100 多年前在华盛顿特区建的真正文化机构，与泥泞的山地车道有什么关系呢？但事实证明，它们有着密切的关系。

James Smithson 是一名科学家和探险家，他为美国人民留下了 50 多万美元用于建设一座促进"知识增长和传播"的博物馆。在年轻时，他是一名勤奋的学生、敬业的科学研究员、而且最重要的一个喜欢冒险的旅行家。他以冒着生命和残疾的风险和著称，这包括在苏格兰北部的赫布里底群岛的旅行中收集地质观察资料差点淹死，而且非常欣赏登山车早期创始人的精力和发明的。

现在，由史密斯家族资助的机构已经演变为世界上最大的博物馆系统，一个容纳美国最重要的历史资料和研究中心的系统，例如国家自然历史博物馆、美国历史博物馆、国家动物园、国家航空航天博物馆、国家艺术和工业博物馆、史密斯杂志以及摆放在国家美国历史博物馆的一个小角落里的 Specialized 的 Stumpjumper。

在 1989 年，史密斯家族发现了山地车，根据它们将改变美国运输方式的最佳示例载入史册的使命，它向 Specialized 拨通了位于摩根山的 Specialized 办公室的电话。麦克说："我们可以寄去一辆摩托吗？"现在，在蒸汽船和宇宙飞船后，史密斯家族的博物馆中又有了一辆 Stumpjumper 将布满灰尘。我们希望他们至少能为车胎充气。

56 & 57
您如何销售您的见解？
Porsche 看上去干得非常漂亮。

此电话来自 Harm Lagaay 本人。他是带有德国口音的荷兰人，很难相信保时捷（Porsche）设计部门的领导是否是真实的。Specialized 能够派遣工程师到魏斯萨赫（Weissach）超级隐秘的工厂探讨有关 Porsche Spider 2.7 磅的碳素钛合金 Epic Ultimate 自行车吗？很难对那样的官员说"不"。

因此，一些 S 团队的成员打好背包、带上护照，前往那位好心的博士所创建的工厂。他们看到的是魏斯萨赫（Weissach）拥有几千名世界顶级工程师的工作间，所有人都对那个辉煌的目标感兴趣：设计与制造最精确。制造汽车纯粹是为了比赛，制造汽车是为了勘测可供选择的燃料，汽车只是设计研究的成果。预算看上去好像奇思妙想的倾泻一般没有止境，尽管魏斯萨赫（Weissach）会定期生产优质汽车，但其它消费产品、任何产品也不必也不仅仅后直接进入市场。这是最纯粹的研究形式。最终，Porsche Spider 自行车只被付诸使用，而然，这一麻森林式的"无用工"却引发了：Specialized 在摩根山制造的自己的魏斯萨赫（Weissach）版本。

最初，该计划是为了让 Specialized 最具天赋的设计师和工程师彻底发挥他们的才能。突破所有的限制并实现预想。不管经济、传统和时间限制，仅仅追求一个简单的目标：制造随处可用的最好自行车。他们成功了吗？S-Works 自行车已经使骑手们在世界锦标赛的公路赛和山地赛中取得了胜利，骑手们赢得了自己的舞台并视觉着环法自行车赛冠军黄衫，骑手们赢得了奥运会奖牌和 X Games 奖牌，骑手们还赢得了"铁人"称号。在还有很多自行车和零件还未制造出来、尽管其中有一些好的想法和许多其它仍不可能在某个时刻问世，而这些都不是 S-Works 所关注的。他们关注的是不顾一切地做到最好。

58 & 59
Specialized 避震？
避震趋势？

当 Captain 获得了 1990 年在 Durango 举办的世界杯比赛时，他将一个 RockShox RS-1 避震前叉模型挂在他的 Specialized Epic Ultimate 前面。事实上，Ned 和其他顶级车手们（如 Greg Herbold）都很信任这一为重大项目发明的新装置，并明确地告诉大家：避震前叉是未来的趋势。

意识到这一机会后，Specialized 开始开发他们自己的避震前叉。试骑并拆分为几个早期的 RS-1 Ultimate 的 Winter 设计和生产，他们意识到制造由 RockShox 的发明者 Paul Turner 开发的气压 - 油压内部零件是很困难的。于是，他们驱车来到位于 Santa Cruz 大街上的 Turner 的商店，进行一次商务谈判：由 Mark Winter 带领的 Specialized 工程队将生产许多外部零件，而 RockShox 将提供复杂的内部零件和生产人员。

1992 年，Future Shock 前叉系列应用到了 Specialized 自己的山地车上，但是事实上，第一批车叉与 RockShox 以自己的商标生产的产品有很多相似之处。下面介绍 Future Shock FSX。在 Winter 设计的碳素钛合金 Epic Ultimate 车架的类似产品之上，它成为了使用碳纤底座的第一款避震前叉，可支架看上支架价值 100 多美元。模铸管和 CNC 制造的铝支架和配件使 FSX 比市场上任何产品都轻便且昂贵。Specialized 的避震权威 Mike McAndrews 和儿时伙伴 Turner 共同开发 RockShox，他说："当时，我们知道 Specialized 的前叉确实比我们的好？""而他们的优越之处正是我们负担不起的"。

但最终，避震器生产商之间的竞争使大家都明白了一个道理：在 Morgan Hill，谁都不会始终在前叉行业中保持领先。于是，他们开始网罗其它公司的最好变速器、轮圈和脚踏板模型。这意味着他们永远退出这个游戏吗？这很难说，但是 S. 先生是一个总爱抓住机会的人。

62 & 63
未来的后避震系统
当 Specialized 的工程师拿到一个奥地利人的后车架时，会发生什么呢？

我们把它命名为 1991 式。在推出最初的 Stumpjumper 后的十年当中，越野世界以每人能想象的速度发展。车尾悬挂的出现，就像 UFO 突然出现在内华达沙漠上空的雷达上一样。可问题是，大多数设计者是沉重和低效的异形怪物。当时，后轮悬挂系统非常复杂和不可靠，以至于 S 总部中的许多人都不相信这是一个好东西。

尽管如此，麦克并不考虑它是什么，而关心它会是什么，这样也让他的团队开始研究一种没有妥协的悬挂山地车。一辆在你用力正确骑行时无论何时都非常舒适和容易控制的山地车。它轻便（不超过 27 磅）、可靠而且维护方便。即便在今天，它也是一个大 BHAG（伟大、危险和大胆的目标）。但在 91 年，能够制造这种悬挂系统的大部分技术甚至还不存在。

在目上花费了一年多的时间后，工程师 John O'Neil、Mark Winter 和 Mark DiNucci 在帮助他们改进的每个设计进行了复制和修改。其中一些还不错，但都不是很完美。于是，他们继续制造 Franken 山地车并听取那些找上门来的、有丰富经验的 Franken 车手的意见，（你如果运上，总有机会向更好了气垫鞋）。最终是 60 世纪 70 年代就职于多家欧洲汽车和摩托车大型集团的奥地利工程师 Horst Leitner 带领该团队发明出魔幻般的多连杆设计，也就是今天的 FSR。对于 DiNucci 和设计师们来说，Horst 是一个摩托车设计权威，他不仅拥有很多专利；对于 Horst 来说，Specialized 拥有微调他的设计和重复别人对 Stumpjumper 所做事情的资金。

拥有多连杆尾部控制的原型车后，DiNucci 和公司从现有的 Stumpjumper 车架上拆掉了后叉，并用 Horst 设计出的一个摇摆臂代替它，制作出了早期的 FSR。在这一个运动场那么大难得的废弃山地垃圾桶后（而且专门为此项目组建了一个新的试验队），开发终于进入了生产阶段。也许有点太快了：1993 年夏天，当发现最初的油压管减震架不够牢固时，不得不将首批几百辆山地车粉碎掉。就像 DiNucci 所说："每个人都将自己的经验抛到一边，而根据自己的直觉来做决定。我们从来没有像制造一辆 FSR 山地车那样需要如此复杂的测试和开发。"FSR 在 Specialized 公司中如此重要的一个原因就是 - 它是一辆超越现有生产机械的山地车，使得 Morgan Hill 不得不重新考虑他们的研发流程。Specialized 的长期营销和研发人员 Chris Murphy 说："突然简单的鸡尾酒组装方式就不够了，您需要真正的设计和测试。"

64 & 65
Cactus Cup
Specialized 发起的一次春游

自行车赛的非正式"春游"风靡了将近整个 20 世纪 90 年代，业山象那 Cactus Cup 阶段赛的召唤令人难以抗拒。这样的召唤令人用几天（或更长时间，如果您能够腾出来）在烤炉般的索诺兰（Sonoran）沙漠进行自行车比赛吗？最坏的结果是什么呢？"有关 Cactus Cup 比赛的具体情况我确实记不太清了 -- 但我记得他们每个人头入奋的样子"，长期从事山地车报道的记者兼最早的车架制造者 Richard Cunningham 这样说。

正如表出哈瓦苏的代托纳，选择 Cactus Cup 的时间是至关重要的。三月中旬的时节不仅可以带给选手平稳、快速行驶的机会，以检验他们在进行冬季培训训的结果，同时还能为自行车企业在当季取得成功创造机会。在其发展的颠峰时期，Cactus Cup 是唯一在该行业每年秋季的贸易展之外能够进行大肆宣传和震惊销售的商业活动。

多年来，这种活动随着 Scottsdale 的北迁而变化多样，吸取了单轨的经验，并增加了活动的细分意识，但有两个要素是 Cactus Cup 永恒不变的，那就是：岩石和沙漠。在有适当的压强和一些粘土时，就可以控制车胎不被扎破，但是，如果道路比以 Umberto Ecco 的小说还迂回曲折，那就不可避免地要被仙人掌如的崎岖道路扎破车胎了。

66 & 67
Stumpjumper Field Guide/1994 Specialized S-Works FS

用于 1994 年的 FSR 的，由 Mark DiNucci 和 Mark Winter 设计的轻便、坚固的直接驱动前三角是 Specialized 在制造悬挂车架方面的一个顶峰。

FSR 悬吊系统是由 Amp Research 创始人 Horst 共同开发的，它的设计目标是为舒适、控制和效率的最大化而完全胜任和完全独立。多年来，FSR 设计被证明有意想不到的多种功能。

由 RockShox 共同开发和制造的前叉，FSX 使用了改良的 RockShox Mag21 内部零件以及 Specialized 设计的碳素低支架和 M2 合金刹车。

变速装置是 1993 年首次生产的，SRAM SRT 500 8-速旋转变速装置是由基于芝加哥的公司制造的首批高端、比赛专用的变速器。

以 Pink Floyd 乐队专辑命名的车胎 Umma Gumma 是第一种采用软复合橡胶的车胎。也许它跑在了时代的前面，因为从此以后再也没有新的产品问世，并且最终停止了生产。

70 & 71
不仅是赛车。更重要的是胜利。
当你胸前有一个"S"时，飞跃变的如此容易。

飞机票？你要谈论买飞机票的事吗？自从麦克将我们第一个赞助的越野车手 Laurence Malone 作为我们的主力后，Specialized 已经花费几百万美元并派出几百名车手和支持人员到全世界，为了一个共同的目标而努力：站在冠军的领奖台上。

翻开这些成绩，你就会发现那些胸前佩戴"S"标记的男女车手们是靠底特律猛犬队的凶猛和丰田 Prius 的效率而赢得胜利的。成绩如何？Specialized 赞助的山地摩托车手赢得了 5 次 UCI 精英组世界赛、多次 UCI 世界杯大赛和世界杯的冠军头衔；以及在 Ned 是赢得所有参加比赛冠军的运动"工厂掌舵人"而我们失去别人注意的时候，赢得了许多 NORBA 全国比赛和全国锦标赛。

夺冠对于一个正在事业高峰期的车手来说就是一切，而对 Specialized 来说，为地球上最挑剔的车手提供为他们创造和提高竞技行了设计的装备是一件随时执着的行为。毫无疑问，如果没有整个团队，就没有 S-Works，而没有 S-Works，不会有轻盈的 Stumpjumper 破纤车架或者能够分辨颠簸和踩踏力回馈之差别的 Brain 避震器。

72
我的 Stumpjumper N.3
Vedran Novak

过去的难民恢复了正常的 Stumpjumper 骑车生涯。

30 岁的 Vedran 过去住在克罗地亚的 Zagreb。当 20 世纪 90 年代内战爆发时，他和成千上万的人一样成了难民，逃到了塞尔维亚。在形成难民营中几乎看不到人骑车，原因很简单，逃离家园的人们将有东西都背在身上，根本没有车子的位置。塞尔维亚、Vedran 和克罗地亚的其它地区都处于 Slobodan Milosevic 的压迫政策统治之下。基本的必需品都很难得到，生活非常艰难，自行车成了无人买得起的奢侈品。那时在塞尔维亚的 Vedran 说："局势如此糟糕，我甚至不能想象什么时候才能再次骑车。"

对于 Vedran（和世界上的其他人们）来说，幸运的是，Milosevic 政府的垮台使巴尔干半岛的生活慢慢地恢复了正常。Vedran 省吃俭用地攒钱，直到可以买一辆旧的 Stumpjumper 职业车，他说这车的车况非常好。后来他每天都骑着它，他说他就是不想停止骑车。"在买新的 Stumpjumper 之前，我真的不知道骑车会给我带来如此多的乐趣！我的自行车不断地提醒我，生活原来可以这么美好。"

73
起飞
Pulp Traction 是第一部反映自由滑行的电影

一个身穿莱卡服装的年轻人骑一辆拖尾登山车从布满碎石的山路上下，只有两英寸冲程的前 Marzocchi Bomber 单叉肩盖？这不是自由滑行。当然尾部翻转或及其凶险下下的坠，但这确实是自由滑行。这就是早期的自由滑行。多亏了 Pulp Traction 的导演，滑雪的传奇人物和英属哥伦比亚省人，Greg Stump，Pulp Traction 成为第一部在 North Shore 拍摄出现山地车镜头的，才诞生了自由滑行镜头的电影。在穿梭松短裤打篮球和长途旅行指直飞中国的时代，Pulp T 和教父 Richie Schley 和 Brett Tippie 在一起共事。

因为那个时代还没有人拍摄山地车的电影，所以 S 营销部便请滑雪摄影师 Stump（他拍摄了 P-Tex、Lies 和 DuctTape 以及其它冰雪运动的经典影片）来拍一部反映超酷的骑行技术、美丽风景和深入这种生活方式的电影。Schley 说："我们中很多人都曾相过滑雪或滑雪板电影，因此当伙计们来到拍摄现场时，我们发现大家就像做像滑雪一样的动作，只是在那些我们可以回转腾跃的地方落下和跳起。""有一天我们回到了拍摄 Pump Traction 中一个场景，我们都在笑我们使用两英寸冲程前叉的硬尾登山车竟然也能成功完成拍摄。"

当然，效果不是很好，但这在荧幕上第一个永远留下了这种运动的镜头。

74 & 75

没什么多余的。绝对没有。
硬尾登山车棺材上的最后一枚铁钉。

训练、训练再训练，训练成为山地车越野赛上最快的速度，而且你会发现除了一组大型车灯外，你就像超级模特一样稀有。这就是 FSRxc 背后的创意：把悬挂山地车的多余的部分全部拆掉，就像一辆 XC 赛车的车体一样。

而且时机才是恰到好处：在 1996 年，山地车正在获得额外的冲程，但同时也获得了很多额外的重量。在此过程中，它们失去了对那些关心速度和效率胜于撞开大石头的人的吸引力。

因此，当其它人都向一个方向的时候，S 团队成员 Ben Capron、Mark Norris、Mike Ducharme 和 Jeff Pint 却决定转向另一个方向。他们打磨、优化、去掉、修改，最后得到了有 3 英寸冲程的 FSRxc，虽然底盘比标准的 FSR 少 1 英寸，但是比 TK 轻而且有灵敏的操作性。Ducharme、Capron 和队员们认真处理了车架上的每一平方毫米，缩短了管子的直径、缩短了对接侧面的轮廓，并且修改了座位的设计。而 FSRxc 最大重量缩减的秘密是避震器、主架和后又都在一个轴上 - 这只有一般零件数量的一半。

最终制出历史上最轻的枢轴山地车；当完全装配优质零件时，FSRxc 的重量达小于 25 磅，而且在 1998 年 Interbike 展览会上推出的赛车样品仅重 20.6 磅。

为什么要相信另？看看 1999 年发布在 MTBR.com 上的一则用户评论，"我不会再骑硬尾登山车了。一旦骑过这种车，你也不想骑别的车了。"

78 & 79

凝固汽油弹！

当世界上最伟大的运动员在山地车现场爆发时，他只留下了焦土和揉皱的保释书。

他不是一名山地车手。这就是问题所在。他从没有真正认为自己是一名摩托车手，而未到这里来坐在山地车上，就像他在滑雪板或摩托车或坐在他十几个卡迪拉克车上一样。

他不是一名山地车手。他是一个摇滚歌星，他从没想过进入脚踏为动力的圈子。自从他在 Donner 滑雪衣场第一天踏上滑雪板后，这个人称 Mini-Shred 的男人就完全彻底拥有了冰雪世界。之后，他完全崩溃了，"1992 年我的祖母去世了，这让我变成一个完全的白痴，在酒吧里打架、酗酒、哪儿也不去。于是我重调转方向，开始将全身心投入运动中，将发泄祖母去世而引发的愤怒。这种愤怒"去他的，我要取得所有的胜利"。于是，Mini-Shred 变成了凝固汽油弹，并开始打败在比赛中的所有对手。他说："这让我感觉很好"。

到 1996 年，他经转入山地车运动，随着奥运会的潮流和流入体育运动的技术资金，他的时机再好不过了。Palmer 成了一个完美和关注的焦点，最终千禧年山地车比赛的前前后后都会留在人们的脑海中。一套金色的金属光泽外套，一辆 Troy Lee 绘制的普雷沃斯汽车和一张六个数字的合同（虽然麦克和几乎所有知道的人都说合同额只不过是大话）。绰号叫 "Buck" 的原机械师兼保释人 Joe Buckley 说："这个家伙从不把赢得大奖当作一回事，但是他总是胡言乱语。"

80

Enduro
因为它叫做 "全山地" 而不是 "轻松的山地"

在千年即将结束的时候，人们预料到会有混乱发生。千禧年问题是人们常挂在嘴边的话题。某些宗教派别声称："世界末日已经不远了。"当然，这是不可能的，否则将会有另外一个完全不同的故事。

对于越野车手来说，混乱表现为他们对摩托和赛道的看法，以及两者如何相结合的问题。由于山地车的普及，那些很容易到达的场点（赛道旁的停车场）面临着巨大的压力，以致还没有足够的重视而逐渐关闭。核心的山地车手想要扩大众，但呼唤赛车手到那些多数人无法进行的更艰难的赛道上，但是因为这些赛道距离较远，所以无疑会增加额外的重量或损失效率。

大量的赛道时间（所幸，Specialized 对汽车进行了研究）和 S 工程师与悬挂权威 Horst Leithner 对 1991 年共同开发的、已经过时间考验的四杆后悬挂设计的重新考虑，促成了第一辆 Enduro 的生产。它在 1999 年夏季才真正离开装载车间正式面世。最初的 Enduro Pro 车架采用结实的 MAX（操控铝挤压成型的）主底盘，4.6 英寸的可调冲程，仅比上一年度的短冲程 FSR 重 250 克。Enduro 同样也有低悬挂 v 形顶管，使车手拥有惊人的骑跨高度，可长时间骑行。在 2000 年，底盘重量进一步减轻，并进行更大的改进，同时增加了挡泥板，更增添了它的魅力。

81

我的 Stumpjumper N.4
Bob Brewer

从后卫到轻量级选手，Stump 使 Bob 减去了 90 磅

两年前是 Bob Brewer 体型最差的时候。5 分 7 秒的检查结果显示，他浮肿的身体达到了 250 磅，并患有高血压，这两者还加重了他的先天性肾病。Bob 那年 40 岁，是 MSM 有限公司的客户代表和两个孩子的父亲，他的医生告诉他应该减肥并保持健康，否则他的寿命不会很长。

Bob 过去非常喜欢骑车，但并未加以重视，他开始骑车是希望能够变得更加健康。但是他的旧车骑起来很不舒服且笨重，总之，没什么乐趣。于是，Bob 上网做了一些调查，并很快发现 Specialized 车具有良好的声誉，并有很多忠实的用户。很幸运，Bob 买到了一款 2004 Stumpjumper Comp 车，他说，它独特的令人惊讶。"不是 '回归自行车'，而是一种新的激情。"

这些天 Bob 没有骑车，因为他不得不这样做，或者这样对他有好处；而他骑车是因为

他觉得总没骑够。"我现在拥有一生中最棒的体型。我已经减去了 90 磅，而且每星期会去参加 4 到 6 次当地的单轨运动。"

Bob 过去总是有病、疲劳、压力大，而且没有一点动力。现在，他很有动力、精力充沛，并且对生活充满了信心。他还高兴地说，他又要当父亲了。好像 Stumpjumper 赋予了他新生。

82 & 83

你能从 "抽筋" 中学到什么？
只有当你愿意的时候，再让悬挂系统工作。

在世界杯比赛开始前，曾为一个越野赛车高手的车装上车把或车库吗？告诉你，他们赛车前面所谓的悬挂前叉没有上下移动很多。事实上，他们中许多人将前叉打到最高，几乎没有冲程。那么，如果他们喜欢这样，而且还可以赢得比赛，那又有什么损害呢？对吧？

问 Specialized 一生热爱悬挂装置的工程师 Mike McAndrews，他会告诉你其中的害处。他多年来一直从事制造工作良好的悬挂装置。所以，当许多 S 车队的车手说他们希望悬挂装置当大块障碍物时才移动，而头脑中一直在思考悬挂问题的 Mick 忽然想到了一个好方法。

在 FoMoCo 工作的一位工程师朋友曾告诉过 Mick，他设计的避震器只有在车轮撞到大块物体时才会收缩。在 Detroit，他们叫它为 "抽筋" 避震器，因为它要重力才可以激活。当 Mick 开始修改他自己版本的 "抽筋" 避震器，但是在摩根山，人们开玩笑地称它为 "衰人" 避震器。

Mick 认为这是个非常好的主意，因为这款避震器更新了碰撞和双头输入之间的差别。他把这一项目称为 "Brain"。他设计了一个很快就能开始运行的原型，但不像预期的那样可靠。后来，他有了一个 "找到了" 的时刻：如果 "抽筋" 避震器的心脏 - Intertia 阀门 - 尽可能地靠近主轴，所有零件可以翻转地更好、更快、更可靠。他进行了实验，并且取得了成功，这一辅助就成了 Brain。在 Fox 的帮助下，终于生产出了 Brain。

另一件事就是 Filip Meirhaeghe - 他习惯使用硬尾登山车比赛，并尽可能地将他的前叉打倒坚硬状态 - 用配有 Brain 避震器的 Epic 车赢得了世界锦标赛的冠军（好的，Meirhaeghe 在接下来的赛季中因某种化学物质不平衡而被逮捕，但是 Epic 车没有使用任何非法的物质）。

现在，麦克配有随路况调整技术的 Brain 避震器非常智能化，在比赛中甚至是在 Stumpjumper 赛车上都能发现它的身影。

86 & 87
Demo

即使为世界上最高难度花招而打造的自行车都是由像积木般拼凑开始

就在这之前的广告上的广告词。Darren Barrelcloth。新自由滑行学校的校长。他需要一个武器来与限制、法律和偏见进行战斗。于是，麦克开始投产 Demo 9，BearClaw 说这款车在崎岖和难走的山路上骑起来非常舒适、灵活、表面保持平衡、重心非常低、要有下垂的顶管来提高操作性，要有超级变速装置，包括前变速器的调节。Mike 说："没问题，我们可以做到"。

于是，一个由 Specialized 工程师、设计师和生产经理（包括 Jason Chamberlin、Brandon Sloan 和 Rober Egger）组成的团队投入到该项目中，在拼装厂房里忙碌。团队将拼装部件组建在一起，研制出一种快速、简单的基于基本的悬挂概念的演示模型。就是在明星工程师 Jason Chamberlin 用电脑完成艰难的设计工作之前，整个团队可进行调整、修改和修改。

不需要火箭科学也知道玩拼装部件是容易的部分。用 Pro/E 3-D 建模软件进行设计，在位于摩根山的 S 总部的机械车间制造原型，测试 Demo 的设计，这些过程耗时多年 - 即两年 - 而且花费了上万美元。

Chamberlin 计算机天分和到 North Shore 多选结果对于产品经理 Brandon Sloan 来说就是 9 英寸冲程、4 杆避震架、由 1 个副摇臂和 6 个支点增加的正常摇臂的山地车。为了使 Demo 结实耐用，Chamberlin 和伙伴们设计了一套专用于自行车的最昂贵的冷锻件，包括最复杂的单锻件容纳避震器的中心承座，需要 500 万磅的压力来生产。

有人曾猜测说用来应付跳下最大深度、最粗糙落差和最强烈撞击的车都是由拼装部件开始的。

88 & 89
30 年的飞跃和冒险
你一直在和谁打电话？

伟大的 30 年。习惯于觉醒而不是庆祝；童年已经过去了，现在已进入成人世界。现在，应该醒醒酒，在中午（虽然是工作日）前少喝点啤酒。然而，没人愿意提起他。最初在 San Jose 的一个穿着猥琐的外套，卖起及类似东西的小家伙快要 30 岁了。伟大的 30 岁。

然而这很好。现在你也即将满 30 岁了。对吗？30 岁就好象还在 25 岁一样。有一件事是毋庸置疑的，那就是 Stumpjumper 的第 30 年庆典（Specialized 的成立纪念日）比以往办得好得多。它的跨越时间、骑着我到任何地方、一个健人都会会微笑完整无缺。车身呢？看看 Dream Silver 底盘的破砖房。就像 Specialized 传奇的首席设计师 Robert Egger 喜欢的那样："如果看上去不错，就可以了。"以意大利的 Dolomites 为背景，它是永恒的。Specialized 的精品车如 Enduro、Hemi 和 Tarmac 的设计师 Egger 说："这款车就需要许多结实的外形，组装的车身应比全部零件看起来更结实。"

90 & 91
骑上 Captain
没有什么能够阻止生活的积极向上。

Captain 的又一个周六之夜。住在每晚 99 美元的世界级酒店里。受伤的右脚下敷着冰块，坐在床尾收看 Speedvision（北美赛车频道）的精彩节目。他要看当地的晚间新闻，喝完也是最后的一点神密的万灵药，即使这样，他还是早上 7 点起床。这就是 Captain 的生活方式。

Ned 于 1996 年正式退役，但他似乎已经记不清了。自从 Specialized 那年秋天为他开了退役聚会后，他又继续参加了世界杯和 NORBA 全国比赛、公路赛、爬山赛、速降滑雪赛（身的、成长胜了他的十几岁的儿子）、铁人两项赛、铁人三项赛、越野三项赛、马拉松赛、越野跑步赛、山地越野赛和其他任何你可以想到的比赛。如果比赛会让你分泌大量的乳酸和脑内肘，Captain 一定会感同身受，兴奋不已。见鬼，在他 50 岁生日的当天，他完成了第四次疯狂的 Mt Washington 爬山赛。

当 Ned 参加完 1980 年 Ironman 获得第 24 名时，或 1983 年当他获得第一个山地车冠军，并和著名的 Ti-Raleigh 队（有 Andy Hampsten、Roy Knickman 和 Steve Tilford）一起获得 Coors Classic 的冠军时，甚至当他 1987 年获得欧洲和 NORBA 世界比赛的两项冠军时，今天被他甩在后面的孩子那时还没有出生。

但是 Ned 不想有特殊的待遇和额外的赞赏，Captain 不想将优美的住宿环境、伤痛的折磨和早上 7 点起床视为一名运动员的命运，他说："我是去那里证明我比那些年轻人骑得快，只是因为我喜欢通过努力而领先 -- 我喜欢比赛。"

92 & 93
Stumpjumper Field Guide/2006 Specialized S-Works Carbon Stumpjumper
跟随最平稳的碳纤潮流。

用有专利的 FACT Y570 混合材料制造的车架，同时，最结实的碳常用来制作车架，S-Works 碳纤 Stumpjumper 因其高效率和出色的刹车系统组合而获得了好评。

带有 Brain Fade 的 Brain 避震器，是第一智能避震器，它知道何时正常启动，何时提高效率。2006 年的亮点 Brain Fade 技术，可使车手自定义调整对 Brain 避震器的感觉。

为快速、全冲程越野车如碳 Stumpjumper 设计的轮胎：Adrenaline Pro 26 x 2.0 轮胎使用可使重量减到最轻的每英尺 120 螺纹的外胎，并拥有双复合配方的橡胶胎，可使良好的转动阻力和摩擦力相结合。

控制杆：对 Carbon Stumpjumper 混合车架的高度评价，Specialized OS Carbon Rise 杆仅重 175 克，是上倾（6 度）下倾（8 度）的完美结合。

座位：2006 模型年的新设备，Rival 采用了 Specialized 独有的车身几何面技术，在试验室的测试中，这一技术可提高血液向敏感区域的流量。

94 & 95
未来发展？

未来总是世事难料。

许多人已经经历了我们仍记忆犹新的千禧年问题。

我们唯一确定的问题是需要对这一文化的尝试和创造者进行保护。为此，我们将把本书的全部收益都捐赠给 IMBA（国际山地车协会）和山地车名人堂。